STORM OVER LEYTE

OTHER BOOKS BY JOHN PRADOS

The U.S. Special Forces: What Everyone Needs to Know

A Streetcar Named Pleiku:
Vietnam 1965, A Turning Point (longform e-book)

Operation Vulture: America's Dien Bien Phu (e-book)

The Family Jewels: The CIA, Secrecy, and Presidential Power

Islands of Destiny:
The Solomons Campaign and the Eclipse of the Rising Sun

In Country: Remembering the Vietnam War (written and edited)

Rethinking National Security (longform e-book)

Normandy Crucible:
The Decisive Battle That Shaped World War II in Europe

How the Cold War Ended: Debating and Doing History

William Colby and the CIA: The Secret Wars of a Controversial Spymaster

Vietnam: The History of an Unwinnable War, 1945–1975

Safe for Democracy: The Secret Wars of the CIA

Hoodwinked: The Documents That Reveal How Bush Sold Us a War

Inside the Pentagon Papers (written and edited with Margaret Pratt Porter)

The White House Tapes:
Eavesdropping on the President (written and edited)

Lost Crusader: The Secret Wars of CIA Director William Colby

America Confronts Terrorism (written and edited)

The Blood Road: The Ho Chi Minh Trail and the Vietnam War

Presidents' Secret Wars:
CIA and Pentagon Covert Operations from World War II
Through the Persian Gulf

Combined Fleet Decoded:
The Secret History of U.S. Intelligence and
the Japanese Navy in World War II

The Hidden History of the Vietnam War

Valley of Decision: The Siege of Khe Sanh (with Ray W. Stubbe)

Keepers of the Keys:
A History of the National Security Council from Truman to Bush

Pentagon Games

The Sky Would Fall: The Secret U.S. Bombing Mission to Vietnam, 1954

The Soviet Estimate: U.S. Intelligence and Soviet Strategic Forces

STORM
OVER
LEYTE

THE PHILIPPINE INVASION
AND THE DESTRUCTION
OF THE JAPANESE NAVY

JOHN PRADOS

NAL
CALIBER

NAL CALIBER
Published by New American Library,
an imprint of Penguin Random House LLC
375 Hudson Street, New York, New York 10014

This book is an original publication of New American Library.

First Printing, July 2016

For more information about Penguin Random House, visit penguin.com.

LIBRARY OF CONGRESS CATALOGING-IN-PUBLICATION DATA:

Names: Prados, John, author.
Title: Storm over Leyte: the Philippine invasion and the destruction of the
Japanese Navy/John Prados.
Description: New York, New York: New American Library, [2016]
Identifiers: LCCN 2015047067 (print) | LCCN 2015047122 (ebook) | ISBN
9780451473615 | ISBN 9780698185760 (ebook)
Subjects: LCSH: World War, 1939–1945—Campaigns—Philippines—Leyte Island. |
Leyte Gulf, Battle of, Philippines, 1944. | Leyte Island (Philippines)—History, Military.
Classification: LCC D767.4.P73 2016 (print) | LCC D767.4 (ebook) |
DDC 940.54/25995—dc23
LC record available at http://lccn.loc.gov/2015047067

Printed in the United States of America
10 9 8 7 6 5 4 3 2 1

Designed by Kelly Lipovich

PUBLISHER'S NOTE
While the author has made every effort to provide accurate telephone numbers and Internet addresses at the time of publication, neither the publisher nor the author assumes any responsibility for errors, or for changes that occur after publication. Further, publisher does not have any control over and does not assume any responsibility for author or third-party Web sites or their content.

Penguin
Random
House

For Natasha,
who pursues her goal
with such determination

Despair is the price one pays for setting . . . an impossible aim.

—Graham Greene, *The Heart of the Matter*

CONTENTS

Map Symbol Key

	Allies	Japanese
Launch Air Attack		
Submarine		
Sighting (submarine)		
Light Unit (or destroyer/s)		
Light Cruiser		
Heavy Cruiser (or unit)		
Battleship (or unit)		
Aircraft Carrier (or unit)		
Track (surface unit/carrier unit)		
Maneuver Area		
Naval/Air Base		
Air Base (on land)		
Ship Sunk		

MAP LIST

INTRODUCTION

The Battle of Leyte Gulf figures among the most important events of the Pacific campaign in World War II. As a turning point it marked a key passage of the war. As a crushing blow to Japanese power it brought an escalation of violence that led to some of the bloodiest confrontations of the war. Though Leyte Gulf is among the more studied clashes of the fight, it still offers space for fruitful exploration. In *Islands of Destiny*, my last Pacific excursion, the intention was to show that, among Pacific turning points, the South Pacific campaign outshone the Battle of Midway as the more decisive development. *Storm over Leyte* extends that story to the moment of the American return to the Philippine Islands and the carnage it triggered.

This account begins with the extraordinary conference President Franklin Delano Roosevelt convened at Pearl Harbor in July 1944. Histories of the period have minimized or even ignored this event, a virtual summit of the Allied proconsuls in the Pacific, Douglas A. MacArthur and Chester W. Nimitz, conjoined with their top leader, FDR. Where histories cover this event they often treat it as a photo op or political stunt from a man about to run for his fourth term as president of the United States. As you will see from the narrative, I believe the meeting at Pearl Harbor is far more important than that, both in the immediate sense and in its longer-term consequences. I will argue that President Roosevelt worked to resolve a real strategic problem, and that the course he charted, taking the side of one of the summit's participants, set up the most momentous military headache of the Pacific war. The question of using the atomic bomb on Japan versus invading the Japanese Home Islands has been prominent in recent writing on the Pacific. Here I argue that the Pearl Harbor conference and the Philippine campaign that started at Leyte Gulf led directly to that horrible dilemma.

Storm over Leyte continues the enterprise I began several books ago of reinterpreting the standard military history of World War II in the light of contributions made by intelligence on both sides. I believe that our knowledge of intelligence in the war, developed late and only gradually released by the keepers of the secrets—even though broad outlines of the story were revealed quite early—has reached the point where our conventional knowledge of these events can be seamlessly reworked into a comprehensive history that offers full scope to all contributing elements. I did that for the South Pacific in *Islands of Destiny*. This tome continues the endeavor.

One thing from World War II that this book demonstrates and that merits celebration is the citizen soldier. The incredible exploits of U.S. naval, air, and ground forces before and during the Philippine invasion were the exploits of ordinary people. In this era of an entirely professional military it is too easy to lose sight of the fact that private citizens proved fully capable of learning everything necessary, as well as exercising competent military judgment, in a modern, technologically advanced conflict. I believe that elements of techno-obscurantism and plain arrogance have crept into the mind-sets of a disturbingly large slice of our serving professionals. The record of Leyte Gulf supplies a useful corrective—brilliant military results were posted by armed services overwhelmingly comprised of civilian volunteers and draftees. In the twenty-first century we may argue the desirability of national service, but events such as Leyte Gulf put beyond question that a citizen force can be as capable as a professional one.

An endeavor that continues between these covers is my attempt to give full play to both sides, the Allied and the Japanese. It is true that histories have been improving on this count in recent years. It is also the case that Leyte Gulf, because of the destruction of the Imperial Navy that occurred there, has been covered in ways that lend more weight to the Japanese viewpoint. I nevertheless believe the literature leaves room for improvement. Following *Islands of Destiny*, I think that what the Imperial Navy took away from the South Pacific was a realization of the need for detailed combat planning and high coordination between planning and battle preparations. In *Storm over Leyte* I make that case by showing in detail the evolution of the Japanese plan and preparations. Commencing their chronologies with the Leyte battle itself, or the preliminaries just ahead of it, existing accounts treat the planning in isolation and fail to capture what the Imperial Navy attempted to do. In my view a full appreciation of the dimensions of the enterprise needs to start with Tokyo's anguish over the Marianas campaign, and that is what I do here.

This is big-picture military history. It contains numerous stories of individuals' bravery or misfortune, but my stance in the memory-versus-history debate is on the history side. That is how I was trained and the kind of history I prefer to read. In my view the purpose of individuals' stories is to enhance and illuminate the narrative. Their purpose is not to *be* the narrative. That said, some of the characters here are people we've met before, in *Islands of Destiny*, and here we continue their stories, plus add new ones. However, make no mistake—the characters populate the story, not the other way around. It is distressing to see readers complain, despite warnings like this one, that the book is short on personal narratives. A primary focus on memory impedes the search for larger meaning.

THE FOCUS HERE on intelligence opened the door to a huge array of information that was unknown or poorly understood. That carried us a considerable way toward providing a fresh view of this crucial battle. Readers will also recognize my agreement—or occasional differences— with such historians as Samuel Eliot Morison, Evan Thomas, Paul S. Dull, Richard Frank, Ron Spector, and others. I want to make special mention of John Toland, whose research on the Pacific war, deposited at the Franklin D. Roosevelt Presidential Library and Museum, remains an important resource. Another historian whose work should be mentioned is Elmer B. Potter, a naval biographer. His oeuvre includes full-scale profiles of several of the key leaders of the U.S. Navy. Largely forgotten today is Edwin P. Hoyt, a popular historian who had friends at Leyte Gulf. He set himself to study the battle repeatedly from angles ranging from the demise of single ships (*Princeton, Gambier Bay*) to the heroics of the pilots of the carrier *Lexington*, plus other points in between.

The work of Gordon W. Prange, with his associates Donald M. Gold-stein and Katharine V. Dillon, becomes less valuable for the period after Pearl Harbor–Midway, although they have contributed a study of the Japanese aviator Fuchida Mitsuo. What Goldstein and Dillon *have* given us that is of tremendous value is a translation of the diary of Imperial Navy admiral Ugaki Matome. Having said that, I should add that another translation of the Ugaki diary, while not of literary quality, is available. This one, done for John Toland and in his papers, fills in many places where Goldstein and Dillon chose to condense material for publication. A careful study of the Ugaki material indicates, as I argue here, that the diarist gave free rein to his predilections and prejudices. There has been a tendency to rely too much on the Ugaki diary primarily because it furnishes the widest-ranging contemporary source we have for the Japanese side. On Leyte Gulf, at least, I shall argue that Admiral Ugaki is not a reliable guide.

Any modern treatment of the Japanese side must acknowledge the contributions of social media, in this case the CombinedFleet.com Web site, mastered by Anthony Tully. A tribe of new historians clustered around that resource site are assiduously adding a new dimension to the information available about our former enemies. A fine example of their work is the book on the Battle of the Surigao Strait by Tully, who previously had collaborated with Jon Parshall on a history of the Midway action. Readers will see instances where I take Tully's side and some where we differ. I nevertheless credit Tully with advancing our record tremendously.

My debts to others are wide and deep. At the National Archives and Records Administration (NARA) I relied upon John E. Taylor until his death in 2008. I still know no one with so comprehensive a view of the sources, both archival and published. This book continues to benefit from records I consulted upon his advice. Also of key assistance at NARA were Richard A. von Doenhoff, whose knowledge of the naval records was remarkable, and Judy Thorne. The National Security Agency records group at NARA yielded a plethora of information, as you will see. Elizabeth Mays of the Navy Department Library, Linda O'Doughda of the U.S. Naval Institute, and Edward Finney Jr. of the Naval Historical Center all provided valuable help. I am indebted to Michael Walker, John Hodges, Kathleen Lloyd, and Gina Akers of the Naval Operational Archives. These archives held not only U.S. Navy records but also copies of important oral histories compiled both by the U.S. Naval Institute and by the National Security Agency, as well as the papers of Samuel Eliot Morison. The Naval Operational Archives have fallen on hard times of late, with the deterioration of both facilities and records, tight budgets, and what has been reported as the pilfering of the Morison papers. There are additional problems pertaining to the transfer of Navy records to NARA in the context of changing policies on who may use the Naval Operational Archives and what records it will continue to house. Overall the outlook seems to be bleak, since the movement of records to NARA takes them out of circulation for an indefinite period.

At the Franklin D. Roosevelt Presidential Library and Museum I was assisted by Susan Y. Elter, John C. Ferris, and Robert Parks. The Roosevelt Library held invaluable resources. I am delighted to take note of the library's progress in putting source material online. Many of the documents I traveled to Hyde Park to examine physically are now available electronically. This is a boon for all researchers. The Roosevelt Map Room files are not yet completely online, but the set should become fully available in the near future.

Many of those who helped me with this research have passed away or moved on to new projects. John Taylor is an example of the first. John Ferris, who has become an intelligence historian in his own right, can stand in for the second. I am deeply grateful that our respective trajectories carried us close to each other at key points for my research. Thank you all.

Ellen Pinzur read and edited the manuscript and made many excellent suggestions. She has been most valuable as a first reader. I am especially grateful for the editing work of Brent Howard and Christina Brower. They saved the manuscript from much silliness. Jason Petho once again ably executed the maps I wanted to illustrate the text. And Michael Congdon held my hand throughout the process. These persons, individually and together, have contributed much to what is good about this book. I alone am responsible for its faults and omissions.

—John Prados
    Washington, DC
    January 2016

PROLOGUE

The Allied juggernaut had momentum. The battles were bloody, fierce. On Saipan, where U.S. Marines and Army troops clawed their way across the Central Pacific, desperate Japanese defenders hurled themselves into the most vicious suicide attack of the war. In New Guinea, where the Australian-American forces of General Douglas A. MacArthur had mastered the strategy of bypassing the enemy's strongholds wherever possible, the Southwest Pacific Command had jumped from the big island on to other targets, leaving Japanese garrisons behind to starve, bereft of the supplies denied them by Allied naval power. That summer of 1944, the question was increasingly one of what to do next.

President Franklin Delano Roosevelt chose this moment to powwow with his theater commanders at Pearl Harbor. He had considered the move carefully. In mid-May, FDR quietly asked his Joint Chiefs of Staff chairman, Admiral William D. Leahy, to arrange the trip, with the president to travel to Seattle, then Alaska and Hawaii. As it turned out, Roosevelt left a little earlier and reversed the order of his destinations, but that hardly mattered. They departed Washington by special train on July 13, with a brief stopover at his New York estate, Hyde Park.

The president, code-named "Duke," arrived in San Diego with no fanfare on July 21. The press that day reported an apparent revolt among Hitler's henchmen. With FDR on his way to the Pacific, he would largely be on his own to speculate upon the meaning of the July 20 Plot.

Accompanied by his son James—now a Marine officer—plus the base commander, FDR visited the naval hospital at Balboa Park. His auto passed Evans F. Carlson, the redoubtable Marine officer, convalescing

after wounds suffered on Saipan. Carlson, who had organized and led
the Marine Raider force, and under whom James Roosevelt had served,
waved. President Roosevelt had his driver stop the car so he and the
Marine colonel could trade compliments.

Then the party moved on to the San Diego–Coronado ferry. FDR
crossed to the island to see the Navy's Amphibious Training Center,
on the Strand not far from the famous Hotel del Coronado. Admiral
Leahy heard a briefing on techniques—newly premiered on Saipan a
month earlier—whereby ships' guns, strike aircraft, and artillery would
all be coordinated in support of troops on the beach. Their arrival
coincided with the graduation exercise of newly trained amphibious
combat teams of the 5th Marine Division, and the president actually
witnessed a landing of 10,000 troops. The mock invasion fascinated
Roosevelt.

Late that afternoon Franklin stopped by his son John's home, about
a mile away, off Alameda Boulevard. John served aboard the aircraft
carrier *Wasp*, but Franklin could greet both his daughters-in-law, along
with his grandchildren. Just after sunset the president arrived at Broad-
way Pier, where the heavy cruiser USS *Baltimore* lay moored on the
south side of the wharf. There were no photographers. No honors were
rendered. The trip had been kept hush-hush, strictly on the q.t. Together
with his Scottish terrier, Fala, and Admiral Leahy, plus other admirals
and White House advisers, FDR boarded the warship. Captain Walter
L. Calhoun raised the president's flag on the yardarm of the *Baltimore*.
The cruiser cast off at midnight and cleared the swept channel just
before 4:00 a.m. Four destroyers escorted the presidential ship. Captain
Calhoun of the *Baltimore* led the entire force. It set course for Hawaii.

For all the security afforded a president of the United States, Roosevelt had a bit of a scare. Less than two days out from the West Coast,
Captain Calhoun received a message from the admiral leading the
Hawaiian Sea Frontier, the local naval command: "POSSIBLE ENEMY
TASK FORCE LOCATED 200 MILES NORTH [OF] OAHU." The dispatch
must have sent shivers down a few spines—but it proved unsubstanti-
ated. In this third year of the war, with the Japanese Navy having just
sustained a major defeat off the Marianas, no enemy should have been
hazarded off the powerful American bastion Pearl Harbor. In any case,

Captain Calhoun, Admiral Leahy, and other top Navy officers decided the cited position lay so far away that, if there were any Japanese, they posed little threat.

The effort to maintain security extended down the chain of command, and the secrecy almost led to a snafu—General MacArthur, in ignorance of FDR's visit, rejected the first invitation to come to Pearl Harbor. Pacific theater commander Admiral Chester W. Nimitz learned of the visit only when Michael F. Reilly, chief of the president's Secret Service detail, arrived to check on security. Techies waited until the last minute to install FDR's dedicated phone and Teletype lines. Leahy asked that only official military photographers be permitted to take pictures. Mike Reilly escorted Nimitz and other military potentates who boarded the *Baltimore* from a tug as she slowed to round Diamond Head at about 2:30 p.m. on July 26.

Despite all this care, Admiral Leahy noticed that everyone on Oahu seemed to know about Roosevelt's visit. An area of about two acres had been cleared, but beyond that stood a throng of people. As Captain Calhoun's cruiser approached the harbor, the sky filled with planes, a veritable air show for the president. Sailors in dress whites manned the railings of ships in the harbor. CINCPAC chief of staff Vice Admiral Charles H. McMorris assembled flag officers in formation on the pier. Two dozen admirals and generals stood at attention.

At 3:00 p.m. the *Baltimore* entered and moored at Pier 22-B of the Navy Yard, riding just astern of the USS *Enterprise*, returned from the fleet only a week earlier to receive a new propeller and a fresh air group. "Soc" McMorris ordered "right face." A couple of the military pooh-bahs turned the wrong way, bringing guffaws from the multitudes of enlisted. The brass marched up the gangway, and aboard FDR's flagship Captain Calhoun held a reception for the visitors.

Forty minutes later, as the party broke up, howling sirens announced the arrival of a long car, led by a motorcycle escort. Douglas MacArthur sat in the backseat wearing a leather flight jacket. The car made the rounds of the cleared dock area before stopping in front of the gangway. Admiral Leahy, who'd known the general nearly forty years, wondered why he sported winter garb in tropical Hawaii. "Dugout Doug" shot back that Australia was cold—and an airplane at altitude worse still.

MacArthur, Nimitz, and Leahy huddled together for half an hour with President Roosevelt in his quarters.

At 4:15 p.m., the big shots emerged to pose for the newsreels and photographers before officers helped FDR ashore. Because of animal quarantine regulations, Fala was left behind aboard the *Baltimore*. A Marine band and guard rendered honors for the president. Roosevelt got into the open car driven by Boatswain's Mate 2nd Class W. F. Reasley, the 14th Naval District commander's regular chauffeur, for the twenty-minute drive to Kalakaua Avenue in Waikiki. The Chris Holmes house, usually occupied by Navy pilots on leave, had been commandeered, and teams from the Pacific Submarine Command had prepped it for the official visit. A palatial mansion in cream-colored stucco, the Holmes House offered a glorious setting on the beach.

Franklin D. Roosevelt's thoughts must be imagined. He had been to Hawaii only once, a decade before, almost to the day. That time the president had visited several of the islands, gone fishing, been greeted by a huge crowd at Honolulu, and dedicated a new gate to Pearl Harbor naval base. This time, there was a war that needed to be won, and the final stage of that endeavor was to start right here. Thus began a fateful meeting.

FRANKLIN DELANO ROOSEVELT had a very particular problem. The question of what to do next in the Pacific war was fraught with consequence. With the new tactic of "island hopping" piled atop huge matériel superiority and a major intelligence edge, Allied offensives were gaining momentum so quickly that actual moves threatened to outrun the planning. The Marianas and northwest New Guinea, specifically, marked a nexus. From the Marianas, Japan itself would be within striking range of Allied heavy bombers for the first time. The way lay open to invasion of the Inner Empire, including Taiwan (then called Formosa), the Bonin and Ryukyu islands, even Japan itself.

As for New Guinea, winding up the struggle for that land freed General MacArthur's Southwest Pacific forces to cooperate with Admiral Nimitz's Pacific-area juggernaut in an unprecedented fashion. The question of what to do became paramount.

Everyone had their own ideas, but the alternatives essentially boiled down to two options. One, to leap from the Marianas to Taiwan, would cut off Japan's supply lines to the resource-rich lands of Southeast Asia, particularly Indonesia, the source of practically all the fuel that ran the Japanese war machine. Invading Taiwan would also make available airfields close to Japan—and it would furnish a platform from which the Allies could strike the Inner Empire, the China coast, or indeed the Philippines.

The other possibility would be to jump to the Philippines. This would succor Filipino partisans, who had been fighting the Japanese for many long years, and liberate a land in which the United States had a direct interest. The islands also offered airfields and an invasion platform, though less centrally located. A Philippine invasion would make good on the American promise during the dark early days of the war, articulated by none other than Douglas MacArthur, to return and free the islands from Japanese occupiers.

Both approaches were already on the table when Admiral Nimitz's fleet descended upon the Marianas, and the capture of those islands crystallized the debate. As a matter of fact, the American and British chiefs of staff—together making the Combined Chiefs of Staff—were meeting in London when the U.S. armada began its Marianas invasion, called Operation "Forager." At those meetings General George Marshall, U.S. Army chief of staff, spoke of the accelerating pace of the advance and the need to nail down a strategy. Admiral Ernest J. King, commander in chief of the U.S. Navy and chief of naval operations, raised the specific idea of gaining surprise and speeding up operations by means of bypassing the Philippines, despite Washington's promise of independence, in favor of attacking Taiwan. The top brass at this conference even toyed with the notion of bypassing all the rest in favor of a direct invasion of the Japanese island of Kyushu.

When they queried the theater commanders, General MacArthur stood firm. On June 18, on the cusp of the Battle of the Philippine Sea, the Southwest Pacific boss rejected any idea of bypassing the Philippines as foolish, insisting that logistics problems made it impossible for him to accelerate his operations any further and that the United States had a moral obligation to liberate Filipinos. General Marshall, wary of the

Japanese building their strength there, remained open to bypassing the Philippines. Once MacArthur understood that King wanted to spring ahead to Taiwan, he put down a marker: If Washington moved toward that option, then MacArthur wanted to come home and make his case in person.

For planning purposes, American war strategists slated the southern Philippines island of Mindanao as the next target, and November 1944 as the date, but neither was set in stone. The Japanese fleet and air force remained powerful and could be expected to fight hard. At Pearl Harbor, Admiral Nimitz had no problem with Mindanao as an objective, but he felt perfectly comfortable presenting Ernie King's Taiwan scheme too. In early July, when representatives of both commands met to hammer out a way forward, Nimitz plumped for invading Mindanao, then skipping the rest of the Philippines to hit Taiwan.

Franklin Roosevelt, in a nutshell, needed to arbitrate between two strategic visions, and it was apparent in three ways that he took the problem seriously. First, the president was prepared to go as far as Pearl Harbor to settle the dispute. It would be the only time Roosevelt went to the Pacific theater in the entire war. Because of his physical disabilities, FDR traveled mostly by train and ship. Visiting Pearl Harbor in that fashion meant being away from Washington for an entire month and represented a serious commitment.

Second, President Roosevelt was serious *about* that commitment. When he initially spoke to Admiral Leahy, FDR wanted to schedule two trips. The other would have been to Europe to see Winston Churchill, who was anxious for a new meeting of the Allies. FDR canceled the European trip—within hours of scheduling it—but the Pacific journey stayed on his calendar.

The third strand of evidence is the trip itself. Roosevelt treaded lightly as a war manager. He was not like Hitler, pushing flags for his divisions around on a map of Europe; nor was he Lyndon Johnson, meeting his Joint Chiefs of Staff to consider schedules for bombing North Vietnam. The president rarely saw his military leaders except when the Chiefs accompanied him to Allied conferences, and he did most of his business through Admiral Leahy. Over the entire length of the Pacific war there were just a handful of times when FDR took a hand in military operations—and one of them was this conference at Pearl Harbor. Roosevelt must have perceived the situation as requiring his personal attention.

DOUGLAS MACARTHUR HAD no use for this meeting. He rejected the invitation—admittedly, before he knew the president would be there, but MacArthur had to be *ordered* to Pearl Harbor. General Marshall knew the score and wanted his American Caesar on board. MacArthur groused that this was all a political stunt. He left Brisbane on a four-engine C-54, not his personal B-17, called the *Bataan*, which he considered not quite up to the long haul to Hawaii, and paced the plane's aisle, openly complaining of his humiliation at being summoned to "a political picture-taking junket." His personal pilot, Major Weldon "Dusty" Rhoades, had set up a cot for the general at the back of the plane, but MacArthur wouldn't go near it. The general brought along only a few aides, none of his senior officers, and no planning documents. At an intermediate stop on Canton Island, MacArthur received a Nimitz dispatch requesting he delay his arrival two and a half hours, likely so that FDR's cruiser could dock. The general refused.

MacArthur's plane landed about an hour before the *Baltimore* docked, but the general would not be there to welcome his president. Only when others had already greeted FDR did MacArthur go to the *Baltimore*. The gesture seemed a calculated snub aimed at Chester Nimitz, a delayed arrival, carefully staged for maximum publicity, after the lesser fry were off the board—all classic MacArthur.

Yet MacArthur's complaints about the trip had some substance. The strategy papers were on file. Planners had discussed them. Why have a conference? President Roosevelt would be seen meeting his top Pacific theater commanders, taking an active role. The photos in the papers would help his upcoming political campaign. But there was more to it than that. In actuality the Pearl Harbor event reflected careful orchestration. The planners *had* had their say. The papers *were* on file. The Combined Chiefs of Staff had commented. Yet whom did FDR leave out of his travel party? Admiral Ernest J. King, the very person who counseled the Combined Chiefs to accept the more cerebral strategy of bypassing the Philippines. While FDR slowly made his cross-country journey by train en route to Hawaii, the Navy chief grabbed a plane and flew out to Pearl Harbor for the ostensible purpose of making a quick inspection of newly conquered Saipan, now declared secure. He huddled with Nimitz, then took the admiral with him to Saipan, counting on the shared experience to cement his arguments with the Pacific theater commander. Then Nimitz returned to Pearl Harbor to receive his president.

Roosevelt, supreme political animal that he was, had to be keenly aware of MacArthur's promise to return to the Philippines, and he certainly knew liberation of the islands would be good for his own prospects in the upcoming presidential election. He also knew that King advocated bypassing the archipelago. Chester Nimitz represented the wild card. The admiral had accepted part of MacArthur's plan while also aligning himself with Ernie King's Taiwan strategy. FDR needed to get Nimitz and MacArthur to play from the same sheet music. Admiral Leahy's presence among the group, as a colleague of Marshall and King, would reassure the other Joint Chiefs.

Formalities had to be observed before the president could get down to business. On July 27, President Roosevelt, together with General MacArthur and Admirals Nimitz and Leahy, toured Oahu military bases in a red Lincoln Zephyr convertible. There were just two like it on Oahu. The fire chief owned one. The other belonged to Jean O'Hara, a flamboyant former Chicagoan who had run a brothel there and now was a landlady and call girl madame in Honolulu. O'Hara had been leery of driving of late—she had been sent to trial on charges of trying to run down a friend's husband. Though acquitted, the madame needed to build goodwill, and lending out the car looked like a good prospect. Admiral Soc McMorris, having forbidden naval officers (who included some of O'Hara's tenants) from attending the salacious trial, rejected the loan. The Navy got its car from the fire chief.

At each base, Roosevelt made short remarks to assemblies of servicemen, and even an impromptu speech to the mustered troops of an Army division on its way to the front. Between stops, riding in the Zephyr, Nimitz sat in the middle of the backseat as FDR and Doug MacArthur talked past him. The president and general had a history stretching back before World War I, when Nimitz was no more than a young engineering lieutenant with the Atlantic Fleet. Now the two men chattered away, with the admiral mostly an attentive listener. MacArthur later bragged to a subordinate that he had talked with President Roosevelt for six hours while the Navy sat mute.

With all the pomp and ceremony, Roosevelt got only a couple of hours to himself late in the afternoon, before hosting the same officers to dinner at the Holmes mansion. Admiral William F. Halsey, who had arrived from the United States just that afternoon, joined the festivities. Afterward the group, minus Halsey, repaired to trade horses.

Early on, in the conversation where MacArthur had been teased about his flight jacket, FDR had said he supposed the Southwest Pacific commander knew what this meeting was all about. The general had professed complete ignorance, though of course the denial was part of his studied posturing. Early in the war, detractors had nicknamed MacArthur "Dugout Doug" for his propensity to wax heroic from the safety of fortress Corregidor. But the sobriquet applied equally to MacArthur's bulldog refusal to budge when he had decided to have his way. He would tell the president he had no idea what this conference was about, but the moment it came time to talk turkey in the huge living room of the Holmes House, its walls now hung with maps, MacArthur stood ready with an articulate, detailed argument for why his approach had to be the one—his case complete with a timetable. The United States, not merely MacArthur himself, he insisted, had made a commitment when he had promised to return to the Philippines. Politician Roosevelt could not miss that point. MacArthur lectured—and he presented myriad details. The island of Mindanao would be just the first step. Then Leyte, and finally Luzon, the prize, with the Philippine capital, Manila.

Roosevelt worried about combat losses. General MacArthur assured him that modern weapons were too deadly for frontal assaults. His losses would not be excessive. He already had the forces needed. Compared to this vision of the Philippines as a low-cost mission, MacArthur held Iwo Jima and Okinawa—and, by extension, Taiwan—out as expensive frontal assaults. Were that option selected, the Southwest Pacific theater that MacArthur commanded stood to be reduced to just a couple of divisions of combat troops. No doubt that irked the general too.

MacArthur argued that seizing the Philippines would block Japanese sea-lanes to the southern resources area. "The blockade that I will put across the line of supply between Japan and the Dutch East Indies will so strangle the Japanese Empire that it will have to surrender."

It is not clear how General MacArthur could pretend a Taiwan invasion would not have the same effect. If anything, because Taiwan lay closer to the mainland, a blockade from there would have been more effective than one based on the archipelago. Aircraft ranges were such that Japanese vessels could skirt the bottleneck of a blockade from the Philippines by hugging the Southeast Asia and China coasts. Such a blockade would have to be enforced by constant naval patrols, and aircraft would need to cover both the Taiwan and Luzon straits.

But MacArthur insisted Taiwan would be a mistake. He thought the people there would be unfriendly—Japan had held the place since 1895—which would make it an insecure base for a blockade. This argument begged the question of the effects of Japanese colonialism, for Tokyo's proconsuls had treated the Taiwanese in a shabby fashion. MacArthur slung mud at King's Taiwan option in hopes something might stick.

FDR told his doctor afterward, "In all my life, nobody has ever talked to me the way MacArthur did." The president demanded an aspirin before bed, but, more than that, another one for morning, when there would be another session of this marathon discussion.

Admiral Nimitz spoke at length too. The most iconic photo of the Pearl Harbor talks features Nimitz standing at a map, holding a bamboo pointer, with the others looking on as he points at Tokyo. He was more analytical, agreeing upon Mindanao but not seeing any advantages offered by Luzon and Manila—with its great bay—that were not available for less cost elsewhere. Having talked with fleet commander Admiral Raymond Spruance, Nimitz spoke authoritatively on the Marianas invasions and the naval battle that had been fought to protect the landings. The Pacific theater supremo then presented Taiwan as a great opportunity. Under Roosevelt's gentle prodding he conceded there might be circumstances that made a Luzon invasion, capping a Philippine campaign, desirable. There he let go of Ernie King's logic, effectively accepting the MacArthur option. Admiral Nimitz felt he could move either way—and that his forces were adequate for the operations. MacArthur, too, had proclaimed his armada sufficient.

Leahy, for one, felt relieved. Rather than the heat expected in a clash between MacArthur and Nimitz, "it was both pleasant and very informative to have these two men who had been pictured as antagonists calmly present their differing views." The friendly atmosphere lasted through the entire discussion. "It was highly pleasing and unusual," he noted, "to find two commanders who were not demanding reinforcements."

Leahy was also impressed with the president's leadership. "Roosevelt was at his best," he recorded, "as he tactfully steered the discussion from one point to another and narrowed down the area of disagreement." MacArthur agreed. In his 1964 memoir he wrote of the president, "He was entirely neutral in handling the discussion."

MacArthur thought that Nimitz behaved with complete evenhandedness and got the impression the president had doubts about the Taiwan option. The general went out of his way to say nice things about Admiral King, whom he actually despised. President Roosevelt's mission had succeeded.

Finally the group sat down to lunch. Afterward MacArthur asked to speak privately with FDR, and then he made his political pitch for the Philippines invasion as fulfilling American promises. He left immediately afterward to begin the long return flight to the Southwest Pacific. The rest of the day passed with an upbeat FDR visiting the naval air station at Kaneohe Bay. Entertainment came at dinner that evening. The Nautical Hawaiians, seventeen sailors of the 14th Naval District led by Machinist's Mate 1st Class Bill Dias, set up on the lawn outside the dining room and serenaded the president. As the sun set, the table was cleared, and the diners went outside, hula dancer Lila Reiplinger and singer Emma Pollack took the entertainment to a higher level, under palm trees, in the bright light of a half-moon. The performance went on until the 10:00 p.m. curfew.

On Saturday, the twenty-ninth, there were more base drop-bys, plus a lunch with Admiral Nimitz at his quarters on Makalapa Hill. One of the Makalapa drop-bys honored the hush-hush Joint Intelligence Center Pacific Ocean Area (JICPOA) and supersecret code-breaking outfit called the Fleet Radio Unit Pacific (FRUPAC). Despite the security surrounding the president's Hawaii visit, the spooks somehow knew about it. Julianne Dilley, a key telephone switchboard operator, had had time to uncrate and clean her best dress for the occasion. Now she stood among a knot of colleagues. President Roosevelt waved. Julianne was thrilled. She and husband, Luther, among the stalwart code breakers who had been at Pearl Harbor since the war began, were going to supply critical support for the next phase of the war. The president understood, even if the spooks, so far, could only suspect. That afternoon Roosevelt held a news conference, and in the evening he reboarded the *Baltimore*. The cruiser cast off its moorings at 7:20 p.m., getting under way for Adak, in the Aleutians.

EARLIER IN 1944, on a visit of his own to MacArthur at Brisbane, Australia, Admiral Nimitz had provoked Dugout Doug's anger by mentioning a Joint Chiefs of Staff directive that required both of them to propose options for accelerating the Pacific offensive. Nimitz had had to wait for his moment, then interject that members of the Joint Chiefs were people like them, trying to do their best. The Chiefs happened to have even more information than theater commanders like MacArthur or Nimitz himself, and the admiral thought they were doing a pretty good job of it. Nimitz would have sympathized with Admiral Leahy, whose view of the Pearl Harbor conference was that President Roosevelt was getting an excellent lesson in geography—among his favorite subjects—and gaining a familiarity with the situation that would be invaluable "in preventing an unnecessary invasion of Japan." The planning staffs in Washington, Leahy felt, were ignoring the steep loss of life that would result from a direct invasion of Japan, which they advocated mindlessly. "MacArthur and Nimitz," Leahy writes, "were now in agreement that the Philippines should be recovered with ground and airpower then available in the western Pacific and that Japan would be forced to accept our terms of surrender without an invasion of the Japanese homeland." Leahy considered that the most valuable result of the Pearl Harbor discussions.

But the real question was, Could that agreement be driven home and made to stick? Navy official historian Samuel Eliot Morison claims the arguments raged for Philippines versus Taiwan for months after the Pearl Harbor conference. That is not quite true. Planners from CINCPAC continued to present lesser versions of the Taiwan option into September. But it was late in August before Admiral Leahy had returned to Washington and could brief the Chiefs on the Pearl Harbor results. The uncertainties disappeared after high-level deliberations in early September. By then the only remaining doubt would be whether the initial target in the Philippines should be the island of Mindanao or that of Leyte.

There were three aspects to making a Philippines invasion work. One, the Japanese fleet remained in play. While the Imperial Navy had suffered crippling aircraft carrier losses—and huge attrition of its naval air forces—in the Marianas campaign, its surface strength remained. So long as Japan possessed a powerful fleet, it would be difficult to isolate the Home Islands sufficiently to compel Tokyo's surrender. Two, Japanese determination seemed undiminished. If they remained stead-fast, ultimately someone would have to go in and dig them out. The Washington planners' point on that seemed well-taken. Last were the positions held by the Allies. Ernie King's attitude here had merit. An Allied juggernaut emplaced on Taiwan posed an absolute block on Japan's sea-lanes to Southeast Asia. Ships could not transit from Empire waters to the south without spending many days within the envelope of Allied bases. MacArthur's preference—the Philippines—offered a favorable position but not an absolute barrier. Naval forces would have to make a blockade of Japan effective, and the power of Japanese naval and air resistance became crucial. Put another way, MacArthur's Philippines invasion plan placed additional weight on other factors.

FDR ended his cruise at Bremerton, Washington. From there he made a radio speech to the nation, declaring the participants at the Pearl Harbor meeting had reached complete accord. At a news conference the president referred to the Philippines and MacArthur in the same sentence. Soon after, he went to a conference with Prime Minister Churchill after all, but paused to dash off a letter to Dugout Doug. Roosevelt told MacArthur that the days in Hawaii had been the highlight of his trip and promised, "as soon as I get back I will push on that plan, for I am convinced it is logical and it can be done."

Everything now hinged on the Japanese variables.

CHAPTER 1

ALL IN

Now in the third year of the war that Japan had herself initiated, the consequences of her decision were palpable. The fight in the Marianas that June crystallized the issue. Here the Allied armada invaded Japanese territory for the first time. The Combined Fleet, heart of the power of the Imperial Navy, sallied to do battle—and had been soundly trounced. Swarms of Japanese airplanes hardly managed to lay a glove on the Americans. Meanwhile, the Allies continued fighting on Saipan, while the neighboring islands of Tinian and Guam tottered at the precipice.

On the evening of June 21, as the Japanese fleet scurried to safety, four senior officers of Imperial General Headquarters gathered for dinner in Tokyo with the chief private secretary to Japan's foreign minister. Naval officers among the group spoke of the battle as a great victory, drinking toasts to the Combined Fleet's glorious achievements. One of the men, forty-year-old Captain Watanabe Yasuji, happened to be among a dwindling number of links between the heady early days and the increasingly ominous wartime present. Watanabe, now with the Naval Affairs Bureau at the Navy Ministry, had been the gunnery officer on the Combined Fleet's staff at the time of the Pearl Harbor attack. Many considered him the favorite of Admiral Yamamoto Isoroku, Japan's great hope. If nothing else, Watanabe had been his constant opponent at *shogi*, a popular strategy board game. Yet Yamamoto's death in a U.S. ambush in the Solomons had been a tragic setback for Japan. It certainly had drained Watanabe's fighting spirit, though as a descendant of ancestors who had lost an epic battle to the feudal Genji clan, the captain had not given up.

But even as Watanabe toasted to Japan's supposed success, he had a new perspective. One of his naval academy classmates commanded an air group being chewed up in the Marianas. Watanabe had seen the same thing before, in the Solomons, where the cream of Imperial Navy seamen and aviators had been skimmed off by voracious Allied combat power. By Tokyo's decision, the Marianas had been central to Japanese plans since the fall of 1943, and now the Allies were there. Another link with the heroic early days, Admiral Nagumo Chuichi, commanded the Navy's forces in the area, and his headquarters on Saipan were in greater peril every day. Men of sound minds could agree something needed to be done. The difficulty lay in deciding what.

When the dinner broke up, Captain Watanabe stayed behind to speak to the Japanese diplomat. Kase Toshikazu held a delicate position in the hierarchy. As confidant to ministers and advisers of the emperor, Kase worried intensely about the ability of the present government to conduct the war. General Tojo Hideki had concentrated much of the power in his own hands by simultaneously running the cabinet, the Army ministry, and the Army General Staff, and by having an associate, Admiral Shimada Shigetaro, do the same on the Navy side. The Tojo government's policy seemed bankrupt. Saipan demonstrated that. But Tojo ruled with an iron fist and brooked no interference. Secret policemen had repeatedly visited Kase to try to induce him to voice opposition. As a result, the diplomat had become ultracautious. Thus it is even more significant that Kase considered Watanabe his trusted friend. Captain Watanabe swore Kase to silence. The captain then told him the toasts they had drunk were to the official version. In reality the Navy had sustained a devastating defeat. Considering their conversation, Kase thought the episode had been hilarious in an ironic way. He decided to sound out some of his senior political contacts.

A RESCUE TOO FAR

Nagumo Chuichi had once thought the Allies would not attack the Marianas. Since the enemy would not attack, Nagumo felt the islands had no need of fortification. He said that to former comrade Kusaka Ryunosuke when the latter passed through Saipan on the way home to become chief of staff for the whole fleet. Now, with his nation's fleet soundly beaten, Nagumo must have wished the great naval battle had come out the way the propagandists pretended.

The reasons for failure had nothing to do with poor advance work or bad luck. Despite Nagumo's proclivities, the Imperial Navy had never been better prepared. Watanabe Yasuji knew it. As gunnery staff officer he had been responsible for tactical flourishes in Yamamoto's plans. Those had featured multiple moving parts coordinated in time but not space, in effect trading concentration for surprise. Admiral Yamamoto had been renowned for breaking with tradition, in this case with the prewar Japanese concept of the "decisive battle," in which the different ship types and combat forces each helped deliver the adversary's main fleet to the guns of the Imperial Navy's battle line in ripe condition to be finished off.

Where Yamamoto had opted for plasticity, his successors, attempting to cope with mounting Allied material superiority, had veered toward the set piece of a Kabuki play. The Combined Fleet command had reconceptualized the Pacific Ocean area as an array of zones, trying to ensure each one had local resources, bases, and airfields, with contingency plans fashioned for rapid deployment of warships and planes to any threatened sector. The various Japanese combat forces would join together, whittling down any Allied force to the point at which it could be dealt with by a Combined Fleet now built around aircraft carriers. This battle plan was all about mass action, and closer to the classic vision of a decisive battle than the Yamamoto template. Koga Mineichi, Admiral Yamamoto's successor, termed this the "Z Plan," invoking the heady days of the Russo-Japanese War, when fleet commander Togo Heihachiro had sailed to a famous victory under the flag for that letter.

Since Imperial General Headquarters (IGHQ), comprising the general staffs of both Navy and Army, considered the Marianas a key sector, plans for them were especially well developed. Nagumo had been sent to Saipan to lead the Central Pacific Area Fleet, the local naval command. Prince Takamatsu of the imperial family, a Navy captain who had been close to Watanabe, told a foreign ministry associate that this might be the last full-scale operation of which the fleet would be capable. Staffers were quietly confident. The Navy had never had such a detailed battle plan.

Japanese planners foresaw that they possessed one significant advantage. Imperial Navy warplanes had a longer striking range than U.S. carrier aircraft. Land-based bombers could fly even farther. Potentially the Combined Fleet could battle the American task forces from distances at which the United States would be unable to respond, and part of the Japanese strength could fight from land bases impossible to sink. The Imperial Navy made specific preparations to take advantage of this. In 1943, many months ahead of time, it created a First Air Fleet, an elite land-based force. It was to be the anvil to hold the American task force that would later be finished off by the hammer of the Japanese carriers. Around that time—before he ever went to Saipan—Nagumo led a survey mission to the Marianas to select new airfield sites for the redeployed air force.

The Japanese carriers, also reorganized, became the First Mobile Fleet, comprising three carrier groups, with the aircraft of each to fly as a single force. Pilots and crews of the carrier air groups, who had not been in action since the end of 1943, were better trained and prepared than previously. In Vice Admiral Ozawa Jisaburo the Mobile Fleet for the first time had a commander with a solid understanding of carrier operations. The Navy General Staff (NGS) also prepared elaborate plans for submarine screening lines that might warn of an approaching Allied fleet and weaken it before the battle. From a matériel standpoint, the Combined Fleet had been about as well prepared as it could be. All the extensive study culminated in tabletop war games rehearsing the operation. Emperor Hirohito personally attended the NGS's postmortem of its version of these war games.

Nagumo's command was remarkable in the way it disintegrated as battle neared. The Fourth Fleet, his surface naval force, which was not so strong to begin with, suffered near annihilation with U.S. task force raids on Truk and Palau in the early months of 1944. On the eve of battle Nagumo really had only a seaplane tender and some patrol boats. A Japanese Army formation, the 31st Army, had been attached to a joint force led by the Navy. American submarines took a heavy toll of its soldiers, sinking a number of the troopships bringing them to the Marianas. Then the general leading the 31st Army refused Nagumo's orders, making his unified command a fiction.

As battle approached, the two air flotillas that had formed parts of Nagumo's force were assigned to Vice Admiral Kakuta Kakuji of the First Air Fleet instead. This left dispositions unchanged and the First Air Fleet headquarters located on Tinian.

No plan survives contact with the enemy, and so it proved with the scheme for the Marianas battle. Much of the land-based air strength of both the First Air Fleet and the local forces fell to the swarms of American carrier planes that raided Truk, Palau, and the Marianas as Admiral Nimitz's invasion began. Half of Kakuta's force evaporated. Allied intelligence put more nails into the coffin of Japan's dreams. It had been code breakers who furnished U.S. submariners with the Japanese convoy positions, enabling the slaughter of troopships bound for the Marianas. Intercepting an instruction from the Japanese Sixth Fleet to its own submarines, U.S. code breakers were able to break out the locations of an entire patrol line of Japanese subs, and an Allied hunter-killer group then rolled up the line, sinking half a dozen undersea craft. The Japanese would be desperately short when the Marianas battle began. They would also lack destroyers—and here the code breakers alerted the submariners to the Imperial Navy fleet concentration, and subs dispatched seven of these precious escorts. More decrypts told U.S. submarines the best places to find Ozawa's fleet, and the boats then confirmed the Japanese sortie with sighting reports. The dearth of escorts mattered when Ozawa lost two fleet carriers, one of them his flagship, to subs.

Admiral Raymond A. Spruance, commanding Task Force 58, the U.S. carrier force, as well as the Marianas invasion fleet, could base his dispositions on both radio intelligence and submarine reports. The most controversial aspect of the battle on the Allied side became Spruance's decision to pull the fleet back as Ozawa advanced. Spruance understood that Task Force 58 protected the invasion and therefore needed to be kept whole. He put up strong fighter defenses. Ozawa's strike aircraft were intercepted many miles away from the American fleet on June 19. Very few got past the defenses and none scored any appreciable damage. So many planes fell to the savage defenses that Americans called the encounter "the Great Marianas Turkey Shoot."

Having defeated the Japanese onslaught, the next day Spruance pursued the enemy. His own carrier strikes wiped out another aircraft carrier. The Imperial Navy lost three flattops and something like 450 warplanes, while achieving nothing. One has to wonder how IGHQ officers could have toasted this "victory" with a straight face. Indeed, Tokyo propagandists made extravagant claims—nine American aircraft carriers and five battleships sunk or damaged—while in reality hardly any U.S. ships were touched.

THE DISASTROUS PHILIPPINE Sea battle left the Imperial Navy in the position of having important forces in a combat zone completely dominated by the Allies. Not only were more than 15,000 sailors caught in the trap, but also those endangered included skilled ship artificers and aircraft mechanics, Japanese communications intelligence experts, naval infantry, and the staffs and commanders of the Central Pacific Area Fleet, First Air Fleet, and Sixth Fleet.

For days, talk of rescue expeditions roiled across Tokyo. Navy staff officials promised salvation. Junior naval officers clamored for action, accusing the Japanese Army command of obstructing a rescue. Many others thought the whole idea ludicrous. The scheme might have had some chance while Ozawa's Mobile Fleet monopolized Allied attention, but the day after Prime Minister Tojo approved the mission the Mobile Fleet went down in defeat at the Turkey Shoot.

Combined Fleet chief of staff Kusaka Ryunosuke, anxious to succor his old boss Nagumo, dreamed up the first scheme for the Saipan mission, revolving around two old battleships. Staffers thought Kusaka's idea silly, but he was determined to go ahead. Captain Yamamoto Chikao (no relation to the great admiral), who led the operations section of the NGS, completed the plan on June 21.

The next day Admiral Ozawa's vanquished Mobile Fleet anchored at Okinawa on its way home. As the fleet neared Japan, C-in-C Toyoda Soemu held the options open by ordering Ozawa to concentrate in the Inland Sea and prepare for an immediate mission. Under a revised rescue plan, the one available fleet carrier, *Zuikaku*, and every other two-bit aviation ship the Navy could scrape up would be loaded with whatever planes could fly, scrounged from both the Army and the Navy. The planes would have to take off only once. They would be expended in the fight.

This improvised carrier fleet would sail several days behind a convoy escorted by the Fifth Fleet, Japan's northeast sea frontier protection force, expected to leave the port of Yokosuka carrying an Army infantry regiment. The carrier force would cover its approach with a one-way air attack. The next day Japan's Second Fleet, the Navy's big-gun unit, would steam in and crush the Allied fleets off the Marianas. The Fifth Fleet would then arrive with the Army's regiment, and a day after that would be another convoy with a full Army division.

The rescue, still merely on paper, already looked shaky. The Ozawa fleet had been smashed in a full-scale battle and could hardly be ready for another. That went for the Second Fleet as well—it had been part of Ozawa's force. Admiral Ozawa himself estimated he needed two months to get the ships back in fighting trim. About the only naval units really at hand were the Fifth Fleet and the old battleships. The aged *Yamashiro* of Battleship Division 2, and a pair of converted battleship–aircraft carriers, the *Ise* and *Hyuga*, were just completing modification to this hybrid status. There was also the *Fuso*, then in the southern Philippines after participating in a similar—but abortive—sortie to aid the Japanese defenders of Biak Island. The two hybrid ships, still working up, were ultimately left out of the plan.

Operations officers wanted to send at least the *Yamashiro*. She could dash to Saipan, deliver the regiment to stiffen the defenses, and then ground herself to serve as an artillery battery. The Army might contribute one of its own transport ships. Cruisers of the Fifth Fleet could carry more troops as well as the landing barges to put them ashore. With a handful of escorts these warships could become a relief mission. The *Fuso*, sailing independently, would shoot up Allied convoys headed to the battle areas. Combined Fleet alerted her for that mission on June 17. But the battleship-only rescue was a nonstarter. Three days later the Navy scrubbed the *Fuso* raiding mission. Combined Fleet commander in chief Toyoda Soemu thought the entire concept reckless and rejected chief of staff Kusaka's proposals. According to Kusaka this was among the few times Toyoda ever did that.

Historian Anthony Tully attributes the rescue to Captain Kami Shigenori. A notorious hothead in the Imperial Navy, Kami might well have dreamed up this kind of scheme. Tully reports that Captain Kami, ready to accept any risk, volunteered to skipper the *Yamashiro* to her destiny. Contrary to some claims, however, at that time Kami was no operations specialist with either the fleets or the NGS. He was captain of the light cruiser *Tama*. That vessel at least belonged to the Fifth Fleet and could have participated, but it leaves the captain as just another advocate, not the planner of this extravaganza. It is true that Kami had spent much of his career in staff billets, but by the same token he had minimal command experience. The *Tama* had been his first ship in many years. Why the Navy should put Kami in charge of a battlewagon goes unexplained. In November 1966, Admiral Kusaka personally claimed credit, regretting the rescue had not been carried out, claiming that with the right timing it could have worked.

Meanwhile the plan had also envisioned that a long-range air unit (the "Hachiman Force") would cooperate with the surface fleet, flying out to strike the Allied armada and paving the way for the surface ships. Cobbled together ad hoc, and composed of crews picked from the Yokosuka Air Group and Twelfth Air Fleet, the Hachiman Force actually deployed to Iwo Jima, but it never comprised more than sixty aircraft, and half those were lost in June and July.

Serious fliers thought this enterprise could only be a death ride. How a small air unit would penetrate the dense Allied umbrella, where the entire Mobile Fleet had failed, remained a mystery. Similarly, an ancient battleship was supposed to sink the mighty Blue Fleet, and another would get through to Saipan and reverse the strategic balance. The rescue plan had no substance. Admiral Toyoda stuck to his guns, and the Army high command dismissed the idea out of hand. The Army had spent six months reinforcing the Marianas with really significant forces—more than a few of which had been sunk en route by Allied subs. A single regiment sent now would achieve nothing, a regiment plus a division not much more.

But these plans, empty as they were, are important for other reasons. Such a degree of desperation now prevailed in Tokyo that the most extreme alternatives suddenly appealed. There is an argument from cultural history that the Japanese held special esteem for showing nobility even in failure. In the Pacific war in late 1944, Japan stood at the brink of that very deep chasm.

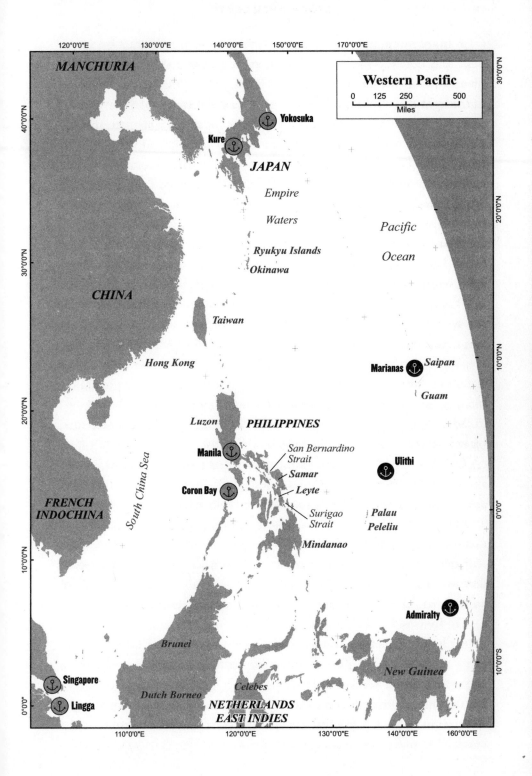

A more mundane reason would turn out to be a distraction in the next real battle. That is, the rescue plan envisioned taking the Fifth Fleet away from its geographic mission, employing it instead as an integral element in a battle concept. Once the Imperial Navy finally finished reconfiguring the force for the next battle, that element stuck—the old northern force would morph into the anticipated vanguard for the Ozawa fleet.

Emperor Hirohito sided with the young Navy officers. He demanded action. He had told Admiral Shimada on the eve of the Philippine Sea battle that with sufficient determination Japan might achieve a success like Tsushima, the glorious 1905 victory against the Russian fleet in the Sea of Japan. Hirohito warned Prime Minister Tojo of air raids on Tokyo if the Marianas were lost. They had to be held. IGHQ chiefs kept bringing him bad news. The emperor *ordered* Navy minister Shimada to craft a rescue. On June 24 Tojo and Shimada united to tell the emperor the bad news that Combined Fleet now felt the plan unworkable. Hirohito countered, demanding a second opinion from the Board of Field Marshals and Fleet Admirals, a military appendage of the *jushin*, or senior statesmen, who had a behind-the-scenes role in Tokyo. When the board also nixed a rescue, the emperor ordered them to put that judgment on paper, turned on his heel, and stalked off. The *Yamashiro* mission evaporated.

One *jushin* with whom diplomat Kase Toshikazu discussed Japan's situation was Admiral Okada Keisuke. Okada had been Navy minister and prime minister in the 1930s. Now he told Kase that a rescue operation would only deepen the disaster, though perhaps that was a *good* idea—"he thought it advisable to let the 'young fellows' have their own way once in order to reconcile them ultimately to their inevitable fate—defeat." Admiral Yonai Mitsumasa, another *jushin*, agreed the loss of Saipan would be a calamity, but he refused a useless gesture.

On June 29 Prince Takamatsu conceded to associates that the recent defeat had stymied the Imperial Navy for the present. The Navy captain's remark, coming from the second brother of Hirohito, suggested the emperor had accepted reality.

The only efforts to rescue the Japanese in the Marianas would be by submarine. The big fleet submarines, I-boats, and smaller medium-range craft, RO-boats, were used in these operations. Two subs went down in futile missions to Saipan to recover Sixth Fleet commander Vice Admiral Takagi Takao. Thirteen Japanese submarines were lost in the Marianas, nearly half in rescue attempts. The sole success came to Lieutenant Commander Itakura Mitsuma's *I-41*. Itakura managed to get his boat into Apra Harbor on Guam and spirit away more than 100 airmen.

RESHUFFLING THE DECK

What did happen after the Marianas debacle would be the fall of Tojo and Shimada. The former had many enemies. There were offices at IGHQ—not just Navy but Army ones too—where the occupants regarded Tojo as an enemy. The prime minister owed a good deal of this to his ruthless approach, brooking no opposition. Officers who spoke up or who said the wrong thing could quickly find themselves sent to the China front—Tokyo's equivalent to Hitler sending an officer to the Russian front or Stalin sending someone to Siberia. When a Tojo intimate, whom he frequently consulted in private, advised the general to give up his second/third job as chief of the Army staff and said something about realigning the cabinet to try to seek a compromise peace, Prime Minister Tojo threw his friend out.

Colonel Tanemura Sato, an Army senior staffer, viewed Tojo as a tool of the Imperial Navy. Many Navy officers saw their own chief, Admiral Shimada, as Tojo's creature. The prime minister had induced Shimada to hold the posts of Navy minister and chief of the General Staff simultaneously, as Tojo did for the Army. Feelings had already run high that the men ought to shed their dual posts.

Colonel Matsutani Sei had been a section chief on the Army staff. Worried sick at the velocity of the Allied advance, that spring Matsutani organized a study group of influential IGHQ officers to coordinate planning. They met regularly at Tokyo's Sanno Hotel. Matsutani's Army counterparts included Colonels Hattori Takushiro and Nishiura Susumu, respectively, a senior operations planner and a former aide to Tojo himself. Navy members included the operations chief Captain Yamamoto; Captain Ohmae Toshikazu, the operations staff officer for the Mobile Fleet, Japan's carrier force; and Captain Fujii Shigeru, a top logistics planner who had earlier been private secretary to Admiral Shimada. Matsutani led the discussions. Over time the growing pessimism became unmistakable. Thus, Admiral Yonai's remarks to Kase Toshikazu reflected wider feelings that were anathema to Tojo.

Colonel Matsutani became another of Kase Toshikazu's intimates. Convinced that an early end to the war had become the only solution, around the beginning of July Matsutani showed up in Kase's office with a paper titled "On the Future Conduct of the War." He had compiled the study together with Colonel Tanemura and another General Staff officer. Matsutani pointedly observed that while Tokyo professed to have a military strategy, it had no diplomatic program. He wanted to argue this with Prime Minister Tojo. Diplomat Kase, fearing the officer would be disgraced, perhaps imprisoned, begged Matsutani not to. The colonel also showed the paper to a couple of senior General Staff officers. Both forbade him from circulating it.

Matsutani did anyway.

On July 2, the colonel confronted Tojo. A stormy argument ensued. The next day Colonel Matsutani dropped by Kase's office in dress uniform to say good-bye. He had been ordered to the China front.

But the press of events overpowered Tojo. The Philippine Sea disaster left Admiral Shimada completely discredited. Hirohito demanded his ouster. General Tojo could not save his close ally, nor even preserve his own multiple posts. Tojo's great advantage had always been loyalty to the emperor.

Saipan stripped that away—or, more accurately, the general's honest evaluation of the uselessness of a fleet rescue sortie led Hirohito to rescind his protection. After that Tojo became fair game. Admiral Toyoda of the Combined Fleet, among the most senior active officers, stood in line to succeed Shimada. Tojo managed to torpedo that idea, insisting he could not work with Toyoda, whose attitude was anti-Army.

Maneuvers against Tojo began in the Diet—significant because the Japanese legislature had long since stopped being a power center. Anti-Tojo forces coalesced around Prince Takamatsu. The Allies' extension of their offensive with landings on Tinian and Guam in July only sharpened the differences. Prime Minister Tojo tried to curb dissent by inviting some of the *jushin* to join his cabinet, then dismissing

Admiral Shimada. The *jushin* met with Lord Kido, the emperor's privy counselor. Finally, on July 18, unable to quiet the clamor for his skin, Tojo gave up his post as Army chief of staff. Later that day he resigned all posts and retired. Tojo finished the war tending his garden.

A new cabinet took office as President Roosevelt made his voyage to Pearl Harbor, empaneled on July 22 under General Koiso Kuniaki. Koiso was also head of the new Supreme Council for the Direction of the War, an inner cabinet/military coordination unit made up of the war and Navy ministers, their respective chiefs of staff, the foreign minister, and the prime minister. This group made the basic policy decisions. The military high command, rather than meeting at IGHQ, would gather at the War Council's offices. The new Navy minister would be Yonai Mitsumasa.

Everyone was aware that heavy bombers flying from the Marianas would be capable of striking Japan. As if to underline the point, a force of American B-29s, temporarily based in China, attacked Japan for the first time since the Doolittle Raid of early 1942. The raid aimed not at Tokyo, but at a steelworks at Yawata, on Kyushu, and it occurred the same day American troops stormed ashore on Saipan. The threat loomed—the target could just as easily have been Tokyo. The Japanese did not know that the Allies were already planning to expand the B-29 force and regroup it in the Marianas for an air campaign against Japan. But anticipating that precise move, General Koiso brought up the matter of evacuating the supreme command from Tokyo.

That subject raised hackles. General Koiso broached it with Marquis Kido after his imperial audience, and Kido took it directly to the emperor. The Japanese had long lived in fear of bombing. Before the war, mass civil defense drills and a constant barrage of media harped on the threat of death from the air. Tokyo watched the 1940 Battle of Britain with apprehension, with the German bombing of London; and the Doolittle Raid had had a powerful effect on the nation's sense of security.

In case of evacuation, Marquis Kido told General Koiso, IGHQ and the Supreme War Council should be colocated and the emperor would take charge as generalissimo. But, Kido added, he had never discussed leaving Tokyo, alone or in concert, with Hirohito. That conversation took place on July 26. The emperor instantly dismissed the idea.

Hirohito feared restlessness and defeatism among the people if he left the Home Islands—which he referred to as "the mainland." Only absolute necessity would induce him to reconsider. "I must remain on the mainland by all means," the emperor declared, "to try desperately to protect the mainland, where our grand shrine reigns." The emperor would not budge.

Too many hard-liners remained in high places, determined to fight. Fleet C-in-C Toyoda later remarked, "While it would not be accurate to say that we were influenced by public opinion, questions were beginning to be asked at home as to what the Navy was doing after loss of one point after another down south."

Perhaps Admiral Suzuki Kantaro's sensibility, applied more broadly, was right: The hard-liners needed to get their way and see it fail, at least once. That could happen in the Philippines.

WHILE POLITICAL MACHINATIONS continued, the military moved ahead with its preparations. Even as American leaders struggled to decide which way to jump and Tokyo reflected the same apprehension, commanders of the Combined Fleet held a conference on measures for the next battle, then sent the project to the NGS for the drafting of an operations plan. Officers at IGHQ wanted to apply the new standard of detailed planning that had been achieved before the Marianas battle.

On July 24 IGHQ informed the Southern Area Army, Japan's operational command for the entire Pacific Ocean area, that it expected to direct a decisive battle against the Allies in the second half of 1944. For the Navy Admiral Shimada laid down broad outlines in one of his last directives as NGS chief. Admiral Oikawa Koshiro, who succeeded him at the head of the NGS, had yet to take up the reins. But Captain Yamamoto's planners applied the standard to *each direction* the Allies might take. He had more than a dozen officers in the NGS operations section, so the work could be spread around enough to avoid overwhelming the staff. The project wound its way through the NGS while the politicos lined up to oust Tojo.

It is striking how closely the Japanese timing matches President Roosevelt's Pearl Harbor strategy deliberations. The Imperial Navy's basic directives for the next campaign emerged from the warren of General Staff offices on July 26, *the day before FDR convened his top commanders at Pearl Harbor.* Some doubt Captain Yamamoto's strategic good sense, but in fact he'd held this job for two years. For fifteen months before that he had been a section chief under Baron Tomioka Sadatoshi, a renowned staff officer under whom fools did not last, and Yamamoto had done a tour with the NGS operations bureau in the late 1930s. His reputation had been shining enough that, at a time when the Pearl Harbor attack plan remained a closely guarded secret, the air staff officer for Combined Fleet had felt comfortable telling him of the scheme. Yamamoto Chikao, then the skipper of a seaplane carrier, had noticed the absence of the fleet aircraft carriers from the southern invasion lists and had made inquiries. The Navy would promote Yamamoto to flag rank and send him on to lead a unit of aviation ships. Historian Samuel Eliot Morison claims the quality of NGS planning deteriorated under Captain Yamamoto, but the meticulous preparations for the upcoming campaign are evident.

The Japanese christened their plan "Sho Go," or "Victory Operation." There were four Sho contingencies, numbered according to the geographic areas to which they would apply. Sho 1 would take effect if Allied forces invaded the Philippines. Sho 2 provided for the defense of Taiwan, the Ryukyu Islands, and southern Japan. Sho 3 would go into effect if the attack were to be against central Japan. Finally, if northern Japan became the Allies' target, Sho 4 would be the response. Each plan provided specific countermeasures. The contingencies replicated the careful approach pioneered in Admiral Koga's Z Plan.

To grease the wheels of action before giving up his posts, Tojo sponsored the Supreme War Council. That group now decided to go all in on the next battle. As Combined Fleet commander Toyoda Soemu explained it to Allied interviewers after the war, Tokyo reviewed the full range of its resources along with its geographic position. If Japan were to be cut off from the southern area, it would no longer be able to find resources for the Inner Empire. The Supreme Council decided to apply 70 percent of Japan's resources to the next battle and husband the rest for the struggle for the homeland. IGHQ now began fleshing out the concepts.

Captain Yamamoto worked on the general schema. The NGS articulated the result in IGHQ Navy Directive No. 431, issued on July 21, as the Tojo government collapsed and the Americans mopped up on Tinian and Guam.

Despite the Marianas disaster, Yamamoto and his colleagues still thought the operational concept perfectly sound: The Imperial Navy could use land bases to shuttle bomb the Allies and hold an umbrella that might cover its surface fleet. If there were a substantial carrier, or "mobile," force, they would be even more potent. One reason the tactic had not worked so well at the Battle of the Philippine Sea, Yamamoto noticed, had been the restricted number of airfields on small islands, which made it practical for the Allies to neutralize the base network. With big landmasses like Taiwan, the Philippines, or Japan, that became impossible. There would always be alternate airfields. Under this concept the strength of land-based air forces became even more crucial to the overall mission.

Admiral Shimada, not yet supplanted from his NGS post, signed the orders. Directive No. 431 provided that the air fleets would be reorganized and massed in the homeland, from where they could sally. The object "of attacking and destroying the enemy fleet and advancing forces" became the goal. Surface naval forces would concentrate their main strength in the southern area, close to Japan's oil sources. Mobile forces—by which the directive meant carrier units—were lumped together with the surface fleet, but the inclusion of language providing that some units would be stationed in Empire waters indicates that the NGS had already begun grappling with the treatment of aircraft carriers—something that emerged as another headache. The fleet should give special attention to "raiding operations"—mounting surprise attacks—including ones designed to catch the enemy in their advanced bases. The NGS envisioned many kinds of raiding operations. The overall concept, like that of the Z Plan, remained one of "intercepting and destroying the enemy within the sphere of the [land-based] air forces."

On July 26 IGHQ Navy Directive No. 435 followed, establishing Sho contingency areas and fleshing out arrangements for air operations. Following the new combined action model (which had not worked in the Marianas, but perhaps had simply been too novel), there would be a unified command—the air fleets to include both Imperial Navy and

Japanese Army units. Navy officers would direct when enemy fleets were the targets. Directive No. 435 specified which Army air units would be controlled by Navy air fleets. Captain Yamamoto's planners had been thorough. The order went so far as to list aircraft types and designate what kinds of enemy forces they should destroy.

Prior to battle, air strength should be dispersed as much as possible to avoid incidental losses from Allied attacks. When the moment came to hurl the air forces, one element would blast Allied aircraft carriers, while the major strength made both day and night attacks against enemy transport convoys and—again—carriers.

Laying down the framework accelerated. On August 1, Admiral Toyoda Soemu issued orders providing for cooperation with the Army "to intercept and destroy the invading enemy at sea in a Decisive Battle." This directive, so far as the Philippines were concerned, envisioned rapid preparation of air bases to accommodate the planes of a re-formed First Air Fleet as well as a newly created Second Air Fleet. Allied carriers were to be sunk by air attack, while warships and planes combined to smash transport convoys. If the Allies' invasion succeeded, their amphibious shipping would then become the primary target. The surface fleet would sortie within two days of any invasion, and air strikes would begin at least forty-eight hours before warships reached the scene. A separate top secret directive specified a new fleet organization for the battle.

By late July, Imperial Army commanders were starting to line up behind the option for putting nearly all remaining resources behind a single roll of the dice. At senior levels of Imperial General Headquarters the discussions climaxed the week of August 9, when planners held talks every day.

Finally everyone agreed, and on August 18 the services jointly sent an IGHQ petition to Emperor Hirohito. An audience with him took place the next day. Apparently unaware of the petition, privy seal Marquis Kido viewed the meeting's purpose as somewhat vague, with a roundtable discussion and the emperor encouraged to pose questions.

After the war Hirohito recalled, "I agreed to the showdown battle . . . thinking that if we attacked . . . and America flinched, then we would probably be able to find room to negotiate." Historian Herbert Bix, a notable Western expert on Hirohito, found this to be an example of the emperor's destructive influence on military operations, but the truth seems more nuanced. The Japanese Army did not change its plans for defending the Philippines merely because of the decision in Tokyo. Rather, its commitment to send additional forces to the Philippines made it possible for area commanders to expand their inadequate defenses beyond the island of Luzon.

THE WATCHERS

The Marianas campaign became an intelligence bonanza for the Allies. For example, with the loss of Sixth Fleet headquarters, the Imperial Navy's top submarine command, the Americans captured thousands of documents. By itself Saipan contained the command posts of Nagumo's Central Pacific Area Fleet, of naval base forces, of the 31st Army, and of the 1st Combined Communications Unit of the Imperial Navy's radio intercept service. Tinian also contained the nerve center for Admiral Kakuta's First Air Fleet. All their records were vulnerable. Not only did the fighting go quickly enough that the enemy had very limited time to destroy papers, but Allied intelligence outfits had gained expertise and their commanders had put new mechanisms in place. Intelligence teams accompanied the combat troops and did triage—making on-the-spot assessments of critical documents for immediate translation. The Marianas battles became the first instance where the take of captured documents could be measured by the ton, and the first time captured Japanese soldiers numbered in the thousands.

A fleet or task force commander—say, Admiral Spruance with the Fifth Fleet in the Marianas, or William F. Halsey, who followed him, in charge of the Third Fleet—had a fleet intelligence officer on his permanent staff. More reporting came directly from Pearl Harbor, or from several sources in Washington, DC, including Army, Navy, and Marine. General MacArthur had his own intelligence organization in Australia and New Guinea, which included radio and photo intelligence shops, its own collection units, and its own interpretation offices, for ground, naval, and air forces. The Australians had a parallel apparatus. The British—in Burma and India—had yet another autonomous spy agency.

And the British had a Far East Combined Bureau (FECB) at Colombo as a kind of fusion center. Subordinate units had less elaborate staffs to do the same. In short, a robust intelligence network supported the Allied offensive.

All agree the most important entity was the Joint Intelligence Center Pacific Ocean Area (JICPOA) at Pearl Harbor. It was a fusion center like FECB, using all-source intelligence, working directly for Admiral Nimitz, commander in chief Pacific Ocean area (CINCPAC). Something like 1,100 people worked for JICPOA. Wags called it "the Zoo." JICPOA sent the intelligence teams that accompanied invasions, and its cohort, the Fleet Radio Unit Pacific (FRUPAC), supplied mobile radio detachments to commanders, to whom they supplied urgent news. The ensemble had just gone through the bedlam of its latest expansion.

Descended from the now-famous Station Hypo—the radio spooks at Pearl Harbor who had divined the Japanese plan to attack Midway Island, leading to a remarkable victory—JICPOA had mushroomed, adding sections for estimates, photographic interpretation, document translation, prisoner interrogation, mapping, terrain modeling, and psychological warfare. They worked to intercept actual Imperial Navy messages, in a code the Allies knew as JN-25, which were decrypted to reveal the thinking of the enemy. The intelligence product was called "Ultra."

The center outgrew its original Hypo basement offices, moved to a large frame building constructed on Makalapa Hill, then outgrew that too. The Navy had begun the war with a small cadre of radio intelligence specialists—code breakers working the intercepted messages—and radiomen (called the "On the Roof Gang" for the erstwhile location of their radio shack atop Navy Department headquarters in Washington) trained to record the letter-characters the Japanese used in transmission. A little over a month before the Philippine Sea battle, JICPOA moved to a matching headquarters just finished next door, while FRUPAC took over the remainder of the first building save for one suite occupied by the Estimates Section. The radio unit had swollen to roughly the size of the rest of JICPOA, about 30 percent of everyone in Navy radio intelligence at the time. (OP-20-G, the Navy's code-breaking organization, had 3,722 civilians, officers, and enlisted sailors in February 1944.)

Messages broken by the code breakers were interpreted by "Japanese language officers," men carefully trained as Japanese linguists. At the beginning there were just a few dozen of these men, with knowledge of Japanese culture and, usually, experience as naval attachés. War brought huge pressures for more language expertise. The Navy started programs to train language officers quickly at Harvard, Berkeley, and the University of Colorado at Boulder. British authorities did the same thing at the School of Oriental and African Studies in London. In the United States the group trained at Boulder would be the largest by far, and "Boulder Boys" became something of a slang reference to the freshly minted language officers. Beginning in 1943 the stream of Boulder Boys arriving at Pearl Harbor became a steady flow. A number of them roomed in apartments rented from the Honolulu madame Jean O'Hara. By day they translated intercepted radio messages or captured documents, or interpreted during interrogations of Japanese prisoners of war. At night, who knows?

All streams of intelligence fed into the JICPOA Estimates Section, under Commander Wilfred J. "Jasper" Holmes. In many ways Jasper Holmes was the glue that held together the entire outfit. Invalided out of submarine service for arthritis of the spine, Holmes had worked in naval intelligence since the Hypo days. He had been the apostle for operational intelligence, creating a "combat intelligence unit" that earned kudos in the Solomons campaign, and had then spun it off into the Estimates Section, a unit that supplied weekly and monthly appreciations of Japanese strength on the land, at sea, and in the air. It maintained an all-source running plot of the locations of Japanese warships, and a watch section responsible for urgent warnings of enemy action.

After the attack on Pearl Harbor, then-Station Hypo had soon identified exactly which Japanese warships had done the dastardly deed. Holmes and others made a huge poster adorned with silhouettes of each archenemy vessel. The poster moved with him to the wall of his new Estimates Section, where it appeared like the FBI "Most Wanted" list. Holmes confessed to "unprofessional vindictive satisfaction" each time he crossed out one of the culprits, and he had a standing offer of a bottle of Scotch for any submarine skipper who sank a Pearl Harbor enemy. He had made good with every sinking until the Marianas—where Commander Herman J. Kossler and his *Cavalla* dispatched the *Shokaku*, the fifth of six Imperial Navy aircraft carriers that had participated. The sub skipper's superior never presented Kossler with his reward, and years later it still pained Holmes that he had not made good on his promise, especially since it turned out *Shokaku* would be the only one sunk by submarine.

As a trained engineer, Jasper Holmes's solutions were practical ones, and despite the exponential growth of U.S. intelligence in the Pacific he kept the Estimates Section on an even keel. They learned from Japanese prisoners, scanned captured documents for important details, and incorporated photo analysis, not to mention the decrypted text of messages supplied by FRUPAC. They added sections when work in subject areas became extensive—an air section, an "enemy land" section, another for "enemy bases," a mine warfare section, and so on. He corresponded with counterparts elsewhere, cheerfully chiding a colleague at Navy headquarters that the Estimates Section would be happy to copy any great idea Washington came up with, or to host visiting staff for temporary duty at its office.

Captain Edwin T. Layton, the redoubtable fleet intelligence officer for CINCPAC Nimitz, had maintained a file of biographic information on senior Japanese naval officers. Pressed with other business, he'd neglected it, and finally turned the file over to Lieutenant John Harrison, one of the language officers in the Estimates Section. Harrison soon endowed JICPOA with the best collection of Japanese naval biography outside Tokyo. For example, the Japanese command turned over again several months before the Marianas battle when Combined Fleet leaders fled Palau ahead of a U.S. carrier raid but the planes carrying the officers crashed amid storms. Fleet commander Koga Mineichi perished. His successor became Admiral Toyoda Soemu. That puzzled a lot of Americans, since Toyoda seemed virtually unknown. Looking into his files, Lieutenant Harrison found a photo of the Japanese admiral and could produce a short biography, so JICPOA put out an intelligence bulletin on changes in the enemy high command. This became the first time most Americans had heard of Toyoda.

Jasper Holmes, soon promoted captain, wore two hats. He worked as deputy to General Joseph J. Twitty, an Army brigadier who had been among that service's Japanese language officers, but also as officer in

charge of the Estimates Section, which swelled to thirty-two officers
and a dozen enlisted personnel, including three women. Their reports
went to Admiral Nimitz at CINCPAC and to other commands. Eddie
Layton functioned as Nimitz's indispensable aide on all things intelligence. When Holmes was away from the Estimates Section, Commander
Donald M. "Mac" Showers ably seconded him. Another key weapon
in the JICPOA arsenal, Mac Showers had played central roles in both
the 1942 breakthrough that had identified Midway as a Japanese target,
enabling the United States to lay a trap there, and the decrypts that led
to the aerial ambush where perished Japanese fleet commander Yamamoto Isoroku a year later. Those were among the most important
achievements of the operational intelligence Holmes championed.

In addition to operational intelligence, biographical reporting, and
estimates of opposing strength, JICPOA did translations from the Japanese. It published special studies that surveyed islands, regions, or
practical subjects based on captured documents. The translation unit
started in the fall of 1943 and at first had little to do. But document
hauls at Tarawa, Kwajalein, and Eniwetok had grown steadily. From
early 1944 on it became impossible to translate every paper that crossed
the transom. Soon the section morphed into as many as fifteen units,
each of which handled documents in a particular subject area.

The fall of the Marianas proved grist for the mill. On Saipan alone,
JICPOA took control of fifty tons of documents, including information
about the defenses on Tinian and Guam. There were codebooks, radio
monitoring schedules, exemplars of Japanese radio direction-finding
equipment, and more. The take included actual diagrams of every major
aviation facility in the Home Islands, a digest of Japanese naval air
bases, and a complete set of Imperial Navy administrative orders.
Translators spoke of laboring in the salt mines.

From them a smart analyst could derive the Japanese order of battle, its fleet organization, its leadership, even post office addresses. To
have any chance at all of finding actionable intelligence, JICPOA had
to deputize officers to scan for hot documents and embargo what they
found. A forward translation team processed them immediately.

Similarly, until the Marianas, Japanese prisoners had been rare. The
1,780 prisoners captured on Saipan alone were more than those taken

so far throughout the war. Coping with the bonanza of enemy soldiers required Admiral Spruance, plus the Army, the Navy, and the Marines, to pool intelligence resources. Prisoner interrogation, an art form Allied intelligence developed to a high level, began by asking each detainee a set of identical questions, designed to produce data that could be compared from one man to another, and elicit whether the prisoner possessed especially useful intelligence and should be questioned at greater length. The challenge seemed insurmountable. The JICPOA Interrogation Section expanded to twenty-four officers and twenty-seven enlisted, but even so most of the actual interviews took place elsewhere. Some 3,500 prisoners were interrogated at Camp Tracy in California (producing more than 1,700 data reports). The most sensitive questioning, usually of senior officers, took place at Fort Hunt, near Mount Vernon, Virginia.

Jasper Holmes and General Twitty kept in close touch with all the other Allied intelligence centers. Those in Washington, including the Office of Naval Intelligence (ONI) across the board, and OP-20-G for radio intelligence, were among their closest correspondents.

As Japanese officers promulgated orders to build strength for the big Sho battles, Commander Holmes wrote to ONI's F-22 section, where Commander William J. Sebald, his counterpart, had charge of ONI's estimates of Japanese strength. Sebald had proposed a new way to categorize aircraft. Holmes objected that available information would often be insufficient to make the choices. "Under present conditions," Holmes wrote, "it is impossible for your people and mine to agree, [even] with 'very wide limits,' how many planes are in the Central Pacific, let alone attempt to classify them."

On August 16, Holmes's people issued a "special estimate" of Japanese fighter strength in the Inner Empire. Of a total of more than 2,200 aircraft projected, JICPOA saw 774 as belonging to combat units in training, with another 830 training pilots and aircrews. Just over 600 battle-ready fighter aircraft were in the assessment. Two-thirds of the fighters were in training!

Whatever else appeared, the intelligence revealed that Japan had begun frantic preparations.

CHAPTER 2

THE LOWDOWN

On July 25, the Japanese NGS operations chief sent out an all-hands warning: "KING HAS CONFERRED WITH NIMITZ IN HAWAII. THE NEXT ENEMY OFFENSIVE WILL BE DIRECTED TO THE PHILIPPINES AND WILL BE CARRIED OUT SHORTLY." While Captain Yamamoto identified the American participants, he did not know that President Roosevelt stood on the verge of greeting his field commanders for the Pearl Harbor conference. He was also unaware that U.S. Navy chief King stood opposed to the Philippines option. It did not matter, though, because Japanese expectations were correct. The question that remained was what the Combined Fleet could do to defeat the offensive.

By this time most of Japan's surface ships had arrived safely at Singapore or Lingga Roads, the southern bases, where they began strenuous combat exercises. Yamamoto's dispatch heralded the fall of the last Marianas outposts. Vice Admiral Ugaki Matome, commanding Battleship Division 1, could imagine how bitterly this news was received at Combined Fleet headquarters. Ugaki had been the Combined Fleet chief of staff when the Allies captured Buna, in eastern New Guinea. His feelings of sorrow and regret had been nearly intolerable. Now, perfecting forces for the next battle became the best thing to do. Victory would not bring back the Marianas, but it might blunt the Allied advance.

There were immense immediate problems, however. Politics between NGS and the Combined Fleet command had often been touchy, and this battle threatened to bring them into play. An equally thorny problem existed between Navy and Army at Imperial Headquarters. The Navy Ministry meanwhile dealt with a host of difficulties ranging from rates of aircraft, engine, and warship production; to finding the metal for the manufacturing; to coping with the Allied technical superiority; to servicing and preparing the fleet for battle. And of course, all the Japanese efforts were under observation by an immensely capable Allied intelligence.

FORCE BUILDING

One reason the Japanese could not send a naval sortie to rescue beleaguered forces in the Marianas is that much of the fleet went through dry dock or construction yards as soon as the ships returned from their most recent battles. Even though the high command was anxious to return its forces to combat readiness as soon as possible, it would be no matter of scraping barnacles off ships' bottoms, touching up their paint, or sticking on a few extra light antiaircraft guns. Rather, the summer and fall of 1944 witnessed the most concentrated burst of armament augmentation the Imperial Navy had ever seen.

Say what you like about the insanity of Japan's war and the resource constraints that so often forced the Imperial Navy to make radical shifts in construction or deployment plans. Despite all of that, there is a certain logic that becomes apparent once the Japanese reached decisions. Even though their goals might be unobtainable, the Navy plotted reasonable directions toward them. After the Midway disaster, senior officers immediately convened to mull over shipbuilding changes and aircraft procurement. Now, two years later, conversions of battleships and seaplane tenders to hybrid or full aircraft carriers were available. New carriers were coming from the shipyards, and converted merchantmen—now escort carriers—were already on the high seas.

Japan had smart people wrestling with the production problems. At the top of the heap, Vice Admiral Hoshina Zenshiro headed the Military Preparations Bureau of the Navy Ministry. Hoshina had spent two years in the States, serving as an attaché in Washington and studying at Yale University, and thus he knew the Americans intimately. Once the captain of the battleship *Mutsu*, which had sunk due to an accidental explosion in September 1943, Hoshina now felt a special sense of duty to protect sailors. His department supervised production of ammunition, along with the radars and new technical equipment that officers hoped would transform the Imperial Navy.

Hoshina's combat preparations specialist was Captain Oishi Tamotsu, chief of the 1st Section. Oishi had previously served as a senior staff officer to Nagumo Chuichi, the swashbuckling carrier boss at Midway so recently lost in the battle for the Marianas, and had also been navigator for one of Japan's most renowned surface commanders, Kondo Nobutake. Though not a pilot, Oishi had a reputation as a close observer, and he listened to reason.

In addition, Admiral Hoshina had close ties with Vice Admiral Oka Takazumi, chief of the ministry's Military Affairs Bureau. Together, Military Preparations and Military Affairs took the lead in shaping the Imperial Navy's doctrine and equipment. Oka's bureau also set the Navy response to general political developments. And in conjunction with the Naval Technical Bureau, the Military Affairs Bureau matched available budgets with the shipbuilding and modification program.

Admiral Oka, a submariner, had gained renown as an oil expert. Well aware that Allied subs were slaughtering Japan's tankers, he faced daily complaints of the difficulties of obtaining fuel in the Home Islands. Basing the surface fleet in the southern area eased the headaches of obtaining fleet oilers for a naval sortie.

The other side of that coin, however, was the hostile aerial environment. In this operation the fleet would need to make a lengthy approach across waters dominated by Allied aircraft. If the Sho contingency materialized in the Philippines, that meant steaming more than 1,300 nautical miles into the Allies' clutches. The other Sho theaters were even more distant. Fleet antiaircraft defense could not be solved by means of fighter interceptors, land *or* carrier based.

The Japanese were aware of their shortcomings in fleet antiaircraft defense and were already taking measures to close the gap. Captain Oishi understood from the Marianas battle that the Navy would face a hostile air environment regardless of its own aerial strength. Tokyo's system made the Naval Technical Department the center of warship design and construction. Oishi and Hoshina cooperated with Vice Admiral Sugiyama Rokuzo, who headed this ministry unit. Much of Sugiyama's experience had come in the China Incident, where at various times he had been both chief of staff and fleet commander, as well as a leader of operating units. But the admiral had been a battleship skipper too. He knew the problems of surface ships in an air age and was an Etajima classmate of such officers as Kusaka Ryunosuke, now Combined Fleet chief of staff; and Mikawa Gunichi, the Navy's top leader in the Philippines.

The Naval Technical Bureau moved affirmatively to strengthen flak defenses. *Akitsuki*-class destroyers, designed as antiaircraft ships, were modified in midprogram to become even stronger, with a complement of eight 3.9-inch dual-purpose guns and forty 25mm automatic cannon. The lead redesigned destroyer, *Fuyutsuki*, joined the fleet in May 1944, right before the Philippine Sea debacle. Similarly the light cruiser *Isuzu*, already in the yard, would emerge in mid-September as an antiaircraft cruiser armed with a half dozen 5-inch antiaircraft guns but no fewer than fifty 25mm weapons. But it would be months until more *Akitsukis* joined the fleet, and the Japanese had no cruisers to spare for conversion like the *Isuzu*.

The Imperial Navy did something more ambitious. Admirals Sugiyama and Hoshina, in conjunction with Combined Fleet commanders, determined to up-gun pretty much the entire fleet. Fleet boss Toyoda, who had headed the Naval Technical Bureau before the war, gave his complete support. Every aircraft carrier, every battleship, nine of eleven light cruisers, and all but four of the roughly fifty destroyers were given strengthened antiaircraft armament. Of the thirteen Imperial Navy heavy cruisers, all but two had construction workers swarming over them immediately after the Philippine Sea battle. The Kure and Yokosuka Naval Districts did most of the work. The yards installed more than 300 additional 25mm flak pieces in the heavy cruisers alone. And the Navy deployed a new weapon, the 5-inch antiaircraft rocket, placed on carriers and battleships. Every major vessel without a radar now received one. Many got additional, more sophisticated sets, including models that could control the fire of heavy guns.

All of this amounted to a huge increase in defensive firepower. The post–Philippine Sea battle fleet upgrade included the installation of more than 1,650 5-inch rocket launchers, 20 dual-purpose 5-inch powered gun mounts, nearly 2,000 of the 25mm antiaircraft guns, and more than 200 13mm flak pieces. Plus there were the antiaircraft ships starting to join the fleet. In terms of air defense, the Combined Fleet rose from the ashes of the Marianas as a more powerful force.

THE AIR ARMADA

The headaches of fitting out the fleet, however, paled next to the dilemmas of refashioning its air arm. The First Air Fleet had effectively been destroyed over the Marianas and had to be completely rebuilt. There was little alternative except to press ahead. Land-based aircraft provided the Japanese Naval Air Force (JNAF) with its heft. The carrier air groups that had been its elite were now so debilitated there was no alternative to emphasizing air fleets over carrier groups.

Vice Admiral Teraoka Kimpei took over a re-created First Air Fleet. Under the Sho plan, which provided roles for multiple air fleets reinforced with Army air divisions, on July 10, Admiral Toyoda reorganized the JNAF and created the Second Air Fleet. This was a major formation that Toyoda hoped would swing the odds in battle. On July 11, the Third Air Fleet, led by Vice Admiral Shunichi Kira, with Rear Admiral Miura Kanzo serving as chief of staff, formed as the JNAF's central training outfit. The reorganization consolidated or eliminated a host of battered fighter or bomber groups. The Third Air Fleet was a key to their future plans. Based in the Home Islands, it would be both the air force reserve and the key organization preparing crews for battle. Admiral Shunichi's mission was simple—to jump-start flight training for the JNAF so that as the Allies began to bomb Japan, his air fleet would become the Empire's sky defense as well.

Despite the reorganization, aerial preparations faced enormous obstacles. In September, Shunichi's headquarters released a study that revealed how deep the problem had become. The paper surveyed aircraft readiness and crew skills in several air groups across the force over the fleet's early months. Of nearly 500 pilots and crews, Third Air Fleet staff evaluated just 77 as fully capable, with 58 others reliable for daytime missions only. All the rest it judged insufficiently trained. In a fighter group with 232 pilots, there were 17 able men and 9 more pilots ready for daytime flying.

The pilot and crew situation may have been a mess, but the aircraft situation looked abysmal. For instance, Captain Fujimatsu Masahisa's 252nd Naval Air Group, a fighter unit bloodied in the Solomons, particularly at the Battle of the Bismarck Sea, had fewer than forty planes—aircraft whose average flight availability hovered around 40 percent. On July 10, the group added several flying units. Some pilots went to another veteran unit, the 201st Air Group. Admiral Shunichi assigned the 252nd to his old northern Pacific command, the 51st Air Flotilla.

The 752nd Naval Air Group, renowned in the JNAF for its actions in the northern theater, at Rabaul and in the Central Pacific from November 1943, had been re-formed in Japan earlier in the year, in February. As a result, the 752nd was a little better off than most, with twice as many planes as the fighter group, and within its twin-engine bomber unit, it accounted for *two-thirds* of the air fleet's qualified crews. However, the average flight ability remained about the same as that of the 252nd.

There were exceptions, of course—the most prominent of which would be the T Air Attack Force. As the war progressed, the JNing Allied superiority and adopted new tactics in an attempt to equalize the odds. One of these measures had been training units to specialize in night attacks, and the T Air Attack Force represented an evolution of that idea.

The unit was activated in March 1944, under the direct command of the Combined Fleet, and Fukudome Shigeru took credit for the development. As a midlevel officer in the 1930s and the top operations planner for the Combined Fleet at the time, Fukudome had championed an idea known as "foul weather training." The Imperial Navy had had to give up the practice after a storm capsized one of its warships with massive loss of life, and Fukudome had been forced to resign his post. But the T Air Attack Force brought back that idea—the T stands for "typhoon"—and the unit came under the Second Air Fleet in mid-June. Led by Captain Kuno Shuzo, one of the Navy's most experienced pilots, who had fought in the Solomons and gained fame at Rabaul, this would be an expert bombing unit. The T Air Attack Force was exceptional for another reason too—for the first time Japanese Army Air Force regiments were assigned to a Navy unit.

Preparing the T Air Attack Force became a race against time. Captain Fuchida Mitsuo, the Pearl Harbor attacker, helped train the Army airmen, but unfortunately, he was called away to join the Combined Fleet staff before he could complete the program. Though the force was not ready in time for the Marianas battles, Captain Kuno continued to drill his crews in bad weather and at night.

For the Army, which usually avoided flying its planes over the ocean, the duty could be terrifying. Admiral Fukudome argued that several years of training were necessary for a special unit like this. By that standard none of Kuno's crews were proficient. The first of the Army's air regiments, the 98th, joined the T Force in April 1944, when there were enough of the new Ki-67 "Peggy" twin-engine bombers to equip it. The 7th Air Regiment received its bombers only after the Sho operation had been devised. Fukudome honestly believed that in a night battle—under conditions intended for the T Air Attack Force—the Army crews would have no idea whom they were attacking. Nevertheless, the admiral records of the T Force, "I placed my greatest reliance for victory upon this unit."

The 343rd Naval Air Group at Tateyama were also an exceptional unit. Its pilots flew Japan's new Shiden fighters. The JNAF created the group at Kagoshima at the beginning of 1944, under Commander Takenaka Masao, a former flying boat driver. The 343rd started with Zeros—since new planes were not ready yet—and only half a dozen of its pilots, just one-tenth of the initial complement, were experienced. But by the time of the Marianas sea battle, Takenaka, who had a reputation as a fine trainer, had whipped them into some kind of shape. But for every unit like the 343rd, there were many JNAF groups challenged just to put a formation in the air.

KISARAZU BASE, WHERE much of the 752nd Group roosted, held an important role for the Navy, in addition to being the air fleet's headquarters: It housed the No. 2 Naval Air Depot, a place where the fleet took possession of aircraft production. Warplane quality figured in flight readiness, in-flight performance, fuel consumption, and combat survivability.

As the war progressed and Allied forces, especially submarines, destroyed more of Japan's resources every day, the Navy had to cut back the amount of steel and aluminum it devoted to aircraft fabrication. Until 1942, the Imperial Navy had not made any effort to calculate the raw material required for programmed aircraft production. That had been a mistake. The first new assessment allotted 4.5 tons of aluminum per plane—which was much too little. In 1943, planners revised the allotment to 5.5 metric tons.

Actual consumption in aircraft built after the Marianas battle reverted to 4.7 tons, near the former figure. But this proved extravagant compared to the end of 1944, when Japan could spare only 2.4 tons of aluminum per aircraft. A Zero fighter toward the end of the war weighed about 6,000 pounds. An American medium bomber like the B-26 clocked in at ten times that weight. Allied aircraft had weight to spare for armor and survivability features.

The Army and Navy ministries regularly coordinated production plans. Officers from both services staffed sections of the Munitions Ministry. Vice Admiral Sakamaki Munetaka led the air materials section of the general affairs bureau. The plan for 1944 would be trashed at the very outset of Japan's fiscal year (April). The new plan lasted just four months, until superseded by another, even more ambitious one. This plan anticipated a production rate of 5,500 aircraft a month by early 1945. Naturally this involved prioritizing aircraft production, with increased labor and raw materials. Employment at aircraft plants swelled by a third through the year.

Herculean efforts brought a slight growth in steel production in the summer of 1944. Even though it was not as high as growth in 1943 or early 1944, this level could not be sustained. Tokyo's stocks of both steel and aluminum were on the brink of precipitous decline. Aluminum supply stabilized only by drawing on strategic reserves. This triggered the tumble. But desperate measures resulted in production, during the three months before the impending battle, of 7,361 aircraft for the armed forces. Peak aircraft production for the entire war occurred that September, when Japanese plants churned out 2,572 warplanes.

Production had to be matched against losses, however. The September deliveries should be viewed against the loss that month—by the

Navy alone—of 773 aircraft. Over the period surveyed previously, between losses in combat and operational ones, the JNAF lost 1,975 planes. Zero fighter production, which stood at 100 in June 1944, reached 115 the next month and 135 in both August and September. It peaked when 145 Zeros left the plants in October. Deliveries of Raiden ("Jack") and Shiden ("George") fighters, plus Gekko ("Irving") night fighters, added about 100 new aircraft on top of that each month. But only in July and August did deliveries outrun losses, and in one month by just a few warplanes. Deliveries of new-type carrier bombers and torpedo planes ("Jill," "Myrt," and "Judy") outpaced losses but, again, only by a few aircraft on average—and the production of twin-engine medium bombers (G4M2 "Betty") consistently ran far behind casualties.

Japan's practice had been to divide effort and raw materials between the armed services. At prevailing percentage rates the Imperial Navy's share of the new production would have been roughly 4,000 warplanes. Between combat losses and wastage over the same period, the Navy lost just under half as many aircraft as new production added. Bottom line: The admirals would have planes to flesh out their air fleets, but the craft were less sturdy—and there were fewer heavy types like the twin-engine Betty bombers on which the Navy relied.

Curtailed resources made testing of production aircraft even more important, since the designers were cutting corners and the factories were doing everything to increase production. In these circumstances, the toll of oil imports lost to the Allies became a huge impediment. Testing programs atrophied under the assault of oil scarcity. Ersatz substitutes like gasoline diluted with alcohol, methanol, and other additives were necessary but not good substitutes because they also damaged the engines' workings. Pine root oil got attention as another substitute. Typically, an engine would be bench tested before installation, the plane would be tested at the factory, and the naval air depot would test it again before accepting delivery. The Navy bench tested engines for nine hours. A test flight would go on for several hours and feature five takeoffs and landings.

By late 1944, though, protocols were upside down. Bench testing began to be applied randomly—typically to just one of five exemplars, though one source puts it at one in ten. Commander Suzuki Eiichiro, the NGS officer responsible for aircraft maintenance, needed to cut every corner to reduce the burden on the system. The flight from factory to air depot began to be counted as the aircraft's flight test, and the depots rarely tested a plane on arrival. Commander Muramatsu Tokiwo estimated that aircraft were being accepted with between two and five hours of testing in total.

Trends already developing at the time of the Solomons campaign were now well established. In general, fighter planes outnumbered strike aircraft. At the Philippines Sea battle, as a result of diligent force building and careful conservation of strength, the Imperial Navy had had a balanced force in its air groups. One more pernicious consequence of the sacrifice of the air groups in the Marianas would be to destroy Japan's last balanced air force.

In short, the JNAF became weaker with every passing day. That meant the current production, with all its limitations, would largely determine striking power in the next battle. On July 6, the JNAF ordered a wholesale reorganization of the fleet air arm. A number of the land-based air groups were disbanded. The existing fighter units, as with the carriers, suddenly shrank to a minuscule force. A baker's dozen of fighter groups became just two. The Americans intercepted the message mandating these massive changes. Unfortunately they did not succeed in deciphering it until October 12.

HASEGAWA KAORU GRADUATED from Etajima in March 1944. Ensign Hasegawa had cottoned to the air corps—every Etajima cadet did a monthlong flight course for familiarization—and he longed to be selected for the JNAF. He got his wish, receiving orders to Kasumigaura for basic flight training. In 1940, due to the pressing need for pilots, training had been accelerated by merging elementary and intermediate courses, with sixty flight hours between them. At that time crews logged hundreds of hours of instructional flight, and just a small percentage of JNAF pilots had had fewer than 500 hours in the air. Now, by 1944, practically no Japanese aircrew had as many as 500 hours. Most of those who did had been moved up to be instructors. Elementary training now came entirely in the classroom. And while advanced combat training

used to take the student up to the 100-hour mark, with half that much
or more added with a unit before a pilot could fly in combat, by the time
Hasegawa moved on to the advanced stage at Usa, in July, he had nothing like that amount of logged air time. By comparison, Ensign Iwasaki
Kaneo, an observer and the plane captain of a Zero floatplane ("Jake"),
had had the same preliminary training at Tsuchiura, had had his advanced
training at Oi, and entered flight service just as Hasegawa began his
advanced stage. When Ensign Iwasaki began flying in combat he had 80
hours in the air. Petty Officer Iwata Daisaburo, similarly, spent 80 hours
and 10 minutes in flight during his training.

American pilots typically had more than 400 hours in the air before
even moving to a unit. Hasegawa and other JNAF pilots got no more
than 80 flight hours—a man was lucky if he reached 100. Lieutenant
Commander Shigeki Takeda, a *trainer* at Kuwa air base a little after
this period, had received 160 hours of instructional flying in his preliminary flight training, then 170 hours with a combat unit before
entering full duty.

"Kate" torpedo bombers (B5N2 or Type 97) were the usual training
aircraft. But with the increasing demands of the front in the middle of
the war, the JNAF often skipped aircrew past the advanced training
to the combat units. That backfired in 1944, since the lumbering 235
mph Kate bore no resemblance to new aircraft—fighters like the J2M
"Jack" (371 mph), N1K2-J "George" (363 mph), and A7M "Sam" (357
mph); or bombers like the B6N2 "Jill" (289 mph) and the D4Y1 "Judy"
(350 mph)—which were now in the units. Airmen needed advanced
training for the new-generation aircraft.

More than that, the growing superiority of Allied airpower made
night attack—when just a fraction of Allied aircraft could fly—the most
desirable tactic. Night attack required the most practice. Yet—because
of fuel—in the spring of 1944 JNAF began imposing restrictions on
flying hours for trainees. Until the Marianas campaign, the training
command had few restrictions on its use of aviation gasoline. By that
summer, however, the NGS began to ration aviation gas, allocating a
certain amount for training.

This was the new JNAF. Japan had been defeated in the Marianas.
There were 4,000 prospective pilots and observers in training in August

1944, the high point for the war. The extensive training of the prewar and early war periods had been telescoped and then further restricted. The yearlong officer course and eight-month enlisted program were both cut by two months. Fuchida Mitsuo called this the "Red Dragon" training. In addition to the shortened training regimens, age requirements to serve as a flier were dropped by two years. A fourteen-year-old "young pioneer" could enlist, spend a couple of years at a special school, then enter JNAF training. Training for ground crews shortened from a year to just four months.

Captain Mieno Takeshi, director of training at naval air headquarters, hated the practice, but reality forced it upon him. Combined Fleet chose how to distribute gasoline among its field and training commands. Commander Terai Yoshimori saw the gasoline situation as "acute" by that autumn. Early the next year Captain Mieno would be forced to resort to limiting the monthly flight hours permitted every training plane. Trainers had also slashed washout rates—from 40 percent before Pearl Harbor to just about 5 percent by 1945. The net impact pained Mieno: Less thoroughly tested—but more dangerous—aircraft were going to units consisting of marginally trained aircrew, in a situation in which JNAF's raw striking power had diminished.

Ensign Hasegawa knew nothing of these calculations. He worried the war would end before he could get into it. Hasegawa also reached the fatalistic conclusion—perfectly rational, given the JNAF situation—that he would die in the air. At least the Kasumigaura trainers had an internationalist orientation and a sense of humor. Every weekend they would have Western movies shown in the auditorium. One Saturday the duty officer's order read, "If we are to win the war, we must first know our enemy. Today, the movie *One Hundred Men and a Girl* will be shown. Attack the enemy!"

THE PARAMOUNT CHALLENGE for the Imperial Navy would be to reconstitute the carrier air groups decimated in the Marianas. Though the fleet had lost two big flattops there, more were now coming on line. The *Amagi* and *Unryu*, full-size carriers, joined the fleet in early August. A sister ship, the *Katsuragi*, still fitting out, would become available in a couple more months. Two Japanese battleships, the *Ise* and *Hyuga*, had been converting to hybrid aircraft carriers and were in sea trials. They could operate floatplane bombers. The behemoth *Shinano*, transformed from a huge *Yamato*-class battleship, would be launched at the same time *Katsuragi* joined the fleet. Half a dozen additional carriers of various sizes were under construction, with two more than 80 percent complete.

On August 10, a reorganization revamped the carrier force. Carrier Division 1, survivors of the Battle of the Philippine Sea, comprised fleet carrier *Zuikaku*—the only vessel remaining from those that had struck Pearl Harbor—the converted light carriers *Chitose* and *Chiyoda*, and the light carrier *Zuiho*. Equipping those ships alone—they constituted Naval Air Group 601—meant qualifying pilots for 174 planes. The group would include a unit of Zero fighters, one of Zero fighter-bombers, and one combining torpedo planes and dive-bombers. The re-formed force would not be ready until the end of 1944. The loss of ships at the Battle of the Philippine Sea brought the dissolution of another full air group, which could not be re-formed until new-construction aircraft carriers joined the fleet. The new carriers soon to join the fleet brought a requirement for 250 additional carrier aircraft. Once re-created they would be Air Group 653. The hybrid battleships, in Carrier Division 3, needed 44 seaplanes. With added fighters they became Air Group 654.

For the short term there would be no new carrier air groups. A Mobile Fleet plan issued on September 10 envisioned that pilots might be ready for daytime carrier landings by mid-October. In general, crews were not considered for shipboard service until they had at least 500 flight hours, but for Japan at this crucial passage, the rule was waived. Since the vast majority of pilots were enlisted sailors, and those ranks were filled with fresh-faced newcomers, Captain Mieno could see no alternative. So for the interim, Carrier Division 1 would have a skeleton group, with the expectation that sufficiently experienced pilots would become available around January 1945, even though current skill levels were so tenuous the fleet did not trust its pilots to fly out to their ships when the carriers sailed. Instead, the planes would be loaded aboard by crane, before the vessels sailed to battle.

DISPELLING THE FOG OF WAR

American spies watched all of this.

The Estimates Section at JICPOA put out regular tabulations of Japanese strength of all kinds. Its air analysis unit became so important it was split off into the Enemy Air Section. Their figures were incorporated into the Estimates Section's tabulations, then forwarded to fleet intelligence officer Captain Layton, who wrote commentaries and sent each package to Nimitz and other senior commanders. The intel provided guided their decisions.

JICPOA had a crackerjack analyst for the Japanese air estimates on its team—Lieutenant Richard W. "Dick" Emory—who tracked the radio call signs of the JNAF air fleets, flotillas, and naval air groups. With his legal mind and Harvard-inculcated precision, Emory accumulated pieces of string until he could compile a Japanese air order of battle. One of Emory's signal achievements came in February 1944 when he was able to estimate the pattern of JNAF air searches out of the Combined Fleet base at Truk, entirely by reasoning from scattered data. Using that intel, the U.S. carrier fleet made a raid on the Japanese base that would have devastated the Combined Fleet had it not already departed. (The Japanese took warning from a U.S. photo recon flight that had scouted the base.)

Other Allied commands had their own air intelligence analysts, duplicating the work being done at Pearl Harbor. Washington split this work up among different units, two of which were the Office of Naval Intelligence's (ONI) Far East Division order of battle unit, known as OP-16, and a combat intelligence branch working directly for Admiral King, housed in OP-20-G, which had an order of battle unit called F-22 under Commander William J. Sebald. These two units regularly exchanged information—OP-16's air intelligence branch answered questions and compiled studies at Sebald's request, and F-22 published Japanese strength estimates.

Throughout this period, radio intercepts were the raw material for the strength tabulations of the Japanese. The Americans were lucky in that JNAF administrators required each base to file a daily activities report, messages that inadvertently furnished the Allies with a window into the Imperial Navy's air arm. In addition, over time a certain number of prisoners and documents were captured. The interrogations and translations afforded new insights. In time, the material filled in the blanks, enabling Allied intelligence to project the numbers of frontline and reserve aircraft, the ratio of pilots to cockpits, standards for staffing, and so on.

Down under, General MacArthur's Southwest Pacific command had the Seventh Fleet and, under it, the Seventh Fleet Intelligence Center (SEFIC). Captain Arthur H. McCollum, who had headed the Far East Division of ONI, went to Australia late in 1943 to survey MacArthur's naval intelligence needs. While there McCollum would be shanghaied as fleet intelligence officer and SEFIC chief. He had eight officers in his Estimates Section and six in Enemy Information—but twenty-two in Translation and four more interrogators. Fleet Radio Unit Melbourne (FRUMEL) would be MacArthur's counterpart to FRUPAC at Pearl Harbor.

MacArthur had something else that was lacking at Pearl Harbor. This was the Allied Translator and Interpreter Section (ATIS), a specialized unit for language translation of both captured documents and prisoner interviews. Many of its staff were Nisei—Japanese-Americans—who fought for the country even while their families were being imprisoned in U.S. internment camps. The Nisei were absolutely indispensable to the war effort. They represented both the largest pool of translators and the most qualified linguists.

Washington and Pearl Harbor clashed over the Japanese air estimates, specifically over the role of the First Air Fleet. Captain Henry Smith-Hutton had sent Commander Sebald, who had charge of the air reporting, to JICPOA to have it out directly. Jasper Holmes introduced Sebald to his resident air expert, Dick Emory. The two mulled over the intelligence. In February 1944, Sebald circulated a paper correctly identifying Japanese units in the First Air Fleet and discussing its purpose.

Despite this effort, aircraft estimates continued to show wide discrepancies. The JICPOA assessments were higher, and they increased considerably that spring. The main reason for this lay in Lieutenant Emory's belief that air groups the Japanese used to train crews could be flown for defense if the need arose.

These arguments illustrate the difficulty of deriving meaningful estimates of JNAF strength. In practice, a projection involved some tabulation of Japan's aircraft production, its combat losses, the loss of aircraft in accidents, crashes, and so on (termed "operational losses"), and an evaluation of planes already in units. All of these were soft figures. Allied intelligence had no hard data on Japan's factories or operational losses, had only its own pilot claims for combat losses, and had just the scattered data for frontline air units, which had been photographed (or had been reported in Ultra message traffic) for unit strength. Pilot claims were famously known to be exaggerated, and both F-22 and JICPOA made conscious efforts to deflate them. Comparison of Japanese data provided after the war with U.S. intelligence estimates from 1944 shows the intel consistently underestimated Japanese aircraft production as well as operational losses, while still overestimating combat losses.

Late in 1944 U.S. intelligence began to devote special attention to Japanese aircraft production. The first report in this series complained of the scarcity of Ultra data, and not long afterward an Army officer who had stopped by at JICPOA on his way to join MacArthur's intelligence staff found a whole series of "consignment" messages sitting in the Ultra files. These intercepts recorded the Imperial Navy's acceptance of new warplanes and what units the aircraft would join. The consignment messages furnished a direct measure of Japanese production and put the aircraft estimates on a new basis.

After the Philippine Sea battle, Admiral King asked F-22 whether the Imperial Navy might replenish its carrier air groups from other existing units, either in Empire waters or the Philippines. Lieutenant Robert L. Suggs, the air estimates man with Army G-2 (U.S. Army intelligence), doubted it. Commander Sebald took his cue from that.

At Pearl Harbor the consignment messages, understanding of which depended upon translation, confirmed that impression. Translation required Japanese language officers. Smith-Hutton, the last prewar U.S. naval attaché in Japan, Sebald, McCollum, and Emory were all Japanese language officers. Jasper Holmes was not. Holmes later wrote, "Had the U.S. Navy been dependent on people like me, Japanese secrets would have been safe; but it was not." The language officers became the basis for U.S. understanding of the Japanese. Each of the language

officers had lived in Japan for periods of several years or more, absorb-
ing culture and mores in addition to the vocabulary. In fact, Bill Sebald
had actually left the Navy to become a lawyer for American clients in
Japan but returned to the service once war came. Even before Pearl
Harbor Albert E. Hindmarsh had surveyed Japanese language teaching
in the United States and found it woefully inadequate, and that led to
the courses at Harvard and Berkeley. In Tokyo as attaché, Henry Smith-
Hutton scooped up copies of Japanese dictionaries, character illustra-
tions, and so forth. They became the basis for the courses.

Once war came, the language program expanded to the University
of Colorado. The first of the Boulder Boys arrived at JICPOA in early
1943, and by the Marianas battle, most of the 250-odd officers in the
Estimates, Enemy Air, and Translation sections at Pearl Harbor were
Boulder Boys. They became the backbone of JICPOA, and they were
about to face their greatest challenge to date.

Japanese preparations for battle could be followed via the intelligence, and in July the radio traffic told the Boulder Boys that Tokyo
was stripping its army in Manchuria of air assets to move them to the
Philippines. Two entire air divisions were overheard making links to
the 4th Air Army, a new entity identified in the islands. One unit con-
sisted mostly of maintenance crews; the other division contained nearly
400 aircraft. Smaller units, fighter regiments, were found to be trans-
ferring from Formosa or Burma to the Philippines. As for ground forces,
the code breakers identified a new 14th Area Army covering all of the
Philippines, and in mid-August, a new 35th Army in the southernmost
islands. The Ultra betrayed no fewer than fifty-two major Japanese
convoy movements over the high summer—and many of them were
bound for Manila. American subs used the intel to exact losses from
the Japanese by sinking their transports, cargomen, and tankers. In
mid-August U.S. intelligence knew that Japanese Army forces in the
Philippines had increased to some six divisions and believed that two
more could be en route. One of these actually went to Okinawa, but
several additional formations added to the 14th Area Army more than
made up the difference. Estimated Japanese troop strength rose from
176,000 in July to 200,000 in early September to 225,000 a month
later.

PLANNING ARMAGEDDON

When Toyoda Soemu rose to the top of the Imperial Navy he was a cypher to Allied intelligence. They had only themselves to blame. For years before Pearl Harbor the U.S. and Japanese Navies traded officer lists and Toyoda's rise could be followed in them. Toyoda had been a language officer too, in his case in London, learning English and then serving as naval attaché to Great Britain at the time of the historic naval arms limitation negotiations in the 1930s. His English might not have been great (he could understand but not speak it), but the Brits had plentiful understanding from encounters with him. Later, when another naval treaty was negotiated at London in 1930, Toyoda went along to shepherd delegation chief Yamamoto Isoroku, who had been a class ahead of him at Etajima.

The renowned Japanese destroyer captain Hara Tameichi found it nonsensical that Admiral Toyoda had reached the pinnacle of the Combined Fleet, for Toyoda had no combat know-how—the only experience that could be pointed to was his role in the China Incident, where Toyoda had led the Japanese invasion at Tsingtao (Qingdao) and supervised a blockade of the coast. But while up to a point there's a certain truth to Hara's gripes, the admiral held one of the top slots on the officers' list, and to appoint someone different would have meant getting rid of Toyoda altogether. The next sailor behind him, Admiral Kondo Nobutake, had been under a black cloud since his defeat leading Imperial Navy battleships off Guadalcanal. There could be no question of Kondo heading the Combined Fleet at this stage of the war, so Toyoda Soemu became the inevitable choice.

But despite his lack of experience, Admiral Toyoda had the reputation of being very sharp—and well informed. Tenth in seniority among Japanese naval officers, Toyoda graduated Etajima in 1905, not at the top of his class but not very far away (26 out of 171), and he prided himself on strict precision. Leading the Fourth Fleet off the China coast in early 1938, Toyoda had his flagship, the cruiser *Mogami*, challenge a Royal Navy vessel that had failed to salute his flag. In 1939, he was picked to head the Naval Technical Bureau—leading on shipbuilding—because Japanese senior officers realized naval construction needed to be energized. Toyoda served two years each on the staff of the Combined Fleet and with the Navy Ministry. In those roles, the admiral showed that he was not necessarily wedded to hoary old ideas.

Toyoda considered the problem of defending the Philippines, realizing full well that fighting the battle might cost the entire fleet, and decided with equanimity to take that course. In making that decision, he and his chief of staff, Kusaka, also moved the Combined Fleet staff from the light cruiser *Oyodo* to a shore post on the outskirts of Tokyo in Hiyoshi—which caused much controversy. Young sailors denounced the admirals for demoralizing the fleet by leaving them for a land base, and old officers complained that Toyoda was breaking a tradition begun by Admiral Togo in the Russo-Japanese War.

By moving command ashore, the fleet commander would have the calm to consider matters without being caught up in an immediate battle situation—plus a shore base would be less vulnerable to interception of its orders sent by radio. And, of course, doing without a flagship meant an additional warship on the front lines.

Putting fleet headquarters in a former women's college dormitory encouraged flippant remarks but made good sense for several reasons. Proximity to Naval War College facilities was one. Another was the chance to build a huge bombproof command complex for the corps of about 600 radiomen that kept Combined Fleet staff in touch with all its far-flung outposts. This kind of expansion space was just not available on a ship. Another advantage was having the staff officers living right at headquarters, with the men available at all hours, if necessary.

When quarters were being assigned, those for Admiral Toyoda were placed right next to those for chief of staff Kusaka. The latter rejected this, telling Toyoda's aide-de-camp to give him rooms as far away from the C-in-C as possible. The move startled Toyoda, who asked Kusaka about it. The chief of staff replied that they should not live next door— it would be too close and the C-in-C was like a boil above the eye—the one man in the Navy Kusaka should be afraid of. Toyoda, open and frank, suggested a compromise. They moved in down the hall from each other. From time to time the C-in-C visited Kusaka in his quarters.

At the morning staff meetings Vice Admiral Kusaka ruled the roost. He would go around the table, solicit views on the day's business, and

make decisions. The C-in-C often said nothing. Admiral Toyoda intervened only sporadically. Kusaka consulted him afterward with a list
of issues and decisions. Sometimes Toyoda asked not to be bothered
with small details. When necessary he changed an order. Kusaka once
asked Toyoda why the C-in-C had so little to say. The admiral replied
that he took the measure of men, and those who were razor-sharp and
great, like Kusaka, needed little attention. This confidence would have
an effect once battle began.

Admiral Toyoda understood that each day the surface fleet spent in
Empire waters amplified the fuel shortage problem. Before the Marianas
battle, Toyoda had gone to the mat with Tokyo authorities and obtained
an allocation of 80,000 tons of tankers specifically to support the fleet.
Some of these had promptly been sunk at the Philippine Sea battle, and
more were destroyed every day. In order to stem the fuel problem,
Toyoda wanted the fleet right down in the oil-producing southern
resource area as soon as its refit had been completed.

To separate the Second Fleet, the Navy's major surface attack unit,
from the Mobile Fleet represented a radical departure. Admiral Toyoda,
however, reasoned that without a supply line to the south, the fleet
would be useless. Takata Toshitane, a senior planner, later observed
that Toyoda was thinking of what had happened to the Italian fleet
earlier in this war, which had kept to its bases awaiting battle, and
wound up just surrendering; or the German High Seas Fleet in World
War I, which had had to scuttle itself to avoid the same result. Rear
Admiral Takata agreed that once the Allied fleet arrived off the Japanese coast, the Imperial Navy would be unable to oppose it with a
balanced force of any size. Much better to go now while the Navy
possessed some power.

Vice Admiral Ugaki Matome, the leader of Battleship Division 1 in
the Second Fleet, opposed the move south on grounds that the round-
trip from Empire waters to Singapore would take twenty days or more.
Ugaki did not realize the fleet would never return. Admiral Ugaki also
objected to using the warships to carry cargoes of troops, equipment,
and so forth for deposit at various ports along the way.

But in the midst of 1944, there were few options. Warships were
faster and better protected, unlike merchant ships, whose losses had

put serious constraints on what the Japanese could move. Strength had
fallen to a level where it had become necessary for the big warships to
do double duty. With no other choice, the Second Fleet began moving
on July 8—its big ships bound for different intermediate ports. Ugaki
sailed in the *Yamato*. While leaving port, he was annoyed when his
superbattleship took extra-long to turn. The admiral knew it had happened because the load she carried—men and equipment bound for
Okinawa—had changed the vessel's trim. As the *Yamato* sailed toward
its destination, the Navy reorganized the Second Air Fleet—one of the
formations Admiral Toyoda expected to be at the center of battle. The
surface ships continued to deploy. Another group stopped at Manila.
The task force with the *Yamato* in it arrived at Lingga anchorage on
July 16.

Takata Toshitane and Yamamoto Chikao were good friends. The
admiral may have been channeling the feelings of his comrade the NGS
operations chief. But that is not likely. Takata himself had become
almost a professional staff officer in the Imperial Navy. He had been
an instructor at the War College, had worked on shipbuilding with the
Naval Technical Council, and had been in the prestigious Military
Affairs Bureau of the Navy Ministry, the NGS, and the Second, Third,
and Combined Fleet staffs. That summer of 1944, Rear Admiral Takata
had been seconded to the Combined Fleet staff. The Sho operational
concept that emerged from fleet staff matched and reinforced the NGS
vision at every level. Admiral Toyoda approved the top secret order. It
provided that airfields be prepared in the Philippines, that two entire
air fleets would be sent into battle, and that within two days of invasion
the surface fleet would leave for the landing area. Its primary target
would be the amphibious shipping that sustained the invasion.

A complementary directive, Combined Fleet Operations Order No.
84, issued on August 1, set the disposition of the forces. Overall com-
mand went to Vice Admiral Ozawa Jisaburo, who had led the Mobile
Fleet at the Philippine Sea battle. He would shepherd a main body from
Japan, with the available carrier strength. The 1st Diversion Attack
Force (also called a "striking force") would sail from the Singapore-
Lingga area. It contained the fleet's primary surface power, Vice Admi-
ral Kurita Takeo's Second Fleet. The Fifth Fleet, Japan's guard force

in the North Pacific, would swing around far to the south, pick up a pair of old battleships and a couple of destroyer divisions, and make a 2nd Diversion Attack Force.

On August 4, Takata added an "outline of operations" that became Directive No. 85. This plan ordained that the Kurita fleet would strike the landing zone in conjunction with the air force, while Ozawa's main body "will . . . assume the mission of diverting the enemy task forces to the northeast in order to facilitate the attack of the First Striking Force." In this case, the Fifth Fleet could function as a vanguard force for Ozawa's diversion.

Preparations continued at a drumbeat pace. Simulated war games at the Naval War College helped validate the Sho strategic concept. Before the evaluations began, Admiral Yonai Mitsumasa addressed participants. He spoke of the upcoming operation, but also of the need for peace. When the games began, Combined Fleet staff and NGS officers took the role of the Allied forces. Ozawa Jisaburo played leader of the carrier fleet and Mobile Fleet, and stand-ins took the roles of Admiral Kurita and his subordinates. The scenario modeled a hypo-thetical Allied invasion of Taiwan, projecting the American carrier fleet would punch at the Home Islands and Philippines before their invasion flotillas unloaded their storm troops. The war games' main finding would be that Japan must conserve attack capabilities until the very moment of action. The JNAF saved its planes in the war game by sending them elsewhere—either to Korea or to northern Japan, where they would be out of range, or to the Tokyo area, where heavy defenses could deter the Americans.

Meanwhile, Admiral Hasegawa Kiyoshi, governor of Taiwan, visited Tokyo in early August to discuss intensifying the island's contribution to the war effort. The Sho plan anticipated using Taiwan as a transit point for air forces by deploying from Japan to the Philippines in an "aerial pipeline." On August 6, the Navy designated Vice Admiral Teraoka Kimpei as commander of its First Air Fleet in the Philippines. That force itself would be reconstituted the next day. The JNAF Second Air Fleet would cover Taiwan.

On August 15, Admiral Mikawa Gunichi took command of the Southwest Area Fleet, the Japanese Navy's regional command for the

Philippines. The same day, the Navy Ministry, responding to the initiative of its Taiwan area commander, issued orders establishing a new Takeo Naval Guard Force that would include five air groups for training.

Mikawa's position was identical to the role that Admiral Nagumo had held in the Marianas. Mikawa had been the naval commander in the Solomons when Allied forces invaded Guadalcanal, and Mikawa had won the signal Japanese victory at the Savo Island battle there. The admiral's assistant chief of staff, Rear Admiral Nishio Hidehiko, had held that same post under Mikawa at Rabaul early in 1943. Another officer seconded to Mikawa's command staff was the attaché to the puppet Filipino government under the Japanese. That man, forty-eight-year-old Rear Admiral Hiraide Hideo, had been the Navy's official spin doctor, who had enraged Tokyo political circles after the Savo Island battle when he claimed in a propaganda broadcast that Japan planned to stage a naval review off of New York Harbor. These were the seasoned officers of the Southwest Area Fleet.

On August 20, Combined Fleet promulgated its Operations Order No. 87, completely revamping the manner in which the Imperial Navy's submarines would fight. Priority targets would be aircraft carriers, battleships, and troop transports, in that order. Submarines should lurk in patrol areas, not be deployed along a line of bearing as before.

Admiral Ozawa issued his first Mobile Fleet orders on August 10. The directives laid down new arrangements for communications, cruising dispositions, standard maneuvers, and other basic fleet routines. He also circulated a paper creating a framework for the Sho plan. Ozawa recognized something the Combined Fleet had not—that there might be a requirement to activate Sho as an air-only operation. In that case, Ozawa's carrier air groups, which had not completed their training, were to act in conjunction with the fleet's land-based air arm. Rear Admiral Obayashi Sueo viewed his boss as pained by this possibility but resigned to it. Vice Admiral Shima Kiyohide, whose North Pacific force (Fifth Fleet) answered to Ozawa under the August reorganization, also affirms Ozawa's reluctance to part with his air groups but resignation at having to do so.

Over the first days of September, Admiral Ozawa held tabletop war games for Mobile Fleet commanders. Due to the projected dates when officials expected the air groups to attain proficiency, game masters allotted the fleet with only enough planes for a single carrier division. The converted battleship-carriers sailed with Ozawa but had no planes. The Mobile Fleet had another battleship division, with the older vessels *Fuso* and *Yamashiro*. That, plus the Fifth Fleet, had little potential for victory in surface attack. The games showed Ozawa that he had no chance of effecting a rendezvous with the Kurita fleet coming from the East Indies. They also suggested that, sailing independently, the Mobile Fleet could exercise very little control over the Kurita fleet. And the Mobile Fleet would be too weak on its own to fight the Allies. Thus the war games revealed that Ozawa's mission—to disrupt Allied rear areas—was too ambitious.

Japan's Mobile Fleet commander did something very audacious—he asked superiors to *reduce* his forces and mission. In a memorandum to Admiral Toyoda, Ozawa argued that the assigned mission exceeded his capabilities, and that, rather than increasing his force (not practical), Toyoda should reduce Ozawa's role to *diverting* Allied strength.

Fuchida Mitsuo, the ebullient Combined Fleet air staff officer, claims that it was he who suggested to Ozawa that the Mobile Fleet be reconfigured for the decoy mission. The two men enjoyed some familiarity. A few years before the war, when Ozawa first led an aircraft carrier division, it had been Fuchida who commanded the air group aboard flagship *Akagi*. The younger officer had taken charge of a practice night torpedo attack where all four of the battleship targets were declared eliminated. At the time, Admiral Ozawa had been personally congratulated by C-in-C Yamamoto. Now Ozawa, according to Fuchida, waxed enthusiastic over the concept of a decoy fleet. The captain quotes the admiral, "Good. I will recommend the idea to the Combined Fleet as my own initiative. You keep quiet."

That's a good story and likely true. Chief of staff Obayashi confirms that the decoy idea came from Combined Fleet. Historian Gordon Prange, whose works include a biography of Fuchida, accepts this claim as well. The degree of collaboration is suggested by Ozawa's senior staff officer, Captain Ohmae Toshikazu, who recalls making no fewer than ten trips to Combined Fleet headquarters to coordinate parts of the plan.

But the matter is more complicated. First of all, Captain Fuchida was fond of talking large. Moreover, Admiral Ozawa was a highly capable officer, perfectly able to intuit the decoy concept himself. Indeed, at the Philippine Sea battle, Ozawa had sent part of his force ahead of the carrier fleet in a decoy role. At the Battle of Midway, the Japanese thrust into the Aleutians had been a decoy mission, and Imperial Navy aircraft carriers had had decoy roles in carrier battles off the Solomons. In addition, Rear Admiral Takata's August 4 operations order had already provided for the Mobile Fleet to function as a diversion. The better way to think of this is to view decoy operations as a standard of Imperial Navy tactics, and Ozawa, whether or not assisted by Fuchida, as looking for ways to incorporate deception into Sho.

Admiral Ozawa also reviewed his involvement with the Kurita fleet, arguing that Toyoda's Combined Fleet should control it directly. With his own tactical role, Ozawa felt he would have little attention to spare for controlling another fleet. In addition, the 2nd Battleship Division, with the old battlewagons, should be sent to Kurita. The battleships added nothing to Ozawa's mission, but they might contribute to Kurita's surface assault. Similarly, he argued that the Fifth Fleet would be ineffective as an advance guard for the Mobile Fleet unit. Ozawa recommended taking it away from him, as well, and employing the Fifth Fleet more usefully. In addition, the admiral felt Kurita would need directly cooperating air units for cover, but Ozawa could do nothing about that. He predicted the Sho contingency would take place in the Philippines. For mid-September this amounted to a prescient recitation.

Admiral Toyoda took some of that advice but not all of it. He *would* take control of the Kurita fleet himself, and strengthen it with the additional battleships from the 2nd Battleship Division. He also removed the Fifth Fleet from Ozawa's force, but its role remained undetermined. As for air cover over Kurita, JNAF assets were so thin that Toyoda preferred to have them attack the Allies rather than protect friendly forces.

That air element proved especially painful for Combined Fleet's chief of staff. Vice Admiral Kusaka had lived and breathed airplanes. When Ozawa had led a carrier division and Fuchida the air group, it was Kusaka who had been the flag captain. One of the most ardent champions of the JNAF, and one of those who argued for the primacy of the air arm and the amazing flexibility of the aircraft carrier, Kusaka had been chief of staff for Nagumo Chuichi at Pearl Harbor and right through Midway and the South Pacific. In a sense he was poacher turned enforcer—but his JNAF dog of war now lacked fangs.

Navy Minister Yonai Mitsumasa had risen through the ranks before aviation had acquired the predominance it now possessed. But Yonai, revered for his astuteness and bravery in the face of political storms, drew the right conclusions. Rising to speak in the Diet on September 9, Admiral Yonai refused to make light of the damage Japan's forces had suffered in the Marianas fighting. He conceded that air strikes to follow up carrier attacks had gone badly. The combination had been "truly action which would make the demons weep." The next battle had to go better.

In its summer-fall issue, the journal *Contemporary Japan* featured an article by the naval writer Ito Masanori titled "Japan's Fleet in Being Strategy." He, too, had words about the next battle. The Marianas had been near the "aorta" of Japan's lifeline. While the Americans still did not dare enter the Imperial Navy's "operational zone," the war situation favored them and they might even be able to command the fringes of Japan's shores. The Imperial Navy, Ito thought, would make its "decisive onslaught" soon. Ito's logic had penetrated the obfuscations imposed by Japan's wartime censorship. His conclusion proved correct. The long-anticipated decisive battle approached rapidly.

CHAPTER 3

BREAKTHROUGH AND EXPLOITATION

Allied commanders continued puzzling over the big picture. Now in its third year, the Pacific war had nearly—perhaps neatly—reversed itself. The Japanese might have an incredible willingness to die for their emperor, and a stoic determination to fight, but the balance had shifted sharply against them.

No longer on the march, Japan struggled to fight on equal terms. Americans called the Philippine Sea battle the "Great Marianas Turkey Shoot," and why not? Hundreds of Japanese planes had been shot down virtually without them laying a finger on the "Big Blue Fleet," as Yankee sailors nicknamed their carrier armada. Similarly, Japanese carriers had been sunk by American submarines without U.S. aircraft touching them. So far in 1944, Japanese combat losses totaled 240 warships, including aircraft carriers, cruisers, and much more. To put it in perspective, the Allies had lost barely 50 ships in the entire Pacific theater—only one as large as an escort carrier and just half a dozen as big as destroyers.

Marines and GIs who slogged through the coral of Biak or the mud of the Mariana Islands, or who slugged it out with the Japanese in their caves, knew the war had changed too. With growing Japanese impotence, there were changes in combat tactics. The Imperial Army became less enamored with defending the beaches where the Allies focused their firepower so easily. Now Japanese troops fought from prepared positions in the interior—often caves in hillsides that were largely impervious to the American bombers and battleships. Only when the Japanese decided they could fight no longer did they revert to the familiar war tactics: The imperial troops would fling themselves at the enemy in fierce suicide charges.

As a result of this transformation, Allied leaders had begun to talk of "accelerating" their offensive. Indeed, the "island hopping" that made Chester Nimitz famous owed equally to the agglomeration of American combat power and the growing ineffectualness of the Japanese. Whether a landing in the Philippines had the purpose of liberating them or of preparing the way for a leap to Taiwan, and where that landing might happen—those things were details. There would be such an invasion. To have airfields to cover such a mission, and to complete the isolation of the Carolines and New Guinea, both Nimitz and MacArthur slated fresh amphibious operations. Nimitz would invade Peleliu, an island in the Palau chain, and MacArthur would plot a move to Morotai in the Moluccas, the storied Spice Islands. A carrier raid deep into Empire waters would cover these offensives. The carrier task force, now under the command of Admiral William F. Halsey, prepared its strike. Halsey intended to assail rear positions in the Ryukyu Islands, as well as airfields in the southern Philippines from which Japanese warplanes might intervene. His carrier raid would have very fateful consequences.

THE BIG BLUE FLEET

This war cruise would be the first time the Americans traded off admirals and staffs for the carriers—Halsey's Third Fleet against Spruance's Fifth—or, in Navy bureaucratese, a "platoon" system.

There were challenges in the transition. William Halsey, who had covered himself with glory in the Solomons, had not held a seagoing post since 1942. While directing the Third Fleet involved some of the same kinds of concerns that Halsey had had as a regional chieftain, his role now was much more involved in the care, feeding, and employment of warships and amphibious groups. In addition, the changes since Bill Halsey's last seagoing assignment were enormous, not just in the strategic situation but also the result of technological and logistical developments. Halsey needed to refamiliarize himself with the rhythms of life aboard a warship at sea. He had never led more than a single aircraft carrier, but now there were four or five in every group, and four different "task groups" working in tandem to make the "task force." Halsey had to accustom himself to new action patterns, as Nimitz advanced U.S. fleet bases across the Central Pacific. In the Solomons, bases had been fixed. By contrast, during Halsey's first month, Nimitz's Pacific Fleet put three new anchorages into service. The fast carrier task force would sail from one base but return to another, closer to the new scene of action. Months of shoreside planning did little to prepare Halsey—nicknamed "Bull"—for this command.

Admiral Halsey had lots of help. His staff—200 officers and seamen—outclassed what he'd had had as an area commander. Fifty were officers. Rear Admiral Robert B. Carney, chief of staff, presided over the lot. "Mick" Carney, who had already been with Halsey for a year, had seen some of the most ferocious fighting in the South Pacific, first from the deck of a light cruiser, then at headquarters. He was known for sharp staff work and jocular "dispatchese." Captain Ralph E. "Rollo" Wilson, the operations officer, proved adept at anticipating the multifarious needs of carriers, juggling orders to the task groups, service squadrons, and amphibious forces. He had a logic the Bull found convincing. Chief for air matters was Commander Douglas Moulton. William Riley, a Marine brigadier general, doubled as the chief planner. Captain Harold E. Stassen, former governor of Minnesota, functioned as flag secretary, keeping track of Halsey's rapid-fire decisions. The communications section absorbed a lot more of his staff manpower.

Captain Michael Cheek served as fleet intelligence officer. Cheek, his cragged face calling attention to his name, usually worked out of his cabin, even though the intelligence staff had a table in flag plot, situated in the conning tower of the New Jersey. Cheek had been a Navy pro but left the service to be a businessman in the Far East. He returned to the service before Pearl Harbor and signed on with the ONI. Uncomfortable among the wild bunch of Halsey's staff, the strait-laced captain had a more outgoing lieutenant, Harris Cox, to front for him.

Commander Gilven M. Slonim led the mobile radio detachment that fed Halsey Ultra intelligence as well as the results of their own radio interceptions. Slonim and Halsey had virtually invented the "mobile radio unit," as those entities were known in the Pacific. Or more accurately, the code breakers of the Zoo (then Station Hypo), led by Joe Rochefort and including Slonim, had had a vague initial idea; then Slonim went to sea with Halsey and made it practical. Gil Slonim had been a budding language officer. He went to Japan for training in the fall of 1939 but never quite finished—his study of kanji was curtailed as the war clouds gathered in the summer of 1941, when the Navy pulled out all its trainees. Lieutenant Slonim went to Pearl Harbor to work at Station Hypo with the fabulous Commander Rochefort. The mobile unit was to have been a temporary assignment while Halsey conducted some carrier raids, but his radiomen became so invaluable that Slonim spent the entire war at sea, alternately serving with Bull Halsey and Raymond Spruance, and finished his career as an admiral.

All these people helped Bull Halsey refashion himself as a fighting sailor. The Navy even had a word for that, "makee-learnee."

The focus for much of their activity would be flag plot on the *New Jersey*. One deck up from Halsey's quarters—and beneath the captain's bridge—flag plot was a veritable command post, complete with communications stations for direct links with the fleet, chart tables to plot navigational data and record positions, a stand-up desk for the intelligence staff to assemble their material, voice tubes to pass orders, and a built-in chair for the admiral to sit in while he stared at the sea. On a routine shift there were twenty or more staffers and seamen in the space. One of the senior staff—Mick Carney, Rollo Wilson, Bill Riley, or Mike Cheek—took turns heading the watch when they were not out on deck playing doubles tennis with the admiral. Bill Halsey liked to step out onto the bridge wing first thing every day, before heading to flag plot, check in, then exercise with tennis. The admiral's partner, Carnes "Piggy" Weeks, staff doctor, very importantly controlled the liquor supply.

What was true for the chief held for his Indians. Like Halsey, many top admirals lacked sea legs as leaders of aircraft carrier formations. The Navy had sent Vice Admiral John S. "Slew" McCain to take the reins as the officer directly in charge of Task Force 38, the Big Blue Fleet, with its four carrier task groups. But he needed to apprentice too. Slew McCain, as a captain, had skippered the carrier *Ranger* before the war, but he had never led a multiship carrier force, much less a multigroup one. McCain's wartime posts had been with land-based air, including a brief stint in the South Pacific, but he returned to the fleet from a slot at the Navy Department. Before he could function effectively at the head of Task Force 38, McCain needed to makee-learnee both modern carriers and fleets of them.

One thing McCain *was* aware of was the mobile radio detachment. He wanted someone like Gil Slonim with him—Slew had been aboard Spruance's flagship during the Great Marianas Turkey Shoot and had seen radio interception in action. But the Navy had only a certain number of detachments and, often enough, none available. The code-breaking organization typically provided mobile detachments only for fleet commanders like Spruance or Halsey. Admiral McCain and Commander Slonim made a private arrangement under which Slonim sent McCain special messages for his eyes only containing Ultra or radio intercept information and tagged "Polecat."

Vice Admiral Marc A. "Pete" Mitscher, who had had McCain's job under Spruance, had just seven months with the task force and didn't want to leave. Mitscher, too, had been in the South Pacific, where he had worked closely with Halsey as land-based air chief. Mitscher's chief of staff, Commodore Arleigh A. Burke, had been there too, as a destroyer leader. Both were formidable men whom Halsey esteemed. McCain had left the Solomons just as Halsey arrived, and he could not escape the apprenticeship.

For Admiral Halsey the choice between Mitscher and McCain was clear. Instead of the full fast carrier force, McCain got temporary duty—makee-learnee as chief of Task Group 38.1. Admiral Mitscher stayed on as boss of Task Force 38, perched uncomfortably over a group leader who felt he should be in charge.

In the meantime the former group commander, Rear Admiral J. J. "Jocko" Clark, stayed in the *Hornet* as the instructor to educate Slew McCain.

PETE MITSCHER SPLIT up the force. Task Force 38 sailed on August 28 and 29. Task Group 38.4 left first, and the next day, Admiral Mitscher's main fleet followed.

Staying behind in Eniwetok were the supply ships of Service Squadron 10, now the mainstay of Pacific Fleet logistics. They were probably relieved to see Mitscher's fleet go. Mitscher's hungry ships had exhausted all its stocks of fresh and frozen food, and emergency rations were all ServRon 10 had left. Thirsty ships drank its fuel oil as well. Admiral Halsey, the fleet commander, anticipated a return to Manus, in the Admiralties, not Eniwetok. More than 4.1 million barrels of fuel oil were required for that maneuver. Only a quarter of that could be found at Eniwetok, where supply officers had to organize a shuttle to the Admiralty Islands base.

All that had been in slow motion now sped past in overdrive. The aircraft carrier *Enterprise*, a stalwart of the fleet, had been at Pearl Harbor to celebrate Franklin Roosevelt's visit. Now the "Big E," as she was known, went with Task Group 38.4, Rear Admiral Ralph E. Davison's unit, to bomb the Bonin and Volcano Islands, mainly Chichi Jima and Iwo Jima. Starting on August 31, the carrier planes spent several days socking them. Davison had a cruiser-destroyer force bombard them too. Fighter Squadron VF-20 of the *Enterprise* kicked off with a sweep over Chichi Jima. Commander Fred Bakutis led twenty-eight F-6F Hellcat fighters on the mission. A dozen SB-2C Helldiver bombers from Commander Emmet Riera's Bombing 20 followed. The Bonins strike would be Air Group 20's first combat action. No Japanese planes opposed them, and shipping proved so scarce, the strikes hit harbor installations instead, strafing and using rockets. Then they went for other Bonins.

For Commander C. L. Moore's Air Group 51 of the light carrier *San Jacinto* the story proved the same. But fierce Japanese flak challenged the Americans. Lieutenant (Junior Grade) George H. W. Bush, piloting a TBM Avenger of Torpedo 51, was swinging in on his attack run over Chichi Jima when flak riddled his plane, setting the engine on fire. Lieutenant (Junior Grade) William White, the carrier's air intelligence officer, had wanted to see Chichi Jima for himself and sat in the tailgunner position. Lieutenant Commander D. J. Melvin, the squadron commander, did not object. The other man aboard the Avenger, Radioman 2nd Class Jack Delaney, regularly flew with Bush, who kept control long enough to drop his bombs and put the plane on a trajectory for a water landing.

Lieutenant Bush bailed out, followed by one other—but nobody knows who he was, for this sailor's parachute did not open properly. Lieutenant Bush himself hit the plane's tail on his way out, slicing open his scalp and tearing the parachute. He made it to the water, though, and some hours later the submarine *Finback* rescued Bush. Commander Robert R. Williams Jr., of the *Finback*, had been assigned to recover downed aviators, and on this cruise returned not only Bush but also a *Franklin* Avenger crew downed over Iwo Jima, and an *Enterprise* fighter pilot. George Herbert Walker Bush would be awarded the Distinguished Flying Cross for his mission; he went on to become the forty-first president of the United States.

Admiral Mitscher had kept the other carriers with him. Rear Admiral Frederick C. "Ted" Sherman with Task Group 38.3 in the *Essex* crossed the equator on September 1. Captain Carlos W. Wieber permitted his sailors to convene King Neptune's Court and initiate those who had never made the passage, a long-standing nautical tradition. From September 6 to 8, Mitscher blasted Palau, a little over a week before the scheduled landing. Commander David McCampbell, boss of Air Group 15 on the *Essex*, led nearly 100 fighters from his carrier and three more ships on the first sweep. Air strikes followed. By this point in the war, the U.S. carriers had evolved a more or less standard strike "package," typically consisting of a dozen SB-2C dive-bombers, eight or ten TBM Avenger torpedo bombers, and a dozen more F-6F fighters.

As Admiral Davison had in the Bonins, Sherman found little aerial opposition at Palau. Meanwhile Davison's group hit Yap on the sixth and then refueled at sea. Second-day strikes at Palau went smoothly, enough so that bombers pasted ground targets to soften them up for the invasion. The lack of opposition at Palau seemed especially odd since just six months earlier it had been the major base of the Japanese Combined Fleet.

Mitscher's intention had been to move up from the Palaus to Mindanao, the southernmost major island of the Philippines, on September 9 and 10. Order-of-battle specialists for U.S. intelligence estimated JNAF air strength at 145 fighters, 140 bombers, and 83 other planes for September 7. The Japanese would be able to send planes to interfere

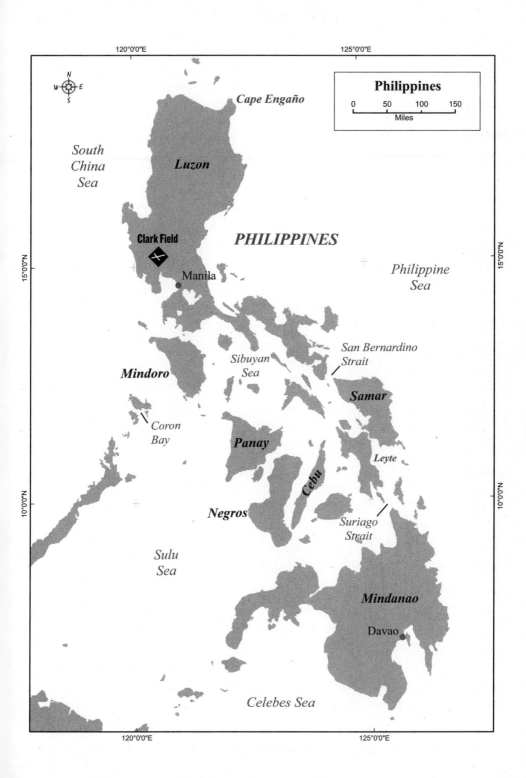

with the Palau landings, and they had to be stopped. Strikes began soon after dawn on the ninth. JNAF observers, who kept close track of Allied air activities, recorded 300 American sorties (in military parlance, a "sortie" equates to one flight of one aircraft). A few Japanese planes were torched in the air, more on the ground. At Tacloban field, on Leyte, several twin-engine "Gekko" night fighters had just taken flight when they were set upon by Hellcats. All perished, but Petty Officer Tanaka Takumi reported he had splashed two of the intruders.

Admiral Teraoka Kimpei's First Air Fleet received a false report of Allied landings on Mindanao and ordered searches from Davao. The scout planes were on the runway when the Americans arrived. Del Monte Field, a hallowed place to American defenders of the Philippines a few years earlier, now faced a U.S. assault. A convoy off the coast was set upon. Lieutenant Commander Harold L. Buell, a dive-bomber pilot from the *Hornet*, led his strike package on a new type of mission: Instead of going for a designated target, they were to find promising prey and attack it. This would be called "armed reconnaissance" in a later war. Buell torched a Japanese warship off Davao, which he thought was a destroyer but turned out to be a landing ship. Once Halsey steamed away, Allied land-based air from Morotai took over, keeping Davao under constant attack.

Teraoka finally gave up trying to keep air units permanently stationed there. In late July, the First Air Fleet had had just 134 aircraft, all but three dozen of which were fighters. The JNAF's reorganization, which included adding such aircraft as remained at Yap and Truk, brought strength up to 120 fighters and 56 other aircraft. Admiral Teraoka's headquarters came to Davao on August 12, and he was moving it to Manila when the Americans struck. That disorganization figured in the paltry JNAF response. So did the weakness of Teraoka's groups. JNAF maintenance had deteriorated so much that the air command had begun using Japanese Army craft for scout missions, while Teraoka even called on Army fighters for air defense. The admiral forbade his Zero units from intercepting marauding Allied B-24 bombers in order to conserve strength. The reported landings at Davao finally induced Admiral Teraoka to order the 201st Air Group into action. Ninety Zeros flew from Manila down to Cebu to prepare attacks. Once the report proved false, half the fighters returned to Luzon. The others would face the Americans. Somehow Japanese communications became snarled, according to Commander Okumiya Masatake, air officer with the NGS. A radar malfunctioned, and an observer's warning radioed from Suluan Island got delayed, so reports on the American strike packages headed for Cebu on September 10 never reached the field.

The initial strikes were led by Commander Theodore H. Winters, boss of Air Group 19 in the *Lexington*. A few Japanese planes were intercepted in the air. *Hornet* strike package chief Harold Buell recalled the situation as "a dream come true" for dive-bomber pilots—all those planes on the ground revving their engines, desperate to be airborne, forty-one Zeros to mix it up with the F-6Fs. The three-ring circus became, by far, Commander Buell's most successful attack of the war. The 201st Air Group lost more than two dozen fighters, and another twenty-five were damaged in the air or on the ground. More JNAF aircraft succumbed over Cebu and Leyte on September 13, and when the U.S. task force left, Admiral Teraoka's fleet had been reduced to thirty-four Zeros and fifty-one other planes. Japanese ships caught along the coast had little chance of survival. Third Fleet wags labeled this action the Cebu Barbecue.

The NGS staffer Okumiya happened to be flying into Cebu—his transport arriving overhead at almost the same moment as the Americans. He witnessed as planes on the ground were slaughtered. At that point, Admiral Davison had rejoined the fast carriers to support the Mindanao hit and participate in the Cebu strikes, bleeding off JNAF strength in the Visayas, Leyte, and Samar.

Back at Manila, to where his plane fled, staff officer Okumiya conferred with 201st Air Group pilots. He found them furious, enraged at their powerlessness, and determined to exact a price at any cost. "It was obvious," Okumiya wrote later, "that there would soon be radical changes in our battle tactics."

In contrast, as the days wore on the American pilots noticed an extraordinary lethargy on the part of their enemy. Oddly enough, a shoot-down led to the key insight. Ensign Thomas C. "Cato" Tillar of *Hornet* was lost off Leyte on September 10. Native fishermen rescued him and took him to shore in their outrigger canoe. Late that afternoon, a representative of the Philippine partisans arrived and told Cato there were no Japanese on Leyte—the Americans ought to land there first. A floatplane from cruiser *Wichita* retrieved Tillar and brought him to the ship, where Rear Admiral C. Turner Joy questioned him. Cato Tillar had never met an admiral before, and the ship's surgeon fortified the young ensign with a tumbler of brandy. The pilot then told Admiral Joy his story. Joy recognized the value of this intelligence right away.

Hornet was flagship of Task Group 38.1, and Admiral Joy commanded its screen. He passed Tillar's intel along to Slew McCain, and the information swiftly percolated upward. Rear Admiral Clark takes credit for ensuring the Leyte intel went immediately to Admiral Halsey.

The fleet commander, who visited Mitscher on the *Lexington*, mulled over the latest reports. Weak Japanese resistance could mean opportunity.

BILL HALSEY REALLY looked like a bulldog. Hard eyes peering from a fierce countenance and a square-set jaw gave others the sense the Bull was about to pounce. And that was fine with him. Halsey cultivated his reputation for aggressiveness. If anyone with the Third Fleet had the ability to appreciate the looming opportunity, it would be him.

At least twice in his life, Bill had made radical shifts to get what he wanted. One came when an anticipated appointment to the Naval Academy failed to come through. Halsey instead went to the University of Virginia, premed, planning to join the Navy as a doctor. When the Annapolis appointment materialized later, Halsey dropped medicine to become a midshipman. He received his commission while sailing the Caribbean aboard a gunboat captured in the Spanish-American War. Then the young officer wrangled an assignment to the new battleship *Kansas* and cruised the globe with Teddy Roosevelt's "Great White Fleet." In World War I, he commanded destroyers, then experienced the intricacies of intelligence work after the war with an assignment as naval attaché to Germany.

His other radical shift came when Halsey became interested in airplanes. Deciding that pilots had a better shot at naval aviation commands, Halsey took pilot training as a full captain at the age of fifty-one.

Just two months after gaining his wings the budding aviator took over the bridge of the aircraft carrier *Saratoga*. After that, he commanded at Pensacola, the very place where the Navy trained its pilots.

William F. Halsey was, indeed, a formidable officer. The sailor showed no fear. As a rear admiral in the last days before Pearl Harbor, Halsey ordered his *Enterprise* fliers to shoot to kill. It did not matter that the Navy had yet to authorize that level of action. Sent to the South Pacific, he ordered a desperate stand by U.S. carriers off the Solomons and ended up in an immediate battle.

At that action in Santa Cruz in October 1942, the Allies were reduced to a single damaged carrier, his old *Enterprise*. The Bull personally supervised efforts to get her back in shape for battle and didn't wait a moment to use her. That November, when the Japanese were turned away from Guadalcanal in the first battleship actions of the war, the Bull quickly exploited the enemy's absence by sending even more ground troops to the island. Even though Allied forces were still thin on the ground, Admiral Halsey began the slog toward Japan's bases. His effort would be crowned in November 1943 by the isolation of the vaunted Japanese fortress of Rabaul. Six months later he received an invitation to one of the get-togethers that Admirals King and Nimitz held periodically in San Francisco. There he learned that his time in the South Pacific was over and he'd be sent back to sea as a combat commander. Halsey's appointment to lead the Third Fleet in June 1944 marked the culmination of a long road—and for the Bull, the chance to get back in the action. He returned to Pearl Harbor, arriving during President Roosevelt's visit, in time to attend one of the ceremonial dinners.

Admiral Halsey had his own ideas about Pacific strategy. He thought the Allies should move next to the central Philippines, develop that as a base, then hop directly to Japan via the Bonin and Ryukyu islands. The Bull thought Admiral Nimitz agreed with his approach, though that is not quite what the CINCPAC told Roosevelt and MacArthur at Pearl Harbor. In any case, Halsey did not like the operation Nimitz had slated for him, a move on Palau and the western Carolines. Halsey chipped away at the fervor of proponents, and the evident lack of Japanese resistance helped his argument.

The Bull asked to be assigned a battleship for his flag, and the Pacific Fleet gave him the *New Jersey*. She left Pearl Harbor on August 24. Escorted by several destroyers, the fleet flagship steadily neared the battle zone. The first week of September, with Mitscher's Task Force 38 pounding Okinawa and Palau, the *New Jersey* was almost there. When Mitscher shellacked Mindanao and the Visayas, Halsey lay just beyond the horizon. His flagship joined its flock on September 11, taking position in Admiral Gerald F. Bogan's Task Group 38.2. The fleet commander could see the mountains of Samar Island from his flag bridge. Excited to be with the fleet, Admiral Halsey hastened to visit Mitscher on the carrier *Lexington*. Sailors rigged a breeches buoy line between the two ships to get Halsey aboard Mitscher's flagship. The Bull marveled that his chair had a surrey top and came equipped with an ashtray. Here Halsey discovered another change from the way things had been the last time he commanded at sea—U.S. warships were competing for who had the fanciest transfer chairs.

While aboard the *Lexington* with Mitscher, Admiral Halsey learned of the intelligence highlighting Japanese weakness on Leyte. The Bull took note but for the moment confined himself to observation. Over the next two days, Task Force 38 hurled no fewer than 2,400 sorties against the Japanese in the Visayas. Cebu and Negros airfields were primary targets. The Japanese now had more warning and put up a stiff fight. Over Negros, Japanese Army fighter aircraft had a dogfight with the Hellcats. A formation from the Japanese Army Air Force (JAAF) 32nd Air Regiment lost a dozen planes from a training flight. General Tominaga Kiyoji's 4th Air Army made a weak counterstrike the following morning with four fighter-bombers. Lieutenant Fujimoto Katsumi of the 30th Squadron claimed a bomb hit on a cruiser. His plane would be the only one that came back—and American sources do not mention any damage to U.S. warships. The JAAF lost between sixteen and twenty more aircraft.

The Third Fleet had one plane crash and lost eight more in combat. But the intelligence officers pegged Japanese losses at 173 planes shot down and 305 destroyed on the ground, plus fifty-nine ships sunk and another fifty-eight damaged. Those were enormous results. The box score seemed incredible. With these results in hand, Admiral Halsey decided he would renew the attack—on Luzon, at Manila, the center of Japanese power. As he wrote after the war, "My decision to poke a strike into this hornet's nest was not made hotly, without forethought. . . . I intended probing just as an infantry patrol probes—finding a soft spot and pressing it until I met resistance that I could not overcome." Halsey signaled the fleet, "BECAUSE OF THE BRILLIANT PERFORMANCE MY GROUP OF STARS HAS JUST GIVEN, I AM BOOKING YOU TO APPEAR BEFORE THE BEST AUDIENCE IN THE ASIATIC THEATER."

FAST TRAIN TO LEYTE

Bull Halsey made another decision too. The Third Fleet had encountered little substance in probing the Japanese defenses. Halsey realized that a whole series of Allied military moves had been pinned to a certain timetable based upon estimates of Japanese strength. Those did not seem borne out by the resistance Task Force 38 encountered. Under the schedule, his own fleet had prepared to fight a series of battles in the Palau group. General MacArthur's forces took Morotai and were to move on Davao, then to Leyte. They expected to arrive there in December. Now Halsey felt that plan was too conservative. As the Bull put it, "The South Pacific campaign had impressed us all with the necessity of being alert for symptoms of enemy weakness and of being ready to exploit them." He decided he could afford to curtail planned landings, skipping Palau and the western Carolines, lending the amphibious ships to MacArthur so the Philippines landing could be accelerated. The XXIV Corps, slotted to be the Third Fleet's principal troop strength, could join MacArthur too. The Bull figured the Allies could skip Davao altogether and move directly on Leyte, reaching it in October and saving two months. The intelligence that there were no Japanese troops on Leyte proved extremely tempting.

Admiral Halsey put his recommendations in a dispatch he sent to Pearl Harbor during the forenoon of September 13. The message, copied to Chester Nimitz and Ernest J. King, arrived on the U.S. East Coast that evening. As it happened, Admiral King and the other members of the Joint Chiefs of Staff were in Quebec to meet with the British at a conference known as "Octagon." They were at dinner when the message arrived. The Chiefs took less than ninety minutes to agree that the offensive could be accelerated. Returning to Washington, they advised the Southwest Pacific commander to accept the suggestion. MacArthur did exactly that. He certainly knew—as did the Joint Chiefs—that Ultra disproved denials that any Japanese were on Leyte. But MacArthur was not about to squander this opportunity.

Meanwhile Admiral Nimitz warned Halsey that securing positions in the Carolines and the Palau group were required to complete the isolation of bypassed islands. Halsey carried out part of the original plan, landing a Marine and an Army division to capture Peleliu and Angaur. The Palau landings were scheduled for September 15. That morning one of his sailors saw the admiral on the flag bridge, perched on his chair, reading a paperback book. Looking back, the officer recalled that day as the only time Admiral Halsey ever did such a thing. The Bull not only felt confident his boys could take care of business, but also felt the invasion seemed unnecessary. At that point, Halsey was already anticipating the next phase—his run to strike at the heart of Japanese strength in Manila and Luzon.

The breeches buoy came into play once more. This time, while the *New Jersey* refueled, Third Fleet staffers left for MacArthur's headquarters at Hollandia. One, General Riley, sought to coordinate the new scheme for accelerating to Leyte in October. The other, Lieutenant Carl Solberg, needed to check the status of Manila. Lieutenant Solberg, of Halsey's air intelligence staff, had last been with the Seventh Fleet Intelligence Center (SEFIC), the naval intelligence unit that served MacArthur.

Top spy Major General Charles Willoughby, suspicious to a fault—and prickly too—tended to see anyone who left MacArthur's command as an enemy, and he took special notice of Solberg now. But with Halsey intending to throw the Third Fleet at Luzon as soon as it rearmed, Solberg's mission to check on General MacArthur's declaration making Manila an "open city"—not to be bombed or shelled—became urgent. He could hardly mince words. The lieutenant got some guidance from Seventh Fleet commander Vice Admiral Thomas C. Kinkaid. His best access came through his old chief Captain Arthur H. McCollum, the

SEFIC director. McCollum affirmed that Manila should not be attacked but went on to say that nearby airfields, ships in the harbor, and fuel stocks serving the port were legitimate targets. Lieutenant Solberg hurried back to Halsey with the scoop.

CARL SOLBERG HAD wanted to be a pilot. He had volunteered, been commissioned an officer on the strength of his education and work as a reporter for *Time* magazine, and completed a brief training course at Quonset Point, Rhode Island. But Solberg couldn't pass the Navy's flight school evaluation. He'd been regraded an aviation specialist instead, and in the summer of 1942, that appointment led to his post in air combat intelligence.

In April 1943, Solberg had had a midfield seat at SOWESPAC headquarters as Ultra intercepts warned Halsey, who was by then leading U.S. forces in the South Pacific, of a big Japanese air offensive. That had led directly to the aerial ambush of the Imperial Navy's commander in chief, Yamamoto Isoroku—an amazing feat. Solberg considered the intercepts, which made that possible, to be the greatest wartime contribution of radio intelligence.

While the young naval reservist was not privy to the contents of Ultra—in the Third Fleet only Halsey saw the intercepts and decided whom to tell about them—as an air intelligence officer working next to radio intel maven Gil Slonim, Lieutenant Solberg knew the Ultra had lost some of its timeliness and fluency of eighteen months earlier. Solberg worked directly with aerial photography, interpreting the photos and writing intelligence reports based on them, and he saw the pictures begin to dominate the data flow. The United States had become so strong that finding targets—Japanese ships and aircraft revealed by the photo coverage or by radio traffic analysis—seemed more important than the enemy's intentions. Halsey's Third Fleet steamed at the tip of the spear.

While Lieutenant Solberg pored over the aerial photos, Admiral Marc Mitscher pulled the fleet from Palau to get it refueled for the Manila strike. Task Group 38.4 crossed the equator on September 19 and, having traveled farther in order to blast the Bonin Islands, would return to Manus for resupply. On the *Enterprise*, Chief Radioman D. C. Gensel took up the scepter as Neptunus Rex to initiate the latest batch of pollywogs. Other sailors focused on the airplanes and munitions to be used at Manila.

Aboard Mitscher's flagship *Lexington*, the air officers scratched their heads trying to predict wind direction the morning of the attack. Off the Philippines' east coast, prevailing winds tended to blow from either north or south in the morning. Which direction made a difference because the carriers needed to be downwind to launch aircraft. Marc Mitscher, an experienced old salt, got the wind right.

The photography suggested Luzon would be a target-rich environment. There were nineteen Japanese air bases there alone, including Nichols and Clark fields, familiar to the U.S. Far East Air Force (now MacArthur's 5th Air Force) from 1941. Intelligence estimated their capacity at more than 1,000 planes. Manila had a huge harbor. Radio intelligence revealed the city had the headquarters of the Imperial Navy's Southwest Area Fleet and its First Air Fleet, as well as the Japanese Army's 4th Air Army and the 14th Area Army. Task Force 38 crept up on the big island. Halsey would attack with three groups. Admiral Davison's carriers would return to port for fuel. But the day of September 21 dawned foul. Neither Chief of Staff Arleigh Burke nor the air officer, Commander James H. Flatley, wanted to put up airplanes in this muck, especially without knowing the weather over Manila itself.

Admiral Mitscher solved the dilemma. He sat in a chair on the wing of the bridge—his customary station in all but the worst weather. Commodore Burke groused about having to rely upon the guesses of weathermen. "The hell you do," the boss piped up. "Keep our radars going, and as soon as we see enemy airplanes in the air, we launch."

Unbeknownst to the Americans, the Japanese had intended their own air attack. Lieutenant General Tominaga of the 4th Air Army wanted action to help the Palau defenders. He inspected Clark Field the night of the twentieth, to stoke morale among his crews. The Japanese at the time gave JNAF responsibility for air searches over the ocean, so the Navy put up the first parcel of airplanes the morning of the twenty-first to find the Allied invasion fleet to the south.

The task force carriers flew their strikes from just forty miles off Luzon's coast. Air Group 15 leader David McCampbell again led the initial wave, off the *Essex* at 8:05 a.m. He flew a new-model Hellcat, improved for ground strikes with the installation of underwing rocket pods. The other aircraft of Fighting 15 were also of this type. Bombing 15 flew SB-2C Helldivers. Some carried 1,000-pound bombs for the concrete runways at Clark and Nichols. Others bore 250-pound bombs in numbers to shatter grounded airplanes and blow up personnel. The TBM Avenger torpedo planes of VT-15 had become used to constantly being armed with bombs. On this day, they carried torpedoes for the first time since leaving Pearl Harbor. There were thirty-six *Essex* aircraft and an equal number from the *Lexington*. The strike aircraft would drop "window" as they approached. Baled strips of tinfoil, cut to sizes related to radio wavelengths, would generate false returns on air defense radars. The Americans took every precaution.

The night before the attack, Halsey called in the *New Jersey*'s Filipino stewards—Filipinos and African-Americans held many of the steward billets in the U.S. Navy—and showed them on a chart the targets that would be hit. Halsey knew his Filipinos had relatives in Manila and would fear they might be injured, or worse. Benedicto Tulao, who had been with the admiral for years, was chief steward. He asked, "Those are Japanese installations there, sir?"

"Yes," the Bull answered.

The steward boomed as he declared, "Bomb them!"

Confusion abounded in Manila when American warplanes appeared overhead. Japanese officers conducting a tour bragged of the power of their air force—until those planes began dropping bombs. Near Rizal Park (then Wallace Field), eleven-year-old James Litton was visiting his friend Henry Chu at the latter's home when both boys saw airplanes practicing maneuvers. They knew this was different when one of the planes began burning up. Then they saw the tracer bullets. Litton watched a dive-bomber dropping almost vertically on a Japanese ship anchored in the south harbor. Chu grabbed him and they both ran to an air raid shelter. Another schoolboy watched from his rooftop near the Quiapo Church. An American plane flew so low, he and his friends could see the faces of its three aviators.

Seaman Jack Miller was a gunner in one of the Helldivers. His plane, of Lieutenant Commander J. F. Rigg's Bombing 15, flew on the second and fourth missions that day. The crews were briefed that the Japanese had more than 500 planes and fifty cargo ships in the harbor. The briefers assessed naval strength at a pair of battleships with eight heavy and nine light cruisers plus lots of destroyers. The reality proved different. Seaman Miller saw a convoy of tankers as they moved in, but no battleships or cruisers.

At the Nichols and Clark air bases, the Americans had a field day, strafing and bombing for ten minutes before the Japanese got their first interceptor into the air. The JNAF 201st Air Group put up forty-two Zeros and claimed twenty-seven enemy destroyed but lost nearly half their own aircraft. Among the JAAF, losses included a squadron leader plus the executive officer of another unit in the 22nd Air Regiment, along with more than twenty warplanes. Early the following morning a formation of seven Ki-61 fighters from the 22nd would be obliterated by attacks from 100 U.S. planes.

For the *Hornet*'s Air Group 2, Lieutenant Commander Buell was about to lead its strike package on the second-wave attack when he was recalled to flag plot. Admiral Jocko Clark told him that planes were being shot up by a Japanese destroyer that had planted itself in the middle of the bay. Flak positions on the shore strengthened her defenses. Clark asked Buell to go after that ship and he did. Planes of Bombing 2, the "Sea Wolves," finished off the *Satsuki*. Buell would receive the Navy Cross for this exploit.

Not the whole day would be a cakewalk. Pilots of the *Enterprise* torpedo squadron, VT-20, were plagued by weather. Prevailing winds obliged the carriers to sail away from them while they flew their mission. They had to fly around the storm on the way to Manila and on the return. No one expected that. Lucky pilots alighted on *Enterprise* with an average of ten gallons of gas apiece. The most skillful, Ensign Eugene E. "Roddy" Roddenberg, had thirty-five gallons left. Luckless aircrews ended up in the drink, putting their TBM Avengers down in Pacific waters and hoping for rescue. One Avenger made it to a different carrier and managed to land, only for its engine to cough to a stop while taxiing away from the arresting gear. Lieutenant Paul W. "Herr"

Schlegel, also forced to land on another ship, had the worst experience, with his engine giving out during the approach for his second pass. Herr Schlegel had to make a "dead stick landing"—one in which the airplane has no power.

The U.S. declarations for destruction—110 aircraft shot down, 95 destroyed on the ground—were exaggerated. First Air Fleet on September 23 had been reduced to 25 Zeros and 38 other aircraft. That limits the loss to less than two dozen. Adding the attrition among JAAF warplanes does not tally to the American number. U.S. fliers had been briefed on a pair of battleships and a passel of cruisers at Manila. The top secret claims reported to President Roosevelt—and instantly released to the press—include a dozen ships sunk (one by submarine) and thirty more damaged. None had been a battlewagon or a cruiser. The largest warship sunk was the *Satsuki*. Two other destroyers listed do not correspond to any Imperial Navy losses. Probably the most disastrous aspect for the Japanese would be attrition among their tankers and oilers. Task Force 38 claimed five of assorted sizes sunk plus two more damaged. Japanese records reveal nine tankers down or wrecked, either at Manila or in the convoy.

Admiral Mitscher's plan had been for a two-day extravaganza, hitting Manila and the air bases four times each day. Instead, on September 22 the weather closed in. Aboard the *Essex* sailors talked about a typhoon bearing down on Luzon. Mitscher ran two early strikes that morning, but the lack of targets and the weather made him change his mind. Teraoka's First Air Fleet mounted a feeble counterattack—six strike planes escorted by nine Zeros and led by Lieutenant Suzuki Usaburo. Half a dozen of Suzuki's planes never made it back, and although the Japanese believe they reached and struck the Big Blue Fleet, U.S. accounts note the lousy atmospheric conditions, not any JNAF attacks.

The ever-aggressive Halsey, wanting, despite the weather, to take advantage of Task Force 38's position off the Philippines, conceived the idea of mounting a different attack, one at Coron Bay in the Calamians, to the southwest of Mindoro. Third Fleet intel officers were telling Halsey that the Japanese used Coron Bay as a way station to shuttle ships, especially their precious oil tankers. Here, they could hole up at a base, briefly stopping between the oil ports in Indonesia, then continue to Manila en route to Japan. It remains unknown whether the more important intelligence on Coron resulted from photo reconnaissance or radio intercepts.

Mick Carney invited Commodore Burke over to flagship *New Jersey* to talk. Halsey employed the breeches buoy, having Burke cross from the *Lexington*. While the task groups refueled following the Manila strikes, Burke and Halsey deliberated. The Bull especially liked the idea because Coron Bay was a likely bolt-hole for Japanese ships fleeing Manila. Planes with extra fuel tanks, Burke calculated, might have just enough legs to make Coron, a 300-mile flight from San Bernardino Strait, the nearest point in the Pacific.

Slew McCain's Task Group 38.1 and Ted Sherman's 38.3 cooperated in the mission. Harold Buell led *Hornet*'s strike package. It would be the last operation for Air Group 2, who called themselves "the Rippers." Hellcats carried wing tanks and 500-pound bombs, followed by SB-2C Helldiver dive-bombers. On this day Buell's SB-2Cs performed excellently. The tally included a pair of oilers, half a dozen supply ships, a couple of escorts, plus the seaplane carrier *Akitsushima*, which had survived close encounters with Allied fleets since the Battle of the Coral Sea.

SPYING ON THE JAPANESE AIR FORCE

Chester Nimitz got most of his exercise walking Makalapa Hill. His house lay only 300 or 400 yards from CINCPAC headquarters, but on most days, the admiral would turn down one street or another to continue his walk. This allowed him to keep up with the intel.

Luther and Julianne Dilley, at 8A Kamakani Place, were not the only folks from FRUPAC or JICPOA to reside on Makalapa. The homes of staffers and the intelligence crowd dotted the hill. Intelligence chief Captain William B. Goggins shared a house with John Redman, CINCPAC's communications chief. Marine Major Alva Lasswell, who had made the crucial translation of the intercept that led to the ambush of the Japanese admiral Yamamoto—as well as a big contribution to the Midway victory—lived in another. Lasswell bunked with Tom Steele, yet another code breaker, and occasionally they were joined by Ham Wright, one of FRUPAC's best. Their house lay at the corner of a street where Nimitz often diverted from his route in the morning. When the admiral reappeared and rounded the corner to head for CINCPAC, Lasswell often joined him for the last hundred yards, going on to his own office while Nimitz disappeared into CINCPAC. The brief walks were a perfect opportunity to trade notes on matters of interest. The intel folks learned about stuff like President Roosevelt's visit, and the admiral got a heads-up on important intelligence issues.

Two issues that boiled through the summer and fall of 1944 would have direct bearing on the Philippines invasion. One concerned security. Officers worried that the weekly summary bulletin on Japanese strength, based on Ultra and put out by JICPOA, circulated too widely and endangered the secret of the code breaking. To correct this, the bulletin series was abolished at the end of June and replaced by a set of weekly summaries issued from CINCPAC (but still based on JICPOA information). This gave CINCPAC the opportunity to widen the scope of situation reports, giving increased importance to overhead photography. But the CINCPAC publication also moved the locus of reporting away from the intelligence analysts, robbing the spooks of their direct dominance of the papers.

The arm's-length relationship assumed greater importance in the context of the other headache, the continuing dispute over estimates of Japanese aircraft strength, which had already been going on for months. The Enemy Air Section of JICPOA, in combination with the Estimates Section, assembled CINCPAC's assessments of the Japanese air force. As seen earlier, Jasper Holmes defended these against charges from the Office of Naval Intelligence that Pearl Harbor's estimates were wrong. In May, an ONI note stung Holmes, who retorted to his opposite number in Washington, William J. Sebald, insisting, "We have never made a dishonest estimate."

A Japanese Navy captain had been captured in China and was being interrogated at Fort Hunt near Washington. His information provided a new basis for the air estimates, but Pearl Harbor could not seem to get hold of details beyond Sebald's notes. Early in September, just before

Bill Halsey's first series of Philippine air strikes and his recommendation to accelerate the invasion, Sebald told Holmes that the CINCPAC situation reports were very well done. But in the same letter, the ONI informed Pearl Harbor that its own intelligence furnished a more realistic picture of Japanese air strength. So JICPOA ultimately lost its battle to OP-16-V of the Navy Department. Aircraft numbers disappeared from the CINCPAC situation reports. For a time, the Enemy Air Section merely maintained its files. Finally it gained renewed importance as the main center for technical details of Japanese aircraft.

Driving JICPOA off the field left only the ONI strength estimates plus those from MacArthur's command, which both Washington and Pearl Harbor felt were excessive. (In an August 12 estimate the Seventh Fleet Intelligence Center put Japanese naval aircraft in the Philippines at 588. ONI on August 10 recorded practically none.) In its September 7 estimate the air intelligence staff in Washington credited the Japanese in the Philippines with 368 Navy and 389 Army warplanes. A week later, after Halsey's Third Fleet was supposed to have eliminated nearly 300 more, ONI estimated Japanese planes at 393 Navy and 366 Army. The American analyses careened between over- and underestimating. The ONI strength tabulation closest to Halsey's round of Manila strikes—this was supposed to have eliminated more than 200 additional airplanes—came out on September 28. The ONI now credited the Japanese with 185 Navy and 182 Army aircraft. Postwar studies indicate that the air strength at that date of all the Japanese services combined stood at less than 200. Japanese sources record that after strenuous efforts at reinforcement, on October 1 Admiral Teraoka's First Air Fleet alone had risen to 230 aircraft, including 132 Zeros, roughly 60 percent of them flyable.

THE JAPANESE WERE hurting. There should be no doubt about that. But the slaughter of their air forces was not so great as Bill Halsey, his aviators, or the Allied intelligence staffs imagined. And the paucity of Japanese warplanes in the sky owed as much to conservation of strength as it did to destruction at Allied hands.

Imperial General Headquarters had done its sums. The calculations were straightforward. Allied advantages were such that only the most intense concentration of the available forces would damage them. The front-line commanders had orders to preserve their forces to the greatest extent possible. The Third Fleet had been in Philippine waters over five days, off Palau for three, one of its task groups in the Bonins—close enough for surface ships to bombard the Japanese-held island. Still the Imperial Navy did not send its Sea Eagles against Halsey's ships. The Allies, exulting over their massive results so easily accomplished, missed that point.

CHAPTER 4

BEST-LAID PLANS

Lieutenant Solberg returned to the *New Jersey* as she rode at anchor in Ulithi's deep lagoon, restocking in preparation for Admiral Halsey's next foray. By now, the preliminaries were accelerating for a Leyte invasion. Before the landings Bull Halsey needed to smooth the way by smashing Japanese air strength, much as he had just done in the Philippines. In particular this endeavor would involve strong blows against Taiwan, the most important locus of Japanese power and Tokyo's link to the southern islands, including the Philippines, and at Okinawa in the Ryukyu Islands. The Third Fleet would range the waters from Japan to the Philippines and hack away at this aerial pipeline. It had become a standard feature of Allied amphibious tactics to strike that kind of preparatory blow.

Lieutenant Solberg brought the latest secret pouch from Pearl Harbor to the *New Jersey*. These CINCPAC pouches contained instructions from Admiral Nimitz not suitable for radio dispatches, private correspondence among top commanders, or intelligence packages and target files from the Zoo. Admiral Halsey reviewed the documents as he made his plans. This time around, the JICPOA folks had a bombshell. It was a report from General MacArthur's Nisei intelligence staff, the Allied Translator and Interpreter Section. The contents were explosive, and the implications went beyond Halsey's powerful preinvasion gambit.

THE Z PLAN

Strange entities abound in war, and the outfit known as the Allied Translator and Interpreter Section (ATIS) was a perfect example. The inspiration of Colonel Sidney F. Mashbir, an Army language officer whose interest in espionage went back to 1904, ATIS was focused solely on Japan. As a Boy Scout, Mashbir had been a bugler at an encampment with the Arizona National Guard and became enthralled with covert affairs when he read a spy story while waiting for a train. A decade later the young Mashbir worked for the Army's John J. "Black Jack" Pershing in a quasi-covert operation from the southwestern United States into Mexico, and after World War I, he had become interested in Japan. He'd started on a compendium bibliography of things Japanese only to have his work wiped out in Japan's Great Kanto Earthquake of 1923.

With MacArthur creating his Southwest Pacific Command in 1942, Mashbir was sent there to take charge of the Signal Corps reference library—until his friend ONI operative Ellis Zacharias told Signal Corps brass that Mashbir's linguistic skills and knowledge of the Japanese would be wasted there. Mashbir's boss, Rufus Bratton, the Army officer who had handled the intelligence source code-named "Magic" in Washington before Pearl Harbor, could not miss a ploy like that.

In September 1942, Mashbir's assignment changed to heading up translation work at MacArthur's headquarters. ATIS already existed, but only as an obscure backwater located at Indooroopilly, a run-down estate outside of Brisbane. At the time, it had eight Nisei linguists and three clerks. Hitching rails surrounded an old frame house. The day after Mashbir's arrival, a stack of captured documents filled his in-box soaked in blood and saturated with grease. That marked the beginning. With Mashbir's impetus, Nisei and Boulder Boys were enlisted. By July 1944, ATIS had 162 officers and 778 enlisted specialists, about 150 of them Nisei. Their rapacious appetite for documents never slackened, while, at Mashbir's initiative, mobile teams accompanied almost all MacArthur ground operations to question prisoners. That year, ATIS interrogated 350 prisoners and translated nearly 4,000 documents.

One document in particular was the extraordinary "ATIS Limited Distribution Translation 4," issued on May 23. That paper of twenty-two pages featured Combined Fleet Operations Order No. 73. Veteran Sunao Ishio, a senior Nisei at ATIS, recalls it as "perhaps the most important single document" translated at Indooroopilly. The document appeared as a result of an eerie repetition of the slaughter of the

Imperial Navy's fleet commander. In 1943, that had been Admiral Yamamoto Isoroku. Now Koga Mineichi held that post.

It happened like this: The Japanese fleet commander gradually became skittish, more and more concerned about American encroachments, and especially irked by the carrier raids. Admiral Koga had been driven out of his base at Truk in February 1944. He pulled back to Palau, where respite lasted all of six weeks.

At the end of March, the Big Blue Fleet struck there too. Japanese radio intelligence pointed to the U.S. task force in motion; then a scout plane from Truk detected it at sea. Koga Mineichi, his headquarters ashore at Palau, ordered the fleet to leave, which it did on March 29— just in time. The next day the admiral had to hunker down as American warplanes smashed his base. That went on for two days. On March 31, as the U.S. aerial assault slackened, Koga decided to move Combined Fleet headquarters to Davao, on Mindanao.

Koga's chief of staff, Vice Admiral Fukudome Shigeru, arranged to move the staff in three big flying boats. Then a scout plane, mistaking reefs and rock outcroppings for ships, reported the American fleet closing in again. Fleet intelligence officer Commander Nakajima Chikataka advised Koga to wait until morning before doing anything, even though the admiral preferred to leave immediately. He boarded one plane while Admiral Fukudome took another. The third plane, delayed, left Palau the next morning and made Davao just fine. But the aircraft carrying the fleet commander and his chief of staff encountered a weather front in gathering darkness. Both lost their way, and neither plane survived the storm. Koga's simply disappeared. Fukudome's aircraft flew too far in its attempt to get around the storm. Once it ran out of gas, the pilot tried a water landing off Cebu Island, during which the plane stalled and broke up. Admiral Fukudome hung on to a floating seat cushion for eight and a half hours, until Filipino fishermen rescued him. There were others, a dozen in all, including staff operations officer Captain Yamamoto Yuji (no relation to the admiral—or to Yamamoto Chikao of the NGS). Two men escaped, but the injured Fukudome and the rest went to Filipino partisans under Lieutenant Colonel James M. Cushing.

Colonel Cushing ended up trapped between the Japanese and General MacArthur, who as soon as he learned of the capture demanded that Admiral Fukudome and the other prisoners be sent to Australia on a submarine.

Meanwhile Fukudome had had a briefcase with him, which the fishermen who rescued him had taken. The briefcase contained papers in a waterproof bag. *That* went to Australia on the sub *Crevalle* (Lieutenant Commander Francis D. Walker Jr.), where it appeared at Indooroopilly. The documents turned out to be Koga's Combined Fleet operations orders for a decisive battle with the Allies, the Z Plan. In fact, they were bound inside a red cover emblazoned with a big Z.

The presentation caught the eye of Major John E. Anderton, ATIS executive officer, and once he was told of the take, Colonel Mashbir immediately called for special handling. All the translation would be after-hours and in total secrecy. Anderton, known for his knowledge of Japanese kanji characters, led the team, which was comprised of Navy Lieutenant Richard Bagnall and Army First Lieutenant Fabian Bowers. Once they had a rough draft, Nisei checked it, with Yoshikazu Yamada and George K. Yamashiro correcting critical translation errors. When they had a completed document, Colonel Mashbir personally ran the copying machine (a mimeograph) to produce just twenty copies, all very tightly held.

The Allied communications system provided for the exchange of secret pouches between SOWESPAC and Nimitz's command. JICPOA sent copies of all publications to MacArthur's intelligence staff. MacArthur's people, including ATIS, returned the compliment. When Translation 4 arrived at the Zoo, Commander Holmes instantly glommed on to it. He recalls being struck by the special handling restrictions, which required General MacArthur's personal approval for copying the document. The Zoo published most of its documents at a lower level of classification and positively encouraged copying—it wanted the intel to reach users.

Holmes saw right away why the translation had been rated the way it had. Not only did the Z Plan contain the Imperial Navy's recipe for decisive battle—right down to the assignment of some forces to divert Allied opponents—but Japanese knowledge that the order had been compromised would lead to changed plans, rendering the intelligence useless. Jasper Holmes showed the document to CINCPAC fleet intelligence officer Layton, who recognized that the ATIS team had not been aware of certain naval terminology. Layton and Holmes pulled an all-nighter retranslating the Z Plan, and a photographic copy of the Combined Fleet order was rushed forward to the fleet. It had to be air-dropped to reach Admiral Spruance. Layton and Holmes implored Chester Nimitz to obtain Douglas MacArthur's approval for wider dissemination. With that in hand, JICPOA made and circulated 100 copies. One of these Solberg took to Bull Halsey on the *New Jersey*.

MacArthur's intelligence people completed the circle by sending the briefcase back to the Philippines. The Japanese needed to think their secret remained safe. Admiral Fukudome's documents were resealed in their waterproof bag. At one point the idea had been to drop the briefcase in the ocean at the crash site for Japanese divers to find, but then Imperial Army commanders began to demand of Colonel Cushing that the partisans give up the documents. In the Imperial Navy, a chief of staff enjoyed much greater power than officers with that post in most Western military services. For someone like Fukudome, who basically possessed the authority of a commander in chief, to be an enemy prisoner was intolerable. And when the Japanese learned what had happened from the escaped sailors, soldiers on Negros and Cebu immediately began patrolling, making harsh threats against the villages about what would happen to them if the Japanese sailors were not returned. Cushing stalled while the Japanese started bombing and shelling Filipino villages to pressure him. Eventually Admiral Fuku-dome, the survivors, and the briefcase were given up.

Fukudome went to a Manila hospital to recover. The Imperial Navy convened a board of inquiry to investigate Koga's disappearance and Fukudome's capture. The board concluded the Combined Fleet com-mander had been lost in a tragic accident and his chief of staff had been the victim of imponderables. Fukudome was cleared for a fresh assign-ment. But Allied knowledge of the Z Plan had played a role at the Battle of the Philippine Sea.

And its story had not ended. Leyte Gulf was yet to come.

THE COMBINED FLEET commander, Admiral Toyoda Soemu, had his hands full coordinating all the far-flung preparations for Sho. He had no time to worry about the Z Plan documents. In Japan, the problem of energizing aircraft carrier construction and the formation of new carrier air groups loomed large. Toyoda was constantly pushing JNAF officials to accelerate their reorganization, and with the Allied carrier raids on the Philippines, it became increasingly necessary to replenish the air strength there.

A continuing quandary for Imperial Navy planners became the role of the Fifth Fleet. This force had conducted Japan's Aleutian campaign and still guarded the Empire's northeast sea frontier. If the Sho threat came across the northern Pacific, the Fifth Fleet would play a major role. But the region had been quiet for such a long time that a threat seemed unlikely. In all other scenarios, this force, built around just a pair of heavy cruisers and their escorts, would have a problematic role. Too weak to be a strike force on its own, too far away from the main surface fleet at Singapore, and too unaccustomed to working in tandem with aircraft carriers to fit easily in the carrier fleet, the Fifth Fleet represented a discordant element. For a time it was expected to operate with the Mobile Fleet, but Ozawa recommended that the Combined Fleet take it over. Admiral Toyoda, on the other hand, could not make up his mind what to do with it.

In August, Toyoda and senior staff went to Manila to huddle with subordinate commanders and their staffs. Attending from the Second Fleet—also called the 1st Diversion Attack Force, but more familiarly known as the Kurita fleet—was its chief of staff, Rear Admiral Koyanagi Tomiji, and the staff operations officer, Commander Otani Tonosuke. Officers from the Ozawa fleet were also present. Admiral Fukudome was late arriving. The JNAF boss for the Philippines, Admiral Teraoka, brand-new on the job, did not know the situation and concerned himself with reestablishing the First Air Fleet. Their host, Vice Admiral Mikawa Gunichi, was also new. He attended as the incoming chief of naval forces in the Philippines, the Southwest Area Fleet. Notably missing were Admiral Ozawa and his staff chief, Obayashi— the importance of their work regenerating the carrier air groups was such that Toyoda kept them focused there.

The command conference opened on August 10, and the scene was redolent with the vapors of times past. The headquarters of the

Southwest Area Fleet, located at the foot of Legaspi Wharf, had been the U.S. Army-Navy Club before the war. The surroundings were opulent: Rooms at the Manila Hotel, where Douglas MacArthur had lived before the war, were impressive. But the food—thin soup and prematurely harvested rice—reflected Japan's difficulties in this third year of conflict.

Japanese officers participated in tabletop war games based on the Combined Fleet directives for Sho. Toyoda's own operations staffer, Captain Mikami Sakuo, briefed the Sho plan, doing a creditable job. Watching him, Toyoda's senior staff officer, Captain Kami Shigenori, very likely felt conflicted. A notoriously aggressive figure, Kami here listened to a scheme that targeted the enemy's means of transport instead of its main strength. Kami had been with another man in this room, Vice Admiral Mikawa, on a glorious night off Guadalcanal in August 1942 when Kami held the same job for Mikawa he now performed for Admiral Toyoda. Kami's advice had been to go for the combat ships, not the transports. At the Battle of Savo Island the Japanese did that. Two years later the decision was universally regarded as a grave mistake.

Imperial Navy officers uniformly believed in the tenets of the fleet's decisive battle doctrine. So it came as no surprise when the Kurita fleet representatives spoke up during a break in the conference. Rear Admiral Koyanagi did the talking. Operations staffer Otani kept silent. Koyanagi objected to the goal. He knew his boss, Vice Admiral Kurita Takeo, took a dim view of targeting mere transports. Koyanagi asked what the Kurita fleet was supposed to do if it encountered aircraft carriers.

Captain Kami gave chief of staff Koyanagi the impression he was convinced the Sho plan was right. But Kami Shigenori believed passionately in decisive battle, the very thing that had guided his advice at Savo. Years later, Koyanagi told historian John Toland of Kami's calm advice to go after the warships. Any Imperial Navy officer would have understood that.

Responsibility for preventing the Imperial Navy's commanders from misunderstanding their orders lay with the Combined Fleet commander. Admiral Toyoda could have intervened. His top subordinate, Kusaka

Ryunosuke, considered Toyoda the best Japanese fleet commander of the war. Chief of staff Kusaka saw his boss as brilliant and very precise. The best interpretation for why the commander in chief failed to step up, permitting officers to think they had contingent permission to go after warships, is that the C-in-C believed in decisive battle too. He realized the Navy had been so steeped in tradition that it could not change—at least not immediately.

WAITING FOR BATTLE

Down at Lingga Roads, an island located about 100 miles south of Singapore, no one questioned the fleet's role. Lingga, a sheltered anchorage off Sumatra, lay practically on the equator. Steamy and pestilent, it had no claims to being a dream base, but the Kurita fleet busily rehearsed battle tactics there from mid-July onward.

During that time, the warships practiced as much as they could. There were damage control practices, underway refueling trainings, towing practices, and antiaircraft and antisubmarine warfare practices. There were exercises by single ships, divisions, and the fleet. Gunnery exercises and night fleet exercises consumed many hours; antiaircraft gunnery received equal emphasis. Tabletop war games rehearsed fleet maneuvers, afforded junior officers a wider perspective. They were able to work out kinks, such as when the Japanese discovered that active sonar interfered with acoustic detectors. I-boats were detailed to the destroyers for them to gain a sense of the noises made by a real submarine. Both destroyers and subs simulated torpedo attacks. In gunnery practice, battleship *Yamato*'s salvo patterns tightened up. Night gunnery shoots. Radar-controlled gunnery practice. *Musashi*'s accuracy did not seem to improve. *Yamato* and *Musashi* often split up and served as flagships for different forces, one to attack an anchorage, the other to defend it. Then there were the exercises by division, when the superbattleships would be together. When they finally sallied forth, Admiral Kurita would say the fleet had crammed a year's worth of training into those few months. The interminable exercises at least had the virtue of getting the warships under way, generating a bit of wind over the bow. In Admiral Ugaki's unit, Battleship Division 1, the boss lost track of the days. The climate and scenery changed so little Ugaki began to think they had arrived in early spring rather than summer. He had to count the days on his fingers.

Battlewagon *Haruna* suffered a real torpedo attack on August 18 in the South China Sea. Escorted by several destroyers and a few days out from Lingga, *Haruna* became the target of the U.S. submarine *Sailfish*. The sub, east of the Spratly Islands and brazenly on the surface, detected the Japanese by radar and launched four tin fish from a distance of 3,600 yards. By this time Allied subs were attacking major Japanese warships with depressing frequency.

In terms of technological advancements, Imperial Navy battleships, including *Yamato*, *Musashi*, and *Nagato* Battleship Division 1, received radars discriminating enough to track targets for gunfire. Sailors at Kure shouted their delight when news of the upgrade was announced. Perhaps, now with radar too, the Imperial Navy's traditional night-fighting advantage might return. At Lingga, the crews worked furiously to attain proficiency. Coordination between radar specialists and gunners was required to make radar fire control practical.

The Imperial Navy, however, did not believe in it. To quote Ugaki, "to depend entirely and blindly on [radar control] should be limited to cases where no other means are available." At a conference in the war room of the *Yamato* on August 20, specialists argued that guns aimed exclusively by radar would never be accurate. Ugaki was a gunner by trade and wholeheartedly agreed with this negative view.

In addition, battleship *Musashi*'s gunnery received special attention. Her skipper went ashore to a staff slot, and a new man, Captain Inoguchi Toshihei, took command. Previously, Inoguchi had been director of the Imperial Navy's gunnery school, and before that, a senior instructor there. By late September Inoguchi had the superbattleship shooting better. Admiral Kurita made him a special adviser on gunnery. In line with a round of promotions throughout the fleet in mid-October, Inoguchi suddenly found himself a rear admiral.

This latter development illustrated the Navy's careful preparations. Constant combat losses had shrunk the number of ships in the Imperial

Navy, and fewer vessels meant fewer commands to go around. And while the Navy had long been abstemious about promotions, with officers serving many years before attaining higher rank, it could be that the Navy Ministry decided a round of promotions might just make skippers fight harder. Virtually every battleship and many heavy cruisers would go into the next battle with a rear admiral at the helm—and every big ship division would be led by a vice admiral.

Another sailor who would enjoy his promotion to rear admiral, Araki Tsutau, had been flag captain of Admiral Kurita's command ship since that fateful day at Rabaul Harbor when the *Atago*, crippled, had had her skipper killed right on the bridge during a savage U.S. carrier raid. Araki's heavy cruiser had been the Second Fleet flagship then too; but then the force comprised only cruisers, its role to weaken an enemy before the Imperial Navy's battlewagons intervened. Now the Second Fleet had morphed into Japan's primary surface attack force, battleships and heavy cruisers together as a juggernaut. The Japanese nevertheless maintained the custom of assigning a heavy cruiser as the flagship. At the end of July Araki had the *Atago* in dry dock at Singapore for fitting of her own gunnery radars plus extra antiaircraft guns. Cruiser *Takao* then got the flagship duty, followed by *Chokai* when the *Takao* drydocked behind Araki's ship.

During that time, periodic gatherings of staff and skippers on the flagship had been devoted to sharpening naval skills practiced across the board. On August 16 Rear Admiral Koyanagi returned from Manila with directives for the Sho venture. A new senior staff officer accompanied him. Captain Yamamoto Yuji had survived Admiral Fukudome's plane crash, which had wiped out many of the Combined Fleet staff. Now Yamamoto had been sent to the front, to the very unit sure to be the tip of the spear in the next sea fight. Revenge wafted on the air.

Vice Admiral Ugaki, for one, felt relieved to have a plan, or, rather, a concrete operational policy. "Now we have something to study," Ugaki told his diary. "It's hard to ask us merely to keep on training when we have nothing to depend on as its basis. It's essential still to hope for victory, whatever difficulty one may be in."

The most controversial aspect of the scheme continued to be the substitution of the Allies' invasion forces—their transports—for their warships as targets. Kurita made the argument that if the Imperial Navy managed to destroy a convoy, the Allies would simply try again. But if Japan sank their fleet—in particular, their "task forces" (language Japanese officers used to refer to aircraft carriers)—the Allied offensive *must* halt at least long enough to replace the destroyed ships and planes.

Before long, Admiral Ugaki expressed concern at the Sho plan's contents. Ugaki had not liked the Z Plan, even with the modifications Toyoda and Ozawa had made for Marianas combat, and he felt the same way about Sho. A week after seeing the plan, he began to complain. Struck by the fact that the Second Fleet would not fight as part of a carrier unit, but act independently as a surface force, Ugaki felt the fleet commander took matters too lightly. He objected that Admiral Kurita had yet to craft any operational plan, or solve any ongoing problems, such as the transition to radar-controlled gunnery. Fleet war games aboard the *Yamato* early in September, followed by a September 6 review on flagship *Atago*, cemented all of Ugaki's doubts. Ugaki's was a simplistic view. The Sho plans fashioned a template to be applied against the Allied offensive wherever it came—anywhere along a perimeter of thousands of sea miles from the Philippines in the south to the Kuriles off northern Japan, not to mention the Home Islands themselves. Kurita felt it premature to lay down detailed operational plans before the Navy had a better idea of the precise Allied intentions.

The admiral happened to be just one of those who expressed concern. When a *Musashi* officer said much the same thing, the behemoth's skipper, Captain Inoguchi, reflected on the importance of engaging the Allies. Admiral Kurita himself, according to a chronicler of the battleship's career, spoke up to provide an explanation. "The war is in its last stages," Kurita declared. "Imperial Headquarters has decided that the Navy is not strong enough to fight a decisive battle with the enemy. That is why, as a last resort, they have opted for a surprise attack. Once the order has been given, all we can do is proceed as planned."

In the meantime, Admiral Kurita *did* work steadily to fix the myriad problems facing his fleet. At the very beginning of his sojourn around Singapore, he had bomb damage to battleship *Haruna* repaired, along with servicing the fleet flagship and other Second Fleet cruisers.

The Imperial Navy had sent electronic technicians with radars, radios, and other new equipment to Singapore, and Kurita shuttled his units through that port and the Singapore naval base, where there were dry docks and specialists to install the new gizmos. That work went on until the very eve of battle.

In addition, he was committed to keeping his officers happy. When the NGS ordered battleship *Nagato* shifted from Ugaki's division to another, Ugaki begged Kurita to intercede. The division commander had served aboard that ship four times in his career, most recently just that spring when taking up the reins of Division 1. Admiral Kurita went to bat for him. The NGS reversed its decision.

The fleet commander also paid careful attention to his sailors. When an outbreak of dysentery occurred aboard battleships *Musashi* and *Haruna*, Admiral Kurita was on top of that. During September, sumo wrestlers competed for best in the fleet. A *Yamato* petty officer won, beating five men in a row. Kurita gave the sailors liberty, too, with a bit of carousing in Singapore. The *Nagato* was detailed to transport groups of Ugaki's men to Singapore for the shore leave. The last transit of the shuttle, returning just a couple of days before battle, brought back a contingent of very happy sailors.

Aboard the *Yamato*, Ensign Kojima Kiyofumi, a newly minted communications officer, had his station on the ship's bridge where a Talk Between Ships (TBS) radio was located. The Japanese adopted communications security measures similar to what Americans did with their Navajo code talkers. For the Imperial Navy this was a secret language, *ingo*, in which radiomen mixed com-room slang with predetermined words and phrases standing for naval terms, plus plain language. Ensign Kojima sent orders and passed reports from the other warships to Admiral Ugaki. He soon found himself able to identify every battleship and cruiser in Kurita's armada.

On September 9, Halsey's carrier raids electrified, particularly on Mindanao and the Visayas. The following afternoon Admiral Ugaki was meeting staff and officers to plan a division maneuver when a Sho alert order arrived. Admiral Toyoda reported that U.S. carriers were striking and troops landing in the Philippines. Toyoda ordered Sho contingency 1. He directed the Fifth Fleet to assemble at Kure to operate with Ozawa's carriers. Submarines were sent to the area. Admiral Teraoka, too important at the head of the First Air Fleet, had to withdraw to Manila, handing over to Rear Admiral Arima Masafumi of the 26th Air Flotilla.

The emergency would be solved before dinner, but there were consequences. Reports of an invasion were false, the Japanese discovered, and the carrier raid was no more than that. Toyoda canceled his Sho I alert the next morning. But the C-in-C also decided to send his last available heavy unit, Vice Admiral Nishimura Shoji's Battleship Division 2, from Empire waters to join the Kurita fleet, and he kept the Fifth Fleet concentrated in support of Ozawa's carriers. As the Allies moved to invade Palau and Morotai, the orders to Japanese submarines were kept in place. Five subs headed toward the landing areas. Two were sunk.

Meanwhile, at Lingga and Singapore, Admiral Kurita dropped plans for the usual exercises and practices. His fleet would stage a war game for the next battle and concentrate on preparing the ships for sea. The war game, held aboard the *Yamato* on September 14, featured the scenario of an Allied landing on Mindanao, and during the afternoon of September 18, there was a detailed briefing to senior officers on the Sho plan. Once again fleet commander Kurita was properly turning his sailors' attention to final preparations for battle when this seemed to impend. Kurita was not taking it easy.

That's not Admiral Ugaki's view, however. After the Sho briefing, Ugaki privately wrote, "How is it that the headquarters attack force, which is going to fight a decisive battle actually commanding the surface force, has no definite idea about answers to basic questions?" A couple of days later, Admiral Koyanagi and Captain Yamamoto of Kurita's staff came aboard *Yamato* for a ceremony to honor recently deceased sailors. Afterward, Ugaki sat with the Second Fleet staff officers for a long talk. The battleship boss advocated an alternative to the single decisive battle, a policy of whittling down Allied strength. If there had to be a battle, Ugaki remonstrated, the object should be the Allied fleet itself, not its transports. On September 29, with senior staff officer Yamamoto at the point of leaving for Manila for another confab with Admiral Toyoda and the Combined Fleet crowd, Ugaki insisted on seeing the staff officer before he departed. The admiral repeated his litany. Captain Yamamoto agreed. After their previous conversation the captain had studied the matter. Now, Yamamoto said, he would make these points to Combined Fleet, but Ugaki was doubtful about whether Toyoda's staff would change their views.

In actuality, there was little space between Ugaki Matome and Kurita Takeo—much less than Ugaki thought. And that went for Kurita's staff too. Koyanagi, who survived the battle and lived to write about it, records, "Our one big goal was to strike the U.S. Fleet and destroy it." Kurita's staff felt that "the primary objective of our force should be the annihilation of the enemy carrier force and that the destruction of enemy convoys should be a side issue." Koyanagi was the one who had posed the question of what to do if the fleet came upon carriers, from the very first high-level meeting, weeks before. Kami Shigenori had advised attacking carriers before going after transports. Indeed, Combined Fleet chief of staff Admiral Kusaka also expressed that he was in support of attacking carriers instead of transports, and the same is the case with Admiral Kurita. Nor was the fleet staff ignorant of concrete conditions in the battle zone. Koyanagi records that they had identified the most likely invasion locales in the southern, central, and northern Philippines—including Leyte Gulf—and "diligently" studied the approaches, navigational conditions, and topographical data for each one. The truth is that *everyone* on the Japanese side wanted to engage warships, not amphibious shipping. Kurita bore no responsibility here, nor did he fail to work out relevant details. The dictum came from on high from the IGHQ directives.

Perhaps it reflected the price Japanese Army leaders exacted for agreeing to Sho. Not to have accompanied the targeting shift with a program to convince everyone of its military desirability remained a glaring weakness in Tokyo's arrangements. For decades, the Imperial Navy had designed its warships and doctrines for a decisive battle against an enemy fleet, strategized for that, and practiced to destroy naval vessels. When they heard the words "decisive battle," officers *thought* of enemy warships. To have that concept suddenly apply to transports, merchant ships, and landing craft was jarring—if not unthinkable.

Thus, shifting the target to amphibious shipping meant asking sailors to rise above their training and experience. Admiral Ugaki's expressions of dismay can be taken to stand for those of the entire naval officer corps.

ONE MAY LEGITIMATELY question what the Japanese were thinking when they calculated that targeting amphibious shipping would obtain superior results. After the war Admiral Toyoda told interrogators forthrightly that shipping had been the designated target. But the former C-in-C articulated no rationale for this tactical move.

In the years since, participants have taken both sides of the question of which target offered the better damage potential. Back at the time of Guadalcanal, when Admiral Mikawa Gunichi had won the Savo Island battle, Allied resources had been so thin that eliminating the amphibious shipping—which Mikawa had failed to do—would indeed have set back Allied offensive action. But by late 1944, there were so many Allied ships that the loss of some of them in Leyte Gulf would hardly seem to matter. Not only that, but with the Allied forces successfully landed in Europe, there were now spare amphibious ships for the Pacific campaigns. Plus the shipbuilders were turning out new craft with incredible speed. Liberty ships, the main type of general cargomen, were coming off the ways in an average of twenty-four days. One had been built in just four (2,700 of these would be launched in the United States alone). The Landing Ship Tank (LST), the most versatile amphibious craft in the Allied armadas, was being built in little more than two months.

The situation with respect to warships would be quite similar. Output from the American shipyards was staggering. During the last half of 1944, four new fast carriers and ten of the little "jeep" aircraft carriers joined the fleet. Newly commissioned destroyers amounted to nearly four-fifths of the total number of these craft in the Imperial Navy at that time. Three heavy and nine light cruisers sailed to war too. Only in battleships and battle cruisers were completions lacking.

While Japanese intelligence did not have these exact numbers, they did have projections that showed anticipated increases in Allied warships. It is true that in these categories it took time to complete new vessels. And a decisive victory that wiped out the battleships with the U.S. fleet, along with perhaps some aircraft carriers, seemed more helpful to Tokyo's cause, exactly as Imperial Navy officers believed. But the other side of the coin was that the Allied fleets could afford to trade that many ships against the Japanese and still win the war.

Admiral Ugaki's suggested recipe, "whittling" operations, seemed completely impractical. Whittling could be done only by pinprick attacks, either from ships or from planes. The experience in the Solomons had been that small units of Japanese ships were at a serious disadvantage. Given shrinkage of JNAF offensive capability, whittling appears unlikely from the air force side too. The idea works only if the exchanges are asymmetrical, such as a plane or two for a destroyer or aircraft carrier. One-for-one trades in types would merely lead to the annihilation of Japanese forces—and with the Imperial Navy already weaker, that simply led to defeat. Ugaki's interest in whittling prefigured the suicide attack, or kamikaze, tactics already being advocated.

But the fundamental point is that neither the formula that Admiral Ugaki and other officers favored, nor the one enshrined in the Sho directives, held much potential for an actual decisive victory. That did not stop Ugaki Matome from streaming stern criticisms, privately recorded. Ugaki had a reputation for humorlessness, and he was nicknamed the "Gold Mask" (ogon kamen). His diaries show someone who was obsessively critical. Indeed, this had been his tone throughout the war. Perhaps the dyspeptic attitude had something to do with the death of Ugaki's wife, Tomoko, in April 1940. Perhaps he was simply cold by nature.

AT LINGGA, THE preparations continued, independent of any strategic doubts. The supply ship *Kitakami Maru* plied a regular route between Singapore and Lingga, provisioning the bigger warships. There were so many vessels that she was able to get to each only at roughly two-week intervals.

In addition, work on the sinews of war continued apace. Cruiser

Division 16, a mixed unit, headed to Singapore in order to be outfitted with modern electronics. Its flagship, heavy cruiser *Aoba*, needed her bottom scraped. The scout seaplanes belonging to battleships and cruisers were also going to be given radars, and Second Fleet staff arranged a rotation for groups of the floatplanes. Light cruiser *Noshiro* went into dry dock right after the arrival of Admiral Nishimura's battleships.

Late September brought a practice exercise with the battleships shooting better. Gunner Ugaki recorded himself as pleased. Admiral Kurita ordered a round of shore leave for the crews. Ugaki went along.

On October 3, there was a brief moment of panic. The *Musashi*, entering Lingga anchorage, had a near-death experience—coming within inches of grounding on a drifted sandbar. She scraped bottom, sustaining minor damage. Sailors' perturbation at the incident would be relieved by the arrival of Battleship Division 2 from Japan the next day. The captain of the *Fuso* dropped by and told Ugaki of conditions at home. Then Vice Admiral Nishimura Shoji showed up too and filled Ugaki in on the downfall of Prime Minister Tojo. Nishimura described Tokyo as plunged into gloom and the NGS as impotent.

A couple of days later the destroyers *Kishinami*, *Shimakaze*, *Okinami*, *Hamanami*, and *Fujinami* of Destroyer Flotilla 2 left the roads. They worked with submarine *RO-23* on an antisubmarine exercise. Crews aboard *Yamato* and *Musashi* took soot from the stack and made it the base for a camouflage coating they swabbed on the main deck.

None of the sailors knew that the waiting had ended.

WILL THEY OR WON'T THEY?

Anchoring the fleet at Lingga put it very close to the oil that was produced at the Palembang fields on Sumatra. The location at Lingga was important, since Japanese authorities were experiencing tremendous difficulties moving oil. The situation with respect to fleet oilers and tankers directly affected the distance from its bases at which the Imperial Navy could engage. In 1941, the Pearl Harbor attack had been mounted—with some difficulty—at a range of more than 5,000 miles from Tokyo—nearly 4,000 from where the fleet actually sailed. The

Midway operation took place 4,000 miles away too. But by the time of the Z Plan, Combined Fleet calculated its operating range at about 2,500 nautical miles. The radius at which the fleet could engage diminished steadily.

Critical fleet oilers sank in growing numbers. When the Big Blue Fleet struck the Japanese base at Truk early in 1944, several oilers went down. The carrier strike at the Palau base some weeks later blasted another five. Two oilers were smashed in the Marianas sea battle. Seven more tankers, including ones that Halsey's carriers caught at Coron Bay during the late September strike, sank beneath the waves over the summer and into that fall.

Allied intelligence was aware of the Kurita fleet's location and speculated about its intentions. In the era before spy satellites and full-time global overhead coverage, one could be fooled. At anchor, Imperial Navy officers got their orders by word of mouth, on paper, or face-to-face—no radio communications were necessary. The Allies had less to work with. The radio spies possessed a marvelous array of instruments, but without photography as a check, their job was more or less a role of assumptions. A glaring example occurred early in October, when Vice Admiral Nishimura Shoji brought his Battleship Division 2 down from Japan to join the Kurita fleet. Nishimura sent a message informing the Second Fleet of his arrival. When the Allies deciphered this dispatch from a unit they knew to be part of the First Mobile Fleet, the Ozawa fleet, they briefly thought the Imperial Navy was reconstituting that formation. Within a day, skilled analysts had corrected the error, but the episode showed what could go wrong.

Watching the Japanese merchant fleet—and Tokyo's tanker situation more particularly—had become an important preoccupation for Allied intelligence. The Zoo at Pearl Harbor, OP-20-G in Washington, and the Seventh Fleet Intelligence Center with MacArthur all kept a close eye on shipping developments, and each of them produced periodic lists of Japanese shipping and losses. In Washington, a joint committee of Navy and Army experts assayed all reports of damage to enemy warships and merchant vessels and kept a running tally of the causes of enemy losses. At JICPOA, Jasper Holmes prodded the organization to create a "*Maru* center" (Japanese cargo ships, commercial or military, all had *Maru* in their names) to follow merchant shipping questions full-time. At both Pearl Harbor and Fremantle (in Australia), where MacArthur's submarines were based, close coordination resulted in a broad flow of intel to the marauding pigboats, as the undersea craft were nicknamed. The intelligence authorities eventually convinced themselves they had exaggerated the losses among Japanese tankers. The code breakers noticed ships listed as sunk that were showing up in the message traffic. Mavens produced revised, higher estimates of Tokyo's tanker tonnage.

But their general sense that the Japanese were facing challenges in moving their fuel remained accurate. The presence and activity of oilers became an indicator of fleet operations. In mid-September a JICPOA weekly estimate noted that large-scale Japanese logistic preparations were apparent. On October 2, the estimate indicated several tankers regularly carrying oil from Sumatra to Lingga and noted the Japanese were training in underway refueling. That report on the observations of tanker activities furnished the best guide to enemy intentions.

THE QUESTION OF whether the Japanese fleet would emerge to fight a Philippine invasion lay at the heart of the entire Allied intelligence enterprise. If the spooks had the right answer, General MacArthur and Admirals Nimitz, Halsey, and Kinkaid would be ready. At the Zoo, the intel folks published a correct general appreciation as early as September. The JICPOA estimate for September 4 observed that the Japanese were acting to restore their fleet and air strength, an ambitious effort that should culminate in about December. Intelligence analysts were aware of the Imperial Navy's lack of destroyers and foresaw five joining the fleet in that time. They knew of the three *Unryu*-class aircraft carriers (but not of the *Shinano*) and expected the Japanese would be able to assemble the largest air force to date. They would then be able to advance with the surface fleet operating under the umbrella of its own shore-based air force to attempt "an all-out decisive battle."

Much can be said of this appreciation. General Twitty's Enemy Situation Section correctly projected the overall Imperial Navy plan— their surface fleet would be used "to complete the destruction of our forces after the air forces have delivered a crippling blow and secured control of the air." The Zoo analysts were almost correct on Japanese strength (twice as many destroyers would join the fleet by December, along with the the *Shinano*). Their main shortcoming lay in tying Japanese action to a date (December, which corresponded to the expected availability of the new JNAF air groups) rather than an event (invasion of the Philippines).

On September 15, the intelligence center issued a new estimate. JICPOA hypothesized accurately that the Japanese would be unlikely to use more than a single carrier division of 175 to 200 aircraft. Intelligence also reported the separation of the Japanese surface fleet from its carrier force along with the reason for it—to get the big ships close to their fuel. But the analysts foresaw the Kurita fleet as not acting independently except for an unusual and unexpected opportunity and with strong air support. They also mistakenly saw the force as entirely composed of heavy cruisers. In Washington, both ONI and OP-20-G agreed in their estimates on Japanese fleet dispositions on September 21 that five Japanese heavy cruisers were located in the Philippines. Thus, Halsey's air intelligence officers during the Luzon carrier raids had briefed their pilots with intel from on high.

Early on JICPOA captured the essence of the Japanese scheme—the use of a surface force under land-based air cover—and it correctly followed tanker activities as an index of Japanese operations. It also scoped out the Japanese concept for decoy forces. The Zoo analysts, however, erred on the specific intentions of the Kurita fleet and on their overall sense of Tokyo's timing.

More aspects of the Japanese plans had been divined too. A Combined Fleet manual, *Striking Force Tactics*, which had been captured in the Marianas, was translated and key passages were circulated in a JICPOA pamphlet series called *Know Your Enemy*. The Japanese manual discussed the use of decoy forces to fool the Allies and illustrated the idea with the example of the hybrid battleship-carriers *Ise* and *Hyuga*. In the coming battle, those very ships would sail as part of Admiral Ozawa's decoy fleet. Also striking, Japanese adoption of the term "diversion attack force," as tactical titles for the Kurita fleet and the Fifth Fleet were known and reported in the estimates. Allied spooks had even caught wind of the code name Sho, though they did not yet know its meaning.

While Pearl Harbor intelligence did well, it could also be taken by surprise at times. The error on the composition of the Kurita fleet is one example. Late in September, Lieutenant Commander Edward J. Matthews visited the Zoo on his way to join the staff of Task Force 34, a special contingency formation of all the Third Fleet's fast battle-ships. Matthews had been assigned as combat intelligence officer to the battleship admiral. Commander Matthews carried data sheets from Washington with intel on Japanese warships that Jasper Holmes had never seen. JICPOA had to apply to Washington for access.

There were other drawbacks too. Holmes agonized over getting the Zoo's intelligence where it was needed "across this wide Pacific." The admirals would hear something that sounded interesting, and then demands for the data would pour in. With its limited numbers of cop-ies of the intelligence studies, JICPOA could never meet demand. More appeals to Washington. "Plans change so rapidly and new commands spring up so quickly that we are having the devil's own time trying to keep the proper people informed." General Twitty asked Admiral Nim-itz if JICPOA could set up forward distribution centers. The CINCPAC agreed. An office on Guam became the first—and it turned into the nucleus for a full-service "JICPOA Forward." But the advance echelon unit had yet to open its doors when the Philippine battle started.

The perspective from MacArthur's intelligence people was equally interesting. Captain Arthur McCollum headed the Seventh Fleet Intel-ligence Center (SEFIC) and had largely the same problem as Holmes. Though not quite so far-flung as Nimitz's Pacific Ocean area, the South-west Pacific still represented a huge region. Distributing publications by pouch often seemed impracticable. Instead, McCollum adopted a hybrid system. Materials like ATIS translations or technical manuals were still hand-delivered. Intelligence estimates for strategic planning appeared on paper initially but would then be modified by radio updates. This system led to confusion regarding SEFIC's view of Jap-anese intentions.

A basic appreciation of the Japanese, published after the Philippine Sea battle, agreed with JICPOA's initial assessment that the Imperial

Navy would avoid action for six to eight months while training new carrier air groups. But from late September onward, Captain McCollum began to anticipate that the Imperial Navy would counter a Philippine invasion with surface forces. A few months later, the Seventh Fleet commander sent General MacArthur a report crediting McCollum's staff memo of September 24 as foreseeing that the enemy would use the bulk of their fleet in defense of the archipelago.

That view, however, remained contentious. The SEFIC administrative officer disputed McCollum's suspicions, and General George Kenney, MacArthur's air commander, also felt Japanese fleet action unlikely. According to Lieutenant Lawrence F. Ebb, of the Enemy Information Section of the fleet intelligence center, the line intelligence experts took McCollum's side. Ebb and his colleagues knew that the Japanese did not expect any threats from the Indian Ocean, so the presence of the Japanese surface fleet at Singapore had to be for its favorable location in relation to the Indonesian oil fields. The SEFIC experts also knew the Japanese *did* anticipate an Allied move against the Philippines.

Several times Captain McCollum petitioned SOWESPAC to ask the U.S. command in the China-Burma-India theater to use a few of its very-long-range B-29 bombers to reconnoiter the Singapore-Lingga area, but General MacArthur and his top spyman, Major General Charles Willoughby, never agreed. The fleet intelligence staff then moved from Brisbane, to Hollandia, to the headquarters ship *Wasatch*, in two groups. The ones who stayed behind when the first wave set off were led by the officer who believed the Japanese would be a negligible quantity in the campaign.

British observers with SOWESPAC, misled or not, gathered that authorities were skeptical the Japanese would risk it all. A British official monograph reconstructing the campaign quotes the observers' report: "It was not believed that the major elements of the Japanese Fleet would be involved in the present operation, but that fast Task Forces might strike at our supply lines taking full advantage of darkness, surprise, and land-based air."

As for the Australians, their Central Bureau functioned in the radio intelligence field, and its intercept organization included nearly 3,400 operators. But they had focused on land warfare. MacArthur asked the Australians to provide him an element to use for the invasion and they responded, forming the Royal Australian Air Force 6th Wireless Unit. Working as a mobile intercept unit in the invasion convoys, the Australians were able to report that their ships had been spotted, but they discovered nothing about the Japanese fleet.

The intelligence impasse continued until the eve of the invasion. On September 24, an update estimated that two major "diversion attack forces" would sally against the Allied invasion, and it tabulated overall Imperial Navy strength that included virtually all of the available Japanese warships. That update went out by radio, as did subsequent versions. The same day, General Kenney issued an appreciation that doubted major Japanese naval activity in the Philippines—an assessment air intelligence repeated on October 4. Captain Raymond D. Tarbuck, the top operations planner at General MacArthur's headquarters, on October 4 expected the Kurita fleet to maneuver in the South China Sea as a preliminary move to attacking via Surigao Strait. Ray Tarbuck later decided Art McCollum was right. Tarbuck wrote a new memorandum some deemed prescient. This time he took SEFIC's point of view completely that all remaining Imperial Navy surface power would operate from west of the Philippines, with a specific threat through the Surigao Strait.

Following the war, both Navy historian Samuel Eliot Morison and the Naval War College concluded that the Sho operation took Seventh Fleet and MacArthur's command by surprise. Arthur McCollum went to his grave in 1976 insisting there had been no surprise. McCollum observed that in the wake of the Great Marianas Turkey Shoot it had been impolitic to put on paper a judgment that the Japanese fleet was about to fight again, so there *had* been an initial mistake, but that this had swiftly been corrected by updates in dispatches. Lieutenant Ebb in the trenches at SEFIC agreed. No matter the paper trail, Ebb recalled, SEFIC briefed the top brass on flagship *Wasatch* that a naval battle impended. How could it be otherwise? Into the summer of 1944, over a period of five months the Japanese fleet had been driven out of three operating bases, creamed in a major battle, then forced to split up. The Imperial Navy had their backs to the wall, and the Allies were going to seize the position that linked the parts of the Combined Fleet. The Japanese were going to fight. Many were sure of it.

Thus, JICPOA noted in September 1944, "The overall tanker movement picture is somewhat confusing insofar as determining fleet intentions goes, but it is apparent that large-scale logistic preparations are in the making." Japanese messages were intercepted that ordered a couple of oilers to the Pescadore Islands, near Taiwan. It was early October. This was important to Admiral Bill Halsey and his Third Fleet, for just then Task Force 38 had gone wild in the Japanese backfield again, slashing at the aerial pipeline in Okinawa, the Ryukyu Islands, and especially Taiwan. Those orders to the Japanese oilers told Halsey that the enemy might be coming after him.

Over the next weeks, decoded messages concerning tankers revealed a succession of key indicators. One early October message, complaining that even with the help of the Japanese Army the Sumatran oil could not be handled efficiently, sent four tankers to Balikpapan, a port on the north coast of Borneo. That place would be ideal for the Kurita fleet to refuel on its way to the Philippines. The command designated one particular tanker to handle all the Palembang-Singapore fuel hauling. Later, that tanker, too, would be sent on to Balikpapan. Another dispatch directed oilers responsible to Admiral Ozawa's main body to take on full loads of fuel from the Imperial Navy's central storage facility at Tokuyama. More messages for this group were intercepted too. Other decoded messages indicated that tankers had been ordered to fuel the Fifth Fleet, and—very suggestively—that merchant ships had been ordered to give up their own oil if the Kurita fleet required it. On October 16, Combined Fleet chief of staff Kusaka assigned half a dozen oilers directly to the Kurita fleet and instructed others to follow the admiral's orders. The OP-20-G comment was "This is the first indication of a possible sortie by [the Kurita fleet] which may comprise the bulk of the . . . units now in the Singapore area."

The stage had been set for a great battle.

CHAPTER 5

DESTROY THE INVADING ENEMY

A dmiral William F. Halsey liked to say he had a destroyerman's nose. By that, Halsey meant he could stand in the wind and foretell the weather. Pete Mitscher possessed a similar gift. The carrier combat commander would often outshine his meteorological staff, making precise predictions, whereas the scientific observations and calculations of his experts led to uncertain forecasts. Both men's skills would be in great demand in early October. Both admirals, with the bulk of the Third Fleet, were at Ulithi atoll, a typhoon bearing down on them. Halsey had wanted his warships to get a week's rest. Instead, the Bull decided he had better order them to sea to be safe from the storm. Fortunately the typhoon, its center several hundred miles to the north and west, dealt only a glancing blow to the Allied anchorage.

Task Force 38 returned to Ulithi and did manage a forty-eight-hour stand-down before going back to sea. Weather remained rough, though. Aboard light carrier *Cowpens* in Admiral McCain's Task Group 38.1, the ship's pitch in the running seas became so violent that six fighter planes and a torpedo bomber broke loose from their moorings and smashed around the hangar deck. The torpedo plane and several fighters were so badly damaged they had to be pushed overboard. In Group 38.3, the *Essex* took water over her flight deck. Airman Jack Miller of the squadron Bombing 15 heard that carriers and battleships both were breaking waves so high the spray splattered their bridges. Rear Admiral Ralph E. Davison's Task Group 38.4 caught even more storm coming north from Palau. On the *Enterprise*, part of that group, sailors found their mess trays sliding off the tables. The vessel's usual slow gyration and stately progress became a sharp lurch and a buck, like a small boat tossed about in heavy seas. In one day alone, the wind force increased fivefold, to near fifty knots, settling back to twenty-five—still a stiff wind—for the next couple of days.

Davison's group rendezvoused with the others on October 7. Radar operators were pleased to see the electronic "pips" of all those friendly warships appear on their screens one, or a few, at a time. All the task groups then sailed in company. This armada comprised seventeen aircraft carriers (eight light), six battleships, seven heavy and ten light cruisers, and sixty-four destroyers.

The fleet followed the storm. Mick Carney, the fleet chief of staff, exulted that the storm lingered in the Tokyo area. Halsey's sailors began to call the typhoon "Task Force Zero" because it advanced ahead of them, smiting the enemy. They imagined the storm and their task force as a one-two punch.

TEMPOS, CUSTOMS, AND COMBAT

The myriad combinations of strategic vision were now going onto the chart table for execution. The plan was to tear up the Japanese rear areas with a carrier raid on the Ryukyu chain and Taiwan, the islands along the Asiatic coast that linked the Philippines with Japan. Any Japanese reinforcement from the Empire would have to traverse this region; in particular ships and planes would need to refuel there. There were too many bases to be knocked out, but at a minimum, Halsey's fleet might cut deeply into Japan's air strength and transportation capacity.

Halsey's plan, simple and daring, provided that Task Force 38 would appear at the northern end of the strike zone, off Okinawa, and hit hard across a 300-mile arc of the Ryukyus. Then Task Force 38 would make its way south, off the Taiwanese coast, finally doubling back along the eastern littoral of the Philippines to provide the heavy cover as MacArthur's invasion convoys entered Leyte Gulf. A surface attack group would divert the Japanese, appearing off Marcus Island to bombard them, making Japanese commanders think "invasion" there. Newly arrived long-range patrol bombers would interfere with the

Imperial Navy's search planes and sink their picket boats, clearing the way for the carrier sweep.

This time, however, the Allies did not achieve the surprise they coveted. Imperial Navy intelligence, while not specifically informed, provided a certain strategic warning. On October 2, the Owada Group, the fleet's radio intelligence unit, noted that message traffic from Pearl Harbor and the Big Blue Fleet indicated that the American striking force would be large, and predicted it might target the Ryukyus or Taiwan. On October 3, the NGS ordered local commands in the Ryukyus to check radars and effect necessary repairs. That same day, the Southwest Area Fleet at Manila reported that its radio traffic analysis indicated a forthcoming attack on either the Philippines or Taiwan. On October 5, Manila ordered an alert for the northern end of Luzon and a withdrawal of shipping from the Taiwan Strait. The next day, the Owada Group noted the departure of a U.S. naval force, which must have been Davison's Task Group 38.4. The Kure Naval District and the Combined Fleet itself issued similar reports. Chatter on the Japanese side attained such levels that the Office of Naval Intelligence, from Washington, informed commanders that Japanese radio traffic reflected expectations for an American attack against the Ryukyu, Taiwan, or Philippine areas. On October 9, the JNAF scout plane on the 140-degree vector from Kanoya stopped transmitting midmessage at 450 nautical miles from base. It had been downed by a U.S. patrol plane from Tinian, though the Japanese assumed the scout had fallen to a carrier plane. The Sasebo Naval District called an alert. The fat had gone in the fire.

BY NOW, THE Big Blue Fleet had the mechanics of carrier operations down to a routine. It could put 1,000 planes into the sky. The task force would start and head toward the battle zone fully stocked and primed for a fight. A specialized supply group existed just to replenish the fleet at sea. This included oilers to fuel thirsty warships, escort carriers with aircraft to replace plane losses, ammunition ships to restock expended ordnance, victual ships to supply food, and fleet tugs to assist damaged or distressed vessels. The logistics group had its own escort, so as not to be a drain on the combat fleet. The usual dance was for the fleet to sortie for action, refuel once before engaging, carry out a wave of attacks, withdraw to replenish, and then attack again. Only after this kind of extended sequence would a task group or fleet head back to base.

Sailors needed to while away the hours before action. Aboard the *Essex*, flagship of Rear Admiral Frederick C. Sherman's Task Group 38.3, special services showed the movie *Follow the Band*, a year-old picture featuring a farmer who goes to New York City and makes good as a singer. Lieutenant John Monserrat on the light carrier *Langley* had a regular poker game under way, his challenge to see how long he could avoid drawing on any of his Navy pay. Bridge and pinochle were popular too. On the *Enterprise*, in Task Group 38.4, the airmen had a card game called "Jacks or Better" that sailors had to pay to learn. Writing letters home always appealed. On all the aircraft carriers, during any kind of decent weather, airmen hung out on "Vulture's Row," a catwalk partway up the ship's island structure, which afforded a panoramic view of the flight deck. By turns gossipy, hypercritical, superstitious, or urgent, aviators watched keenly as their comrades took off or landed.

Every air group on a carrier had its own tempo and customs, for training and for operations. During the Third Fleet's October cruise, Commander David McCampbell's Air Group 15 on the *Essex* flew a total of 1,829 sorties. Of those, 138 were for search or liaison purposes, 16 figured in rescue missions, 539 were for defensive patrol over the task group, and the rest were for attack or cover during offensive strike missions. Aboard the *Enterprise*, the attack squadrons of Air Group 20 practiced attacks against major warships at least once a week. The routine practices soon paid big dividends.

The men who flew the airplanes all had their reasons for taking on that dangerous job. Patriotic, romantic, dramatic, ambitious, vengeful, picayune, every kind of motive propelled the airmen. Take Lieutenant Frederick M. "Wistar" Janney, executive officer of Torpedo Squadron 13 (VT-13) aboard the *Franklin*. From a Main Line Philadelphia family, Janney had gone to Phillips Exeter and Princeton but went out for naval aviation after seeing the 1940 movie *Flight Command*, in which actor Robert Taylor starred as a young pilot in an elite Navy fighter squadron. The enlistment angered his investment banker father, but Wistar Janney reasoned he would be drafted anyway and preferred to chart his own course. Trained at Corpus Christie Naval Air Station, Janney had soon gravitated toward torpedo bombers. Now he flew a TBM Avenger on his second tour of duty in the Pacific.

Carrier groups had a well-oiled operational template. War service pilots were now so practiced that air groups could exchange ships—and did so with some frequency. Air Group 8, on the *Bunker Hill*, had flown from the ill-fated *Yorktown* back at the Battle of Midway. The groups could form and head out quickly on missions, responding to changed circumstances in midflight. The air group commander from each ship actively managed his planes in formation. Every strike now had a "target coordinator"—an aerial field marshal and usually an air group or squadron leader—who controlled the unfolding mission. On a bigger scale, the target coordinator filled the same boots as the forward air controllers of later wars, like that in Vietnam.

There were standard formations and details. A certain number of dive-bombers, torpedo planes, and fighters made a package, or "deck load strike." The packages differed in size and composition for the big "fleet" or "fast" carriers, the light carriers, or the little "escort" carriers. One or a few strike planes, usually with twice that number of fighters, were typical for a scout detail. Each detail would cover a "vector," or wedge-shaped slice of the sea to be searched for the enemy. The task group commander would assign search vectors to his carriers or designate which ships should put up strike packages and who should be the target coordinator.

All the aircraft carriers put up groups of defensive fighters called "combat air patrols" (CAPs). At times one carrier functioned as a defense ship and operated all its aircraft in CAP or antisubmarine roles. Ships controlled their own CAPs, but one vessel—often the flagship— had the air defense command. Radar and radio were the keys. The inputs from the electronic scanners of radar, and the radio intercepts of the mobile communications intelligence teams, came together at the Combat Information Center (CIC), where yeomen crayoned the data on transparent plotting boards while officers directed the CAP fighters.

The defensive controller, in turn, assigned major sectors or specific targets to the CICs of the other carriers. By this time in the war, the Big Blue Fleet had a cadre of specially trained fighter director officers to handle this function. The Battle of the Philippine Sea gives an idea of the fleet's defensive proficiency.

Allied defensive practices evolved with the threat. With CICs installed in ships down to the size of a destroyer, for more than a year already the U.S. Navy had been experimenting with using picket ships, vessels that would extend the diameter of a fleet's active air defense envelope by pushing its radar horizon beyond that of the core vessels. As the Japanese moved to emphasize night air attacks, the Allies developed night fighters. By 1944, many carriers in Task Force 38 had at least a flight of interceptor aircraft equipped with their own radars for night combat. Some ships had a full squadron. Captain Edward C. Ewen's light carrier *Independence* had an entire air group composed of night-fighting aircraft, both fighters and torpedo bombers. Commander Thomas F. Caldwell's Night Air Group 41 had first gone into action in Halsey's September carrier raids on the Philippines. After rapidly gaining experience, Caldwell's fliers were now ready for action.

On October 8, the task force joined up with a fuel group of nine oilers and spent the day replenishing. The *Cowpens* lost a fighter that crashed on landing and a scout bomber that had to ditch. The carrier *Wasp* had an accident when a torpedo plane crashed and burned in a night landing. At noon on the ninth, Halsey began a high-speed run toward the first targets in the Ryukyus. Poring over intelligence estimates of JNAF strength, Admiral Mitscher decided the first wave should be a fighter sweep. Ted Sherman's Task Group 38.3 had Okinawa for its target and launched from about 125 miles southeast of the island, beginning at 5:43 a.m., half an hour before sunrise, on October 10. For a time, the fleet shut down its radars and radios to avoid tipping off the Japanese, but at 6:40, a Japanese scout made further control of electronic emissions worthless. Fighters from light carrier *Cabot* were sent to intercept a "bogey," or unknown target.

Admiral Sherman put up his first team. He approved Commander David McCampbell, the *Essex* air boss, as coordinator of the first strike. Thirty-two fighters from *Essex* and *Lexington* made up the sweep. Right behind them two attack waves combined fighters with bombers. All four carrier groups of the Halsey fleet participated in this aerial circus. They smashed Okinawa and the other islands with 1,396 sorties.

On the Japanese side the commander of the Okinawa defense forces reported his airfields under attack at 6:40 a.m. A little after eight o'clock he added that he was engaging more than 100 enemy aircraft. Nearby islands in the chain confirmed they were under attack too. At 9:39, Okinawa reported the appearance of surface ships, which was a wild exaggeration.

That afternoon the officer commanding the 22nd Torpedo Boat division admitted that a baker's dozen of his PT-type fast torpedo boats plus two other watercraft had been sunk. There were other victims too. In the air, the only claims made for the JNAF were from Warrant Officer Ema Tomokazu of the 254th Air Group, who was credited with one plane shot down and one probable. On the Japanese Army side, half a dozen "Tony" (Ki-61) fighters of Captain Kimura Makoto's 23rd Interceptor Unit engaged the Americans. All were shot down.

Japanese scout planes produced their first sighting report of Task Force 38 at a quarter past noon. After that they kept in fair touch. Captain H. W. Taylor's light carrier *Cowpens* was providing the combat air patrol for Slew McCain's task group that day, and she recorded sinking two Japanese patrol boats and downing a scout. The *Essex* records dealing with at least two "snooper" flights in the morning plus a host of bogeys and "raids" that night, and splashing a couple of Betty bombers.

According to Samuel Eliot Morison, the Japanese losses were "more extensive" than pilots had claimed. Those claims included a submarine tender, 4 cargomen, a couple of midget submarines, and a dozen PT boats, in addition to 111 aircraft. Halsey's losses were 21 planes, including five pilots and four aircrew, of whom half a dozen were rescued by the submarine *Sterlet*.

But Morison's figures were, in fact, cleaned up. Airman Jack Miller of the *Essex* flew with Bombing 15 in the lead attack, and he recalled sinking both a heavy cruiser and a light cruiser. Seaman John Yeager of the same ship noted sinking a cruiser and four destroyers. No such ships were present in the Ryukyus that day. Lieutenant Wistar Janney of the *Franklin* won the Distinguished Flying Cross for leading Torpedo 13 bombing raids.

Essex officers were disappointed. The lack of aerial opposition startled them. Flak proved plentiful but badly aimed, leaving the aircrews with a feeling of anticlimax. What had begun as an adventurous foray seemed to have become a routine mission.

They had no idea that shortly after the first reports of the attack arrived from Okinawa, the Combined Fleet headquarters had issued an alert to execute the Sho operation, or that it had followed up by activating and redeploying air units and carrier air groups.

A battle royale would shortly take place.

AIR-ONLY SHO

The essential, basic directive for the Japanese dictated that they must annihilate the enemy. Admiral Toyoda had issued Combined Fleet Top Secret Operations Order No. 83 back in early August, and by now, the Imperial Navy had had some time to prepare. Decisive battle, discussed explicitly in the directive, remained the fleet's instrument to attain its goal. But the battle orders fudged the objective by failing to clarify what "decisive battle" now meant. The central problem—beyond immutable disparities in strength—was that Imperial General Headquarters had ordained that the forces should target the Allied invasion transports, whereas the Navy had been designed and trained to sink an enemy battle fleet. Toyoda had faced that challenge when the Sho plans were first promulgated, and again at the Manila conference, where fleet commands critiqued the scheme. Both times he had failed to rise to the occasion. Observant and thoughtful, Toyoda knew that.

Years after the war, the U.S. Naval War College would assemble a massive study of the Leyte Gulf battle, one so enormous it could never be completed, despite five years, five volumes, and thousands of pages of material. That study faults Toyoda for his absence from Combined Fleet Headquarters at the moment of the Taiwan air battle. The War College analysts observe that the Japanese had correctly surmised that the Allies would strike at the Philippines, and they had gotten the time frame generally correct, while appreciating the likelihood of an Allied carrier raid on Taiwan before the invasion. This was the time. How could Toyoda have absented himself at such a critical moment?

The complaint joins those of some Imperial Navy line officers, among whom Toyoda Soemu was never universally admired or respected. Yamamoto had been like a god. Koga Mineichi had been the logical successor. Unlike chief of staff Kusaka, some thought Toyoda just a four-star retread. He looked more like a railroad conductor than a fighting admiral. Toyoda Soemu had taken up the reins at Combined Fleet from command of the Yokosuka Naval District, largely an administrative and technical post. Frontline sailors did not know him. Admiral Toyoda had no combat experience in the war.

Aside from that his fleet experience was limited. Toyoda had led the Second Fleet and skippered battleship *Hyuga*, the light cruiser *Yura*, and a division of submarines. Most of his career had involved higher naval affairs. Toyoda had been with Yamamoto at the London Naval Conference in 1930 and then served as Combined Fleet chief of staff. He had been a language officer and naval attaché in London and Berlin, had worked at the Navy Ministry and on the staff of the emperor's special inspector.

Perhaps the key connection is the last one. The war had passed the point of decision. Fighting in the Pacific, from Japan's point of view, now had the object of holding on long enough that the Allies would negotiate peace. Tokyo had already moved to install a cabinet amenable to putting out peace feelers. The Imperial Palace had need of Navy and Army officers who would keep their services in line when the conflict moved to a close. Toyoda Soemu had a reputation as an intensely patriotic man—likely to deflect the hardliners—plus he was able and technologically oriented. As Combined Fleet commander, he would prolong resistance as much as possible.

Soon after the Koiso cabinet took office, Admiral Toyoda spent several days at IGHQ exploring issues with the NGS and checking NGS data on many things. He took the opportunity for a drop-by visit with Admiral Yonai, with whom he had worked closely in the mid-1930s when Toyoda headed the Naval Affairs Bureau at the ministry.

Yonai immediately asked about the war situation. He wanted to know if the Navy could hold on through the end of the year. The Combined Fleet commander replied that it would be extremely difficult to do so.

Behind the euphemisms, Admiral Toyoda understood Yonai to be talking about war termination. Toyoda was taken aback. The fleet commander refused to manifest defeatism, and for him to engage in a peace maneuver was out of the question. "I was hardly in a position," Toyoda wrote, "to say outright that the situation was hopeless."

This brings us back to Toyoda's absence from headquarters at the instant of the Taiwan air assault. He would later agree with the criticism of the U.S. Naval War College, reflecting that he had taken himself away from headquarters for too long at too critical a time. But the admiral *did* have a purpose for this trip. Toyoda regarded it as virtually certain that the Philippines were going to be the next Allied objective. He billed the foray as an inspection and tour of the front, but the truth was that travel to the Philippines might soon become impossible. This represented a last chance to fire up the sailors. More than that, Toyoda's mission was *political*. He knew how the fleet salivated for decisive battle. The admiral also knew that this time IGHQ had deviated from doctrine by aiming at Allied shipping—the measure that was calculated as the one most likely to prolong the war. Admiral Toyoda's duty was to be an apostle, seizing this opportunity to proselytize for the objective that was so disorienting to the fleet.

Combined Fleet officers accompanying the admiral on his trip included deputy chief of staff Rear Admiral Takata and the air officer Captain Fuchida. Toyoda had reached the Philippines, visiting units and holding talks there. They arrived at Manila on October 7. The Combined Fleet C-in-C wanted to go on to Davao, Cebu, and Leyte. But the islands were under intermittent air attack and further travel would have meant diverting First Air Fleet fighters for his protection. Toyoda also felt out of sorts. He had caught a cold in Taiwan on the way down.

So the admiral wrapped up his Manila sojourn on October 9 and flew to Taiwan, intending to head for fleet headquarters the next day. Instead, American carrier planes appeared out of nowhere and began to rain destruction upon Okinawa and nearby islands in the Ryukyu chain. A flight to Japan suddenly seemed too dangerous.

Taiwan, of course, held many Japanese forces. It was a stronghold of the Second Air Fleet, which had begun moving in early in September, and Toyoda would be protected there. Vice Admiral Fukudome Shigeru of the air fleet, recovered from his ordeal of capture in the Philippines, could work in tandem with him. But Toyoda found the radio gear at air fleet headquarters insufficient and his access to communications intelligence inadequate. The Combined Fleet commander could not develop an adequate picture of the overall situation, and beyond that, he could not even ascertain the disposition and posture of his own forces.

In the heat of this crisis, a cable arrived from Toyoda's chief of staff, Kusaka. The latter wanted to know if it would be all right to activate the Sho plan just for the air force. Out of touch, Admiral Toyoda concluded he could not make a proper decision. He asked Vice Admiral Kusaka to do so and issue appropriate orders after consulting the NGS and IGHQ. This matter of the "air-only Sho" is central to understanding what happened at Leyte Gulf.

The Imperial Navy had spared no effort to reconstitute its air arm following the debacle at the Philippine Sea. The JNAF had mobilized large numbers of planes, but in a strategic context, its fuel supply and aircraft production were beginning to flag, its pilots' skills were withering, and current losses were threatening force levels. The decline in the JNAF's quality also meant its ability to cooperate with the surface fleet had all but disappeared. Execution of Sho, therefore, necessarily involved separate air and surface fleet sorties. It would be the fate of the air forces to fight first.

This sequence had not been cast in stone. For months, the Combined Fleet had been deliberately conserving JNAF strength. All the top leaders anticipated the big battle in the Philippines and soon. One more conservation-of-force operation was perfectly feasible. If Second Air Fleet commander Vice Admiral Fukudome Shigeru needed to escape combat by surging his planes into the Philippines, it would only have improved the Japanese deployment there. Even keeping warplanes in the Home Islands remained an option, because there were so many bases along the aerial pipeline to the Philippines that Task Force 38 could not neutralize them. In the Philippines itself the same condition existed. It was a true "unsinkable aircraft carrier."

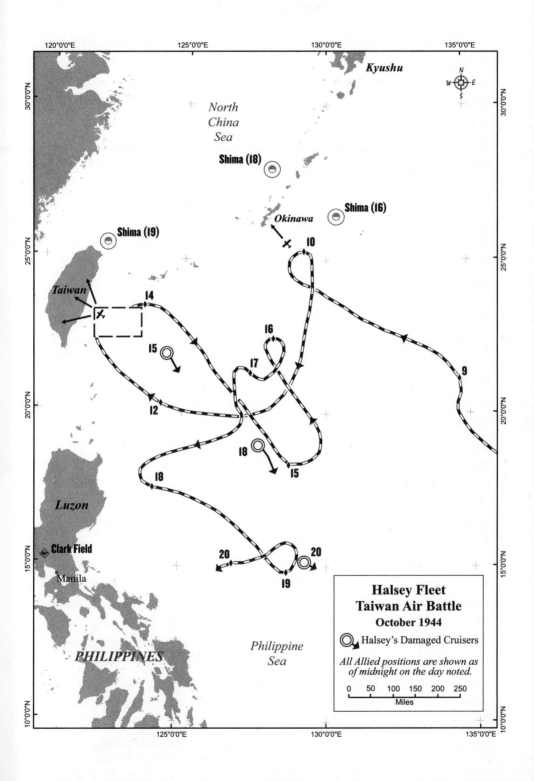

120°0'0"E   125°0'0"E   130°0'0"E   135°0'0"E

Kyushu

*North
China
Sea*

Shima (18)

Shima (16)

Okinawa

Shima (19)

10

9

Taiwan

14

16

15

17

12

18

15

18

Luzon

Clark Field

Manila

20   20

19

PHILIPPINES

*Philippine
Sea*

**Halsey Fleet
Taiwan Air Battle
October 1944**

Halsey's Damaged Cruisers

*All Allied positions are shown as
of midnight on the day noted.*

0   50   100   150   200   250
Miles

A robust air fleet in the Philippines, launching attacks as the Allied task forces and invasion flotillas neared Leyte, would have covered the approach of the Kurita fleet. Even supposing the JNAF inflicted no losses whatsoever on Halsey's carriers, that offered at least two immediate possibilities. First, Halsey's fleet would have been unable to stand off and punch at Japanese surface forces passing through the Philippines. Allied air attacks would have been reduced by the distraction of simultaneously defending their own forces. The same preoccupations would have reduced the potential for Allied air strikes aimed at the JNAF's bases. Equally important, the assaults of the Sea Eagles, successful or not, would require Task Force 38 surface ships to focus on fleet air defense. That would have made it impossible for Halsey to order the concentration of his own surface action group, Task Force 34. This might preclude Halsey from using heavy ships to bar the Kurita fleet's passage through the Philippines.

Both contingencies awarded the advantage to the Japanese. Admiral Toyoda could have squelched the air-only Sho and held the planes back. He did not.

The Imperial Navy had some very smart officers at the center of these events. At Hiyoshi, Kusaka Ryunosuke, while not actually a pilot, had been around airplanes so long that he might as well be considered one. Kusaka thought of himself as an aviation broker. The air fleet leader on Taiwan, squarely facing Halsey's carriers, Fukudome Shigeru, was Kusaka's friend and colleague, classmate at the Naval War College; not a pilot either, but an officer whose aviation experience included helping plan the Pearl Harbor attack. The other JNAF fleet commanders *were* aviators. The air staff officer with Combined Fleet headquarters, Captain Fuchida, was a skilled pilot—and he had been air group commander aboard carrier *Akagi* when Kusaka skippered that ship before the war. Air officer at the NGS was Captain Okumiya Masatake, who probably had the most varied experience of any Japanese aviator.

A year earlier, at Rabaul in the Solomons, Kusaka had been chief of staff of the air fleet that conducted a series of embarrassingly ineffectual air battles in response to the Allied invasion of Bougainville. Captain Okumiya had been the air staff officer of one of the carrier division air flotillas that participated. At home the Bougainville air battles had been portrayed as a brilliant victory. It is not clear whether Kusaka and other line officers believed that, but what *is* true is that the JNAF had called off the operation when its air groups ended up virtually destroyed. Now the same danger existed at Taiwan.

Admirals Kusaka and Fukudome, Rear Admiral Takata Toshitane, Fuchida and Okumiya, and Captain Inoguchi Rikihei, the air staff officer for the First Air Fleet, were all highly professional staff officers, flexible thinkers who had absorbed the fine points of aviation operations. All knew the score in terms of the decline of the Sea Eagles. Skill and potency were much diminished. Any one of them could have advised against the air-only Sho. No one did. Japanese aviation leaders' hearts were set on their own decisive battle.

WHEN THE FIGHT began at Okinawa, Toyoda mandated consultations with the NGS and IGHQ. Colonel Hattori Takushiro, a senior operations planner for the Japanese Army, notes that the power to decide which version of the Sho plan would be implemented was supposed to be reserved for Imperial General Headquarters. Instead, Vice Admiral Kusaka issued the alert order for an air-only Sho at 9:30 a.m. on October 10.

Not only did the Navy take away an IGHQ prerogative; it *had no plan*. Neither the NGS nor Combined Fleet had ever reviewed contingencies for an air-only Sho. There was an NGS directive to govern air activities overall, attempting to foresee what form the scheme might take in each region where Sho might have to be implemented, but this amounted to an operational policy, not a battle plan. This air-only decisive battle would be entirely improvised. Kusaka believed in its absolute importance. That faith marked the beginning of a terrible nightmare, one punctuated by Bull Halsey's invincible striking force.

At the moment Task Force 38 began its onslaught, U.S. intelligence (JICPOA) assessed there were 125 JNAF aircraft in the islands, about half bombers, a quarter fighters, and the rest mixed types. On Taiwan, JICPOA believed there were 241 combat aircraft but a whopping 560 trainers. The warplane estimate broke down as 100 fighters, 64 twin-engine bombers, and 39 single-engine attack planes. Captain McCollum's

Seventh Fleet Intelligence Center estimated Taiwan air strength at 223 combat aircraft and more than 600 trainers. Against Halsey's 1,000 aircraft, these JNAF forces stood no chance whatever.

At midafternoon, Japanese scout planes first sighted the American carriers.

For the Combined Fleet, Admiral Fukudome—and the NGS, if they were to conduct a battle—the first order of business had to be regrouping scattered air units. On October 10, JNAF planes in the southern Philippines were ordered to Luzon airfields. The NGS reassigned several attack units to the 762nd and 763rd Air Groups of the T Air Attack Force.

At 2:25 p.m. Captain Kuno's elite bad-weather fliers were ordered to carry out a night attack on the Halsey fleet. A little while later, their base at Kanoya was heard requesting torpedoes. Admiral Fukudome ordered rigorous searches by his units—but no new sightings came in. Kuno Shuzo's bombers had no weapons with which to strike. An hour after midnight, JNAF commanders canceled the attack orders.

On October 11, the Americans disappeared from the Ryukyus. Some carriers hit the northern part of Luzon. Again, the Allies achieved no surprise. At 6:50 p.m. the previous day, the Japanese command responsible for that sector received orders to be ready for battle the next morning. The strikes kept the Japanese on edge while groups of Task Force 38 refueled for the Taiwan air battle. Mostly Admiral Mitscher occupied himself with preparations for that. That twenty-four-hour reprieve afforded the Imperial Navy commanders one last chance to reconsider their course. Fukudome and Kusaka could have stripped Taiwan of JNAF aircraft, protecting the planes in the Empire. Those were the tactics favored in the war games held in the summer, before the new crisis. They now knew from Imperial Navy intelligence that Halsey's fleet had no transports and therefore no invasion impended. And Japanese analysis had also indicated that carrier attacks in surrounding regions presaged invasions elsewhere. Here was the moment to play the long game against a Philippine invasion.

Instead, the Japanese continued to concentrate for a Taiwan battle. Right into the evening of October 10, the radio circuits hummed with details of which air units would shift to what fields, and where they might refuel en route. The Third Air Fleet would provide staging bases for movement of 170 warplanes of the 51st Air Flotilla from northern Japan. Admiral Ozawa of the Mobile Fleet received instructions to make all his aircraft available with the exception of a small number that were to sail with his carriers. The less-trained fliers preparing for future carrier assignment would be thrown into the fray. Ozawa had anticipated an order like this. His staff had already held meetings with Fukudome's planners regarding what bases Mobile Fleet's warplanes should use. Meanwhile, the T Air Attack Force shifted from Third to Second Air Fleet command. On the evening of the tenth, Vice Admiral Shima Kiyohide, commanding the 2nd Diversion Attack Force, received orders to have his warships ready, with steam up, in the morning.

While Mitscher's task force gulped down precious oil from a replenishment group, it held to a westerly course. Captain James T. Acuff's oilers dispensed 331,000 barrels of oil and 542,000 gallons of aviation gasoline. Lost planes were replaced from the escort carriers *Nehenta Bay* and *Nassau*. Bill Halsey later reflected that the Luzon attack had been a mistake, simply giving the Japanese another day to reinforce Taiwan. The mistake would have been bigger had the enemy used that time to pull their aircraft back to safety.

On the Japanese side, shortly before noon on October 11, Captain Kuno of the T Air Attack Force received the order reinstating his instructions to smash the Big Blue Fleet. His bombers should leave Kanoya and move to Taiwan, refueling on Okinawa and striking the U.S. fleet on the way.

But the headaches of mounting this mission continued. Next to the torpedo shortage, there were weather problems from the typhoon. Kuno could not overcome them. Rear Admiral Sugimoto Shie, Fukudome's chief of staff, was obliged to accept another delay of the planned attack. That night an *Enterprise* night fighter splashed a Betty scout fifty miles away from the task force. While the Japanese struggled to cobble together their response, Admiral Mitscher's wolfhounds leaped forward and struck Taiwan.

THE SUN ROSE on October 12 at a quarter to seven. Weather watchers on the *Essex* noted a moderate sea, visibility at twelve miles, with broken clouds starting at 2,000 feet. Wind was from the northeast at sixteen to twenty knots. Admiral Halsey had all four groups of Task Force 38 on line. *Essex* reckoned her position at seventy-five miles off the Taiwanese coast.

As usual the Air Group 15 boss led the way. Commander McCampbell would be target coordinator for *Essex*. Defended by a flight of three other Hellcats, he would control the laydown of the strike. McCampbell found ground fog and haze over the western side of Taiwan together with partly cloudy conditions. A fighter sweep began the action.

This time it would be the Americans who were surprised. Taiwan had been on alert since the predawn hours, defensive radars lit, so even a launch at 5:44 a.m. afforded the Americans no shock value. A radar-equipped scout from the JNAF 901st Air Group, a unit that specialized in detecting submarines, filed the first sighting report at 2:10 a.m. Air raid sirens on Taiwan first sounded twenty minutes later. With early radar detection (at 6:10, more than half an hour before the Allies engaged), the JNAF could scramble fighters, and American planes arrived over Taiwan to find the Japanese stacked above them, with the critical dogfight advantage of altitude.

Even with this promising beginning, the air-only Sho quickly hung on a razor's edge. One version has Admiral Toyoda stepping from the shower in bathrobe and sandals, learning of JNAF preparations with glee, then finding the Second Air Fleet in extremis by the time he dressed. Admiral Fukudome has left his own account of an emotional roller coaster that starts from exuberance and descends to despair.

The Second Air Fleet had yet to complete its concentration—so far just 100 or so fighters and a dozen flying boats had moved down from Japan. There were more than twice that many Japanese Army planes, mostly at two aerodromes, that had come under naval command. Fukudome did not think too much of their quality but nevertheless felt somewhat reassured because he would have a mass force for defense—more than 230 fighters, which he figured for at least a 3:2 advantage over any U.S. airstrike—and the pilots would be defending their homeland.

Despite knowing of "the manifest inferiority" of JNAF airmen, Admiral Fukudome had been expectant. One new trick would be that some Second Air Fleet fighter-bombers were armed with incendiary bombs that they could sling at the Americans while maneuvering.

With their height advantage, the Japanese dropped down through the American formations and got off a first burst. It looked at first like the Japanese might fight by sections and divisions—the kinds of units that conveyed flexibility and power to aerial combat. Unit tactics were scripture by now to the U.S. Navy and most other air forces. But the JNAF pilots were not proficient enough to keep close on their wingmen through the acrobatics of a dogfight. One after another the flights of Japanese fighters peeled apart, to be engaged by units of American warplanes. At medium altitudes, the U.S. planes had speed and agility to match, and armor for survivability. Few JNAF aircraft made it to low altitude, where the maneuverability profiles reversed, or if they did, it was with masses of American fliers on their tails. It was almost a no-win situation. Fukudome lost a third of his fighter strength, including many of his best pilots, to Task Force 38's first wave.

The scenarios played out repeatedly when flights of sweeping Americans encountered Japanese fighters or bombers that had just taken off or were forming up over their bases. Lieutenant Cecil E. Harris flew an F-6F with the Fighting 18 squadron aboard *Intrepid* and participated in the fighter sweep that kicked off the Taiwan raids. As he crossed the coast, Harris took his flight of four Hellcats down from 15,000 feet to check out an enemy airfield. They found half a dozen twin-engine Japanese bombers had just taken off. As the American fighters began to engage, JNAF Zeros dropped on them from above. Harris flamed a pair of the bombers, then turned to the Japanese fighters. He blasted a couple of those as well. His formation as a whole tallied four of the bombers and three fighters, losing one plane to the twenty Zeros that had jumped them.

Fred Bakutis of Fighting 20 on the *Enterprise* was inbound with his sweeping fighters when combat controllers on the carrier recalled him to CAP positions, as they flung fighters into the air that were slated to escort the next attack wave. The Japanese seemed to be closing in for their strike—but nothing happened.

Once the fighters were released, Bakutis led them back, finding a mixed group of Japanese Army and Navy interceptors scrambling to climb. With the altitude advantage, the Americans destroyed nearly half of a twenty-plane enemy formation. Ensign Douglas Baker got three.

A Japanese Army flight entirely composed of aircraft instructors claimed to have shot down five U.S. planes for two of their own. On the other hand, only eight of thirty-two interceptors of the Army 32rd Fighter Group returned to their base, and all eight planes of an Army training unit were blasted when they tried to fight. Over Taiwan, a unit of nearly forty Navy Zeros engaged a similarly sized U.S. formation only to lose seventeen planes. They claimed seven Hellcats downed, plus several probables. Admiral Fukudome clapped when he saw planes fall from the sky, assuming them to be American. He soon found out otherwise: "Our fighters were nothing but so many eggs thrown at the stone wall of the indomitable enemy formation."

Essex Hellcats encountered the Jack, or Raiden, for the first time. The American pilots were amazed to see it outclimb them at 18,000 feet. They held formation while the Jack made a firing pass and then went after it, putting it down. Ensign C. W. Borley of Fighting 15 flamed four of the enemy in just a few minutes. This combat also proved the first for the Shiden, or George, about thirty of which battled double that number of Hellcats. The JNAF 401st Air Group claimed ten F-6Fs shot down but lost fourteen of their own planes. Petty Officers Hirakawa Hideo and Yamada Takeo were each believed to have accounted for four American aircraft.

Scenes like this played out all across Taiwan. William F. Halsey thought Fukudome's tactics were rather erroneous—the Japanese, he later wrote, should not have bothered defending at all but should have gone after Halsey's fleet with every single plane. Admiral Ted Sherman of Task Group 38.3 agreed. Fukudome Shigeru actually thought along similar lines, recalling his conviction that the best way to get at the American carriers would be with a mass formation accompanied by the strongest possible fighter escort, with the confusion serving to screen the approach of the T Air Attack Force. But when the moment came, the Second Air Fleet commander committed his fighters to a defensive role instead. Fukudome noted that his planes had been able to rehearse the large-scale attack tactic only a few times, and only immediately prior to Halsey's onslaught.

Many interceptors opposed the first U.S. sweep. Only about 60 aircraft rose to contest the second wave. The third and succeeding waves encountered little opposition. The bombers went in after the fighters to plaster Japanese airfields and other targets. Task Force 38 flew 1,348 sorties on October 12. Halsey estimated destroying 200 Japanese planes.

At Takao, fleet chief of staff Sugimoto suggested that Fukudome stay away from his bomb shelter, remaining instead in aboveground administrative offices. The C-in-C snorted. Any morale impact of showing bravery through vulnerability would surely be strictly limited, since they were on just one of dozens of airfields. Admiral Fukudome moved to his underground command post, recently installed in a cave about four kilometers from the offices. Sure enough, American bombers obliterated the administration building. Rear Admiral Sugimoto admitted, "If we had stayed in the administration office, all of us—the admiral and all other headquarters personnel—would have been finished." Sugimoto and Fukudome could only laugh ruefully at their good fortune.

The Americans came in little packets of twenty or so aircraft, with larger formations of thirty to fifty planes sent against specified targets, under the watchful eyes of strike coordinators. Planes broke formation and commenced individual attacks while still outside the flak perimeter. The Japanese countered with a fixed barrage—antiaircraft shells fused to burst after intervals of two to five seconds. Seaman Jack Miller, the Bombing 15 turret gunner from *Essex*, flew in the second wave and recorded the antiaircraft fire as heavy. His flight attacked before 8:00 a.m. The squadron suffered no losses.

Others were not so fortunate. A third wave hit around 10:30. Damaged aircraft tried to ditch at sea where there was a chance U.S. submarines or seaplanes might rescue the crews. Task Force 38 lost forty-eight planes on the first day. The rescue subs would do a brisk business. They retrieved almost two dozen airmen over the following week.

Japanese commanders worked frenetically. The Second Air Fleet reported engaging the enemy at 6:30 a.m. The First Air Fleet took over the scouting mission, mounting air searches from the Philippines. The

Third Air Fleet sent some 250 aircraft to southern Japan bases on Kyushu. But Okinawa reported the weather had closed in. Orders for the T Air Attack Force changed so that it should skip landing on Okinawa and come directly to Takao after striking the U.S. fleet. Kanoya base was to launch five search planes and several intruders to harass the Americans.

At about noon Admiral Kusaka, still acting in place of Combined Fleet commander Toyoda, who was stuck on Taiwan, ordered the main air strength of the northern fleet to Kanoya. At least 250 more aircraft were involved. (Allied intelligence estimated 130 bombers and 150 fighters.) The NGS ordered JNAF air depots at Omura and Kanoya to hand over every plane that had completed repairs or been accepted from the manufacturers to active units. Two fighter groups, which constituted the bulk of JNAF strength in China, were also ordered to Taiwan.

Having done all he could to assemble strength, shortly after 12:30 p.m. Tokyo time, Admiral Kusaka ordered the First Air Fleet to attack from the Philippines and have its planes recover on Taiwan. Air fleet chief of staff Captain Odawara Toshihiko flew to Clark Field to organize the assault. With strength estimated at thirty fighters and fifty bombers, First Air Fleet had trouble putting the mission together. No strike took place that day. Late that afternoon Taiwan reported all airfields still usable.

The Supreme War Council met in Tokyo, and talk there was generally about peace feelers. Prime Minister Koiso complained of glacial movement. Gloom hung over the gathering.

T Air Attack Force launched earlier to begin its torpedo attack. Captain Kuno sent forty-one twin-engine Francis and Betty bombers from Kanoya. Fifty Army bombers were supposed to fly from Okinawa. It is not clear what happened to that group.

At 6:37 p.m. Admiral Sugimoto of Second Air Fleet informed other commands the T Force had engaged. Some attack planes flew from Taiwan. Fukudome records that 101 Sea Eagles assailed the Americans. Carriers *Essex* and *Lexington* experienced JNAF suicide tactics for the first time. A Jill dive-bomber approached first, hidden in clouds but tracked by radar, pushed over above *Essex*, but changed his mind midway and pulled out of the dive, only to repeat the maneuver against the *Lexington*.

Soon after eight in the evening, air fleet ordered its elite strike unit to hit Halsey's fleet again the next day, recovering on Taiwan. Captain Kuno protested that the Americans would be bombing Taiwanese bases. The order stood.

"STRONG COUNTERATTACKS WERE DELIVERED"

On the first day, Task Force 38 struck airfields and rail yards. The next brought more airfield attacks, but there was a concentration on ports. The scale of the attacks diminished—just under 1,000 sorties in place of nearly 1,400 from the first day.

Admiral Fukudome's Sea Eagles behaved like angry bees whose hive had been kicked over. You could see the Japanese energy in the intercepts. At FRUPAC, Julianne Dilley worked the telephone switchboard that day and the place hummed—there were more phone calls than during the Great Marianas Turkey Shoot. If it wasn't Zoo officers checking for the latest scoop, it was the code breakers passing the word on new decrypts, or Nimitz's people asking for confirmation or for more reports.

Most unusually, this air battle involved Imperial Navy shore-based commands, with Combined Fleet headquarters also ashore. Thus, radio was vital to circulating orders to the widely distributed JNAF formations. That meant Allied intelligence intercepted and decrypted numerous air unit movement instructions, many JNAF sighting reports, a number of Kusaka's or Fukudome's mission orders, plus some of the responses. Lags between times of origin and when FRUPAC or OP-20-G broke out messages, translated, and circulated the information were mostly under twenty-four hours. When T Force boss Kuno objected that his airplanes arriving over Taiwan would find the Americans attacking it, that intel appeared in Pearl Harbor's Ultra summary the next day. An unidentified denizen of the Zoo wrote right into that report, referring to Captain Kuno's protest, "Right he was!" In an afternoon dispatch Halsey proclaimed his strikes had eliminated 396 aircraft and sunk fourteen cargo ships.

Now, after two days, IGHQ officers finally decided to inform Lord Privy Seal Kido of the huge air battle. As for Admiral Toyoda, he had returned to Taiwan, to Taibei (Taihoku), and was there when the assault began. Toyoda did not attempt to fly to Japan during the time Task Force 38 rained destruction on Okinawa and the Ryukyus. He stayed in a bunker when Halsey's fliers unleashed their terrible power at Taiwan. In his Taibei command center, Toyoda railed at the dangers that trapped him. With staff officers Takata and Fuchida, the Combined Fleet C-in-C did what he could to contribute, but the role of beekeeper stayed with Fukudome.

The angry bees of the First Air Fleet also swarmed. Vice Admiral Teraoka went to Clark Field to see off a strike—thirty attack planes covered by seventy Zero fighters plus an equal number from the Japanese Army. Their mission proved futile. The aircraft were supposed to refuel at a base in northern Luzon before pressing on, but the operation fell apart there. Problems refueling the Army aircraft took most of them off the board. Then weather closed in over the Taiwan Strait, with a northwest-bound low-pressure system tracking right across the strait, and the naval aircraft found nothing. To compound the sorrow, the Sea Eagle leading the escort fighters, Lieutenant Suzuki Usaburo, suffered an engine failure and had to ditch, lost at sea. Teraoka lamented, "I am sorry to say the 'escape of the big fish' is to be an undying regret." The Washington Ultra summary commented drily on the fourteenth, "These planes failed to find our fleet."

But in flag plot on the *New Jersey*, frustration grew. The first night as it sailed with Bogan's Task Group 38.2, the flagship had been in the thick of the fighting as Japanese bombers hovered in the dark, suddenly attacking from different points of the compass. No damage was sustained, but JNAF would be back.

The day's big discovery, though, came from the strike waves: Fukudome had *many* more airfields than believed. Ted Sherman's pilots, briefed to expect four JNAF bases in their sector, found fifteen. Admiral Mitscher made some quick back-of-the-envelope calculations and told Halsey he could not neutralize all those fields. Mitscher sent no strike waves after noontime in order to avoid being caught landing returning aircraft at dusk, when everyone expected the Japanese attack. Halsey suddenly realized this was Friday the thirteenth.

American intelligence might have minimized the Sea Eagles, but no one told the fliers of the T Air Attack Force. As dusk approached, a constant series of "bogeys" appeared on Ted Sherman's radar screens. The fighter direction officers went into emergency mode. A fighter CAP from Slew McCain's light carrier *Belleau Wood* was vectored to initiate contact. Group 38.3 sent interceptors from three of Sherman's four carriers. The Japanese went down one after another. But more hid in the clouds until dark forced most defending fighters to land. Smaller numbers of CAP night fighters kept up a cat-and-mouse game against the intruders for nearly four hours.

Nothing stopped several Sea Eagles from aiming torpedoes at the *Essex*, and only Captain Carlos W. Wieber's radical turns kept the ship from harm. A flight of Bettys at low altitude went against McCain's 38.1, which knew nothing until the planes were so close a lookout on cruiser *Wichita* spotted them. A journalist aboard the *Lexington* thought the torpedoes were everywhere, and he cringed in fear as a bomber lined up astern of the next carrier. It was destroyed at only the very last moment. The admiral immediately ordered an emergency turn to port. One bomber, shot out of the sky, splashed so close to flagship *Wasp*'s starboard bow that fire scorched the ship's exterior paint. The plane's wingtip damaged a radio antenna. Another Betty on its attack run lost the *Wasp* and went instead for the carrier *Hornet*. With the torpedo launched and churning through the water, that ship cleared— but instead the tin fish plowed into the stern of Captain Alexander R. Early's heavy cruiser *Canberra*. She suffered grievous damage.

Rear Admiral Davison's 38.4 group also had a hard time. It began well, with *Enterprise* fighters still aloft after dusk splashing some attackers, and others brought down by antiaircraft fire. But a Betty braved the flak curtain to dive at the carrier. By luck the bomber went down in between two other ships.

A group of Bettys sought Captain Joseph M. Shoemaker's carrier, *Franklin*. They popped out of low clouds at one-minute intervals. Lieutenant A. J. Pope, flying in the queue of airplanes waiting to land on the ship, found one in front of him and blew it away. Another fell to screening warships. Its torpedo went right under the big carrier—the tin fish had been set to run too deep. One Sea Eagle got a torpedo in the water, hot for *Franklin*'s bow. Captain Shoemaker evaded that by ordering the helmsman to full right rudder and personally ringing up "back, full" on the engine repeater for the starboard engine. The combination swung and slowed the ship just enough for the torpedo to pass ahead. It continued on through Davison's flotilla. The Betty that had launched the torpedo, already aflame, came in from the port bow of "Big Ben," the *Franklin*. The bomber crashed just behind Big Ben's island superstructure, slid across the deck, and tumbled into the sea.

Lieutenant Albert J. Roper led flak crews in the gun tubs right where that plane blazed over them. Roper leaped from his chair. The plane's wing ripped the seat of his pants. A steeper angle on this crash, a shallower depth setting on that other torpedo, and the damage would have been extensive. Ralph Davison's group had superb luck that night. The Japanese Sea Eagles were unrelenting, if outmatched.

The plight of cruiser *Canberra* forced Bull Halsey into a command decision. Captain Early's vessel, dead in the water with flooded engine rooms, could not move. She wallowed less than 100 miles from Japan's stronghold of Taiwan, and only a few hundreds of miles from an entire arc of enemy bastions. The closest place *Canberra* could get even temporary repairs—Ulithi—lay 1,300 miles distant. Early's cruiser could get there only by towing—and that would be at the glacial pace of just a few knots. Meanwhile, covering the cruiser's withdrawal would oblige Halsey to tarry within range of all those enemy bases, with Japanese reinforcements surging in. His original plan had been to spend just two days near Taiwan anyway. Halsey knew from Ultra that the JNAF were being reinforced and that the C-in-C of the Combined Fleet actively opposed him. As the Bull recounted, "We were squarely in the dragon's jaws, and the dragon knew it."

A logical solution would have been to take off *Canberra*'s crew, scuttle the ship, and get the hell out of there. But the Third Fleet commander lived up to his bulldog image. Admiral Halsey ordered cruiser *Wichita* to take the *Canberra* under tow, beginning to move her slowly out of the area. Halsey informed Nimitz by dispatch late in the day on the thirteenth. The Third Fleet commander had Mitscher mount a dawn fighter sweep the next morning to keep Japanese air down for as long as possible. Fukudome's response would also be hampered because CINCPAC had previously arranged for heavy B-29s to raid Taiwan from China. The original idea had been to cover the withdrawal of Task Force 38. Now the mission became even more important. Again there would be no surprise for Admiral Fukudome. Both the Yangtze Base Force and a local command sent warnings that the big bombers were in the air and headed toward Taiwan.

The fights of the past few days had led Bull Halsey to conclude that, strong as it was, the Big Blue Fleet needed even more fighter protection. Flag plot on the *New Jersey* hummed with activity as planners concocted a new scheme under which air groups henceforth would comprise at least half fighters, while the aircraft carrier *Bunker Hill* sported a unit composed entirely of fighters. Because the Hellcat worked well in a fighter-bomber configuration, this change could be made without much loss of striking power. Nimitz approved and CINCPAC began to arrange shipment of the additional F-6Fs required to effect the change.

By now, the Combined Fleet had concentrated all its air forces under Admiral Fukudome, setting the stage for a major aerial confrontation. Halsey tried to head this off with his early-morning fighter sweep—with enough success to double down with a 100-plane bombing raid. But Fukudome Shigeru attained his dream of mass air attack on the Americans—daylight strikes and night missions too, by up to 400 aircraft. Pearl Harbor sent a dispatch outlining JICPOA's analysis of the form and composition of a likely Japanese attack. But the state of JNAF training, diminished quality of aircraft manufacture, and reduced flying practice combined to stymie the air fleet. The abject failure of Teraoka's attack on the thirteenth pointed up the true conditions. It happened again now.

Events proved so confusing that even JICPOA had trouble reconstructing them. In a special review it later produced on the Japanese in the Taiwan air battle, analysts estimated roughly 437 JNAF aircraft had participated. Many came from the carrier air groups that Combined Fleet had seconded to Fukudome. Large numbers of fighters escorted single-engine attack planes or dive-bombers and a small number of medium bombers. Fukudome issued attack orders shortly before 8:00 a.m. Within an hour, the T Air Attack Force reported it would have some of its Japanese Army bombers up and flying soon.

The biggest attack waves formed from planes moved down from the Tokyo region, that is, JNAF groups 653 and 654, the carrier air groups. One formation, picking up its fighter escort over Okinawa, found nothing and turned back. As it flew *away* from Task Force 38, the Americans pounced.

More typical was a midmorning crack at Admiral McCain's carriers. Here were eight to twelve dive-bombers screened by somewhere between twenty and forty fighters. A *Hornet* CAP of eight intercepted them, still many miles from Task Group 38.1. The Navy fighters turned back the Japanese, destroying thirteen aircraft with five more probables, against a loss of four. Lieutenant Charles R. Stimpson, awarded the Navy Cross, chalked up five of the aerial victories by himself. Rear Admiral Obayashi Sueo, who had led a unit of Imperial Navy carriers at the Battle of the Philippine Sea and now moved up to be Ozawa's chief of staff, lamented the slaughter of the neophyte carrier groups. Taiwanese waters, he decided, were "a graveyard."

By dint of the mass attacks, carriers *Hancock* and *Hornet* and the light cruiser *Reno* sustained minor damage. The *Reno*'s flak batteries were so effectively controlled by her gunnery officer, Commander Arthur R. Gralla, that they splashed eleven Japanese attackers.

The T Air Attack Force accomplished the most. Assailing McCain's Task Group 38.1 near dusk, a Francis of the JNAF 762nd Air Group put a torpedo into Captain William W. Behrens's light cruiser, *Houston*. The torpedo struck amidships and flooded the engine rooms with 4,500 tons of water, nearly breaking the ship's keel. That afternoon a T Force dispatch indicated its planes had sunk three to five American aircraft carriers, adding to between six and eight already sent to the bottom. These claims were fiction, but they thrilled Combined Fleet chief of staff Kusaka, who issued a special operations order sending the Shima fleet to sea so it could mop up the supposedly dazed remnants of a crippled U.S. strike force. Allied code breakers in Australia (FRUMEL), confirmed by OP-20-G in Washington, deciphered the message.

Fukudome and the land-based air forces were to support the surface naval attack. Japanese radio direction finders located Task Force 38 at 5:30 a.m. the next morning, followed by repeated aircraft sightings. Here came a moment the Imperial Navy suffered badly from Admiral Toyoda's absence at the head of the fleet command.

Meanwhile on the *New Jersey* the wounding of the *Houston* rekindled all the issues first raised with the torpedoed *Canberra*. Fleet Admiral Halsey at first wanted to get out of harm's way, removing the danger by scuttling both ships. Halsey credits Mick Carney and his operations officer, Rollo Wilson, with convincing him these damaged ships could serve a useful function, bringing Japanese, hopeful of sinking them, in like lambs to the slaughter. Halsey's basic orders provided that if he had a chance to engage the Japanese fleet, that mission could take precedence over his assignment to support the Leyte invasion.

While three task groups covered the crippled cruiser, Halsey sent Ralph Davison's 38.4 group ahead to blast Luzon. The fleet commander informed Pearl Harbor that he was disposing his forces for an engagement and until further notice would be unable to cooperate with the Leyte invasion forces. Submarine *Besugo* saw an Imperial Navy surface force sally forth from the Bungo Strait in Empire waters. The description of several cruisers plus a light cruiser was close to the actual strength of Vice Admiral Shima Kiyohide's Fifth Fleet.

More to the point, after the war we learned that Shima's force actually lay in the Bungo Strait and sortied at that time. But something happened with Combined Fleet's orders. Admiral Shima aborted that mission on October 16, when Kusaka came to his senses and sent out a further dispatch noting that "REMAINING ENEMY STRENGTH IS COMPARATIVELY LARGE" and probably would strike, making necessary several more days of JNAF softening-up attacks. Shima turned west and north for Amami Oshima, where he anchored later. Allied search planes from China saw two "battleships" (Shima had a pair of heavy cruisers). Shima did not leave until October 18.

Halsey's notice that he was configuring for a fleet engagement brought a swift rejoinder from Seventh Fleet commander Admiral Thomas C. Kinkaid, who warned that the landing was proceeding and required carrier support. Halsey relented and brought the rest of his groups in behind 38.4 to add weight to the Luzon attack, assuming position to back the invasion forces.

A seed planted off Taiwan would affect a huge fleet battle just ten days hence.

Meanwhile, both the damaged cruisers were under tow, and they and their close escort were dubbed "Cripple Division 1" or "Bait Division 1," with Rear Admiral Lloyd J. Wiltse tagged to lead them. Halsey instructed Wiltse to stream out phony distress messages. On October 15, JNAF aerial scouts dutifully reported a unit of almost a dozen vessels that looked like destroyers but were practically immobile, discharging fuel oil into northwest Pacific waters. Japanese attacks proved fruitless. Two of three strike waves on October 15 returned without finding the Americans. The last received a shellacking from Slew McCain's airmen. On October 16 one attack wave came up empty-handed, but another, with more than 100 carrier-type aircraft, found the "CripDiv." The *Houston* suffered another torpedo hit. Combat air patrols claimed more than forty JNAF aircraft. By October 19 Halsey could report to Nimitz that he expected the damaged warships to arrive at Ulithi, where they could receive preliminary repairs, about a week later.

One last footnote to the Taiwan air battle relates to Arleigh Burke. Once the smoke had cleared from the big Philippine actions, Spruance and his staff returned to the States on leave. Passing through Washington, Commodore Burke stopped by the Pentagon to upbraid JICPOA for delays in delivering accurate target charts to the fleet, and for under-counting the airfields.

Burke's complaints stunned the spooks at Pearl Harbor. Jasper Holmes knocked down the criticism strongly—during September JICPOA had delivered more than 60,000 copies of various items specifically to support the Taiwan operation, including target maps, analyses, and information summaries. Commander Holmes estimated the share of these intelligence reports delivered just to MacArthur's headquarters at fifteen *tons*—at one point three transport planes had flown to Hollandia just loaded with this stuff. If the spooks underestimated the number of Japanese air bases it was only because photo reconnaissance over Taiwan was in its infancy.

A MOST CRITICAL ERROR

At a desk listening to Radio Tokyo before leaving Taiwan, air staff officer Fuchida was startled to hear the chords of the "Battleship March," which the Imperial Navy had adopted as a kind of anthem, and which always introduced big war reports. An announcer then declared that the Navy had achieved a stupendous victory off Taiwan.

There followed exaggerations of damage inflicted on Task Force 38. First were claims that nine American aircraft carriers had been sunk. By evening the box score had been raised to fifty-three ships, including sixteen carriers—essentially all of Halsey's fleet. Worse, the next day Emperor Hirohito wanted to issue an imperial rescript to commemorate the Taiwan battle results. Lord Kido watched with growing concern as the Koiso cabinet held a special session to inform the emperor, Hirohito received them in audience, and the emperor's return statement congratulated the Navy and Army for acting in unison and for greatly damaging the enemy fleet.

Admiral Toyoda's rotten luck held up a serious inquiry. The C-in-C finally got away from Taiwan on October 18, but then, as he landed at Omura in the Home Islands, the weather closed in, stopping him for two more days.

Upon Toyoda's arrival back at fleet headquarters, the first thing Captain Fuchida did was to initiate a review of the Taiwan battle claims. He convened T Air Attack Force senior staff officer Lieutenant Commander Tanaka, NGS intelligence expert Captain Suzuki Suguru, and Combined Fleet staff officer Commander Nakajima Chikataka, his colleague and the fleet intelligence officer. Captain Suzuki had been responsible for a remarkable report issued in the midst of the Taiwan air battle. This dispatch from the NGS Third Bureau, its intelligence staff, identified the Third Fleet and Task Force 38, accurately described its strength and organization, placed tactical commander Admiral Mitscher aboard the carrier *Lexington*, and even discussed the methods the Americans used to keep the fleet at sea by means of underway replenishment groups. Suzuki's report also ripped away any shred of deception that remained in the Big Blue Fleet's use of the Third Fleet/

Fifth Fleet designators by specifying that the Halsey/Spruance carrier fleet was the *only* U.S. aero-naval task force.

By the numbers being circulated in Tokyo, the JNAF had battered Halsey's fleet practically to death. The daily tolls were striking: four aircraft carriers sunk and another damaged on October 12; three and two, respectively, on each of the next two days; a carrier sunk plus three damaged on the fifteenth; then one more damaged on October 16. That tallied eleven sunk and eight more injured—the entire force of the Third Fleet. Captain Suzuki doubted it, and Fuchida, more so.

The Navy might be cautious, but nothing prevented the Japanese media from indulging in claims of the most lurid sort. The *Asahi Shimbun* headlined, "DESPERATELY FLEEING ENEMY WARSHIPS COMPLETELY DESTROYED," then used italics in a subheading: "ENEMY TASK FORCE HAS BEEN *TRULY* DESTROYED." The *Yomiuri Hochi* proclaimed, "TRIUMPHAL SONG RINGS." Emperor Hirohito opened Hibiya Park for public celebrations.

But the fleet review group discounted most pilot claims. For example, one officer pilot, Captain Saito Kan, almost the only senior flier to return to his base, related how "circling around at an altitude of two thousand meters, I released the torpedo, which hit the enemy aircraft carrier amidships." The carrier supposedly sank instantaneously. No torpedo plane crew in anyone's air force would launch at such an altitude and no torpedo like that—at night especially—could be considered "aimed." Saito spoke of "instantaneously" sinking a battleship, two cruisers, carriers, eight warships in all. Not every claim seemed that preposterous, but the overall picture appeared exaggerated.

At best, Fuchida's group decided, the Japanese could not have sunk more than four aircraft carriers. Judging from the radio intelligence, JNAF might not have destroyed any at all. For future operations Combined Fleet would assume that four American aircraft carriers had gone down. Captain Fuchida decided the Army bomber regiments with the T Force, never before in a battle at sea, had reported all kinds of foolish things and were responsible for the exaggerations. However, the Navy's chief spokesmen, captains Kurihara Etsuzo and Matsushima Keizo, lent their names to communiqués affirming the lurid results.

The radio announcements that stunned Fuchida outraged the Bull.

Admiral Halsey sent a message to Nimitz at Pearl Harbor, deliberately not encrypted, so the Japanese could read it: "THE THIRD FLEET'S SUNKEN AND DAMAGED SHIPS HAVE BEEN SALVAGED AND ARE RETIRING AT HIGH SPEED TOWARD THE ENEMY."

Japanese claims were also addressed directly, in secret. The daily Ultra summaries pointedly noted that intercepted JNAF radio traffic seemed not to contain damage claims until the very last of the fighting. The publication *The O.N.I. Weekly* made a focused analysis of the Japanese claims. Published by the Office of Naval Intelligence, throughout the war the *Weekly* would be the go-to current reports compilation most widely available to U.S. (and Allied) officers. Hedley Donovan, a *Washington Post* reporter recruited to OP-16-P-4 a couple of years earlier, supervised a team of fifteen similarly sheep-dipped civilians pressed into service to keep frontline commanders apprised of the straight poop. One was the historian C. Vann Woodward, brought in from the University of Virginia, and who became an avid follower of the Pacific theater. Woodward worked up the *O.N.I. Weekly*'s article on the Taiwan air battle.

The Japanese public releases, the *Weekly* said, were "a campaign of mendacity unprecedented since Napoleon proclaimed the destruction of Nelson's fleet at Trafalgar." The victory had been "synthetically fabricated" and "an attempt to rekindle the fading memories of Tsushima." Why? the ONI analysis speculated. Without ground truth or any means of establishing it, the *Weekly* postulated that the Japanese were attempting to conceal the high comparative losses Tokyo simultaneously admitted, or it was claiming that the first Allied foray into true Empire waters—long feared by Japan—had been defeated; or Tokyo simply sought to mislead the *Allies* on what it thought had been accomplished. ONI dissected the chronology of Tokyo's announcements, seemingly tapping each piece of the puzzle against a tabletop to see what fell out. The naval spies noted that Tokyo pretended the reprinting of its claims in Western newspapers was confirmation. A vague congratulatory message from German Grand Admiral Karl Dönitz represented another alleged confirmation. The presence of crowds of Japanese hovering around the newsstands for the latest editions was supposed to be mass approval.

What the Imperial Navy had truly been up to remained a mystery—
so much so that after the war C. Vann Woodward went back over this
ground to write one of the first great books on the Battle of Leyte Gulf.
There Woodward noted, "In order to understand the state of mind of
the Japanese at the time the final decision was made to commit their
fleet in this desperate enterprise, even after the evidence of the overwhelming superiority of our naval forces was in, it is necessary to
examine their curious propaganda during and after the air strikes made
by the Third Fleet." Woodward went on to detail material that had
appeared in the ONI article.

Others besides ONI probed the mystery. The Federal Communications Commission had its own spy agency, specializing in monitoring
shortwave radio transmissions, called the Foreign Broadcast Information Service (FBIS). It, too, produced a classified analysis of the Japanese
claims about the Taiwan battle. Instead of the hyperbole of setting up
the Japanese exaggerations as the biggest since Napoleon's day, the
FBIS found a ready comparison from Tokyo's own practice.

Just a year earlier, during the Bougainville battles that had climaxed
the Solomons campaign, the Imperial Navy had flung its air groups at
another Allied invasion force and claimed huge successes. FBIS pointed
out how Emperor Hirohito had involved himself in both episodes. FBIS
suspected an effort to drown out skeptics who doubted the claims. The
radio broadcast analysts quoted approvingly a statement from retired
admiral Nomura Kichisaburo once the frantic celebrations had died
down: "It is erroneous to think that we have completely upset the entire
enemy strategy and that Japan has suddenly won an advantageous
position."

Viewed from a broader perspective, the ravages of war had affected
the Imperial Navy deeply. It had lost cohesion as a unified force. Officers including Admiral Nomura recognized this. Japan no longer possessed an integrated, multidimensional weapon. Toyoda had an air
weapon, a surface force, a fractional submarine weapon, and so on.
The essence of the Sho concept had been to obtain synergistic effects
by employing the distinct weapons at the same time and within related
spaces, if not mutually supporting, at least related. Activating an air-
only Sho vitiated that strategy. Because of the tremendous losses at the

hands of Halsey's carriers, the weight of the Japanese air weapon, as we shall see, went from considerable to ephemeral. To trade the air weapon for glancing damage to a few Allied warships made sense only if the timing were such as to achieve, by this sacrifice, a safer advance of the surface forces. But the air admirals had not waited. The true mystery of the Taiwan phase revolves around why the air admirals thought they should conduct battle without the surface fleet. The sea fight would now be doubly hazardous.

Admiral Halsey's carriers, meanwhile, savaged the Luzon coast, giving Manila another dose of their lightning. The tensions of saving the "Cripple Division" were receding. Surgeon Piggy Weeks broke out the scotch and bourbon in the *New Jersey* wardroom for the Bull's staff to party, celebrating the Taiwan strike results long into the night.

Douglas MacArthur stood poised for his return to the Philippines, and William F. Halsey had smoothed the way for him. But for all their careful preparations, the road would be harder than either man anticipated. The curtain now rose on the main action.

CHAPTER 6

MacARTHUR RETURNS, SHO UNLEASHED

The invasion began assuming its final shape, though there were many pieces to the puzzle that had to fit precisely to ensure Operation "King II's" success.

The slowest units began to sail on October 10, just as Admiral Halsey's Third Fleet commenced its aerial assault on the Ryukyus and Taiwan. The invasion forces destined for Leyte—dubbed "Cyclone" because of its Allied code name—were concentrated primarily at Manus, in the Admiralty Islands (north of the Solomons), and at Hollandia (on the north coast of New Guinea).

While the action climaxed at Taiwan, the Seventh Fleet's 738 vessels sailed and began converging on Point Fin, a rendezvous planners had selected off Leyte Gulf. Vice Admiral Thomas C. Kinkaid had never led such a huge armada. Most of his ships had cleared port by October 13. Kinkaid, with General MacArthur and their staffs, sailed from Hollandia in a fast cruiser group on October 15. Worried that Bill Halsey had gotten carried away with his successes, Tom Kinkaid cabled: "CENTRAL PHILIPPINES ATTACK FORCE WILL PROCEED WITH SCHEDULED OPERATION K-2. REQUEST ASSISTANCE FROM FAST CARRIERS SOONEST PRACTICABLE CONSISTENT WITH DEVELOPMENTS."

The first preparatory operation would be for Rangers to land on Dinagat, Suluan and Homonhon islands, at the mouth of Leyte Gulf, overwhelm any Japanese defenders, and permit technicians to place navigation beacons. The Allies compensated for their lack of surprise with the sheer force of their combat power.

On October 3, Lieutenant Honda Yoshikuni's submarine *RO-41* spotted a unit of small escort carriers the Americans called "jeeps" a few dozen miles east of Morotai. Under Rear Admiral Clifton A. F.

Sprague, this force was to support one of the preliminary landings, MacArthur's Morotai invasion, which aimed to obtain airfields closer to the battle zone. Honda crept up and loosed his last torpedoes. They missed the carriers but split open the stern of destroyer escort *Shelton*, whose buoyancy deteriorated so badly that U.S. commanders scuttled her. To make matters worse, the U.S. boat *Seawolf* happened to be passing through when Sprague's escorts counterattacked a sonar contact they assumed to be Japanese. They sank the American sub. *Seawolf* went down with all hands. Adding to the injury, *RO-41* survived to warn Combined Fleet that Allied aircraft arrived that day to use the Morotai airfields.

The indications continued piling up. At Ulithi on October 7, the *RO-46* scouted and reported just one carrier along with some cruisers or destroyers anchored there. This clearly indicated that the Big Blue Fleet had sailed. Indeed, Halsey stood at the brink of initiating his strikes into the Japanese rear.

Two days later, a Japanese Army plane overflew Hollandia, reporting a fleet plus more than 200 transports. On October 12, the Americans intercepted a Japanese dispatch indicating they expected Allied forces at Hollandia to leave shortly for operations. Japanese radio spies also linked developments there with Pearl Harbor and Manus, suggesting a major operation. When a JNAF scout reconnoitered Manus on October 14, only warships remained at anchor. The invasion fleet had flown the coop. By then, the Japanese were fighting hard around Taiwan. The battle would become far-flung.

A GATHERING STORM

The last days of the Kurita fleet passed in a blur. The admiral and his cohorts labored to whip the armada into shape and update the vessels with the latest technology. Admiral Kurita had electronic gear mounted on his floatplanes and needed to complete radar and other installations on the vessels themselves. Battleships *Kongo* and *Haruna*, with their brand-new electronics, had to be kept away from prying eyes and were restricted to liberty at Seletar Naval Base, which had tighter security.

Vice Admiral Ugaki's *Yamato* and *Musashi*, whose technical features were held secret even from their crews, were not permitted to leave Lingga. Instead Ugaki relied upon his older battlewagon, the *Nagato*, to take contingents of their crews on liberty. The admiral also rejected Singapore as a liberty port because of its allure for young sailors, so they, too, were restricted to Seletar.

Kurita's other units were more fortunate. His cruiser and destroyer formations took turns at Singapore. From October 5 to 8 the pleasure went to cruisers *Myoko*, *Haguro*, and *Mogami* plus most ships of Destroyer Flotilla 10. Over the next several days the liberty parties would be from cruisers *Takao*, *Chokai*, and *Maya*, and the fleet flagship, the *Atago*, with their escorts from Destroyer Flotilla 2. From October 11 to 14, it would be the turn of sailors from the *Kumano*, *Suzuya*, *Tone*, and *Chikuma*. Still, with a day to sail to Singapore and another to steam back, the seamen would get only ten hours to enjoy themselves.

On October 10, when the Combined Fleet activated the air fleets for the Taiwan battle, Admiral Kurita took notice. Not long after, Combined Fleet chief of staff Kusaka sent further word that he intended Ozawa's Mobile Fleet to remain on standby. Kurita took that as a hint. Though he did not immediately alter routines, the admiral demanded a speedup at Singapore dockyards. The next day U.S. intelligence reported that there were no indications in Japanese radio traffic of a sortie by Kurita's fleet. The same or similar notices would circulate for several days.

By October 15, the fleet remained divided between Lingga and Singapore, but Admiral Kurita took new measures to prepare. The cruiser *Chikuma* and a number of destroyers fueled from *Yamato*. The *Kumano* plus other destroyers got their oil from *Musashi*. Vessels of Cruiser Division 5 drank from the oil barge *Hayatomo* at Singapore, while ships of Cruiser Division 16 drew on the Singapore Naval Base. Oiler *Fukuan Maru* topped off the rest of Cruiser Division 7. Light cruiser *Noshiro* went through upkeep in a blaze of dockyard activity. Scheduled to follow her, heavy cruiser *Aoba* would have her dry-docking canceled instead.

Anticipating action, on October 16 Kurita ordered a tanker convoy to Brunei Bay on the north coast of Borneo. At midday, Combined Fleet instructed Kurita to prepare for sea and be ready to join the Taiwan battle. Admiral Kusaka amplified later, telling Kurita that the Second Fleet might be ordered to fall upon the American task force and augment its losses from the air battle. Kusaka added that because a Kurita fleet sortie would consume a considerable amount of precious fuel oil, Combined Fleet would hold any execute order unless it seemed necessary. Chief of staff Kusaka followed up by confirming orders for tankers to head for Brunei.

Preparations became urgent. Admiral Kurita instructed *Aoba* and *Noshiro* to prepare for twenty knots' speed on two hours' notice—a battle indicator. Just a little earlier Kurita had ordered his fleet to Readiness Condition 1. He summoned another oiler to Lingga, as well as the cruiser *Kinu* and destroyer *Uranami*, the remaining ships of the unit to which the *Aoba* belonged. Kurita also instructed floatplanes to return to their ships by morning, including those whose new radar installations were not yet complete. Late that afternoon, Kurita told Combined Fleet that he stood ready to sortie with all of his units—save *Noshiro* and *Aoba*, which would rejoin the fleet by noon or evening the following day.

As late as October 16, the radio summary from Washington recorded no unusual activity around Singapore. The Allies detected high volumes of traffic on communications channels used by the Sixth Fleet, Japan's submarine force, which corresponded to the Imperial Navy directing available subs to positions off the Philippines.

At 8:00 the next morning, American troops first stepped ashore on Suluan Island in the entrance to Leyte Gulf. Nine minutes later the Combined Fleet issued a warning dispatch for the contingency Sho 1. At 8:30, an execute order replaced the alert. An hour later, at 9:28, Combined Fleet affirmatively ordered Admiral Kurita to Brunei.

News of the landings naturally threw Imperial General Headquarters into an uproar. The IGHQ chieftains immediately sought an audience with Emperor Hirohito. Admiral Oikawa Koshiro, Navy chief of staff, accompanied General Umezu Yoshijiro, the Army chief, to the palace. After praising the Taiwan air battle, they asked permission to unleash

Sho 1 and promised to work in complete harmony. "Since this is the important battle to decide the fate of the Empire," Hirohito pronounced, "the Army and Navy will work as one to destroy the enemy."

Allied radio intelligence intercepted the message in which Combined Fleet activated its "S" operation. Though Allied spooks had no direct knowledge of Sho that day, within twenty-four hours, ONI used that name and added that it represented Japan's overall defense plan for the Philippines.

Japanese radio traffic volume continued to be extraordinarily high into October 18. Mikawa exchanged many messages with Fukudome on the Manila-Takao circuit. Other traffic concerned tanker assignments and showed movement not just in Singapore, but in Empire waters also. Oilers that had left for distant ports were suddenly recalled. Submarine frequencies buzzed. Intercepted messages to surface escort units, which the Ultra summary noted on October 18, indicated "that a sortie from Singapore . . . has taken place or will take place shortly." Kurita had actually sailed just after midnight. That day every circuit lit red.

One bit of the Ultra that must have startled Allied officers who learned of it was that the Japanese, *"based on an analysis of U.S. communications,"* had deduced that Allied attacks in Leyte Gulf aimed at seizing an airfield, not necessarily "a major scale occupation of the Philippines." But the Japanese orders for air attacks also tipped their hand on what the target priorities were to be. The Ultra summary reported the Imperial Navy's targets as transports, destroyers, landing craft, cruisers, and battleships, in that order.

Gears had begun to move that would culminate in the greatest sea fight in history.

AT THE SAME time, Bull Halsey and the Third Fleet headed toward the Leyte invasion zone. The end of the Taiwan air battle left Task Force 38 off the Philippine coast, northeast of Luzon, so the Big Blue Fleet had little distance to cover. Ever aggressive, always pushing his advantage, Admiral Halsey took the opportunity to crush the Japanese air arm while he steamed ahead to support the Leyte operation. In the initial planning for the King II operation, Halsey's fleet had been expected to make its way down to the Leyte area by the time of the landing.

But Admiral Halsey's laserlike focus on the Imperial Navy's surface fleet led him to hold his Third Fleet in readiness east and north of the archipelago. His plan was to have Mitscher's carrier groups take turns touching port and refueling at Ulithi, while he kept the bulk of the fleet at sea, clobbering the Japanese. From now familiar waters, Task Force 38 attacked the airfields around Manila on October 15. Planes from Japanese Army Air Force (JAAF) groups rose to intercept or escort counterattacks on Halsey's fleet. Admiral Teraoka ordered dispersal of transports and medium bombers, while scrambling to assemble a JNAF interceptor unit to defend Manila. JAAF became convinced it had accounted for more than forty American warplanes. *Enterprise* Hellcat pilots alone claimed a dozen kills over the city plus twice that many defending the fleet. The claims were wild on both sides.

After Japanese Navy scouts found the fast carriers, the First Air Fleet assembled a half dozen bomb-laden Zeros under Lieutenant Sashijiku, with an escort of nineteen fighters. In a bid to strike by surprise, they took off at 9:15 a.m., and an hour and a half later, they struck an American task group. Pilots claimed to have hit a cruiser and scored a near miss against a carrier, along with shooting down some planes. Just one fighter-bomber survived from the Sashijiku unit.

Several flights also launched from Taiwan and the Ryukyus. One left with ten Bettys and nine fighters. Only three returned. Losses included the chief of a JNAF fighter group. In another unit, thirteen of sixteen escorting Zeros *all* suffered engine trouble and aborted the mission—a testament to JNAF's increasingly poor maintenance. Task Force 38 recorded no damage.

The main JNAF strike went out at midafternoon, after a fresh sighting of Halsey's fleet. At Manila, Admiral Teraoka, calling on General Tominaga at his 4th Air Army headquarters, obtained the help of more than seventy Army fighter planes from Lieutenant Colonel Shindo Tsuneo. With ten more Zeros, Shindo escorted another half dozen Zero fighter-bombers, a dozen Jill bombers, and several twin-engine Betty torpedo planes. Two-thirds of the Jills and all of the Bettys perished.

Rear Admiral Arima Masafumi, who headed the 26th Air Flotilla, sat in one of those cockpits as the Navy's mission leader. Tired of sending crews out to no effect, Arima had advocated crash-diving tactics for months to no avail. The NGS, Combined Fleet, and First Air Fleet had all opposed the idea. With desperation born of despair, Admiral Arima, in full uniform, ripped off his rank insignia before launching. He had decided not to come back. As luck would have it, Arima's target that afternoon would be Joe Shoemaker's carrier *Franklin*, which had been through its fair share of trials during the recent Taiwan battle. The fast carrier indeed sustained a hit—the bomb broke through a corner of the deck-edge elevator and burst just beneath the flight deck, inflicting fragment damage and igniting a gasoline fire. But Captain Shoemaker's damage-control parties were highly efficient, and the following morning, the *Franklin* was back in business, launching aircraft as usual.

Aboard the *Essex*, Seaman John Yeager felt that the Japanese were really out for blood this time around. The ship had to dodge several torpedoes and one plane that crash-dived the stern and missed by only a few feet. In addition, sailors were wounded when JNAF warbirds strafed the carrier.

A Japanese Army scout plane monitoring the engagement radioed that a fast carrier had instantly blown up. That night General Yamashita Tomoyuki, leading Army forces in the Philippines, sent some sake to Teraoka to celebrate the victory. American records note no ships sunk and no damage other than that to the *Franklin*. Radio Tokyo announced Arima's demise on October 20. Counted a hero, in death he would be elevated to the rank of vice admiral. In Tokyo Captain Genda Minoru of the NGS awaited final approval of orders approving creation of the "special attack" (kamikaze) force of which Arima dreamed.

Despite the celebrations in Tokyo, every day there were fresh strikes at the Japanese. And every day they exacted a heavy toll. Admiral Mikawa tabulated the First Air Fleet's entire strength on October 18 as amounting to fewer than three dozen warplanes, nearly a third of which were Jill bombers just arrived from Taiwan. General Tominaga's 4th Air Army was only a little better off and had about seventy aircraft. Bomber types were scarce. Here can be seen the real impact of the Japanese rush to air battle. With the surface fleet in motion, the Japanese needed their umbrella, or at least the challenge their air force could have posed. But the depleted air arm left the Imperial Navy's surface fleet naked before the enemy.

Naval air commander Teraoka felt the terrible weight of the situation. Though he'd been at the front for just a couple of months, the experience had been so charged, and the Allied attacks so fierce, the admiral was spent. He had lost the equivalent of two air fleets to Bull Halsey, one in September and now again. With no viable solution to American superiority, his time expired.

Admiral Teraoka would be given leave and reemployed. His replacement, already en route, was Vice Admiral Onishi Takijiro. Onishi had left Tokyo on October 9, stayed at home for a night, then headed for Kanoya and the flight south. But when Halsey struck Okinawa, that itinerary became impossible. Onishi reached Taiwan on October 11 by diverting through Shanghai, but of course, Halsey followed, striking the big island the next morning. The Japanese officer awoke to the U.S. assault, and he joined Toyoda, who was also stranded on Taiwan, as they both were forced to seek safety in cellars. It was not until Halsey turned his attention back to the Philippines that Onishi was able to resume his travel. It proved to be just in time for MacArthur's return. Onishi reached Manila on the afternoon of October 17. He burned with the determination to fight.

Rear Admiral Davison's task group refueled while the *Franklin* fought off the enemy. Fliers with *Intrepid*'s Air Group 18 got only a few hours' rest. Intramural basketball went ahead in the forward elevator well, a Ping-Pong tournament in the junior officers' wardroom. Later, as the task group began a high-speed run toward Luzon, the air intelligence officer called a briefing, apprising aircrews of expected battle conditions. Once he finished, airmen began a spontaneous jazz improv. Off of Leyte the invasion had begun.

LEYTE LANDINGS

Around 8:00 a.m. on October 17, the American light cruiser *Denver* fired the first shots of the Philippine campaign.

Captain Albert M. Bledsoe of the *Denver* would win the Navy Cross for his actions over the next week, and he began at the entrance to Leyte Gulf—6,500 yards off the islet of Suluan. In company with sister ship *Columbia* and four destroyers, Bledsoe's warship would shoot in support of an important preliminary to the Leyte invasion. Eight destroyer transports steamed in column behind, preceded by several minesweepers. They were the Dinagat Attack Group, carrying Lieutenant Colonel Henry A. Mucci's 6th Ranger Battalion, and reinforced by a company of the 21st Infantry Regiment. The force was to seize Dinagat Island, on the eastern side of Surigao Strait, and the islets of Suluan and Homonhon, which lay astride the entrance to Leyte Gulf, locations of a lighthouse, and a Japanese radar station.

The ground troops, who were the first to report the invasion and effectively triggered the Combined Fleet's alert order, were located on Suluan Island. They resisted briefly, most notably catching the Rangers in an ambush. Private Darwin C. Zufall, killed, and Private Donald J. Cannon, wounded, became the first American casualties of the Philippine campaign. Afterward, the Japanese fled into the jungle.

On Dinagat, Rangers found a unit of Filipino partisans led by an Army Air Force captain named Hemingway already controlling the place. Colonel Ruperto Kangeleon headed a Leyte area command of several thousand partisan fighters, mostly on Leyte itself but also throughout the sector. The partisans on Dinagat did away with the Japanese pickets who had held an outpost there. They'd even captured papers, including hydrographic charts, which they gave to the Rangers, who passed them on to the U.S. Navy. The Filipinos sailed the waters often and assured Americans there were no minefields, but the Allies ignored their advice, taking three days to troll for Japanese mines.

Arthur McCollum's Seventh Fleet Intelligence Center also had reported a minimal enemy setup. The SEFIC experts believed there were no minefields, while the ground intelligence thought Dinagat was defended by about 500 Japanese troops of the 30th Division. (Minesweepers verified a lack of explosive devices *inside* the gulf but destroyed some 227 mines seeding the approaches to Leyte waters.) Once the Rangers had cleared the islets, the invasion fleet began entering the gulf. Ahead of them lay Leyte's beaches.

There was some confusion about Allied intentions. The oceanic storm had muddled Japanese communications. Tokyo's troops on Leyte scrambled to clear away the storm damage. General Tominaga, the Army air boss, decided by the evening of October 17 that the goings-on signaled the invasion and ordered a full strike by his warplanes. But the next morning, bad weather grounded the 4th Air Army.

That afternoon the battleship *Pennsylvania*—one of the recovered victims of Pearl Harbor, back to exact her revenge—opened fire on landing beaches. Two cruisers and several tin cans joined in, and frog-men swam in to do beach reconnaissance. The frogmen, grouped into recently perfected Underwater Demolition Teams (UDTs), would scout the beaches for obstacles or land mines. Although some of the UDTs complained later of the inadequacy of fire support, nevertheless the reconnaissance discovered firm beach and Japanese obstacles were nonexistent.

Mounting air strikes proved harder than the Japanese had supposed. Limited flight envelopes of JAAF flying machines required them to reposition to airfields in the Visayas before they could hit Leyte Gulf. Lieutenant General Terada Seichi's 2nd Air Division, which was sup-posed to take the lead, found his path blocked, first by the storm, then by muddy airfields, and finally by suppressive actions from Rear Admi-ral Thomas L. Sprague's Seventh Fleet. The "Little Giants" spent the days before the invasion countering the Japanese air network. Airstrips on Leyte were deserted. The JAAF concentrated at Bacolod on Negros Island. In the end they had hardly done so when American troops set foot on land.

The initial Japanese air attack into Leyte Gulf—the preordained target of the Sho plan—was comprised of several JNAF Zeros on the evening of October 19. They were but a pinprick. The First Air Fleet had a handful of warplanes with Onishi, its new commander, scheduled to take over the following day. The high command had not yet ordered Fukudome's air fleet to move forward. Japanese Army troops were thin on the ground too. Only one large unit held Leyte—Lieutenant General Makino Shiro's 16th Infantry Division—and only a fraction of its force occupied the sector where the Americans landed. If there were to be a decisive battle for Leyte, the Japanese would have to feed reinforcements in by sea. It could be Guadalcanal all over again.

General MacArthur took no chances. He entrusted the invasion to his 6th Army under Lieutenant General Walter Krueger. The latter had a corps of his own plus the XXIV Corps that Admiral Halsey had given MacArthur. Those two corps possessed seven divisions between them and Krueger planned to land four on the first day. There would be two full divisions in reserve afloat, and the last one, still en route, would be a reinforcement. Allied ground forces enjoyed a marked superiority.

The fleet began entering the gulf an hour before midnight on October 19. The bulky transports slowly made their way to anchorage areas off two coastal towns—Tacloban in the north and Dulag in the south. The next morning, A-Day, when the landings would be made, dawned clear and crisp. The core gunnery ships of Seventh Fleet—destroyers, cruisers, and half a dozen battleships—began a preparatory barrage. One hundred forty aircraft from Rear Admiral Sprague's escort carrier force threw their weight into the scales. At 9:45 a.m., shortly before landing craft were scheduled to hit the beach, gunners redirected their fire to the flanks and rear of the positions.

The experience of destroyer *Bennion* on the gun line was typical of the naval support effort. The ship's first casualties were her assistant gunnery officer and the controller of the Mark-37 director that aimed the ship's main battery. Both died when a Japanese gun scored a direct hit on the Mark-37. Next to *Bennion* was the destroyer *Ross*. She hit a mine while providing support fire and subsequently hit another, becoming the only American destroyer in the war to survive successive mine detonations.

The *Bennion* was of the classic *Fletcher* class and an example of America's productive strength—U.S. shipyards produced seventy-seven destroyers of this single type during 1943 alone, 50 percent more destroyers than Japan commissioned during the entire war. *Bennion* convoyed transports across the Pacific, then joined Kinkaid's fleet. She helped defend Leyte Gulf against the Japanese air raids. Even with the troops ashore there were rich targets in the gulf, for MacArthur rotated Liberty ships through the Tacloban anchorage. At any given time, thirty or more merchantmen were unloading ammunition, weapons, food, and the other appurtenances of modern warfare. While this was not the target-rich environment the Japanese imagined, one that could stymie the Allied cross-Pacific offensive, it was a substantial objective. Still, *Bennion* and plenty more like her stood between the Japanese and their goal.

Officers in *Bennion*'s Combat Information Center (CIC) commented that there were rarely fewer than fifteen or twenty bogeys on the radars. They believed the Japanese weren't very serious. Raids of as many as fifty or sixty aircraft often seemed to turn away just a few minutes from the gulf. But at other times, the enemy was determined. Despite help from Tom Sprague's "Little Giants," Japanese fighter sweeps crossed the gulf repeatedly. Recognizing the continuing aerial opposition, the Navy relaxed its regulations on ammunition transfer, permitting unloading even during alerts. Even so, not much seemed to be getting ashore. *Bennion* officers observed Japanese planes almost always overhead. On October 24, there were between 150 and 200 attackers, mostly twin-engine bombers of General Terada's JAAF 2nd Air Division.

This moment held multiple meanings for Douglas MacArthur. He could see the sandy beaches, the waves breaking upon this hostile coast. They were clear even aboard flagship *Nashville* two miles away. The general stood on the bridge with the cruiser's skipper, Captain C. E. Coney. They were off "Red Beach"—Tacloban town—where as a lieutenant fresh from West Point the young Douglas MacArthur had come on his first duty assignment, to survey for new docks. Now Tacloban, which was the location of an airfield MacArthur was anxious to convert to Allied use, would be the place where he returned. More than that, he would reinstate the Philippine government that had gone into exile. The invasion would be a war event, political development, and personal achievement all rolled into one. One may forgive General MacArthur his histrionic exclamation, "I have returned!" when stepping ashore, and his breathless follow-up, addressed to all Filipinos: "The hour of your redemption is here."

What is more striking, however, is what happened afterward. It shows the general in his political colors, calculating every gesture, measuring every advantage or slight. MacArthur steered the Filipino leader, President Sergio Osmeña, off the beach and into some brush, where they were conversing when it began raining. Japanese planes bombed the beach for the first time. General MacArthur noticed the rain had stopped, so he and Osmeña inspected the now captured Tacloban airfield. Then and there, MacArthur wrote a letter to Franklin Delano Roosevelt. The general explained that he wrote "from the beach near Tacloban where we have just landed." He fancied this a historic missive: "It will be the first letter from the freed Philippines." MacArthur told Roosevelt, "I thought you might like it for your philatelic collection."

Imagine—a frontline general at a key moment in combat, having just invaded enemy territory, takes time out to sit down and write a letter amid the noise. Apart from a trivial reference to FDR's stamp collection, the general goes on to advocate that the president take this opportunity to make a dramatic declaration granting independence to the Philippines ahead of the already scheduled 1946 date. More than that, General MacArthur suggests that President Roosevelt should come to the Philippines and personally make the grant himself. In a fast cruiser, MacArthur says, FDR could be out and back in less than a month. The political suggestion seems like an excuse, a presumptive reason for the note.

MacArthur's letter is really an invocation of Roosevelt's decision at the Pearl Harbor conference—the confidence the president placed in the general's judgment. Only such a purpose could justify MacArthur loosening his grip on the battle to scribble private thoughts on the government's dime. The bit about the fast cruiser, by the way, does not appear in this letter as MacArthur published it in his 1964 memoirs. But it is in the original.

MacArthur also dropped other key language. Referring to Japanese political ventures, specifically their so-called Co-Prosperity Sphere, the printed version of this letter states that U.S. arrival in the Philippines "severs the Japanese completely from their infamous propaganda slogan." Awkward. In his authentic text MacArthur declares, the Allied invasion "severs completely the Japanese from their great spoils in the South Seas and completely explodes their infamous propaganda slogan."

By 1964 the war had ended and it was apparent the Philippine invasion had not fully isolated Japan. The general could not bear that his own words might show him either manipulating the president or making a questionable claim for military achievement. MacArthur passed away that April, and in the sadness no one noticed the odd text of his letter to FDR. Meanwhile, what President Roosevelt might finally think of his decision at Pearl Harbor depended on how the battle turned. The Japanese had much to do with that.

AS LUCK WOULD have it, Japan's troops on Leyte were in confusion at the time of the invasion.

First came the storm. The 16th Infantry Division, the Japanese garrison, was alert and ready for battle on October 17 as Imperial General Headquarters instructed. Lieutenant General Makino Shiro, division commander, watched as the storm tore up beach defenses and caused havoc in the Gulf. When Allied ships appeared the next day, Makino was not certain they were simply weathering the storm. He sent the 14th Area Army, the top Philippines command, ambiguous reports. Once Makino became convinced the invasion was happening, he realized his headquarters at Tacloban town lay in an exposed position. General Makino moved it to a village inland. The move occurred while the Allied fleet entered Leyte Gulf, and not only did it mean the Japanese tactical commander was out of place at a key moment, but it also put the 16th Division out of contact with higher authority for forty-eight hours at a crucial instant—not just for the Battle of Leyte but for the entire Sho operation. The defenders never quite regained their balance.

After that, everything else went haywire too, starting with Japan's strategy. The Army's original plan for Sho 1 ordained that Luzon was to be the centerpiece. When IGHQ activated its plan, the Army staff responded in a yawning manner—telling the Navy it had no troops ready to reinforce that sector and advising that the naval sortie be canceled. Later on, the Army ordered that island be made the focal point. But since the order went by radio, and since Makino was out of touch with the 14th Area Army during headquarters movement, for

that important moment, the frontline leader had no idea he had suddenly become the tip of the Japanese spear.

The Army high command's decision to fight on Leyte also unbalanced
the entire Japanese ground force in the archipelago. When IGHQ committed to enacting the Sho plans, a steady reinforcement had taken place,
with Luzon holding more than half the Japanese troops in the islands
(five divisions and a brigade, close to 100,000 Army troops plus another
13,500 Imperial Navy sailors). Not long before MacArthur's invasion,
General Yamashita Tomoyuki, the victor of Malaya and the Army's most
renowned field commander, arrived to take charge of the 14th Area
Army. Under Yamashita, the ground commander for the southern Philippines, Lieutenant General Suzuki Sosaku, had about 78,000 men scattered over many islands, with about half his force on Mindanao.

Little of Tokyo's strength in the Philippines had been concentrated
on Leyte. To conduct the main ground battle there required that everything beyond Makino's 16th Division be brought in from outside. A
strait about fifteen miles wide separated Leyte and Mindanao, though
the separation between suitable coastal towns on each made the real
distance something close to ninety miles. Suzuki also had troops at
Cebu in the Visayas. There the water crossing would be about thirty
miles. The necessity for water movement, and the potential that Allied
naval forces could isolate Leyte, complicated fighting there. To add
even more complications, Tokyo held only one division and one brigade
outside the Philippines as a strategic reserve. Structurally this situation
bore ominous similarities to the Guadalcanal campaign, where the
Japanese also had to reinforce the main fighting from across a water-
way. The Army's decision to fight the main battle on Leyte was on a
par with the Imperial Navy's leap to a premature air battle off Taiwan.

As far as the landing at Leyte is concerned, Makino had assessed
the terrain well. His soldiers had some months to prepare defenses. On
Leyte, there were half a dozen airfields. Four of them lay near the
middle coast and the town of Dulag. General Makino put his largest force
there, two of the three regiments in his division. The remaining infantry defended the Tacloban sector, where another airfield beckoned. The
other Leyte airstrip, situated near Ormoc on the opposite side, protected the port serving as Japanese supply base.

Nothing was particularly wrong with these dispositions. It was simply that Douglas MacArthur put four full divisions ashore on the first day, overwhelming the Japanese defenders where encountered, and pressing inland where no enemy forces were located. By nightfall, at a cost of fewer than 250 casualties, the 6th Army was solidly ashore, had captured key terrain, and had landed 107,000 tons of supplies. Only at Dulag, where the U.S. 7th Infantry Division was able to capture just part of the airfield, were the Allies seriously held back.

The Japanese response to this action built slowly. General Yamashita ordered Suzuki's 35th Army to conduct an offensive. But Makino's division, already battered, had very limited capabilities, and a series of small counterattacks near Palo village failed to dislodge the U.S. 24th Infantry Division. In the predawn hours of October 24, Colonel Suzuki Tatsunosuke (no relation to the general) had the colors of his 33rd Regiment burned and took his last seventy-five men on one more desperate charge against the Palo River bridge. Their failure left the Americans free to break into Leyte's interior.

Since General Suzuki had first to collect small boats to move nearby forces, and to arrange shipping to transport the strategic reserves, help arrived late. Four Japanese Army battalions reached the island by October 25, but by then Allied forces were well established. On October 23, at a ceremony in Tacloban, General MacArthur ostentatiously approved President Sergio Osmeña's reinstating of the Philippine government. The next day General Walter Krueger's 6th Army headquarters established itself at the village of San Jose. Allied engineers were already working on refurbishing the Leyte airfields.

A HAWK ON THE YARDARM

Japanese commanders refused to be distracted from the fighting on the Leyte front, as became evident the very first day of the invasion preliminaries.

The British suddenly struck with their Eastern Fleet almost 2,000 miles to the west. Coming from the Indian Ocean, a Royal Navy task force carried out an attack on the Nicobar Islands, up the Malacca

Strait from Singapore. The British, under Vice Admiral Sir Arthur Power, the deputy C-in-C, behaved as if they, too, were about to make an invasion. The aircraft carriers *Victorious* and *Indomitable* participated, and there were not one but two surface bombardments, from a fleet that included battleship *Renown*, four cruisers, and a dozen destroyers, two of them Australian and one Dutch.

Operation "Millet" went on for three days, so the Japanese had plenty of time to react. The Japanese had no idea the move was a diversion, and the Kurita fleet, closer to the British than they were to the Philippines, could have responded. Instead, they did nothing.

The first sighting reports arrived shortly before 10:00 a.m. on October 17 and were soon amplified. But the Combined Fleet's standby order for Sho had reached Lingga an hour and a half earlier, and its instruction to proceed to Brunei occurred only minutes before the sighting report. Admiral Kurita Takeo did not ask Combined Fleet if he should do anything differently, and when fresh reports arrived of the British bombarding Nicobar again, the Japanese were already at sea, heading for their rendezvous with destiny.

THE KURITA FLEET remained the key. When the initial alert message arrived from Combined Fleet, the admiral instructed his ships to raise steam. Vessels were to power up sufficiently for a cruising speed of twenty knots while maintaining twenty minutes' notice for twenty-four. That meant battle speed—an early indication that Admiral Kurita expected nothing less. Kurita had time to get cruisers *Aoba* and *Noshiro* ready to join the sortie. Floatplanes from Cruiser Division 5 scouted waters off Lingga. He also recalled a pair of destroyers that had been sent to Manila. A nighttime departure was preferable, frustrating any Allied submarines that might be lurking offshore. Japanese intelligence estimated that half a dozen Allied submarines were located in Philippine waters. In reality there were seventeen, a dozen of them based in MacArthur's zone, the rest sent from Pearl Harbor.

The distances involved in this operation—1,750 nautical miles— were daunting, especially for a Navy whose fuel and oiler situations were critical. If Kurita had sallied as early as the sixteenth—when Allied intentions remained unclear—he could not have reached the battle area until at least October 20, not taking into account the need to refuel, plus any zigzagging or other evasive maneuvers that slow progress. The Second Fleet did not actually depart Lingga until 1:00 a.m. on October 18, which made the Japanese arrival date October 21 or later, and as a result, Admiral Toyoda had trouble selecting X-Day, the moment for Japanese battle action.

A destroyer unit, the "Red Force," exited first and conducted an antisubmarine sweep as more ships steamed from the roads. Following them were the battleships *Kongo* and *Haruna*, cruisers, and other warships. Japanese preparations had been so thorough that officers had even rehearsed a fleet sortie by means of tabletop war games, for example, aboard heavy cruiser *Tone*. The behemoths of Ugaki Matome's battleship division brought up the rear, clearing their anchorage a full hour behind the lead vessels. Admiral Kurita set an east-southeast course to transit the Tempa Channel, came about to almost due north to pass along the west coast of Borneo, then traveled east-northeast following that coast. The Kurita fleet passed between Borneo and Natuna Besar, assuming a formation for defense against subs at 6:50 a.m. Delays passing navigational reference points indicate that the force had already fallen more than an hour behind schedule.

The day dawned sunny but quickly turned cloudy. With the fleet under way, Admiral Kurita permitted captains to tell crews that, this time, he intended no exercise. This would be Sho. There were both good and bad portents to this announcement. On the *Yamato*, almost immediately after the public address system fell silent, a hawk perched on the main battery range finder. Crewmen felt the bird was a symbol of victory. On the other hand, that day brought a submarine scare when the *Noshiro* saw a periscope at midafternoon. Antisubmarine experts evaluated the contact as real, but it was not so. The U.S. submarine *Gurnard* actually held position between Malaya and Borneo at that time. She even had a mission of heading for Brunei to lay mines, but she had stopped to attack a convoy and the Kurita fleet skirted past her.

At 11:10 a.m., a Combined Fleet dispatch, among Kusaka's last before Admiral Toyoda's return, informed Japanese commanders of the overall plan. The message observed a strong possibility of an Allied landing in the Tacloban area. The Kurita fleet "WILL ADVANCE THROUGH SAN BERNARDINO STRAIT AND ANNIHILATE THE ENEMY INVASION FORCE." That penetration of the "ENEMY LANDING POINT" would happen on X-Day. In support of this maneuver, the Mobile Fleet "WILL LURE THE ENEMY TO THE NORTH AND DESTROY REMNANTS OF HIS FORCES IF THE OPPORTUNITY ARISES." This was Ozawa and he would act on X-1. Vice Admiral Shima's 2nd Diversion Attack Force, along with Cruiser Division 16 of the Kurita fleet, would be attached to Mikawa's Southwest Area Fleet "AS THE BACKBONE OF MOBILE OVER-WATER COUNTER-ATTACK OPERATIONS" (in essence, the Tokyo Express). Land-based air forces "WILL COMPLETELY WIPE OUT THE ENEMY CARRIERS." The submarine fleet "WILL DESTROY DAMAGED ENEMY VESSELS AND TROOP CONVOYS."

Combined Fleet's operational plan specified that X-Day would be fixed by special order but, recognizing Kurita's fuel problem, tentatively set it to be October 24. That timing meant that many Allied transports and supply ships at Leyte would have unloaded and left. With the Kurita fleet barely at sea, the Sho plan had already been overtaken by current events. Other factors were also in play. The high command assigned some of Kurita's ships to Admiral Mikawa for a Tokyo Express. Naturally they were physically located with Kurita. Mikawa ordered them to Brunei, the same as the Kurita fleet, to await orders. General Yamashita had no troops ready to be carried on a Tokyo Express. Mikawa turned around and argued to Toyoda that units assigned to him—Shima's 2nd Diversion Attack Force and Cruiser Division 16—should be used instead in the main raiding operation.

During the predawn hours, with Kurita's fleet more than 400 miles from Brunei and a convoy of tankers following about seventy miles behind, the horizon to the north and east showed an odd luminescence. Another portent.

The portents for October 19, however, were not so good. During the forenoon the destroyers *Akishimo* and *Hayashimo*, the two warships recalled from Manila, sighted a surfaced submarine and gave chase. They evaded its torpedoes but the boat got away. That was the submarine *Darter*, which would very shortly inflict grievous harm on Kurita Takeo and his sailors. The encounter had been a fateful one.

For the moment, though, all remained well. From early afternoon onward, the Kurita fleet enjoyed antisubmarine warfare (ASW) protection from land-based aircraft, though its battleships kept floatplanes on the catapult ready to reinforce them. After midnight, the task force altered toward its final course for Brunei and changed its zigzag pattern. Kurita's destination was now only 165 miles away. By morning, the fleet neared its goal. Reefs and shallows lay as far as 40 miles offshore, so Admiral Kurita hastened to instruct ships to proceed independently to their planned anchorages, which he did at 9:18 a.m. on the twentieth. Most ships reached their berths at noon or soon afterward.

At this critical time, Allied scouts detected the Imperial Navy task force. This had to do with Arthur McCollum of Seventh Fleet intelligence, who worried about a Japanese sortie from Singapore and had asked for a special watch on Brunei. That morning a B-24 search plane saw what it identified as a battleship, three light cruisers, three destroyers, and half a dozen other warships off the north coast of Borneo. This important sighting seems to have been lost in the confusion. Though Pearl Harbor radio repeated the Seventh Fleet message, and someone denigrated it with an "open to doubt" notation, the sighting was real. The Japanese picked up the plane's signal. Admiral Ugaki noted that radio operators on *Yamato* overheard a nearby transmission that took the form of a sighting report. Destroyer Flotilla 10 recorded no less than *nine* sighting-type messages from before noon until late in the day. Most likely on the basis of the aerial sighting, at 11:29 p.m. on October 20 the Owada Group warned of a high probability the Kurita fleet had been discovered. After the war, Captain Arthur McCollum would reflect that the whole Japanese fleet had passed under the Allied search umbrella without anyone noticing anything. He would be wrong.

Though the ball was dropped on the sighting, the Allies never yielded advantage to Japan because Ultra continually updated Allied commanders. The radio intelligence summary for October 19—with Kurita on his way to Brunei and the invaders at Leyte poised to land—accurately related the composition of the Kurita fleet and observed that it had already or would soon sortie from the Singapore area. The code breakers were wrong only in continuing to place Nishimura's battleships and Shima's 2nd Diversion Attack Force with the Ozawa fleet.

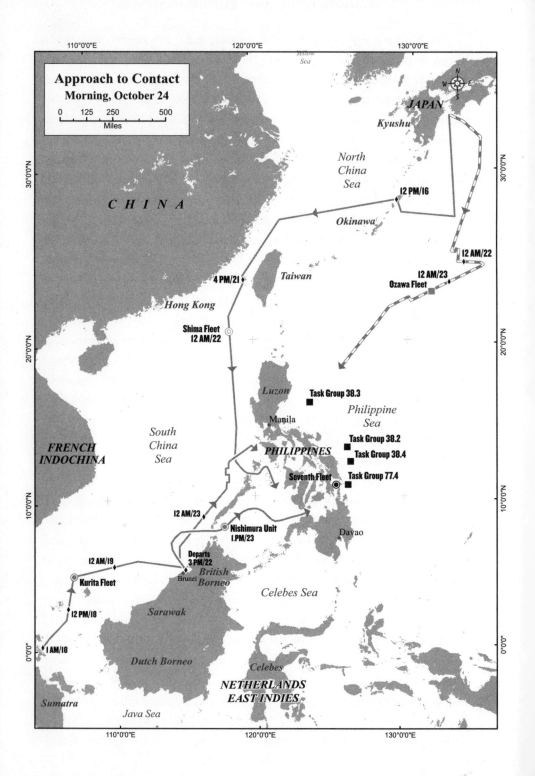

Approach to Contact
Morning, October 24

0   125   250   500
Miles

Yellow
Sea

JAPAN

Kyushu

North
China
Sea

12 PM/16

Okinawa

12 AM/22

12 AM/23
Ozawa Fleet

CHINA

4 PM/21

Taiwan

Hong Kong

Shima Fleet
12 AM/22

Luzon

Task Group 38.3

Philippine
Sea

Manila

South
China
Sea

PHILIPPINES

Task Group 38.2
Task Group 38.4

FRENCH
INDOCHINA

Seventh Fleet

Task Group 77.4

12 AM/23

Nishimura Unit
1 PM/23

Davao

12 AM/19

12 PM/18

Departs
3 PM/22

British
Borneo

Kurita Fleet

Brunei

Celebes Sea

1 AM/18

Sarawak

Dutch Borneo

Celebes

NETHERLANDS
EAST INDIES

Sumatra

Java Sea

The bigger development at Brunei would be an improvised move that eventually determined the way Sho 1 finally unfolded. Vice Admiral Shima Kiyohide's Fifth Fleet—the 2nd Diversion Attack Force—had been kicked around among the NGS, the Combined Fleet, and the Southwest Area Fleet. Shima had sailed to run down Halsey's supposed remnants. Combined Fleet considered simply assigning Shima to Kurita, but then attached him to Admiral Mikawa as the main force for the Tokyo Express. But Mikawa discovered that the Japanese Army had as yet no troops ready to "express" into Leyte. On the afternoon of the twentieth, he cabled Shima asking that the Fifth Fleet, or at least someone of Shima's staff, come to Manila and consult General Yamashita before making any further decisions. A stop risked losing the opportunity to strike, Shima replied. He held out for an assignment to follow Kurita into Leyte Gulf.

Late on invasion day Admiral Mikawa sent a further dispatch observing that a smaller unit—Kurita had given up Cruiser Division 16—would be sufficient for the Tokyo Express–type missions. Kurita, who had earlier opposed the assignment of Division 16 to the area fleet, also registered unhappiness at being given Shima's command because it had never exercised or operated with his Second Fleet. Meanwhile, Admiral Mikawa freely yielded control of the Shima fleet so it could participate in this supporting maneuver.

Anthony Tully writes that Kurita "was vaguely aware" that the Fifth Fleet might join him in the raid because he "probably intercepted some of the traffic between Manila, Tokyo, and [Admiral Shima]." In fact, Admiral Kurita had remained completely informed—the detailed action record for Cruiser Division 16 shows the Second Fleet as an addressee for all messages concerning employment of the Shima fleet save the ones where Mikawa and the Army hammered out whether troops were ready to go to Leyte.

Then came an intervention from on high. Admiral Kusaka weighed in with a suggestion that Kurita detach a unit to infiltrate Leyte Gulf from a different direction, through Surigao Strait. This would mean a double penetration of the Gulf. That made Kurita Takeo think carefully about Rear Admiral Nishimura's old battleships *Fuso* and *Yamashiro*. Slower and less heavily armed, Nishimura's unit had been an awkward attachment from the beginning. Admiral Kurita liked the double-penetration idea much better. After preparing to receive his captains and unit commanders aboard flagship *Atago*, Kurita Takeo resolved to go ahead with that option and use Nishimura's battleships as the core of that force, adding heavy cruiser *Mogami* and a screen of four destroyers.

The written directive handed to Rear Admiral Nishimura on the evening of October 21 instructed him to cross the Sulu Sea, enter Leyte Gulf via the Surigao Strait, and attack invasion shipping there in the predawn hours of October 25.

IN TOKYO, AT the eleventh hour, the Japanese Army suddenly got cold feet. At an IGHQ conference, Navy chief of staff Oikawa informed the Army of the fleet's preparations for the Leyte raid. General Umezu of the Army responded that the Navy should cancel the operation and protect its forces. The Army recognized there was little chance of success. The most likely outcome would be destruction of the fleet.

Army staffers were particularly incensed at the Navy's sudden demand for four additional tankers and their fuel. The Army saw this as a breach of a previously agreed-upon schedule for oil supplies to the Empire, and a threat to the war effort. To give up the oil for a decisive battle in which the Army knew practically nothing about Combined Fleet's operational movements was unacceptable.

The dispute led to a nighttime skull session at which planners from both services met at the Navy Club in Tokyo, ranging over the same ground. The NGS was represented by its top operations people: Rear Admiral Nakazawa Tasukichi, the bureau chief, and Captain Yamamoto Chikao, the section chief. Colonels Sanada Sadamu and Hattori Takushiro carried the ball for the Army staff. The services each repeated their arguments. Sanada added that the Navy's lack of carrier air groups would force the Army to divert planes from attacks on Leyte.

"If the fleet does not take the offensive now," Captain Yamamoto fired back hotly, "the war will be lost!"

The Navy insisted that if it did not act, the fleet would suffer the same fate (total destruction) that had befallen Mussolini's Italian Navy.

Sanada objected, "Stop talking nonsense!"

The next morning, Colonel Hattori went to Army chief of staff Umezu to report their failure to reconcile with the Navy planners. Umezu thought for a moment, but he conceded the issue: "If Combined Fleet were to suffer defeat the consequences would indeed be serious. However, since this matter is up to the Navy, and since Navy Minister Yonai has already approved it, there is no ground for the Army to put up any further opposition."

The entire episode is a measure of the dysfunctional nature of the Japanese high command. The Army had secured a Sho plan in which the Imperial Navy put aside its traditional goal of destroying enemy fleets to serve an Army purpose of reducing Allied invasion capabilities. Then the Army upended the strategic plan of centering its own defense on well-prepared Luzon, for a scantily held Leyte. Now the Army wanted out altogether.

But the Navy was in motion and was not going to stop. The die had been cast.

AT BRUNEI BAY, the Kurita fleet rode calmly at anchor. The admiral knew nothing of the squabbles among the high command. He knew only that his Second Fleet would have the main part in the elaborate scheme that the Imperial Navy had concocted to get at the Allied shipping. The central role of Kurita's fleet loomed large, and it was underlined when a Combined Fleet dispatch announced that Admiral Toyoda would assume direct control.

At midmorning of the twenty-first Kurita summoned unit commanders, senior staff, and ship captains to convene aboard his flagship at five o'clock. Tankers arrived after eleven, and at half past noon, they began refueling the battleships. A full loading might require nearly a whole day, but to comply with Toyoda's X-Day dictate, Kurita must leave Brunei by 8:00 a.m. on the twenty-second.

Timing also bore on the choice of a route to the target. There were several possibilities, and of course, all of them had drawbacks. No matter what route Admiral Kurita selected, he would have to make a daylight crossing of waters that were dominated by American carriers. Combined Fleet had decreed the Kurita fleet must debouch from the San Bernardino

Strait, so all his alternatives led there. The island of Palawan defined the possibilities, for the fleet could advance to either side.

The shortest route lay to its south, with Kurita hugging Palawan's east coast until passing Mindoro to enter the Sibuyan Sea. Kurita's shorter-legged ships might possibly make this voyage without refueling. On the other hand, the admiral believed his fleet had been seen off Brunei and that Allied airmen would be extra-vigilant here. Crossing on the south side of Palawan would place Kurita in the Sulu Sea at the same time as the diversion force under Nishimura. The danger was that both fleets could be spotted simultaneously and attacked together. A second route kept to the north of Palawan, then skirted Mindoro to enter the Sibuyan Sea. One more possibility—let us call it the "indirect approach" (also the longest)—took the north side but angled back northwest and sliced ahead to Mindoro, the Sibuyan Sea, and finally the San Bernardino Strait. This track kept Kurita away from Allied air scouts longer, but it took his sailors through dangerous shoal waters, consumed the most time, and required a final approach to battle under daylight air attack. The northside standard track gave Halsey's and Kinkaid's airmen their shot, but in the afternoon, when darkness would eventually end the agony.

Fuel also presented its persistent problem. Tankers had to be positioned to fuel ships returning from the mission. Combined Fleet ordered some tankers to Coron Bay, situated in the Calamian Islands at the east end of Palawan. The sea-lane from Manila to Leyte and Kurita's route from Brunei both passed nearby, while Nishimura's voyage to the Surigao Strait lay close enough that a warship in extremis might harbor there. Once Admiral Shima's force joined the scheme, it, too, would sail near Coron. This became a key support base for the Sho operation.

Back at Brunei Bay, Vice Admiral Kurita stood before his officers. It was late afternoon on the quarterdeck of *Atago*. The sun sank toward the horizon. Staff had already handed out written materials. The assembled group drank a toast to success. The session went on for almost three hours. Subordinate commanders would have their own meetings with skippers once the parley broke up. Kurita acknowledged that many found their mission distasteful, but the admiral insisted, "The war situation is far more critical than any of you could possibly know."

There would be shame for all if the nation perished but the fleet survived. The admiral continued, "I believe that Imperial General Headquarters is giving us a glorious opportunity." (In the particularly Japanese style of *honne*, author Evan Thomas tells us, private thoughts left unsaid or merely hinted at are often more important than actual remarks.) Some of Kurita's captains no doubt took the admiral to mean that they were being given an opportunity to die. "Because I realize how very serious the war situation actually is," Admiral Kurita exhorted, "I am willing to accept even this ultimate assignment."

Kurita Takeo explained his decisions to his senior officers. He composed a lengthy dispatch informing Combined Fleet of the final plans. Kurita explained that Nishimura's assignment would be to penetrate Leyte Gulf from the south, the Surigao Strait. His own, much bigger force would break in from the northeast, from waters off the island of Samar. Vice Admiral Ugaki, so garrulous about so many things, does little more than note this momentous occasion.

Kurita handed Nishimura a written directive. For his penetration mission, Kurita beefed up Nishimura's battleships with heavy cruiser *Mogami*, of Cruiser Division 5. She had been modified after Midway as an aviation cruiser, thus giving Nishimura more floatplane scout capability. Kurita also detached destroyer *Shigure* from Destroyer Flotilla 2 to give Nishimura a little additional escort strength. Tin-can boss Vice Admiral Hayakawa Mikio told the skipper of the *Shigure* that he was sorry to lose her. She had been known as the "Miracle Destroyer" during fighting in the Solomons, where she had survived every battle. Later, when Vice Admiral Nishimura convened his own explanatory session, he drew the destroyer captain aside and told Commander Nishino Shigeru much the same thing. Nishimura then made an emotional appeal to his own assembled officers, followed by chief of staff Rear Admiral Ando Norihide, who outlined the plan.

That day the JNAF had gotten some solid sightings and the Japanese sent airplanes into Leyte Gulf for actual attacks—enabling them to view the Allied armada. Observations from radio intelligence located more Allied task groups. Before talking to his commanders, Kurita Takeo learned that the phony claims from the Taiwan air battle were just that. The actual number of aircraft carriers with Halsey's Third Fleet and Kinkaid's Seventh remained unclear, but it was definitely considerable. Kurita learned that the Allies had as many battleships as he had inside Leyte Gulf alone. Beyond that, the Allied fleets outnumbered the Japanese in almost every category. Kurita, his staff chief, Koyanagi Tomiji, and many of their officers were uncomfortable with their declared purpose—to sink transports, not enemy fleets. Some groused that fleet commander Toyoda should come and lead the sortie himself. Koyanagi, who, as chief of staff, was actually the person responsible for fleet planning, had collaborated with his boss on an implicit, private plan—if they came across an enemy fleet, they would go after it.

"What man can say there is no chance for our fleet to turn the tide of war in a decisive battle?" Kurita asked. "You must all remember there are such things as miracles." Officers leaped to their feet with shouts of *"Banzai!"* The Kurita fleet would storm Leyte Gulf.

EVERYONE CONCERNED SOON got a glimpse of the realities as a result of the experience of Cruiser Division 16. Rear Admiral Sakonju Naomasa's unit had been assigned as the Tokyo Express—the equivalent of the Leyte run, with control given to Vice Admiral Mikawa, who put Sakonju on standby alert. His ships refueled from battlewagons *Fuso* and *Yamashiro* at Brunei.

On October 21, Mikawa ordered Sakonju to the Philippines to move Army troops to Leyte. Rear Admiral Sakonju received the order at midafternoon. He ordered his ships—the heavy cruiser *Aoba*, light cruiser *Kinu*, and destroyer *Uranami*, to sail at a quarter to five, just as the fleet's senior officers gathered to meet Admiral Kurita. As it turned out, the *Aoba* did not clear Brunei at the appointed hour. Sakonju began his mission twenty-five minutes late.

An intelligence expert and political operative for much of his career, Sakonju had had his big moment in this role back in 1941, when he helped convince the government of Thailand to cast its lot on the Japanese side. He seemed an unlikely combat commander, but during the spring Sakonju led his cruiser division on a raid into the Indian Ocean and ran down some merchantmen (sealing his fate as a war criminal when he had crewmen execute sailors from the captured ships). Afterward, Toyoda put him in charge of the Tokyo Express unit on an abortive attempt to reinforce the island of Biak before the Marianas battle. Now he would serve the same function in the Leyte action.

But he never got the chance to do so. Near midnight, Cruiser Division 16 was en route, approaching the western end of Palawan, when it was attacked by the American submarine *Darter*. Admiral Sakonju, seeking safety in speed, raced ahead at twenty-three knots.

David H. McClintock, the young captain of the sub, knew his only chance would be to chase Sakonju on the surface. He tried but could not pull it off. But Commander McClintock's position reports tipped off U.S. submarines.

Just over twenty-four hours later, during the predawn of October 23, Admiral Sakonju approached Manila with the sub *Bream* in front of him. Like McClintock, Lieutenant Commander Wreford G. "Moon" Chapple was running on the surface when his radar detected the Japanese vessel. Moon pursued until he attained a satisfactory attack position, and he loosed a spread of six torpedoes. Two smacked Captain Yamazumi Chusaburo's *Aoba*. Moon Chapple dived deep as Sakonju's other ships counterattacked. The *Aoba*, which sustained a hit in the starboard forward engine room, lay dead in the water. She had to be towed to Manila. That delayed Cruiser Division 16 badly, and Sakonju did not make port until night. There the admiral moved his flag to Captain Kawasaki Harumi's light cruiser *Kinu*.

SHIMA KIYOHIDE, ANOTHER Japanese officer who needed to pay special attention to the Allied submarine threat, had finally succeeded in straightening out his assignment. Admiral Shima's Fifth Fleet had been seen by an American sub back in Empire waters, only hours after setting off.

Originally, his force would have been the vanguard of Ozawa's Mobile Fleet. Fortunately Admiral Ozawa did not participate in the ill-founded mop-up operation. With just a pair of heavy cruisers and one light cruiser at the core of his flotilla, Shima had little real gun power and would have been outclassed by a single one of Halsey's task groups, much less the whole Third Fleet. Instead, Shima was recalled after he had been spotted by aircraft and submarines.

Instead of returning to the Home Islands, Vice Admiral Shima made for Taiwanese waters. The Mobile Fleet commander had long argued that the cruiser force would be better employed elsewhere, and the sortie to catch cripples had been a special exception. Shima paused briefly at Amami Oshima but sailed again not long after the Kurita fleet departed Lingga. Shima next called at Mako in the Pescadore Islands, west of Taiwan, jumping into the dialogue-by-dispatch concerning how his unit should be employed. Admiral Kusaka instructed Shima to head for Manila under orders of Vice Admiral Mikawa, there to help with Japanese counterlandings. Mikawa, dismissing Army delays in providing troops to lift to Leyte and satisfied with Sakonju's even smaller cruiser division, advised that Shima's warships should be used to augment the assault of Admiral Kurita. Combined Fleet responded.

Aboard heavy cruiser *Nachi*, which had been the flagship of the Imperial Navy's northern fleet for as long as anyone could remember, the fateful message arrived at noon on October 21. Combined Fleet ordered Shima to cooperate with the Kurita fleet by means of penetrating Leyte Gulf via Surigao Strait, the same entrance toward which Kurita had aimed Nishimura's battleships. Admiral Shima sailed again, toward Manila, about an hour before Sakonju's cruisers left Brunei. That evening Shima joined the conversation, objecting that a stop in Manila to confer with Army commanders risked losing the opportunity to join the Leyte attack. From Manila, the area fleet commander Mikawa added his own endorsement. The 2nd Diversion Attack Force would make for Surigao Strait, stopping along the way to fuel at Coron Bay.

THE IMPERIAL NAVY had now begun pushing hard. The last piece on the board, Vice Admiral Ozawa Jisaburo's Mobile Fleet, had sailed too.

In the evening of October 20, Ozawa cleared Kure and exited the Bungo Strait. Admiral Ozawa had the aircraft carriers—not all the ones Japan possessed but enough for a show of force. The Ozawa fleet headed southward at a leisurely pace, giving time for Admiral Toyoda—finally back in the driver's seat—to move the other pieces on his board.

The question would be, How would the Allies respond?

Pearl Harbor, July 26, 1944. President Franklin D. Roosevelt sits for a portrait photograph, flanked by General Douglas A. MacArthur on the left and Admiral Chester W. Nimitz on the right. They are aboard the heavy cruiser *Baltimore*, which traveled 2,285 miles to bring the president to meet his key commanders.

The Pearl Harbor conference, morning, July 28. General Douglas MacArthur presents his plan to invade the Philippines as the next stage of the Allies' Pacific campaign. MacArthur has his pointer aimed directly at Manila.

All photos courtesy of the National Archives except where noted.

During his Hawaiian visit, President Roosevelt made use of a very unusual automobile. Here the presidential motorcade arrives for one of the many morale-boosting stops on FDR's itinerary. Note the president's Secret Service protection. Presidential detail chief Michael F. Reilly is on the running board at the left, with an unidentified agent on the driver's side and a truckful of Secret Service agents following. Reilly's body obscures General MacArthur and President Roosevelt behind him. Admiral Chester Nimitz is just visible behind the waving flag.

Admiral Bill Halsey's fleet became the nemesis of the Japanese. Here American striking power is manifest, at rest, anchored at Ulithi atoll. The five fleet aircraft carriers in the center are the most evident, but another big carrier and two light carriers are in the left rear. Carriers lined up at the center include the *Wasp*, the *Yorktown*, the *Hornet*, the *Hancock*, and the *Ticonderoga*.

Japan's war effort depended upon the output of oil rigs in Indonesia. This facility in the Netherlands East Indies lay not far from the port Brunei, where the Kurita fleet would stop to fill its bunkers on the way to battle.

The intelligence nerve center of the Pacific War lay behind security fences on Makalapa Hill alongside Pearl Harbor. The nearest of the two wood-frame buildings in the enclosure is the Joint Intelligence Center Pacific Ocean Area (JICPOA). The one behind that is the Fleet Radio Unit Pacific (FRUPAC), den of the code breakers. *Naval Historical Center*

First moves. The fateful campaign began with Halsey's Third Fleet attacking Okinawa and Taiwan. Dive-bomber pilot Lieutenant Rupert Weber, of Air Group 13 on the *Franklin*, stands next to his damaged plane, looking unhappy. Two days later, on October 14, Weber would not come back from the Halsey fleet's attack on Taiwan.

The target. MacArthur's transport force inside Leyte Gulf on A-Day, the moment of the invasion. Japan's sudden switch to making transports the main target of its operations stunned and disturbed Imperial Navy officers, who were accustomed to thinking of warships as the objects of decisive battle.

Filipinos in outrigger canoes paddle alongside U.S. Navy Patrol Torpedo (PT) boats. The PTs would play an important role in the Battle of the Surigao Strait. The outriggers would move U.S. troops around islands at the mouth of Leyte Gulf.

October 20, 1944. General MacArthur debarks from a landing craft on the beach on the island of Leyte. At the left, in military uniform but tropical helmet, is Philippines president Sergio Osmeña. MacArthur would be sensitive about the letter he wrote to President Roosevelt once ashore.

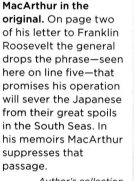

MacArthur in the original. On page two of his letter to Franklin Roosevelt the general drops the phrase—seen here on line five—that promises his operation will sever the Japanese from their great spoils in the South Seas. In his memoirs MacArthur suppresses that passage.

Author's collection

the center of his defensive line extending along the coast of Asia from the Japanese homeland to the tip of Singapore and will enable us to envelope to the north or south as we desire. It severs completely the Japanese from their great spoils in the South Seas and completely explodes their infamous propaganda slogan of the Greater East Asia Prosperity Sphere. Tactically it divides his forces in the Philippines in two and by bypassing the southern half of the Islands will result in the saving of possibly 50,000 American casualties. He had

This is in reply to No.
(Insert Sig Corps No. to which this reply refers.)

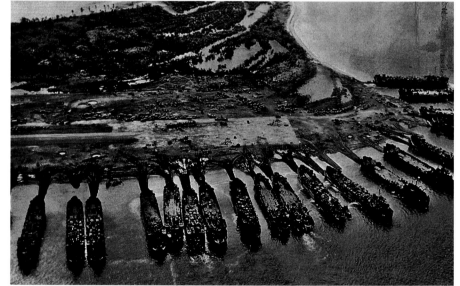

Logistics. By this time in the war, Allied forces were expert in landing large quantities of troops and supplies very quickly. Here, road-grading equipment has been used to bulldoze berms of sand on the beach at Tacloban to serve as temporary docks to unload the Landing Ship Tanks (LSTs) you see in the picture. Many vehicles can be seen, both waiting on the LSTs and in a truck park ashore.

Ready for anything. The Australian cruisers *Australia* (*middle left*) and *Shropshire*, with a U.S. heavy cruiser (*center, distance*) in Leyte Gulf. They are seen through the gunsight of a flak piece on the U.S. cruiser *Phoenix*. The warships would fend off Japanese attackers. *Australia* would be damaged by a kamikaze strike. The *Shropshire* would participate in the hurricane bombardment at Surigao Strait.

Death in the night. The Nishimura unit is destroyed by Allied naval forces inside Surigao Strait during the predawn hours of October 25. This was the cannonade that marked the crescendo of the action.

The Ozawa fleet maneuvers off Cape Engaño on October 24. In the foreground steams one of the Imperial Navy's hybrid battleship-carriers, in the middle distance a light aircraft carrier. The carrier is trailing smoke from fires on board. Near misses of rockets and bombs can be seen both next to the ship and farther away. The many disturbances on the surface of the sea are the impacts of machine guns fired by aircraft or the fall of spent flak shells.

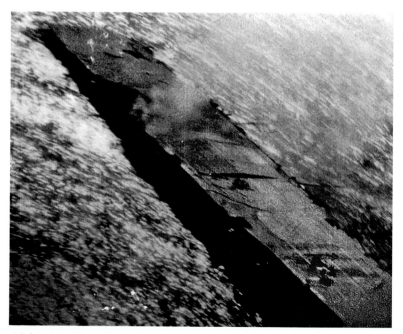

Light aircraft carrier *Zuiho* settles by the bow before sinking. Attacked at Cape Engaño by planes from the USS *Franklin*, the Japanese ship had little chance.

Another view of the action. Ozawa's aircraft carrier *Zuikaku*, by now the only one left in the formation, is at the center and surrounded by bomb splashes.

Planes from the *Franklin* also took this photograph on October 24. It is identified as a *Nachi*-type heavy cruiser in the Cape Engaño action. The ship does look like that type, but Ozawa had none of those ships. In the Ozawa fleet, light cruiser *Oyodo* bears the closest resemblance. The *Nachi*, actually Admiral Shima's flagship, was sighted that day but not attacked.

Japan strikes back. The light carrier *Princeton* suffers grievous damage from Imperial Navy bombers. Here the cruiser *Birmingham* closes alongside to help with its water hoses. Later the *Birmingham* would be badly damaged from an explosion aboard the stricken carrier.

The ready room of aircraft carrier *Franklin*, with pilots and crew of Torpedo Squadron 13 being briefed for attacks they will make in the Sibuyan Sea on October 24.

Battle of the Sibuyan Sea, October 24. In this photo taken by airmen of the USS *Enterprise*, Japanese superbattleship *Musashi* is in extremis. Dark smoke from raging fires alternates with white smoke of detonating bombs. Beside the ship there are circular ripples from near misses. Beyond the *Musashi* the water spouts of other bombs are visible on both sides of an escorting destroyer.

Battle of the Sibuyan Sea. U.S. Navy planes attack the Kurita fleet. American pilots believed the warship in the foreground to be a light cruiser, likely the *Yahagi*. If so, the battleship *Kongo* would be the vessel at middle left and the one commencing a turn at the right would be heavy cruiser *Chikuma*.

Battleship *Nagato* bracketed by a pair of bombs hitting the water. The Japanese ship is firing special antiaircraft shells from her main battery.

The Imperial Navy's superbattleship *Yamato*. The first good overhead photograph of the Japanese warship would be taken only the day following the battle off Samar.

Battle of Samar, early morning, October 25. Battleship *Yamato* is in the foreground, with an Imperial Navy heavy cruiser, probably the *Haguro*, at center, top. They are in hot pursuit of Taffy 3. While not certain from the grainy photograph, it appears that several American planes are going at the *Yamato* from different angles off the ship's bow. The picture was taken by a plane from the escort carrier *Petrof Bay*.

Slowly but surely the Japanese gain on the little American escort carriers with their thin protective screens. Here Taffy 3 vessels desperately make smoke, hoping the screens will hide them from the Japanese.

Kurita loses control. At the height of the battle, the Japanese admiral's most powerful battleships turn to evade torpedoes and take themselves away from the action. The Japanese leader would never regain the commanding position he had been on the brink of achieving. This picture looks very much like it was taken at that very moment, near eight a.m. That was the only instant in the battle when Kurita's flagship, *Yamato*, held to a course diverging from other Japanese vessels, such as the heavy cruiser in the distance to the left. In the center an American plane is pulling up after an attack run on the *Yamato*.

A Japanese heavy cruiser of the *Tone* class under weigh at speed during the Samar battle.

The smudge at the center of the Japanese heavy cruiser in this photo, combined with the light patch just ahead of it, indicates the warship has just been struck by a bomb. Splashes in the water to the right of the ship are likely expended antiaircraft shells falling into the sea. An off-color stretch of sea surrounding the ship indicates leaking oil.

Taken by a plane from the escort carrier *Natoma Bay*, this picture shows the same Imperial Navy warship as in the previous shot. Judging from the oil slick, the silhouette of the heavy cruiser, and the Japanese destroyer standing by in the lower right, American aircrews are witnessing the final moments of the Japanese cruiser *Chikuma*.

The Japanese find a weapon. Later that day, jeep carrier *Santee* is struck by a kamikaze suicide bomber. This picture records the instant of the strike, with debris of the airplane flying through the air and American sailors crouching for shelter.

Above: Santee crewmen fight fires resulting from the kamikaze strike and try to keep the planes spotted on the afterdeck from becoming involved in the conflagration. The kamikaze weapon introduces a new factor into the Pacific war.

Right: **Aftermath.** On the deck of Seventh Fleet flagship, *Wasatch*, fleet intelligence officer Captain Arthur H. McCollum briefs fleet commanders and staff on the course of the Leyte Gulf battle and its consequences.

United States Naval Institute

CHAPTER 7

"WITH CONFIDENCE IN HEAVENLY GUIDANCE, THE ENTIRE FORCE WILL ATTACK!"

Denizens of the Zoo at Pearl Harbor were electrified by the display of events unfolding in signals intelligence, and they helped detect unusual activity in some of the intercepts. There were multiple indications of Japanese fleet movements, different moves spread over thousands of miles, and odd pockets where nothing seemed to be happening at all.

Allied capabilities for radio interception had increased considerably—with more sites and more receivers—in comparison to the far-off days before the war. The old-timers of the On the Roof Gang had seen a lot and knew they needed even more resources. Petty Officer Albert M. Fishburn, one of the On the Roofers, became part of a migration to Guam that opened a fancy new station there. First, they worked in Quonset huts, then switched to newly constructed A-frame buildings. Though still halfway across the Pacific, the listening would be better than from Wahiawa, the Fleet Radio Unit Pacific (FRUPAC) facility in Hawaii. The new unit, almost as big as Wahiawa too, would have a three-shift schedule, which meant 240 radiomen. Guam had a couple of Marine lieutenants who were Japanese linguists, and a couple of code breakers who'd been associated with Albert Einstein—one had solved math problems for him. The Guam station had a new traffic analysis unit as well, the Radio Analysis Group Forward (RAGFOR).

Predictably, the move to new quarters ended up happening at exactly the moment of the big battle. Fishburn spent the first day in the back of a Marine mobile radio truck FRUPAC used to keep the intercept work going even with the regular receivers unplugged. Then he settled into a chair at a new receiver table. The petty officer stayed glued to the 7,910-kilocycle frequency the Imperial Navy employed. "It just operated all day long," he recalled. "It was just one ship after another." The spooks were fond of comparing notes on traffic volume and urgency—and this day was right up at the top.

The Japanese were up to something, and the indications mounted steadily. On October 18, it became clear from transmissions of Japanese intelligence reports that the enemy were aware of the move against Tacloban on Leyte. JNAF plane movements converged on Kanoya Air Base, the first link in the chain from the Empire to the Philippines. In a message the morning of the nineteenth, Combined Fleet's Kusaka revealed tanker movements toward Coron Bay and others with a convoy from Hong Kong to Mako, the latter specifically linked to fuel for the Shima fleet. The next night came a message from Ozawa, sent so as to disguise the originator, and it took the form of an operation order and went for information to all the Imperial Navy commands participating in Sho.

By the time JICPOA assembled its Ultra summary for the day, the radio spies reported "good indications" that Ozawa was at sea and headed for the Philippines. Around 10:30 p.m. on the twentieth, a radio fix—which was admittedly "poor"—located one of the Mobile Fleet units at a specific location. In fact, the Mobile Fleet had steamed out of base in the Empire only three hours earlier. Submarine *Trigger* saw Admiral Shima's 2nd Diversion Attack Force in the Taiwan Strait, as FRUPAC reported at 5:15 p.m. on the twentieth. The size of his Fifth Fleet force would be slightly exaggerated, but the radio spies clearly linked the move with the tanker convoy approaching Mako, concluding that Shima would refuel there. When the Japanese base at Mako sent extra escorts to help bring in the tankers, the radio spies were on top of that too, and a FRUPAC dispatch just after 1:00 a.m. on October 22 alerted the Allies that the tankers were under submarine attack.

The radio spies missed some key events of October 22, however, while they were recording others. That morning, for instance, the Zoo warned that the Second Air Fleet and the T Air Attack Force had been ordered to the Philippines. That evening JICPOA reported a dispatch from a detached element of Kurita's fleet—without doubt Nishimura's battleships headed for Surigao—regarding where their floatplanes should shelter. The following day the Zoo noted that submarine and aircraft had, for the moment, supplanted Ultra in furnishing the best picture of Japanese locations and intentions, making an example of the Ozawa fleet, which kept radio silence and had not shown up in the day's traffic. By then, Kurita Takeo could have said volumes about subs.

TORPEDOES IN THE NIGHT

The Kurita fleet sailed from Brunei at eight o'clock in the morning on October 22—one event FRUPAC missed. The admiral appreciated the clouds that hampered Allied scout planes. Slightly after noon Kurita turned the fleet to a course just west of north to make the track off Palawan, and he altered at 6:00 p.m. to his final course. The fleet varied speed between sixteen and eighteen knots, alternating zigzag patterns, and for part of the day avoided zigzagging. Kurita's course took him near where an Allied submarine, based on radio observations, was believed to be located. Several more were overheard on the radio. The sequence suggested a sub might actually be trailing Kurita. Jumpy lookouts reported periscopes. Around 9:00 p.m. light cruiser *Yahagi* made an emergency turn and fired a red flare, signaling a sub contact. Admiral Kurita considered these imponderables. The truth, about to blast the hull of his flagship, lay submerged right ahead.

Commander David H. McClintock skippered the American sub *Darter*. He led a mini-unit with another boat, Commander Bladen D. Claggett's *Dace*, which clever sailors dubbed the "Double D's." They were on patrol between Palawan and the shoal area known as the "Dangerous Ground." The boats, based in Australia, had been at sea for several weeks, and Claggett had already claimed two merchantmen from a Japanese convoy. McClintock had detected and chased Admiral Sakonju's cruiser division but had not been able to get a good attack position. This night, McClintock had both boats riding on the surface, barely under way, signaling by lamp and megaphone to preserve radio silence. He contemplated heading home. But then, at 1:16 a.m., McClintock's radar detected a gaggle of large ships, which resolved into two

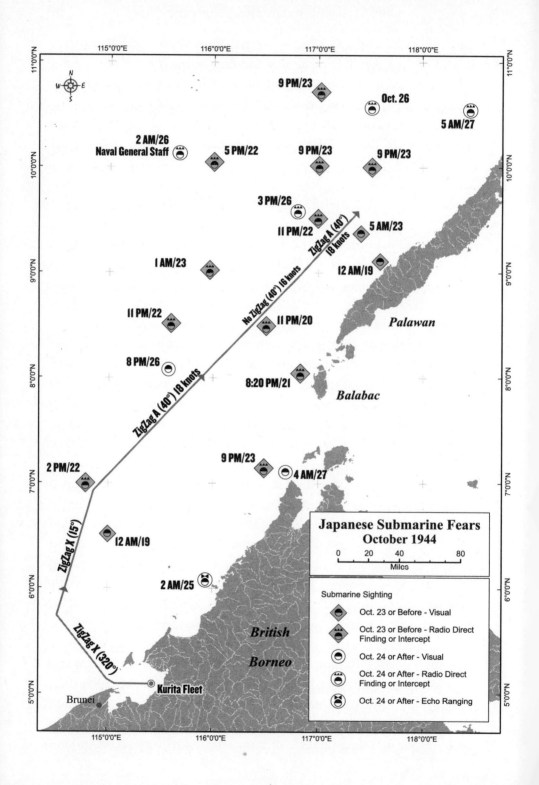

(actually three) columns of the Kurita fleet. The senior skipper passed the word to Claggett and both pursued the quarry.

Admiral Kurita's warships were making sixteen knots, zigzagging. McClintock's subs dashed from their port side, doing nineteen on the surface on a straight course, scrambling to get out in front. The chase went on for hours since McClintock wanted to strike from ahead—and from underwater. He sent a contact report, then two more, estimating at least eleven heavy ships (there were actually fifteen).

Aboard the *Yamato* radio operators overheard an urgent submarine report at 1:50 a.m. At about 4:30, *Darter*'s crew went for coffee; then Commander McClintock sent them to battle stations. He dived the boat, taking the *Darter* deep to check depth and water density, then brought her back to periscope depth. Bearing down on him, flagship *Atago* led the closest column of Japanese ships. Right behind her steamed heavy cruiser *Takao*. McClintock took quick glances through his periscope, describing what he saw to the sub's exec, Lieutenant Commander Ernest L. Schwab. They set up torpedo firing solutions. The skipper planned to fire all six bow torpedo tubes, then swing the boat around to unleash the four tin fish in his stern tubes. He estimated the distance to target to be about 3,000 yards. Clocks registered about 5:30 a.m.

Suddenly the Japanese warships turned in a zig. The *Darter* needed to establish the new course and recalculate the solution. McClintock realized the enemy had turned *toward* him. He would be able to use torpedoes at point-blank range, less than 1,000 yards. The submariner could see a signal lamp blinking from the *Atago*'s bridge as he loosed his first fish. McClintock went through his sequence, then turned and emptied the stern tubes.

The sound of explosions was unmistakable, but crewmen were uncertain whether they were depth charges or torpedoes. McClintock thought torpedoes. He would never forget what he saw when he turned the periscope back to look at the *Atago*. "She was a mass of billowing black smoke from the number one turret to the stern. No superstructure could be seen. Bright orange flames shot out from the side along the main deck from the bow to the after turret. Cruiser was already down by the bow, which was dipping under. . . . She was definitely finished."

From the Japanese perspective, disaster immediately overwhelmed the flagship. Rear Admiral Araki Tsutau, noticing his heavy cruiser had begun listing to starboard, ordered counterflooding of the port engine and boiler rooms, accepting that would mean a shipwide loss of power. Araki ordered full right rudder, but without electricity the rudder could not function. Then telephones died, and engineer officer Commander Domen Keizo could do nothing.

Four of the *Darter*'s torpedoes had struck home. One, near the bow, merely damaged storerooms, but the second strike hit the number one boiler room, broke steam lines, started fires, and opened the vessel's seams. Junior officers' quarters began to flood. The number six boiler room caught the third hit, with such force that the bulkhead buckled between it and the adjacent boiler room and the flames roared through. Above it lay one of the cruiser's torpedo mounts. Its own fish had to be jettisoned, save for one that stuck and threatened to ignite from the heat. The last torpedo hit with the ship's list already increased to thirty-two degrees, flooding the aft generator room, shorting out transformers, filling a propeller shaft, and sending a muck of seawater and oil through the crew's quarters.

There could be no question of saving the *Atago*. She sank in just eighteen minutes. Commanders barely had time to summon destroyers *Kishinami* and *Asashimo* to take off the crew. Radiomen did have the time necessary to destroy *Atago*'s code machines and lock most secret material securely in spaces beneath the waterline. Remaining communications material would be sealed in weighted sacks and thrown overboard.

When sailors were summoned topside, water had begun pouring into the number five turret, killing crewmen there, and the list increased to fifty-four degrees, more than halfway toward leaving the cruiser on her beam ends. Admiral Kurita and his staff decamped amid this disaster, swimming to the *Kishinami*. Kurita was among the first over the side. Amazingly, skipper Araki managed to save 43 officers, 667 petty officers and sailors, and 2 civilians. Commander Domen was not among them, nor were 18 other officers and 340 men. Kurita later sent a destroyer back to ensure that none of those sacks of classified documents had survived. None were found.

Behind the flagship, heavy cruiser *Takao* suffered two torpedo hits.

These opened large gashes in the ship's hull, but the wounds were less grievous and Captain Onoda Sutejiro's damage-control efforts were more successful. Though the engines stopped, the steering was lost, and the ship listed to the starboard side, Onoda was able to right the vessel, and the crew restored power and steerage. Only 33 sailors were killed and another 30 injured. Destroyers *Asashimo* and *Naganami* stood by, mounting depth-charge attacks on the *Darter*. The *Asashimo* rescued 5 sailors who were thrown overboard by the explosions. Combined Fleet sent the *Mitsu Maru* and torpedo boat *Hiyodori* from Brunei to assist.

Meanwhile, on the other flank Commander Claggett's *Dace* got in her own knocks. The boat had used up the fish in her stern torpedo room in previous operations. Claggett listened to the sounds of the *Darter*'s battle with the enemy until 5:54 a.m., when the opposite flank column of warships entered his danger zone. Claggett thought he had a *Kongo*-class battleship; she was actually Captain Oe Ranji's heavy cruiser *Maya*. The *Dace* loosed half a dozen torpedoes. Four of them hit, and the *Maya* began to break up almost immediately, capsizing in just seven minutes. Under the circumstances, it is astonishing that 769 sailors—more than 70 percent of the crew—were saved. Much of that had to do with destroyer *Shimakaze*, which reacted immediately and closed with the hapless cruiser, so that sailors could begin evacuating down makeshift gangways. The 29 seriously wounded men were sheathed in bamboo carriers. Fortunately the sea was calm.

At a certain point, the *Darter*, convinced the Japanese counterattacks were only going through the motions, returned to periscope depth. Commander McClintock found the *Takao* immobile, with assisting ships around her. Late in the day she seemed to come to life. If he got another crack, the submariner thought, he might finish her off. Bladen Claggett was of the same mind. In daylight, Japanese destroyers fended off their attempts to maneuver. The next night McClintock, seeing *Takao* had gotten under way, still slowly, decided to run in on the surface. The Dangerous Ground lived up to its name. *Darter* suddenly stuck fast on a reef known as Bombay Shoal. Hours of efforts failed to dislodge the boat. Commander Claggett abandoned his pursuit of the *Takao* to come to the rescue of McClintock and his crew.

After dawn, a JNAF scout found the two subs and identified one as hard aground. At that point the *Dace*, full with two crews, had to flee. Once the *Takao* neared Brunei, Captain Onoda sent *Naganami* and *Hiyodori* back to see what they could find. The intelligence taken from the boat included blueprints, instruction books, ordnance items, communications procedures, and radio and radar material. American sailors had destroyed their code materials, so the take lacked the dimension of the equivalent Japanese loss of sub *I-1* off Guadalcanal in 1943, but it still amounted to a windfall for the Imperial Navy.

Tokyo paid a stiff price for the intel, however.

IT WOULD TAKE hours for Admiral Kurita to transfer to another warship after the *Atago* debacle. During the transfer, command was entrusted to the outspoken, strident Ugaki Matome.

At the moment of the torpedo attack Ugaki had been standing on *Yamato*'s bridge, in the column behind the *Chokai*. The fleet had been making a simultaneous turn. Off the port bow, against the lightening horizon of dawn, Ugaki suddenly saw flames, explosions, and a waterspout. At first, he thought a destroyer had been hit. "They've done it!" was his unthinking response. A lookout asked if Cruiser Division 4 had been attacked—that brought Ugaki back to reality. Both the victims were from that unit. Admiral Ugaki went outside on the port wing of the bridge structure. He saw the *Takao* dead in the water belching white smoke, and—horrors—the fleet flagship listing, heavily damaged, and suddenly afflicted by what seemed an internal explosion.

Ugaki heaved a sigh of relief once he learned that Admiral Kurita had made it to destroyer *Kiyoshimo*, but in the meantime, he took charge of the Second Fleet. That was a simple matter—he outranked the senior officers present and received orders to that effect at 8:30 a.m. Admiral Ugaki immediately ordered the Second Fleet to battle speed— twenty-four knots—even though Kurita had been maintaining a fleet speed of eighteen. It meant considerable strain on machinery and high fuel expenditure. The fleet had to clear submarine waters, Ugaki thought; it could not be helped. Later he would reduce the speed slightly.

Torpedoed, the *Maya* disappeared. When the smoke cleared, the warship had already gone. That stunned Ugaki. He believed he could see where the torpedoes had originated and thought if *Yamato* had been situated just a little differently, the superbattleship would have taken three or four torpedoes. That kind of thinking soon had grave repercussions. Ugaki thought there were four enemy submarines—he, too, was prone to exaggeration—and that he saw a periscope in the minutes after the torpedo strikes.

The admiral informed Combined Fleet, Mikawa at Manila, and Admiral Ozawa at sea of the disaster that had befallen the 1st Diversion Attack Force. Ugaki indicated that he would continue the operation. Destroyers *Shimakaze* and *Naganami* had meanwhile rescued many crewmen. At midafternoon the rescue destroyers discharged their passengers. *Shimakaze* and *Naganami* sent surviving sailors of the *Maya* to superbattleship *Musashi*.

Before sailing, Kurita had wanted to wear his flag in one of the superbattleships, but Admiral Toyoda forbade it. Senior staffer Yamamoto Yuji and Ugaki's top staff officer, Captain Noda Rokuro, had made a study of the best vessel for fleet flagship, and both had agreed that would be the *Yamato*. Ugaki hated the idea. But Combined Fleet anticipated a night surface battle, according to Kurita's chief of staff, and the Imperial Navy had always considered the heavy cruiser the key ship for that sort of action. So Kurita stayed on the *Atago*.

Now he had to move. Survivors included Vice Admiral Kurita and his staff. The *Kishinami* deposited them aboard *Yamato*. Kurita resumed fleet command, also supervising Battleship Division 1. Ugaki Matome complained to his diary that Kurita had had a secret desire to lead the big ships—a wish that would now come true under the worst imaginable circumstances. It appears that battleship leader Ugaki permitted his resentment of Kurita Takeo to run wild. That would have consequences.

Discharging her cargo of hapless survivors, the *Shimakaze* rushed to catch up. She was a big destroyer, at 3,600 tons the biggest in the fleet, but at forty knots *Shimakaze* was also the fastest. She bent on speed now. Commander Doi Hiroshi's vessel rejoined the formation as the sun set.

By 9:30 p.m. Admiral Kurita had the fleet headed due east, passing

Mindoro. It entered the Sibuyan Sea at 6:00 a.m. on October 24. Kurita ordered his Second Fleet into ring formations suited for antiaircraft action. *Yamato* took the center position in the lead unit. Surrounding her was a ring made up of cruisers, plus the other ships of Battleship Division 1, with a ring of destroyers outside them. The second formation followed about seven miles behind, with battleship *Kongo* at its center, the *Haruna* and other cruisers for the inner ring, and destroyers along the outer perimeter.

American scouts soon found the Kurita fleet. The Japanese logged this at 7:30 a.m. Kurita expected action. He would not be disappointed.

"FIRST AIR FLEET IS TO PROVIDE LAND-BASED AIR COVER"

What chance the Japanese had to protect the fleets headed for Leyte resided with their air forces. The action started poorly on October 17, when air fleet commander Teraoka could scrape up just a baker's dozen of airplanes to harass Leyte Gulf. Only one came back to Clark Field. A few landed elsewhere due to bad weather or mechanical troubles.

On the morning of the invasion, at least one plane would be shot down in front of MacArthur's staff. That afternoon the 331st Air Group managed to launch a pair of Jill strike aircraft. The Japanese claimed to sink a transport when actually the light cruiser *Honolulu* received a torpedo hit, and the *Louisville* a couple of near misses. The sixty sailors lost aboard the "Blue Goose," as crewmen knew the *Honolulu*, astonishingly were the first casualties the ship had suffered in the whole war, even though she had been at Pearl Harbor and in countless battles, and even torpedoed in one of those fierce naval scraps in the Solomons.

The JNAF turned its focus the next day, October 21, to the escort carriers. The *Sangamon* suffered slight damage from a partially detonating bomb. Another "jeep" carrier endured near misses.

But the Japanese were about to reshuffle their entire air operation. At Mabalacat, part of the Clark Field complex around Manila, the senior staff officer of the First Air Fleet, Captain Inoguchi Rikihei, was meeting with Commander Tamai Asaichi on the evening of October

19 when a Packard limousine with the hood pendant of a three-star admiral drew up. Vice Admiral Onishi Takijiro stepped out of the car. Onishi watched airfield activity for a time, then asked to speak to the two of them at 201st Air Group headquarters. Located in one of the few Western-style houses in the town, "headquarters" was a glorified name for a building where thirty or more JNAF pilots lived, with the homeowner and his own family in two back rooms. When Tamai and Inoguchi arrived, they summoned a couple of squadron leaders, and a staff officer of the 26th Air Flotilla, who sat around a table in a room on the second floor that overlooked the yard. Onishi began to speak.

"As you know, the war situation is grave," he explained. "The fate of the empire depends upon the outcome of the Sho Operation, which Imperial General Headquarters has activated to hurl back the enemy assault. . . . Our surface forces are already in motion. . . . The mission of the First Air Fleet is to provide land-based air cover for Admiral Kurita's advance and make sure that enemy air attacks do not prevent him from reaching Leyte Gulf. To do this we must hit the enemy carriers and keep them neutralized for at least one week."

Captain Inoguchi understood the difficulty. The American aircraft carriers were plentiful and powerful. The JNAF had barely been able to scratch them, and now the high command wanted the aviators to hold the enemy at bay for a week. Inoguchi, whose brother sailed with Kurita as captain of the superbattleship *Musashi*, had a personal stake here. Yet, he recalled, "it seemed idle even to hope that we might succeed."

The odds were slim. Onishi looked hard at his younger cohorts. "In my opinion, there is only one way of assuring that our meager strength will be effective," the admiral went on. "That is to organize suicide attack units composed of Zero fighters armed with 250-kilogram bombs, with each plane to crash-dive into an enemy carrier."

Coming from Onishi, this pronouncement could only be seen as a main-line calculation. The vice admiral had long been one of the Imperial Navy's apostles of airpower. His stature was equal to that of such wizards as Genda Minoru, and his technical knowledge far beyond that of famed officers like Nagumo Chuichi. Admiral Onishi had been a behind-the-scenes adviser to the planners of the Pearl Harbor attack, had run the staff of the air fleet that trapped Douglas MacArthur's heavy bombers on the ground in December 1941 and sank the British battleships *Prince of Wales* and *Repulse*. A carrier advocate too, Onishi had been instrumental in making the JNAF an element of naval power. He came to the Philippines from the Navy Ministry, where the admiral had been in charge of ordnance and production, pushing the new-generation aircraft out of the factories.

But for each officer who considered him a visionary, a skilled innovator in a novel field, another thought Onishi a bully whose actions sullied the Navy's reputation. After Pearl Harbor and the British battleships, Onishi had joked that the Navy should trade its anchor symbol for a propeller and become an air force. He'd been publicly critical of the Tojo cabinet and the government planning boards. The Navy minister and others were idiots. The *Yamato*-class ships Onishi derided as buggies in an age of automobiles.

Once, under an assumed name, Onishi had entered a national mahjongg tournament and won it. He'd been criticized in the mid-1930s, as a captain and executive officer of the Yokosuka Air Corps, when seen pulling a rickshaw with a geisha in it. Some had trouble deciding whether pulling the cart or Onishi's open consorting with a lady of the night had been the greater offense. An even more notorious incident— when he slapped a geisha in the face for not sufficiently entertaining his men—resulted in official sanction. Yamamoto Isoroku, another officer with an eye for the geisha, had not been able to protect him. Onishi and Teraoka Kimpei, the admiral he replaced in the Philippines, had been classmates and buddies at Etajima and planned to take the entrance exams for the War College together. Teraoka got in; Onishi did not—and probably not because of his test answers.

In any case, Vice Admiral Onishi Takijiro offered not only a sounding board for anyone with a novel idea but also a willingness to embrace new thinking and a voice for ideas he believed in. Such was the case with "body-crashing" (*tai-atari*) tactics—the notion of using the aircraft itself as a weapon. JNAF pilots had long since come to the idea of perishing in crash-dives when they were wounded or their planes so damaged that survival seemed impossible. The new wrinkle was to make *tai-atari* the normal, standard tactic, and to create whole units—a "special attack" (or kamikaze) force—to carry them out. These ideas were in the wind within the Imperial Navy. It had developed miniature submarines for special attack even before the war, and by this time, it had begun experimenting with explosive boats and special attack divers. The JNAF lagged behind. But there were outspoken advocates for special attack—and all of them went to Onishi.

Captain Jyo Eichiro, former aide-de-camp to the emperor, who skippered light carrier *Chiyoda*, had discussed body-crashing tactics with both Onishi and Ozawa as early as 1943. And after the Great Marianas Turkey Shoot, Jyo had sent Onishi a cable arguing that they had just witnessed the failure of the last chance of hurting the U.S. carriers by conventional means. Because of Jyo's close relationship with the emperor, Hirohito had also seen that dispatch. At the helm of the *Chiyoda*, Jyo was now headed into battle at Ozawa's side. In addition to Jyo, there was also Captain Okamura Motoharu, the leader of the 341st Air Group. He, too, pressed body-crashing tactics on both Onishi and Vice Admiral Fukudome. Okamura went so far as to assert that with 300 special attack planes he could turn the tide of the war.

Admiral Onishi had started by thinking it too much to ask crews to fly deliberately to their deaths, but the reality of current events wore Onishi down. He himself had written a paper toward the end of 1943 arguing that commanding the sea without controlling the air was no longer conceivable. But if control by means of conventional tactics had become impossible, what else was there? On his way to the Philippines, Onishi stopped on Taiwan and conferred with C-in-C Toyoda, who also supported the kamikaze idea. Onishi thus learned that the NGS had reached the final stage in creating a special attack corps.

All of which brings us back to Mabalacat on October 19, 1944. Admiral Onishi discussed the practical feasibility of damaging carriers with a 550-pound bomb strapped to a Zero. The admiral then proposed that the 201st Air Group should organize the first special attack unit. Commander Tamai responded that he would have to consult the group commander, Captain Yamamoto Sakae. As it happened, the boss and his air staff officer, Commander Nakajima Tadashi—were returning to Mabalacat from Manila, where they had fruitlessly gone to see Onishi while he was off visiting them. Nakajima piloted their Zero. Its

engine had not sounded right. The commander ordered a change of
spark plugs, but once they were airborne the landing gear refused to
retract, and the engine died—perfectly encapsulating the state of JNAF
maintenance. They crash-landed in a rice paddy, with Captain Yamamoto breaking his ankle. By telephone from Manila, Yamamoto gave
Tamai leave to respond to Onishi's proposals.

Commander Tamai selected Lieutenant Seki Yukio to lead the special attack unit and by the next day had two dozen pilots for the suicide
mission. They had breakfast and were saluted. Vice Admiral Onishi
addressed them: "The salvation of our country is now beyond the power
of the ministers of state, the General Staff, and lowly commanders like
myself. It can come only from spirited young men such as you. . . . You
are already gods." Onishi promised their deeds would be reported to
the emperor. When Admiral Onishi went back to Manila on October
20, he relieved his old friend Teraoka at the head of the First Air Fleet.

The situation was in shambles. The Manila headquarters, which
had been set on fire by Allied aerial attackers just as Onishi took over,
offered little welcome. Many satellite airfields were in disrepair or mired
in bottomless mud. The main bases were holed, smashed by repeated
attacks from Halsey's carriers. Area fleet boss Mikawa recorded First
Air Fleet strength on the day of the invasion as 24 Zero fighters, 11 Jill
attack planes, 2 Betty and 2 "Ginga" bombers, and 1 scout plane.
Thus, even though the JNAF had created its special attack force, it
could not manage a mission for days. Tominaga of the 4th Air Army
did a little better. He possessed 25 fighters, 10 attack planes, 30 twin-
engine bombers, and 5 or 6 scout planes.

Japanese aerial response the day of the invasion was minimal. Onishi rushed to prepare his special attack. Commander Nakajima Tadashi
went to Cebu with eight of the precious Zero airplanes. Several were
to be kamikazes, others escorts, but Nakajima also had orders to recruit
fliers at Cebu for the special attack corps. At the base command post,
echoing Onishi at Mabalacat, Nakajima spoke of the desperation of
the situation, the importance of Sho, and the impossibility of success
with orthodox tactics. Except for men in the infirmary, every pilot
volunteered. Some even went to Nakajima complaining that they had
been excluded earlier.

It did not take long to find suitable targets. A sighting of American carriers on October 20, which were too far away, merely whetted the appetite. The morning of the twenty-first, Lieutenant Seki led the first kamikaze mission out of Mabalacat. They found nothing, and returned.

That afternoon, Cebu received word of another Allied fleet and prepared another mission. American fighters appeared over the field with the planes ready to launch. The special attack machines were shot up. Commander Nakajima managed to come up with a few flyable aircraft and they flew off late in the afternoon. They, too, found nothing, and one of the planes failed to return.

For the next several days, Halsey's carriers went undetected. On October 21, Leyte Gulf became the target for General Tominaga's Army aircraft, and the HMAS *Australia* was wounded when one crash-dived her bridge, killing twenty sailors, including the captain, with another fifty-four wounded, including Commodore John A. Collins, the senior Australian commander in the Leyte invasion. The damaged *Australia* and *Honolulu* soon left for Manus and temporary repairs.

Admiral Fukudome began funneling his surviving squadrons from Taiwan into the Philippines. On the day of the invasion, there were almost 400 planes with the Second Air Fleet on Taiwan. Nearly half were not flyable. The large bulk—about three-quarters of the overall number—were fighters. By October 23, Fukudome had sent about as many aircraft as he could afford: 126 fighters (mostly Zeros but also 21 "Shiden" interceptors), 35 dive-bombers (mostly "Vals" but also ten "Suiseis"), 25 twin-engine bombers (mostly Bettys but also five Gingas), and 10 Jill torpedo bombers. Vice Admiral Onishi would hurl these planes at the Allies. If he could keep Halsey and the other Allied carrier commanders busy, the Japanese surface fleet might be able to approach unscathed.

Assembling the force was the easy part, though. JNAF leaders were pained at how many planes kept malfunctioning. The cost of the Taiwan air battle now became evident: The combined JNAF forces possessed fewer than 100 bombers. Even including the Japanese Army air forces, there were barely 125 strike aircraft. Halsey's Third Fleet could put up more planes at once than all the Japanese air forces combined. To make matters worse, the heavy losses had weakened Japanese search capabilities.

As a result of this fumbling, when Halsey's carriers were sighted once more on October 24, their power remained undiminished. Instead of a Japanese aerial assault that would force Task Force 38 to hunker down in defense, the sides traded strikes, and the American ones would be far more powerful far.

Despite the discrepancy in power, the Imperial Navy did get in some good licks. Three (of seven) of the available JNAF scout planes were big, radar-equipped patrol bombers of the 901st Air Group. With the JNAF forces now concentrated, the Japanese used their big seaplanes for a night mission. Twenty minutes past midnight on the twenty-fourth, one of the 901st's bombers acquired a contact due east of Manila, about 250 miles distant. Admiral Onishi decided on a full attack. The JNAF's main force, 63 strike aircraft and 126 fighters, began flying from Clark Field at about 5:30 a.m. Ten Suisei dive-bombers followed. Suddenly, between eight and nine o'clock the sightings came fast—three different groups with different numbers of aircraft carriers. Task Force 38. The JNAF strike groups converged on the first sighting. It had been reported with four "regular" aircraft carriers and two escort carriers. The Sea Eagles claimed a solid hit to a fleet carrier and to have set fire to a cruiser and a battleship.

The Japanese target was Rear Admiral Ted Sherman's Task Group 38.3. For Lieutenant (Junior Grade) Paul Drury, it would be the longest day of his life. Drury was one of eight Fighting 27 pilots selected the evening before for morning CAP. Before Drury settled down to sleep, he knew that Japanese night "snoopers" were everywhere, trying to track them. The patrol pilots were awakened at 4:00 a.m.; they took off before dawn. Drury flew as wingman for the ship's biggest ace, Lieutenant James A. "Red" Shirley, who had seven and a half planes to his credit. This was not Drury's regular division or his usual flight, but at this point, all hands went where they were needed. Controllers sent Red Shirley's division after a snooper they'd seen on radar. The interceptors switched off, chasing scouts until controllers sent everyone after a big formation.

As had become routine, radars picked up the enemy approach and intercept officers vectored fighters to them. Shirley's division had the height advantage and saw the Japanese first. "TALLY HO," he radioed. "EIGHTY JAPANESE PLANES. BETTER SEND HELP."

Commander David McCampbell led seven Hellcats from the *Essex* and engaged the JNAF at 8:33 a.m. The Japanese bombers escaped into cloud cover. McCampbell and the other F-6Fs picked at the Japanese fighters. Another dozen planes from light carrier *Princeton* joined the fracas. Drury's Fighting 27 and McCampbell's *Essex* interceptors showered themselves with glory. Shirley added five planes to his score, Drury became an ace that day, and two other *Princeton* pilots got five each. Dave McCampbell, smoking a cigarette as he worked (it was a different era then), flamed nine. Many Sea Eagles did not return. The Japanese admitted to losing sixty-seven aircraft in the morning attack alone.

Lieutenant Drury made for his carrier to rearm. The defenders were sixty or seventy miles from home and out of ammunition.

Just as the U.S. fighters began landing, a single Suisei dive-bomber took aim at the *Princeton*. Captain William H. Buracker, her skipper, had been scheduled for rotation, and his replacement, Captain J. H. Hoskins, was manning the bridge too as a "makee-learnee" understudy. The ship had turned into the wind and moved some loaded Avenger torpedo planes to the hangar deck. The JNAF dive-bomber, sighted and reported, would become lost among the confusion. Suddenly, at 9:38 a.m., the Judy reappeared on the port bow already in her attack run. Captain Buracker ordered, "Hard left rudder," but it was too late. The 550-pound bomb ignited fires on the hangar deck, in the ship's bakery, and in the scullery. The Avengers on the hangar had open bomb bay doors and, inside, torpedoes slung. The flames threatened to cook off the explosives in their warheads.

Among the last *Princeton* pilots to land, Lieutenant Drury had just walked into the ready room when the compartment shook. A blast of black smoke blew into the room through the ventilator. The public address system announced that the carrier had been struck by a bomb. He awaited instructions. There would be no more flying for Fighting 27.

What had first seemed routine suddenly loomed as disaster. Ted Sherman sensed the danger immediately. Just fifteen minutes after the bomb hit, Sherman ordered several destroyers to stand by the carrier.

Ten minutes later the light cruiser *Birmingham* closed in and used her hoses to fight the fires on the stricken vessel. At 10:10 a.m., Captain Buracker ordered a partial evacuation, followed by a more complete one. Less than an hour after the Judy dived on the *Princeton*, her crew had been removed save for firefighters.

Lieutenant Drury, who had been a member of the swimming team at the University of Pennsylvania, went over the side and down a rope to swim to destroyer *Irwin*. But Drury, who was exhausted by that time, barely made it. *Irwin* sailors slung a cargo net, then came down it to help survivors climb to safety. Drury was grateful. Reaching the deck, he promptly fell asleep.

That marked just a waypoint in a tragic day. The destroyer *Morrison*, alongside, got parts of her superstructure wedged between two of the carrier's air intakes and was stuck there when an explosion dislodged an airplane tractor and a jeep from *Princeton*'s flight deck. They fell on the lower ship's bridge and bounced to hit the main deck. With help from the destroyers, the *Birmingham*, and light cruiser *Reno*, Buracker's crew made progress containing the fires. Then the Sea Eagles returned—this time a strike Ozawa had launched. The JNAF aircraft were driven off without further damage, but as *Birmingham* prepared to take the crippled carrier under tow, the fire reached a torpedo storage room, triggering a devastating explosion.

The noise of general quarters alarm bells startled Paul Drury awake. The disoriented pilot first thought he had slept through the next night, then realized only one hour had passed. The JNAF rolled in, followed by the eruption from the *Princeton*. The explosion destroyed the after flight deck and most of the stern, causing grievous casualties aboard the *Birmingham* too (241 dead and 412 wounded, more than half her crew). On the carrier, the supernumerary captain, Hoskins, had his foot blown off. The ship, still afloat after all this, demanded more effort and attention than admirals Sherman or Halsey could afford. That evening American vessels torpedoed the *Princeton* to scuttle her.

Amid this tragedy, luck befell some American radio spies. Mobile radio detachments placed on warships provided instant readouts on enemy activity, and it had become a feature of Allied tactical practice. FRUMEL (the Fleet Radio Unit Melbourne), the radio spies who worked for Captain McCollum, had formed two detachments to support the invasion. One had been slated for the *Princeton* and left Brisbane for Kossol to pick up the ship. But when they arrived, they discovered she had already sailed. Radioman James B. Capron Jr., a card-carrying member of the On the Roof Gang, was disappointed his team missed the *Princeton* and felt left out when relegated to command ship *Wasatch*. But on the *Princeton*, they might have all wound up dead.

Ships in Leyte Gulf suffered at least two air attacks on October 24, but no ships were hit despite near misses on command ship *Blue Ridge* and the British cruiser *Shropshire*. Nothing slowed down the landings. By that day, 144,000 men and 244,000 tons of supplies had been landed. The Allies had apparently gotten the practice of amphibious landings down to a science. The supply tonnage landed at Leyte the first day had been remarkable, and the flow continued. The success was partly owed to capacity, especially that of the Landing Ship Tank, or LST. Each of these were capable of carrying dozens of loaded trucks, a smaller number of tanks, or pallets holding a couple of thousand tons of supplies, and they could push right up onto the beach. The gulf posed a particular challenge because it was shallow pretty far out. But Allied forces were relatively resourceful: Seabees overcame these difficulties by bulldozing sand into ramps that went right out to meet the LSTs and by tying together pontoon bridge sections into makeshift piers—some that were hundreds of feet long—where the supply ships could dock.

On the *Wasatch*, Radioman Capron had no more reason to feel left out—instead he had a ringside seat as General MacArthur waded ashore for his return to the Philippines. Meanwhile, Kinkaid followed reports of the fighting between Allied aircraft and the approaching Japanese fleet.

A bit after noon, the admiral warned his fleet that there could be a surface naval battle. At half past two, Admiral Kinkaid ordered his heavy unit leader, Rear Admiral Jesse Oldendorf, to prepare for a probable night action in Surigao Strait. An advance unit of thirty-nine PT (patrol torpedo) boats, which had staked out search areas inside the strait, would report in if the enemy were really approaching.

MEAT FOR THE ENEMY

A perfect illustration of the degree to which technical means had come to dominate the "Mark I Eyeball" in the war in the Pacific was the detection of the Kurita fleet. Both the first submarine contacts and the first air sightings began with radar contacts.

The submarines carried the ball through the first quarter. News of the enemy armada reached Admiral Halsey in the form of a dispatch from Australia reporting the *Darter-Dace* submarine attacks, before dawn on October 24. Thereafter, many messages amplified the first: three battleships . . . at least nine big ships . . . then eleven ships, with a speed and a heading. Moon Chapple reported torpedoing the *Aoba* along with the presence of another cruiser and a destroyer. The *Angler* chimed in. The *Guitarro* followed, reporting a task force including probably three battleships. The *Angler* came back with a sighting, indicating the Japanese were skirting Mindoro, soon to enter the Sibuyan Sea.

As the sub reports piled up, Admiral Bill Halsey prepared to receive a determined enemy. From the *New Jersey*, he ordered Third Fleet task groups to move closer to the Philippine archipelago, make dawn searches stronger, and search out to 300 miles. Communications relay planes would repeat their reports. The scout-bomber flights were strengthened, with each search aircraft accompanied by a pair of fighters. Halsey took no chances.

So it was that, at 7:46 a.m., Lieutenant (Junior Grade) Max Adams, a Bombing 18 pilot from the *Intrepid*, radioed his fighter wingmen that he had a suspicious radar indication about twenty-five miles away. They altered course to investigate. Soon enough, the searchers spotted ships off the southern tip of Mindoro. From 9,000 feet in his Helldiver, Lieutenant Adams could not mistake the wakes of two large groups of warships on an easterly heading, entering the Sibuyan Sea. He carefully tabulated five battleships, nine cruisers, and thirteen destroyers. Lieutenant Adams's contact report reached Admirals Halsey and Mitscher and his own group commander, Rear Admiral Bogan, by 8:20 a.m. It sent a shudder through the Third Fleet. Adams had spotted the biggest Japanese surface fleet ever seen.

Bill Halsey would not have been "the Bull" had he not responded aggressively. Halsey had previously been tag-teaming Task Force 38, with two or three task groups on the line and others replenishing. Now he summoned everybody.

Within minutes, Halsey's flagship had rebroadcast the Adams report. Then the Bull ordered Sherman's and Davison's groups to join Bogan's Task Group 38.2. At 8:37 a.m., Halsey ordered all three groups to attack. Ten minutes later, he recalled Slew McCain and Task Group 38.1. Admiral McCain missed the first part of the party, since he was refueling at sea the morning of the twenty-fourth, and he began a high-speed approach to the battle area. Regardless, the Third Fleet had most of its strength available to smash Kurita.

As recorded by the *Essex*, the weather remained cloudy (scattered high clouds and broken cumulus ones nearer the ceiling), but the visibility was twelve miles. The sea was moderate, from the northeast with a slight swell. Over the Sibuyan Sea flying conditions were fine, with scattered cumulus at 1,500 feet but ceiling and visibility unlimited.

Carriers *Intrepid* and *Cabot* began to launch their initial strike package shortly after nine o'clock.

REAR ADMIRAL INOGUCHI Toshihei stood on the bridge of his behemoth *Musashi*. The superbattleship steamed on the starboard quarter of *Yamato*, about a mile away. Inoguchi had sent the crew to eat early. He also assigned *Maya* survivors now aboard his ship to help his own sailors. Like others in the fleet, Inoguchi expected action. As early as 5:30 a.m., he had executive officer Captain Kato Kenkichi dispatch Ensign Shimoyama Fukujiro with a contingent of radiomen down to the number two radio room. Normally the radiomen worked in a communications center just under the bridge, but the other compartment was protected by the ship's armored deck and a hatch nearly a foot thick.

Inoguchi learned from the flagship of an American contact message. At 8:10 a.m., the skipper ordered battle stations. A bugler called the crew to their posts. The ship tried to jam radio signals from the Allied scout. Then came a message from Admiral Kurita: "ENEMY ATTACKERS ARE APPROACHING. TRUST IN THE GODS AND GIVE IT YOUR

BEST." Admiral Inoguchi went on the public address system and passed the information to his sailors. About 9:30 a.m. Petty Officer Hosoya Shiro saw three planes together, which he believed to be the scouts.

They began waiting. It would not be long. Aboard the *Yamato*, staff had calculated roughly when Halsey's fleet might respond. Admiral Kurita sent Mikawa an appeal for air cover. Records indicate that the First Air Fleet sent nine fighters to his defense, but no one in the fleet ever saw them. It was the Americans they saw instead. *Musashi*'s radar picked up the first wave of incoming raiders at 10:00 a.m. Radarmen estimated forty planes, and Admiral Kurita increased formation speed to twenty-two knots.

At 10:18 a.m. lookouts first put eyes on the attackers. With careful selection of sailors for this duty, long training, special vitamins, and very good binoculars, the lookouts spotted incoming raiders more than twenty-five miles away. Though the Japanese did not know it, *Intrepid* and *Cabot* had sent a standard strike package—a dozen each of dive-bombers and torpedo planes covered by twenty-one fighters, under the air group boss, Commander William E. Ellis. The planes closed in steadily, hiding among the cumulus clouds off the starboard beam. Petty Officer Hosoya saw the *Yamato* surrounded by tall geysers of water, but the flagship sailed through them. At 10:25, *Musashi*'s flak batteries went into action. There were simultaneous dive-bombing attacks from starboard at both stem and stern. Moments later torpedo planes launched from starboard. One bomb hit atop the number one main battery turret, causing no damage. A torpedo hit amidships, and there were four near misses, resulting in leaks below the waterline. Ensign Hoshi Shuzo, leader of one of the flak groups, died in strafing. Medium-caliber guns expended forty-eight 6-inch and sixty 5-inch rounds against the attacking planes.

The torpedo hit and leaks caused the huge vessel to list about five and a half degrees to starboard. As exec, Captain Kato took charge of the damage-control efforts. Kato had the longest service on the ship, with four successive skippers. Under him, Lieutenant Kudo Hakari led the unit responsible for balancing the ship, with junior lieutenant Naito Masanao as his action officer. They operated a complex network of pumps, pipes, and compartments that could be flooded or emptied.

Kudo's unit had fifty sailors in several control rooms. They were able to return the vessel to near-normal aspect, with a mere one degree of incline.

Of course, the counterflooding system depended on the ship not having taken on too much water, and having empty compartments available to fill along with electric power for the pump system. *Musashi* had also been designed with independent electrical systems fore and aft. Lieutenant (Junior Grade) Asami Wahei, the electrical engineer who supervised the forward system, had forty sailors and eight 800-kilowatt generators at his disposal. Each system also had an emergency team of six men who could be sent where needed to reconnect electrical cables. Asami was busily supplying power to counterflooding efforts when the situation began deteriorating. Vibrations from the near misses jarred cables and disrupted power to the flak batteries. The fans cut out. Asami rushed to compensate. Without fans the heat spiked. With herculean efforts, Lieutenant Asami kept the generators going.

But the *Musashi*'s ordeal had barely begun. Roughly an hour later, there was another attack. Radar spotted incoming aircraft at 11:54 a.m. This assault had major consequences. The two bomb hits accomplished little, but three torpedoes all struck portside. Launching at little more than 450 yards, the Avengers were at point-blank range. Only fish that were set too deep missed. This time, *Musashi* developed a five-degree list to port and lost a key machinery room. Main battery turrets had to switch to an alternate hydraulic power system. Captain Kato hastened to establish a flooding boundary. The most serious damage came from a bomb on the aft port quarter that severed steam pipes from the number two engine room and cut off one of the boiler rooms. The battleship's inner port shaft had to be locked down.

On the bridge, the skipper had his hands full. With a stopped propeller, maneuvering became tougher as *Musashi* filled with water and became sluggish. In addition, he faced arguments from chief gunner Commander Koshino Kimitake. Koshino wanted to unleash the ship's big guns—he had a supply of special "beehive" antiaircraft shells for the 18.1-inch guns, which might blow attacking planes from the sky many miles away.

At first, Admiral Inoguchi—a gunner himself—resisted using his main armament in a flak role. He wanted to save the guns for cannon-ades in a surface battle. Inoguchi knew from experience that a chance of malfunction exists with every discharge of a big gun, and there would certainly be wear on the rifling in the barrels.

But Commander Koshino was persistent and focused on the air threat. Until then, Inoguchi's experience with air threats had been limited. In 1942, he had escorted convoys in East Indian and Burmese waters, where no enemy air existed, and the next year he drove heavy cruiser *Takao* in the Central Pacific under Admiral Kurita—again a safe sector. He had relinquished command in the autumn of 1943, only days before *Takao* had steamed into Rabaul to be blasted by that American carrier raid. Inoguchi must have pondered his fate in avoid-ing the slaughter at Rabaul, but it was really only at the Philippine Sea battle that he first faced an air threat.

(Historians Robert Hackett and Sander Kingsepp argue that Rear Admiral Inoguchi himself prepared detailed plans for air defense of the ship based on the beehive antiaircraft shells. Perhaps they refer to a contingency plan. At his lookout post, Petty Officer Hosoya overheard his superiors' argument over the voice tube. In view of Inoguchi's gunnery expertise and knowledge that the fleet was headed for a gun battle with himself in command of one of its two strongest ships, it seems unlikely that he intended from the outset to employ the special ammunition.)

Koshino returned to reargue his case. As the *Musashi* fell behind, she lost the protection of the fleet's powerful antiaircraft array. Koshi-no's associate, the ship's flak boss, Lieutenant Commander Hirose Eisuke, agreed they needed everything they could muster. Strafing Amer-ican planes were taking a toll on his gun crews. Ammunition supplies were dwindling. A torpedo from the second attack knocked out the main battery's forward fire director. The guns might not be all that great in a surface battle anyway.

Admiral Inoguchi finally relented. The main battery loaded 18.1-inch *sanshiki-dan* shells, as the beehive rounds were known, and fired a nine-gun salvo at the third-wave assailants. The middle gun of the number one turret failed. One account attributes this to a hot fragment from a bomb flying down the barrel and detonating the round, another to the shell itself sticking in the barrel. That turret fell silent.

At the third strike, a torpedo hit starboard sent smoke and fumes surging into the forward sick bay, which had to be evacuated. Several sailors were overcome by carbon monoxide poisoning, including Ensign Suzuki Yakaku, leader of the forward damage-control party. Concussion from a bomb that missed close on the aft quarter blew two men from posts in the aft flak-control station to the aircraft hangar. A sailor suffered an injury and later died, but Ensign Kanechika Hisao miraculously emerged unscathed. Counterflooding efforts failed, and *Musashi*'s bow began drooping.

The next American strikers, launched at 10:45 a.m., attacked at 12:45 p.m. The Japanese estimated twenty planes. The beehive rounds seemed to bother no one—and *Musashi* used up seventy-nine in all that day. Among the attackers in this wave were four TBMs with torpedoes; every one of them hit. With the latest strikes, the superbattleship flooded up to the middle deck forward, now down four degrees. A torpedo hit to starboard and collapsed shoring put up to counter previous damage. A pair of bomb hits to port, meanwhile, wiped out almost all the damage-control men in the forward part of the ship.

Aft, Lieutenant Kudo Hakari's damage-control party held their position with difficulty. Kudo mustered sailors to help put up cofferdams and hold back the sea. Desperate pumping reduced starboard list to just one degree. But Lieutenant Naito had run out of tanks to fill. He had reached the point where counterflooding could continue only by sending water into spaces meant to stay dry. With Kudo preoccupied by his frontline actions, Lieutenant Naito headed for the bridge to explain their predicament to Admiral Inoguchi and obtain his decision.

Musashi gradually lost speed. Lookout Hosoya estimated the distance to her formation at the time of the second attack at more than six miles. By early afternoon, it had doubled. Heavy cruiser *Tone* stood by the stricken behemoth. After the third attack, Inoguchi's unit commander, Admiral Ugaki, ordered the battleship to make for Coron Bay. A little later Vice Admiral Suzuki Yoshio, commanding the second of Kurita's two ring formations, the one built around battleships *Kongo* and *Haruna*, instructed *Musashi* to approach it for cover from his defensive umbrella. But that, too, became impractical as the fleet pressed ahead and *Musashi* lost headway. Finally Ugaki ordered Inoguchi to make for the nearest port if he could proceed under power or be towed—either that, or to beach the ship.

Early afternoon brought the moment of decision. A huge attack wave—the Japanese counted seventy-five planes—came into sight. Commander Theodore H. Winters Jr. of the *Lexington* coordinated the strike initially. Planes from that ship and the *Essex* were joined in midaction by another formation from Admiral Davison's Task Group 38.4. Accounts are confusing in terms of the numbers of aircraft, times of launch, attack, and so on. Together there were 259 sorties against the Kurita fleet that day. By Samuel Eliot Morison's account, there were at least 39 torpedo planes, 26 dive-bombers, and 34 fighters in this strike overall.

On the Japanese side, the majority of Commander Hirose's flak guns now lacked either crews or ready ammunition—or both. Ammunition expended against this wave included thirty-five beehive rounds and seventy-nine 6-inch shells. Inoguchi progressively reduced the ship's speed—from twenty-four knots to twenty-two to sixteen, and now twelve knots. A higher speed would flood the ship even faster, and *Musashi*'s stem was already nearly awash because of the trim forward. Water in the hull that could have been pumped to restore buoyancy was not—Captain Kato may have been unable to keep up with the string of emergencies, or the ship's power supplies (several firerooms were no longer operating) were no longer adequate. Whatever the case, it was a major setback.

The new attack proved decisive. In a matter of minutes, ten bombs and eleven torpedoes blasted the *Musashi*. One bomb from an *Intrepid* plane hit the top of the conning tower and demolished the bridge (and another hit portside, further down the tower), seriously wounding Admiral Inoguchi in the right shoulder and starting a fire there and in flag plot. Sailors put that out immediately, using water from an emergency barrel on the bridge. But Commander Hirose, the ship's navigator, Commander Kariya Minoru, five other officers, and thirty-two men were killed and more injured. Lieutenant Commander Nagai Teizo, a survivor and former executive officer of the *Maya*, perished on the flag deck. They were only some of the casualties. Bombs inflicted extensive damage on aviation facilities; others destroyed radio rooms. A couple of the torpedoes were duds, but those that weren't inflicted grievous damage. Firerooms were out, another engine room was lost, magazine compartments of two lower decks had to be flooded, the starboard list increased ten to twelve degrees, and speed declined to just six knots, which was not enough for the ship to steer.

Rear Admiral Inoguchi scribbled in a notebook he handed to Kato Kenkichi. He had been deeply shaken by the air attacks. The gunner wrote that he regretted having put too much faith in big guns and big ships. At that moment, Inoguchi must have thought his brother, with the First Air Fleet, and his son—a young JNAF pilot then in Japan—had found the path of the future. He instructed Captain Kato to make sure the notebook reached Admiral Toyoda, and also put him in charge of making sure the crewmen were saved and the *Maya* survivors rescued for the second time. Inoguchi shut himself in his cabin, never to be seen again.

Four more hours passed before the *Musashi* actually sank, a little after 7:30 p.m. Kato had time to assemble the crew on deck and hold a roll call. But it was without a doubt that the airplanes had doomed the superbattleship.

WHAT HAPPENED ON the *Musashi* was just a small part of a larger tapestry. Kurita's fleet making its way across the Sibuyan Sea represented the other panel.

The fleet continued its voyage. At 9:23 a.m., in case there was a fight at the San Bernardino Strait, Admiral Kurita ordered the torpedo crews on all ships to be ready by nightfall. Kurita and his chief of staff, Koyanagi, expected to face air attacks. Admiral Ugaki's rough estimate of the time the Allied planes might show up turned out to be accurate. A dispatch from Kurita to Combined Fleet at 10:55 reported attack by about thirty planes.

At the moment of the first wave, *Musashi* had been steaming in column behind the heavy cruiser *Myoko*. Rear Admiral Ishihara Itsu's cruiser had the lead slot in the starboard wing of Admiral Kurita's ring. When the American planes swung in for their attacks, one torpedo slammed into Ishihara's warship. At the very moment Kurita informed Toyoda of their peril, Ishihara was recording the torpedo hit in *Myoko*'s aftermost starboard engine room. The engine room crew were completely wiped out—an officer, a warrant officer, and eleven seamen were killed, and three sailors injured. The ship stopped and began to list. By 11:05 a.m., salt water had contaminated the main-feed water tank serving the number four engine, forcing it to be shut down. The *Myoko*, which had been reduced to one working propeller, could not manage more than twelve knots—though she could pump out at a rate of a couple of hundred tons an hour—and became a clear liability. Vice Admiral Hashimoto Shintaro, commanding Cruiser Division 5, shifted his flag to its other ship, the *Haguro*. Kurita ordered Ishihara back to Coron Bay, radioing the news to Toyoda.

A second strike materialized, then a third one. Many of Kurita's sailors had gone to battle stations without breakfast, and the new raid came at lunchtime. By now, the *Musashi* had begun dropping back. At first Admiral Kurita ordered speed reduced from twenty-five to twenty-two knots so the superbattleship could keep up. Later, he decided to press on and left the *Musashi* behind. Frustration levels rose steadily. Kurita wondered what had become of Ozawa's decoy mission and the air attacks that were supposed to support him. At 1:15 p.m., under renewed attack, Kurita sent a dispatch to Ozawa and Mikawa, with copies to Toyoda and the air fleets: "WE ARE BEING SUBJECTED TO REPEATED ENEMY CARRIER-BASED AIR ATTACKS. ADVISE IMMEDIATELY OF CONTACTS MADE BY YOU ON THE ENEMY."

Imperial Navy officers paid a steadily mounting personal price for their participation in this death ride. "We had expected air attacks," chief of staff Koyanagi records, "but this day's were almost enough to discourage us." Admiral Ugaki, who had lived on the *Musashi*, known to the fleet as "the Palace," felt that losing her "is like losing part of myself." He went on, "Nothing I can say will justify this loss. . . . Today was *Musashi*'s day of misfortune, tomorrow it will be *Yamato*'s turn."

Admiral Kurita's message demonstrates the strain.

NO ONE WORE the mantle of command more easily than Kurita Takeo. The Second Fleet commander bore it as if it were gossamer, despite lacking such rites as graduation from the Naval War College. From Mito

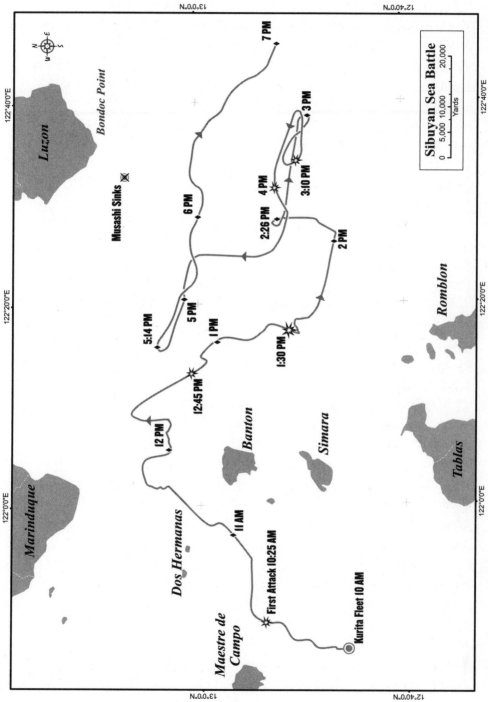

Sibuyan Sea Battle

town on Honshu, northeast of Tokyo, Kurita came from a family of scholars. The town had long been known as a center of support for Japan's shoguns, the strongmen who ruled in the name of the emperor, and Takeo's grandfather, a professor at the University of Tokyo, had authored a famous history of the Meiji Restoration. His father chose classical names—of women mostly—for six brothers, but "Takeo" meant "warrior." Still, his father insisted Takeo read into Confucianism, poring over volumes written in classical Chinese ideographs and imparting an attitude combining charity, gentleness, and kindness. Kurita's sailors uniformly agreed their admiral always looked out for them.

That did not mean Kurita lacked an edge. He could be very competitive. Apart from his command qualities, another way Takeo impressed colleagues was as a competitor. Like Bill Halsey he played tennis. When his ships were in port Kurita went for baseball. Once Takeo became senior enough to command big ships and fleets he would have targets put out for him on the quarterdecks of his flagships. Wherever he was, the admiral practiced archery, peppering the targets with arrows. In the U.S. Navy society of his era Kurita would have played polo. Chief of staff Koyanagi considered him a great athlete. He stood out.

Kurita became a torpedoman, for the Japanese in those days the equivalent of a fighter pilot. According to Koyanagi, Takeo had very sharp reflexes and short reaction times. In the Navy that made a difference—Kurita became a good ship driver. Come the war, his record was remarkable. Admiral Kurita entered World War II holding pennant number 107 on the Navy List (Ozawa Jisaburo was at number 66, Mikawa Gunichi at number 69, Shima Kiyohide at number 154). At the time of Leyte, Kurita was a fifty-five-year-old vice admiral.

In a Navy that prized aggressiveness, Kurita Takeo still stood out. At the Battle of Sunda Strait in February 1942, Kurita's ships had helped sink U.S. and Australian cruisers. The admiral had then led his cruiser division on a raid into the Indian Ocean, even though the British Eastern Fleet had battleships, and he had none. At Midway in June 1942, Kurita's flotilla had been the only Japanese force other than Combined Fleet's carriers to be bombed. Kurita had raced ahead to comply with orders to bombard Midway Island, though his request for support had been rejected, and he had made an extraordinary effort to keep the unrealistic schedule given to him by higher command—so much so that his cruisers outran their escorts. In the Solomons, Kurita's battleships had shelled Guadalcanal. At the Battle of Santa Cruz, he had actually had the U.S. aircraft carrier *Hornet* (by that point a derelict) under his guns. At Rabaul in November 1943, his Second Fleet—then composed entirely of Imperial Navy cruisers—had been famously smashed by U.S. carrier planes. At the Philippine Sea battle, conversely, Kurita's task group had been the only Japanese flotilla to lose no aircraft carriers.

In *Combined Fleet Decoded*, my framing of the Pacific war in light of the first intelligence revelations, I wrote that Kurita had been bombed, shelled, torpedoed, and generally harassed more than almost any other Japanese commander. And that is true—but it was because he kept putting himself in harm's way. I used the phrase "gun-shy" to suggest that Kurita, by the time of Leyte Gulf, had developed a healthy apprehension for Allied aircraft. Historian Evan Thomas, drawing his picture of the admiral, portrays Kurita as super-gun-shy—the "Zelig of sea battle." Overall, he casts Kurita as conservative, a man preoccupied with the "fleet-in-being," or rather, force protection. I disagree with the proposition that Kurita was a Zelig—that is, someone near harm's way, but more often at a distance than in the thick of the fight, hiding from the action. It is easy to take that analysis too far. The fact of the matter is that Kurita could not have been bombed, torpedoed, and whatnot more than other commanders *without* being at the center of the action.

In early 1943, the Imperial Navy promoted Kurita to command the Second Fleet. That unit was *the* one that in the Japanese vision of the "decisive battle" was supposed to dash at the enemy to weaken it with gun and torpedo action so the Imperial Navy battleships could finish off the adversary. By putting Kurita in that role it appears the Japanese were not casting him as a "fleet-in-being" man either.

The personnel officers who did that had known Kurita a very long time. Yamamoto Isoroku, still alive then—and thought to be an excellent judge of talent—shared with Kurita a taste for Johnnie Walker

Black Label scotch. Kusaka Ryunosuke, now chief of staff to Toyoda, had been at Santa Cruz too, in the same role for the Japanese carrier admiral then. He knew Kurita as "an exceedingly intrepid sailor." Mikawa Gunichi, who was renowned for his aggressiveness and also reprised the role he had had in the Solomons, considered Kurita his best friend, unlikely if his Etajima classmate had really been a coward.

In deciding whether to count Kurita Takeo as gun-shy, the most important period is the interval he held the reins of the Second Fleet. The Allies had certainly administered a shock in the cruiser massacre at Rabaul. The Combined Fleet had been driven from its bases at Truk and then Palau. On the other hand, Admiral Kurita had led one of Ozawa's major flotillas during the Philippine Sea battle, and in that action it is fair to suppose he gained confidence—a concentrated attack by the Big Blue Fleet succeeded in inflicting only minor damage on one of the carriers Kurita protected, and one of his surface ships escorting her.

PERSONAL CHARACTER IS one thing, but experience is another, and Kurita Takeo in the Sibuyan Sea that day had been through thirty-six hours of sheer hell. He had had to escape from his sinking flagship—drenched and ruining a very good pair of shoes. One of his two strongest gunnery ships, the *Musashi*, had dropped out of formation. Celebrated as unsinkable, she was on the verge of foundering. The damage to heavy cruiser *Myoko* made her the fourth vessel of her type to be lost—and all of this before any contact with the enemy fleet. The air attacks of early afternoon brought bomb damage to battleships *Yamato*, *Nagato*, and *Haruna* plus one of Kurita's scarce destroyers. And on top of that, the admiral still faced the mystery of what the Imperial Navy was doing to support him—the air attacks and the Mobile Fleet's decoy sortie lay beyond the event horizon so far as Kurita was concerned.

Kurita's situation in the Sibuyan Sea bore a marked resemblance to his forlorn cruiser mission off Midway. There, Admiral Kurita had been put on a limb in the face of the Allied air armada. Here, too, Admiral Kurita had to make a very concrete decision regarding tactics. In his original plan, his own force and that of Vice Admiral Nishimura were to break into Leyte Gulf at the same time—before dawn the next morning—from different directions. The Second Fleet could no longer make that schedule, slowed by submarine and air attacks plus efforts to conserve fuel; delays only mounted. By now the fleet was running six hours late. Giving up the advantage from the simultaneous storming of Leyte, Kurita now pondered how to maximize his weight acting alone.

The air assault after one o'clock inflicted decisive damage on *Musashi*. The *Yamato* also endured a bomb hit. Two more waves of carrier planes hit during the three o'clock hour, crippling *Musashi*, inflicting more bomb damage to *Yamato*, and wounding battleship *Nagato* enough to reduce her to twenty-one knots. Light cruiser *Yahagi* also lost speed due to a few near misses.

Staff chief Koyanagi records that Admiral Kurita had, from an early point in the Sho preparations, spoken of historical precedents, among them the great Battle of Jutland in World War I. A feature of that 1916 action had been the German fleet's use of turning away in midbattle to rob the adversary of targets and perhaps confuse them. An old sea dog like Kurita had to be attentive to what had been the most remarkable torpedo work of the world war—it was hard also not to be impressed by their use of the battle turnaway. It is likely that Kurita intended, in advance, to use a similar tactic under air attack en route to Leyte.

In the Sibuyan Sea on October 24, 1944, a turn to the west, away from the San Bernardino Strait, would permit Kurita to regroup and hopefully allow his damaged warships to lick their wounds. The last American attackers flew away by about 3:30 p.m. One scout plane remained, watching. At four o'clock, Admiral Kurita ordered a westward turn. Commander Ishida Tsuneo, the *Yamato* paymaster, who had been seconded to act as deputy to Koyanagi Tomiji, thought the turnaway brilliant. Others were less impressed.

Kurita intended from the beginning to reverse course again once the coast was clear. Given that intention, it might have been best to say nothing, but senior staff officer Yamamoto and operations staffer Otani advised him to inform the high command. Kurita then sent a radio dispatch to the Combined Fleet:

OUR DAMAGES ARE NOT LIGHT. THE FREQUENCY AND NUMER-
ICAL STRENGTH OF THESE ENEMY ATTACKS ARE INCREASING.
IF WE CONTINUE OUR PRESENT COURSE OUR LOSSES WILL
INCREASE INCALCULABLY, WITH LITTLE HOPE OF SUCCESS
FOR OUR MISSION.

Another version of this message makes more colorful reading:
"UNDER THESE CIRCUMSTANCES, WE WOULD MERELY MAKE OF
OURSELVES MEAT FOR THE ENEMY." Either way Kurita Takeo reached
the same conclusion:

THEREFORE, HAVE DECIDED TO WITHDRAW OUTSIDE THE
RANGE OF ENEMY AIR ATTACK FOR THE TIME BEING, AND TO
RESUME OUR SORTIE IN COORDINATION WITH SUCCESSFUL
ATTACKS ON THE ENEMY BY OUR AIR FORCES.

The description of this measure as temporary, and even more, the
prompt return to the base course when Halsey's air attacks ended, both
suggest the employment of a premeditated tactic.

Consternation prevailed when Hiyoshi learned what Kurita had
done. Chief of staff Kusaka records that Combined Fleet headquarters
was at a complete loss. Events that day had already afflicted command
staff with deep foreboding. The operations room went silent when word
came that *Musashi* had been damaged. Then even more so when the
Yamato was hit by bombs and torpedoes, when *Musashi* fell out of
formation, and with the reports of damage to other vessels. Then the
operations staffer Captain Mikami Sakuo showed him a draft he had
hurriedly scribbled on a message form. Addressed to Kurita, the message ordered him to attack.

Mikami took his draft to C-in-C Toyoda, who had the ultimate
authority. Admiral Toyoda understood how Kurita might find the air
attacks unbearable and be tempted to turn back. But Allied air could
pursue the fleet just as easily. Toyoda reasoned the losses would not
differ much no matter what Kurita did. Commander Mikami's message
struck Toyoda as the right thing to say. But his decision to send the

dispatch, Toyoda reflected, seemed as difficult as choosing to swallow molten iron.

The message went out as Operations Order No. 372: "WITH CON-FIDENCE IN HEAVENLY GUIDANCE, THE ENTIRE FORCE WILL ATTACK!" Kurita thought this was idiotic—something out of a play. Instead of information on the situation, he was given homilies.

As Admiral Toyoda put it to interrogators after the war, "The meaning of that order was, while it does not appear in the wording . . . that damage could not be limited or reduced by turning back, so advance even though the fleet should be completely lost." Toyoda here freed Kurita from any concern over the extent of his losses, and the C-in-C felt confident his Second Fleet commander would not turn back after getting such a message.

In retrospect, Kusaka decided it had been an impossible mission. C-in-C Toyoda and Kusaka and their subordinates were completely aware the Kurita fleet had become an exposed force with no fighter escort. On the other hand, a successful defense of Leyte meant holding all the Philippines. They supported Kurita's appeals to Japanese air commanders for fighter cover. Admiral Onishi replied with a dispatch asking if X-Day could be pushed back a few days for him to bring up additional fighters. Kusaka knew that limited oil supplies rendered delay impossible. Toyoda knew how difficult preparations had been. If it was called off, there could be no revival.

The story of the "divine guidance" message created controversy. Admiral Toyoda sent off his message, only to receive the Kurita dispatch quoted previously not long afterward. The C-in-C could not believe his field commander would spurn an order like that. He had the message repeated. Communications officers checked and determined that Admiral Kurita's 4:00 p.m. dispatch definitely had followed Toyoda's battle order. But the report Kurita filed after the battle records the "divine guidance" message at 6:15. The dispatch had been delayed for several hours (as was the repeat transmission). Japanese communications were fouled up throughout the Sho operation, and that would be a serious weak point.

In the meantime, no more Task Force 38 strike waves appeared over the Kurita fleet. Admiral Kurita, quick to take advantage, ordered a resumption of the original course at 5:15 p.m. The Imperial Navy armada aimed again at the San Bernardino Strait, and it would arrive there around midnight. Kurita Takeo would have his day of battle after all.

CHAPTER 8

THE FIRST TEAM VERSUS THE RISING SUN

I t's hard to imagine today, when the U.S. military is entirely professional and widely regarded as the most skilled on the planet, that World War II was a time when the nation called its citizens to arms, blended them with a small professional force, and created a military that was the equal of any in the world. But it happened. And the events surrounding this climax of the Pacific campaign display this expert citizen military. Task Force 38 alone, dominant over the Japanese at every stage since Bull Halsey's first Philippine sally weeks before, convincingly demonstrates U.S. proficiency. Carrier air over the Sibuyan Sea had sent the unsinkable *Musashi*, the best the Imperial Navy had, to the bottom of the ocean.

During the next twelve hours the Allies would show their prowess again—but the Japanese would face the dawn in a breathtakingly superior strategic position. Allied might. Japanese stratagem. A tale for the ages.

OPPORTUNITY OFFERED OR CREATED

All this began with Admiral William F. Halsey. Days away from his sixty-first birthday, Bill Halsey found himself immersed in the biggest aero-naval battle to date. The decisions required were commensurately huge. Halsey had previously expressed himself regarding Pacific war strategy and not only had played a role in Roosevelt's selection of the Philippines over Taiwan as a goal, but also had been instrumental in accelerating the plan and in making the invasion possible by lending his own ground forces to General MacArthur. Now it became a matter of proving the validity of that choice in reality—against a Japanese reaction that can only be described as monumental. Bull Halsey had made a fine start, tearing across the archipelago with his carrier raids and hitting at the Inner Empire. In the Sibuyan Sea on October 24, Task Force 38 warplanes had seemed invincible, the Kurita fleet merely prey.

But then something happened. While some of Halsey's airmen were away pummeling the Japanese fleet, Task Force 38—more specifically the *Princeton*—engaged a second wave of JNAF attackers that had come from a direction that indicated they were *carrier* planes.

All along Bull Halsey had been wrestling with the question of where the Japanese carriers were, while Marc Mitscher and others tried to answer it. The location and activities of Imperial Navy carriers remained an item on the menu at every skull session of Halsey's "Dirty Tricks" staff. In flag plot on the *New Jersey*, the instant demand was: Find the Jap carriers!

Of course, Admiral Ozawa wanted to be found. The admiral decided to confirm a JNAF sighting of American carriers with a search plane of his own. It did—but the reported position turned out to be 80 miles off, so Ozawa's precaution proved fortunate. American sailors—both ship interceptor directors and air officers—often tracked back Japanese search planes to discover what forces had sent them. This time they did not. Ozawa gave up radio silence and broadcast a welter of messages from *Zuikaku*. That ought to have been a dead giveaway. Indeed, OP-20-G reported from Washington that radio direction finding and analysis placed the C-in-C of the Mobile Fleet within 250 miles of a point east of Luzon on the twenty-fourth. But radio snafus (the same ones that bedeviled Ozawa with Kurita and others) precluded Third Fleet from intercepting his messages. Gil Slonim's monitors, hearing nothing from the carriers, focused their all on the Kurita fleet and Nishimura force. That night, Ozawa would put his two hermaphrodite battleship-carriers into an advance force under Rear Admiral Matsuda Chiaki and send it ahead of his fleet. They reached within 100 miles of Halsey's nearest ships before being detected. Ozawa's force maneuvered east and north of the point on Luzon known as Cape Engaño.

At 4:40 p.m., Japanese efforts were rewarded. Ted Sherman of Task

Group 38.3 had sent a fresh set of scouts off to the north a couple of hours before, and now a *Lexington* search plane found the Ozawa force 190 miles away, northeast of Cape Engaño. Task Force 38 commander Marc Mitscher stood on a bridge wing watching the agony of the *Princeton* through binoculars. His chief of staff, Commodore Burke, suddenly burst out of flag plot, running a copy of the sighting report to the boss. Mitscher, like Halsey, had been following the plight of the stricken carrier and trying to make sense of the confusing pilot claims. The sudden appearance of Japanese aircraft carriers crystallized all the questions that had for so long been purely hypothetical.

The fleet might have been full of citizen soldiers, but the men who made the decisions were professionals all the way—and remarkably, they were afflicted with a sense of purpose that was the mirror image of that of the Imperial Navy admirals, with their obsession with enemy fleets as opposed to invasion convoys. Admiral Mitscher had suffered an immense disappointment at the last great naval battle—Philippine Sea. He had sent out his attack groups, only for them to find the Japanese carriers as the sun set, at the limit of their range. The enemy had escaped then. Mitscher wanted them now.

As Third Fleet commander, Bull Halsey would make the ultimate decision; the ball was in his court. Halsey's entire experience led him to value the aircraft carrier as the ultimate weapon of this war. He had been able to operate after Pearl Harbor because he'd been in a carrier. In the South Pacific, Halsey had saved Guadalcanal on the strength of the single carrier flight deck left to him after the Japanese won their last aero-naval victory. A year later, Halsey had turned the tables and inflicted a Pearl Harbor on the Japanese—on Kurita Takeo as a matter of fact. William Halsey was conditioned to gravitate toward taking out carriers.

Admiral Chester Nimitz, Halsey's direct superior, had been perfectly aware of the Bull's proclivities. He employed Halsey precisely *because* of his aggressiveness. And Nimitz, too, had a bit of the carrier fixation in him. His orders governing Third Fleet's role in MacArthur's invasion contained an escape clause—the support mission could be set aside to destroy major Japanese naval forces. The text read: "In case opportunity for destruction of major portion of the enemy fleet is offered or can be created, such destruction becomes the primary task." The key word was "major." Halsey parroted that text in his own operations order. It could be foreseen that Bill Halsey would view an Imperial Navy carrier flotilla as a major force. The sequence of events that followed showed Halsey's sensibilities perfectly.

None of this was a bolt from the blue. Halsey's hair trigger is demonstrated by constant skull sessions among staff on how to deal with Japanese aircraft carriers. Americans did war gaming too, and the Dirty Tricksters had repeatedly gamed engagements with enemy carriers on a play area created on a deck in *New Jersey*'s admiral's country. And since the beginning of Halsey's rampage, the issue of his predilections had already arisen—when the Combined Fleet had briefly sent out Shima's unit to dispose of supposed Allied cripples. Admiral Halsey had readied Third Fleet for a big aero-naval battle.

While making preparations, on October 24 at 3:12 p.m., the Third Fleet commander sent a message he considered to be a contingency alert. It specified which ships (six fast battleships, two heavy and three light cruisers, and thirteen destroyers) would make up Task Force 34 *if* he ordered its activation. CINCPAC received an information copy of this dispatch, which Halsey thought of as internal housekeeping. The arrangements should have worked well. He provided a contingency plan for Leyte—preparations to form Task Force 34, his surface attack force led by Vice Admiral Willis Augustus "Ching" Lee. The fast battleships plus Bogan's carriers could be left, if necessary, to defend the San Bernardino Strait, while the rest of the fleet went in search of the enemy carriers. In his mind, Kurita's fleet had been badly wounded, and now Halsey wanted to take on the Japanese carriers.

General MacArthur's command arrangements helped create the eventual problem. They permitted no direct channel for communication between Halsey and his opposite number in the Seventh Fleet, Vice Admiral Thomas C. Kinkaid. That put a premium on listening in to the other fleet's circuits. Halsey thought himself speaking only to his own Third Fleet in warning for the contingency just mentioned. But Kinkaid's radiomen copied the Halsey messages, and the Seventh Fleet commander decided these moves had actually been made, not that Admiral Halsey had been sending warning messages. The outsiders were not even supposed to know about that message, much less reach conclusions based on it. But Nimitz and MacArthur's commands both took the signal as Halsey's affirmative instruction to Admiral Lee to form up the battleships.

Equally significant, it was not a given that had Halsey detached his battleships they would block the San Bernardino. The controversy over "Bull's Run" begins with this alleged failure. What Halsey could have done on the afternoon of October 24 was force a fleet-to-fleet engagement—*after* Kurita's naval assault off Samar, and certainly before the Japanese retraced their steps and escaped; or about when Kurita re-transited the San Bernardino *with a much reduced force.*

A lot of officers thought as did Kinkaid—that Bogan and Lee (and Halsey, since his flagship belonged to Lee's task force) would be staying to guard the San Bernardino Strait. Up until the time they went to bed, that remained the impression of both operations chief General Riley and mobile radio detachment boss Gilven Slonim. But they discounted the developments that Admiral Halsey put at center stage, those discoveries that *Lexington*'s spotters induced him to reconsider.

Flagship *New Jersey* received word of Kurita's battle turnaway only minutes ahead of the news that another enemy stood off Cape Engaño. Not only that, but the Ozawa sighting contained news that the Imperial Navy force contained carriers *and* two battleships. From Halsey's perspective, that sighting put things in a different light. Though the enemy possessed but four carriers—just one of them a big fleet carrier (against the Americans, with a dozen of assorted sizes)—they had battleships. This certainly comprised a "major" force.

As he saw it, Admiral Halsey had three options. He could stay and guard the San Bernardino with his entire force, but that seemed to concede freedom of action to Japanese air forces, both sea and land based. It would also have breached his core instruction to seek battle with a major Japanese fleet. Alternatively, Halsey could detach the battleships of Task Force 34 to guard San Bernardino and head north with his carriers. The admiral viewed that as a half measure and a dilution of his force. And because the flak defenses of his carrier groups would be greatly weakened, Japanese aircraft might achieve much more

than if the Third Fleet stayed together. The third option was to go after
Ozawa with all three carrier groups in hand.

Halsey's reasoning is worth quoting: "It preserved my fleet's integrity, it left the initiative with me, and it promised the greatest possibility of surprise. Even if the [Kurita fleet] meanwhile penetrated San
Bernardino and headed for Leyte Gulf, it could only hope to harry the
landing operation." Elsewhere the fleet commander argues, "We had
long since decided the carriers were potentially the most dangerous
ships the Japs had. . . . We named them our primary targets." And as
for the Japanese in the Sibuyan Sea, "We knew Kurita's ships had suffered damage from our attacks, particularly to their upper works and
probably to their fire control instruments." The admiral stormed into
flag plot, stabbed at Ozawa's position marked on a chart, and declared
to chief of staff Robert Carney, "Here's where we're going. Mick, start
them north."

There is the sense here that many tried to keep Halsey from "Bull's
Run"—as the wags were soon calling it—but that he persevered. First
up was the Bull's own staff, or at least his junior fleet intelligence officer Lieutenant Harris Cox. Carl Solberg, Harris's cabinmate and colleague, gave us a detailed account of how Cox looked at captured
documents—those Japanese Z Plan translations—ruminating over
them for days, finally concluding they portended a whole new enemy
strategy: to go for the transports. Lieutenant Cox made the argument
to fleet intelligence officer Captain Mike Cheek. The purpose of the
Japanese carrier force just discovered must be to facilitate attacks on
the invasion force. It had to be a decoy, in this case to open the way
for the Kurita fleet. Cheek had already had a run-in that evening with
the staff duty officer. "They're coming through, I know," Cheek declared, referring to Kurita through San Bernardino Strait. "I've played
poker with them in Tokyo."

When Captain Cheek came back to make an argument based on
the Z Plan documents, that went over no better. Cheek disappeared
into admiral's country, where Halsey and Carney had their sea cabins,
and spoke to the chief of staff. Carney remained adamant but, recognizing the serious nature of Cheek's deduction, gave him leave to
awaken Halsey if he dared. But "the Mick" warned the intelligence

officer that their boss was unlikely to be swayed. Taking Carney's point, Captain Cheek desisted.

Ironically, this is one of those moments when one could be right for the wrong reasons. The Z Plan translations are clear: Allied convoys *were* to be targeted, but only *after* elimination of the enemy "task forces"—in Japanese usage, the carrier fleet. Transports were the contingent target, fleets the primary one. But there were other indicators too, some receiving better attention from Art McCollum at SEFIC.

Just a couple of weeks earlier, SEFIC's *Seventh Fleet Bulletin* publication had carried an article drawn from another captured document called "Striking Force Tactics." That had advocated using empty aircraft carriers as a diversion. A Japanese sailor captured from the sinking light cruiser *Nagara* that summer had attributed the same role to the Imperial Navy's battleship-carriers. One of those vessels appeared in the first sighting of Ozawa. Both of them were, in fact, there. Bottom line: There *were* intelligence indications pointing to a proper interpretation of Ozawa's part; they were just not the ones Lieutenant Cox singled out.

Shortly before 8:00 p.m., Halsey had his chief of staff draft messages to array the force and inform counterparts. Mick Carney's message for Kinkaid was: "CENTRAL FORCE HEAVILY DAMAGED ACCORDING TO STRIKE REPORTS. AM PROCEEDING NORTH WITH 3 GROUPS TO ATTACK CARRIER FORCE AT DAWN."

The assumptions continued. Admiral Kinkaid—and apparently Nimitz also—decided Halsey had meant he was pursuing Ozawa with three groups less the fast battleships. They further inferred that, if Ching Lee's battleships were detached, their mission would be to block the San Bernardino.

Mike Cheek and Harris Cox were not the only men to divine the true Japanese scheme. Also on that list were the admiral's chief subordinates, Marc A. Mitscher; his chief of staff, Arleigh Burke; and Ching Lee, the battleship driver. Mitscher had brainstormed a way to hit Ozawa and double back—detach Task Force 34, send Admiral Lee north on a high-speed dash after the Mobile Fleet, then launch him at Leyte. Ching Lee should be able to catch Kurita either before or just after the Japanese reached the gulf. Task Force 38 carriers could finish off anyone who was left. Commodore Burke proposed a variant: to use only the two fast battleships with Ted Sherman's group. Admiral Mitscher went so far as a preparatory order to make the detachment after nightfall. Staff urged Mitscher to sell the plan to Halsey.

Chief of Staff Burke also thought more deeply on Ozawa's role. He was convinced the enemy carrier force was so weak it must be a decoy. "I think you're right," Mitscher replied, "but I don't know you're right. . . . I don't think we should bother Admiral Halsey. He's busy enough. He's got a lot of things on his mind."

In some versions of this story, Pete Mitscher had suffered a heart attack during these weeks of campaigning, shielded by Halsey, desperate to get Slew McCain up to speed. Regardless of the veracity of that, Mitscher *was* slowing down and doing less. When he received the fleet commander's "three groups north" order, Mitscher concluded Halsey had assumed tactical control and at that point had withdrawn. He went to bed.

Then there was Vice Admiral Lee. He, too, worried about the disposition of the Third Fleet. Prepared to pull together the elements of Task Force 34 that afternoon, Ching Lee became alarmed when no "execute" order followed. When the night search reported Kurita back on a course for San Bernardino Strait, Admiral Lee went on the TBS, the short-range radio system that linked Allied vessels, and asked the *New Jersey* if the fleet commander knew what was happening. "ROGER," came the answer.

The issue sharpened. Light carrier *Independence* had been armed with a night-capable air group completely composed of radar-equipped planes. Admiral Mitscher ordered out a night patrol. One scout saw the Kurita fleet and shadowed it. The Japanese were headed for the San Bernardino Strait after all. American fliers kept watch until Kurita entered the strait. Their final report was timed at 11:05 p.m. The lighthouse there had been fired up. The last pilot on the mission, Lieutenant Bill Phelps, told colleagues Imperial Navy warships had turned on their navigation lights and were using searchlights to bathe the shore in illumination as they nosed into the strait. Kurita debouched into the Philippine Sea soon after midnight. Receiving the night shadow reports,

Ching Lee communicated with the flagship anew. Were they aware? "ROGER." Sarcasm almost dripped from the sparse reply.

The final report of Kurita, now inside the San Bernardino Strait, also went to Commodore Burke. Once he received confirmation, Burke took air officer James Flatley and woke up the task force leader, renewing the recommendation to detach Ching Lee with Task Force 34 and aim him at the strait. Mitscher asked if Halsey had the same report. Assured that he did, Mitscher turned over and went back to sleep.

Rear Admiral Bogan, who commanded the task group that actually contained the *Independence*, discussed the scout reports with her skipper, Captain Edward C. Ewen. When he learned the San Bernardino lighthouse had been lit, the admiral was convinced Halsey was making a mistake, and he began a message to the fleet commander noting the lighthouse information. He intended to recommend that Task Force 34 be detached and that a couple of carriers go with it to furnish air cover. *New Jersey* replied laconically over the TBS that staff already knew about the light, and Admiral Bogan was so put off at the sanguine response, he never made his recommendation.

Admiral Halsey finally took a hand again after midnight. The Third Fleet continued Bull's Run. In fact, at 1:00 a.m., Mick Carney passed instructions to Arleigh Burke for another night search, this one to the north. The noise of the searchplanes launching from the *Independence* woke up Pete Mitscher, who joined Rear Admiral Carney in the flag plot. Sightings of the Ozawa fleet started after about an hour. Some were less than 100 miles away. Halsey reverted control of the task force to Mitscher with orders to form Task Force 34 after all. Ching Lee would have his day with the fast battleships, but they were being sent after the Japanese decoys, not Kurita's fleet. Bull's Run might as well have been in Pamplona. Meanwhile, as the Americans were floundering about, the Japanese remained purposeful.

At 12:08 a.m., the Southwest Area Fleet radioed Combined Fleet headquarters: "TONIGHT EVERY EFFORT WILL BE MADE TO CARRY OUT REPEATED NIGHT ATTACKS, FOLLOWING WHICH THE MAIN ENEMY TASK FORCES WILL BE DESTROYED TOMORROW."

DIVERSION ATTACKS

Mikawa Gunichi would have a tough time making good on this promise to Admiral Toyoda. His best weapon that night bent steam to speed up the Surigao Strait at that very moment. "Weapons" is probably a better term, for there were two distinct Imperial Navy formations plying these waters. Americans labeled them the "southern force" and never really understood why the Japanese, in the face of Allied naval superiority, would operate an inferior force divided rather than united. One, the smaller flotilla, Allied intelligence had been tracking for days. This was Vice Admiral Shima Kiyohide's Fifth Fleet, variously known as the northern fleet, the Northeast Area Fleet, or the 2nd Diversion Attack Force.

Shima's fleet had continued its nomadic life. American submarine *Trigger* reported it in the Pescadores; the radio spies had tracked Shima to Mako port, then followed the tankers sent to refuel him. OP-20-G reported when Shima finished taking on oil, and that he had asked Kurita to send a tanker to Coron Bay. There is no indication, however, that FRUPAC or SEFIC intercepted or detected any of the sequence of messages exchanged among admirals Toyoda, Mikawa, and Shima about the 2nd Diversion Attack Force's mission. Japanese naval journalist Ito Masanori wrote in his postwar history of the Imperial Navy that Admiral Shima had led a "stepchild fleet," and related how it had been repeatedly reassigned until it was finally thrown into battle.

Because Shima's warships were designated a regional fleet, the Combined Fleet controlled them directly, and when Shima anchored at Mako, Toyoda first put the Fifth Fleet under Mikawa's command. However, the fleet's original assignment, a Tokyo Express–type mission to get Army reinforcements to Leyte, didn't pan out because the Army had no troops ready to transport. Thus the Mikawa and Toyoda debate over Shima's mission. Shima took a hand too, proposing that he support the raid into Leyte Gulf. That became their focus. So sure of the outcome was Shima that he summoned captains to confer aboard flagship *Nachi*, where they drank toasts with sake the emperor had presented to the ship. Meanwhile the transport mission led to Shima losing nearly half his destroyers when a division of three ships went ahead to move JNAF ground crews and maintenance equipment.

Shima's force could have been put under Admiral Kurita, but Combined Fleet apparently reasoned that Fifth Fleet represented only a minor augmentation. It would not increase Kurita's power by much, while at the same time requiring so much radio coordination the Japanese might tip their hand. Rear Admiral Takata Toshitane, senior staff officer, affirms that reasoning, adding that Kurita had finalized his plan. Incorporating Shima into it when Kurita was already preoccupied with sortie preparations might throw the entire scheme into confusion. This seems logical enough, except that Combined Fleet had not hesitated to improvise an air-only Sho or, for that matter, to suggest to Admiral Kurita that he change his operational concept and send Nishimura through the Surigao Strait.

At midafternoon on October 21 Combined Fleet advised Southwest Area Fleet that it had approved Mikawa's advice to support the Kurita fleet by means of an attack through Surigao Strait. Shima received instructions to proceed there and to coordinate with Nishimura. The latter, still with Kurita at Brunei, would lead the way into Surigao Strait.

At the point when OP-20-G reported that Admiral Shima had asked for tankers at Coron Bay, his assignment had finally been settled. At noon on October 22, when Vice Admiral Nishimura had barely set out from Brunei, Shima, because of his abortive Tokyo Express mission, was already halfway to Manila. Nishimura's anticipated schedule reached Shima only around sunset, with the Fifth Fleet nearing Coron Bay. Once he understood Nishimura's plan and knew his itinerary, Shima designed his own mission: to follow at about a five-hour interval, in a position to exploit results obtained by *both* Nishimura and Kurita, whose delays were as yet unknown.

In the morning, Nishimura received Shima's dispatch stating his intentions (messages both ways seem to have been delayed by hours). At that point, Admiral Nishimura could have modified his sailing schedule to effect a rendezvous, but he did not. This signal from the Shima fleet is the only one known to have been sent, even though communications were Admiral Shima's naval specialty. And yet, it is impossible to believe that Shima would have further altered his arrangements without transmitting that fact. By contrast, Nishimura proved to be good at updating colleagues, yet he never prodded Shima for better cooperation.

Why Admirals Shima and Nishimura did not coordinate their plans better has consumed a great deal of ink over the years. Historian Anthony P. Tully dismisses the argument that Nishimura, the junior admiral, wished to avoid falling under Shima's command, making the point that both men were subordinate to different chains of command (Nishimura under Kurita and Shima under Mikawa) and therefore not free to set their own rules. While that is a plausible explanation, in 1966, Kusaka Ryunosuke, the Combined Fleet's chief of staff, told historian John Toland he had *expected* Shima to send Nishimura an order to wait for him. That would not have been possible unless their ranks *did* apply.

Shima Kiyohide was a communications specialist and knew the importance of ample and timely information. Admiral Toyoda, as he had shown in the Taiwan air battle, did not fancy himself a microman-ager, and the Sho operation had steadily gained complexities. Toyoda left these matters in the hands of his seagoing admirals. On the other hand, the Surigao Strait tentacle of the Japanese plan, a last-minute improvisation by Combined Fleet—both in Kusaka's suggestion of a role for Nishimura and in its dickering with Mikawa over Shima's mission—demanded more central coordination. An error occurred here.

One possible explanation is that Shima wished to avoid the confusion that a rendezvous in the dark, in the presence of the enemy, could invite. And such confusion could be potentially disastrous. A second alternative emerges from Admiral Ugaki's diary, where he speaks of Shima's finally decided role as that of a "reserve" force. This suggests that the separation in space between the Nishimura and Shima flotillas may have been intended, *at the time*, by the Japanese high command, and not simply something Admiral Shima decided for himself.

Another possibility, proposed by the noted military historian Han-son Baldwin and favored by other chroniclers of this action, such as Thomas Cutler, is that Shima and Nishimura were competitors who disdained each other. The men were classmates at Etajima, and the way that the Japanese naval academy structured its physical education and certain other technical programs required students to compete (and cooperate) in order to get ahead. Between 1917 and 1923, Nishimura had outranked Shima, but thereafter their positions had been reversed. Kusaka Ryunosuke speculated that that day in the Surigao Strait, Rear Admiral Nishimura reasoned to himself that he had the bigger force, so why put himself under someone else?

Nishimura certainly did have a fierce streak, as Kusaka attests. The former was a couple of years ahead of Kusaka at the academy, where hazing rituals were commonplace. Freshman duties included weekend cleanups. Upperclassmen had a right to supervise. Nishimura decided Kusaka, who had gone to the bathroom, had been deficient. The upperclassman waited for Kusaka to emerge and then punched him two, perhaps three times. After Etajima, both officers served in the same gun room on the cruiser *Yakumo*, where they were good friends.

Nishimura Shoji became an old salt, spending most of his Navy career at sea. Ozawa Jisaburo, who had commanded the younger officer when Nishimura had had a destroyer, and who later taught at the Naval War College when Nishimura arrived there as a special student, thought highly of him. So did the hypercritical Admiral Ugaki. Koyanagi recalled Nishimura as a lively person with a sunshiny face who enjoyed his duties and required little or no help. Kusaka saw him as possessing a one-track mind, inflexible perhaps, and stubborn, but honest. Commander Terauchi Masamichi, skipper of the destroyer *Yukikaze*, saw much of Nishimura, who trained many destroyermen. Terauchi recalled the admiral as gentle, and a gentleman too—rare in the Imperial Navy. Historian Tully quotes Lieutenant Ezaki Hisato, paymaster aboard Nishimura's flagship, to the effect that his admiral was every inch a real warrior, with "something dignified and inaccessible in his bearing, but . . . warm-hearted and . . . very attractive."

The sunny disposition served Nishimura well, for in this war his lot had been a hard one, merely beginning with his son's death. In December 1941, during the Japanese conquest of the Philippines, when the world was going another way, Nishimura's was the only invasion force that suffered losses—in two successive operations. During fighting in Indonesia, when the Japanese took the Netherlands East Indies,

Nishimura's weak handling of his destroyer flotilla permitted American warships to gain a victory at the Battle of Makassar Strait. At the Battle of the Java Sea, Nishimura's flotilla had used up its torpedoes too soon and without effect. Not long after that, at Guadalcanal, as he gallantly led a division of heavy cruisers to bombard the Americans' notorious Henderson Field, Nishimura's gunners were so ineffective that U.S. planes rose with dawn to strike back, sinking seven transports and a light cruiser. Another Solomons cruise, in the summer of 1943, left him with two destroyers lost plus damage to heavy cruiser *Kumano*, especially painful to someone who had once commanded her.

Now, crossing the Sulu Sea, Nishimura seemed to be out of luck again. A scout from carrier *Enterprise* found him. Battleship *Yamashiro* detected the planes by radar shortly before 9:00 a.m. Admiral Nishimura had the warning circulated by flag signal. Sister ship *Fuso* had no hesitation breaking out the special antiaircraft shells for her 14-inch guns. On cruiser *Mogami*, Captain Toma Ryo called his ship to action stations in the Japanese style by bugle over the PA system. Destroyer *Asagumo* brought more boilers on line for battle speed. Oddly enough, the lead ship of the escort, Destroyer Division 4's *Michishio*, missed the warning and first learned of the threat when the battleships opened fire.

The circumstances proved odd all around. The scouts were from Rear Admiral Davison's Task Group 38.4. They had been in tough actions pretty continuously throughout the campaign. Air Group 20 from the *Enterprise* had had its worst day ever on October 18 over Manila, losing fifteen planes and six pilots. The carriers were headed for Ulithi and some rest when Bull Halsey summoned them, and the searches that morning were at maximum range—375 miles. They were also "heavy"—rather than the usual three or four aircraft, the Big E and the *Franklin* each put up a pair of scout units composed of half a dozen dive-bombers escorted by eight fighters. Lieutenant Raymond E. Moore led the unit that discovered Nishimura. Another search-strike group led by Commander Robert E. Riera, the Bombing 20 squadron commander, flew a nearby vector. He would join in upon notice. Moore sent the contact report and waited for Riera to come up. Once he did they made an immediate attack.

The squadron commander had his crews climb to 15,000 feet and roll in from there. To have an Imperial Navy formation like that in his sights was "something you dream about as a dive bomber pilot," recalled Ensign Robert J. Barnes. "The anti-aircraft was terrific."

A scout mission limited ordnance to, at most, 500-pound bombs, which could not seriously injure Nishimura's big ships, though they could wound a destroyer. Commander Riera dived on flagship *Yamashiro*, while Lieutenant Moore led the attack on the *Fuso*. Riera claimed hits on both battleships, which was not quite accurate. The flagship sprang leaks from near misses and twenty sailors were killed. Rear Admiral Ban Masami's *Fuso* got the more serious damage. One bomb impacted abaft number two turret, destroying a dual-purpose secondary gun mount. Belowdecks some seams opened and water seeped in, gradually becoming a serious threat. A second hit on the quarterdeck ignited aviation gas, incinerated floatplanes, and destroyed the ward-room just below. Admiral Ban had to put his battleship into a turn so the wind could blow smoke and flames away from the ship. Cruiser *Mogami* sustained minor damage to her plane-handling deck—her most recent refit had converted her to an aviation-cruiser like the *Chikuma*. Destroyers were attacked, but none incurred any serious damage. The worst danger for destroyer *Shigure* came from the *Fuso*, whose deck fire sent flames flaring toward the smaller warship. One bomb grazed her number one turret but bounced and exploded in the sea.

The sole American loss was Fred Bakutis, skipper of the Big E's fighter squadron, who had been leading the escort. His Hellcat, raked by flak, lost gasoline and he had to ditch. But Commander Bakutis would be rescued days later by the submarine *Hardhead*.

ADMIRAL NISHIMURA PRESSED on, seemingly unconcerned. Soon after the attack he set formation electronic watch patterns. An hour later Nishimura informed Admiral Kurita of the attack, pronouncing his own fighting ability unimpaired. Anthony Tully assesses the damage to the Japanese battleships as "far more than credited" in most accounts. But here Nishimura Shoji experienced a burst of good luck. Having gotten in a solid lick against him, Task Force 38 turned to confront the Kurita fleet. Bill Halsey felt confident that Kinkaid's Task

Force 77 could handle the Nishimura unit, which he believed heavily damaged. But, as per General MacArthur's plan, Task Force 77 focused on air defense of Leyte Gulf and support for the troops on the ground.

Early in the morning, even before Nishimura had been spotted, there was a succession of Japanese stabs at Leyte, perhaps 150 sorties in all. None inflicted serious damage, but the hunting that day would be the best of the war for the air groups. Rear Admiral Thomas Sprague headed Task Group 77.4, the escort carrier flotilla, and the pace of the Japanese attacks obliged him to suspend combat air support for MacArthur's troops on Leyte at one point. But that would be all the Japanese accomplished—*except* that, contrary to Halsey's expectations, Sprague had no forces to spare for the Nishimura unit or Shima fleet, now starting to come in behind it.

The tale of the diverted escort carrier air effort suggests what JNAF might have accomplished to support the Japanese surface fleet had it avoided the Battle of Taiwan.

Meanwhile Admiral Nishimura passed between Negros and Mindanao islands in the early afternoon and expected to enter the Mindanao Sea, which leads to Surigao Strait, at about 8:00 p.m. His floatplane reconnaissance, launched from *Mogami*, returned a report from Leyte Gulf that revealed how impossible this mission would be. The report credited the Allies with 4 battleships—twice as many as had Nishimura—a couple of cruisers, 4 destroyers, 15 aircraft carriers, and 14 PT boats. And the aircrew had undercounted wildly—Seventh Fleet's true strength included 6 battleships, 5 heavy and 3 light cruisers, 26 destroyers (plus several destroyer-escorts), and 39 of the pernicious PT boats. The battleships, cruisers, PT boats, and 20 of the destroyers would deploy with Oldendorf into Surigao Strait.

During the afternoon, while under way, Nishimura gathered his captains aboard the *Yamashiro* for a final massaging of plans. The officers affirmed their dedication to the mission. Their admiral worried about a torpedo ambush from PT boats or destroyers as his battleships entered the narrow strait, and to counter that threat, Nishimura decided to have the *Mogami* plus his own destroyers sweep ahead as his battleships neared the Surigao.

Vice Admiral Shima, meanwhile, had gained two hours on his

schedule and steamed about 100 miles behind the Japanese battleships. Admiral Shima thought he had not been seen, which happened to be untrue, but like Nishimura, in this instance he proved lucky. A long-range 5th Air Force scout from Morotai filed a contact report on Shima just before noon, but the same plane later saw Nishimura, and its follow-up reports seem to have confused the two Japanese units.

Admiral Thomas Kinkaid received the second report at about 2:15 p.m., shortly before the Seventh Fleet commander confirmed his final arrangements for receiving the Japanese inside the Surigao. His action message half an hour later to Rear Admiral Jesse Oldendorf put Japanese strength at two battlewagons—accurate enough—but went on to enumerate *eight* cruisers (four heavy, four light) and ten destroyers. Nishimura and Shima combined had half that strength in big ships, and fewer destroyers. Kinkaid also anticipated the Japanese were running a Tokyo Express–type mission, as he revealed in a 3:43 p.m. dispatch informing Halsey of the latest developments, which called the Nishimura force a "PROBABLE ENEMY LANDING FORCE IN CONVOY."

So it would be the fifty-seven-year-old Oldendorf who led the slaughter of the Nishimura unit in Surigao Strait. Heavy cruiser *Louisville*, the flagship, happened to be rearming from an ammunition vessel when the word came down: Deploy a large force in narrow waters to meet an enemy who must transit in column, while you put your battle line across his path. Put cruisers on the flanks and destroyers along the edges to make torpedo attacks. It was a dream assignment, and Oldendorf carried out his orders perfectly, setting the formation to "cross the T" on the oncoming Nishimura. Oldendorf stationed PT boats farther down the strait to report the approaching enemy and attack them in passing.

This night would be the ultimate revenge for the events at Pearl Harbor. Five out of six of Oldendorf's battleships had been sunk or badly damaged on December 7, 1941. Now every one of them, refloated, repaired, or refurbished, would be in the battle line to smite the Japanese. Late in the day, the warships began moving into position. The only difficulties they had were instrumental ones. For example, Lieutenant Commander J. D. White Jr., navigator of the battleship *Maryland*, possessed only old charts for the strait—ones that had not been corrected in many years. Whatever recent obstructions there might be, no one knew. The *Maryland* drew an average of thirty-four feet of water, so there were places she could not go. Similarly, Captain Herbert V. Wiley's battleship *West Virginia* actually touched an underwater obstruction with one screw. She would eventually have to go far into the South Pacific, to Espíritu Santo, for repairs.

Nishimura's flotilla, still nearly 200 miles away, passed between Negros and Mindanao as the Allied fleet took position. Captain Toma's *Mogami* and the Japanese destroyers began speeding up, maneuvering to get ahead of the battleships and slot into their scout mission. The cruiser's navigator, Commander Murokawa Takeyoshi, rose to the challenge of plotting a course to take the scouts through the dangerous waters off Panaon Island without obscuring the battleships' fields of fire. This would have been the moment when Admiral Nishimura learned that the Kurita fleet, heavily attacked, had reversed course in the Sibuyan Sea. Paymaster Ezaki—who was on the compass bridge with Nishimura, his chief of staff, Rear Admiral Ando Norihide, and the *Yamashiro*'s skipper, Rear Admiral Shinoda Katsukiyo—recalls none of the commotion that would surely have followed such news.

It is fair to speculate that Nishimura did not learn of Admiral Kurita's turnaround notice, but the battleship division leader *did* receive Combined Fleet's exhortatory order in which Toyoda invoked the deity to demand advance. Fleet headquarters had been in an uproar and had sent this message without knowing Kurita had already returned to his base course, but the sense of Toyoda's message, in a demanding and even insulting tone, was that the Kurita fleet had abandoned the Sho mission. Anthony Tully notes that this news had crucial implications for the Nishimura unit, a minor force whose purpose was instrumental to helping Kurita reach his goal. If Kurita had given up, what value remained in Nishimura's mission? Historian Tully concludes that Nishimura made the correct decision, to press ahead. The admiral even chided Kurita somewhat in a dispatch reporting when he expected to break into Leyte.

BATTLE NOW LOOMED. Nishimura's information message suggests he expected to fight soon and closer to the mouth of Surigao Strait than he had before. It remains puzzling what Nishimura expected to happen before that—he spoke of "charging" into Leyte Gulf, but he worried about PT boat and destroyer attacks, so it is clear that Nishimura did not think he could simply waltz into Leyte. Moreover, the Japanese admiral knew he had been discovered. The Allies were aware of his approach. And Nishimura had aerial scout reports of Allied battleships and other vessels in Leyte Gulf.

The Imperial Navy chieftain could not have expected to get past the enemy merely on the strength of Japanese mastery of night battle tactics. Above all, Japanese combat experience in the Solomons showed that Allied technology—radar—had trumped night action. Nishimura himself had been in the thick of some of those fights. Commander Nishino of the *Shigure* recalled that fighting off New Guinea earlier in 1944 had convinced him, at least, that night was the *worst* time to engage an Allied fleet. Nishimura's staff chief, Ando Norihide, a gunner, had been gunnery officer of cruiser *Chikuma* and had taught the subject at the naval gunnery school in Tateyama. Rear Admiral Ando had to know that the advantages of "crossing the T" were guaranteed if the Allies took position within the narrows of Surigao, but would have to be won by maneuver if they permitted the battle to occur inside Leyte Gulf. Nishimura must have known that too. Kinkaid's warships had had ample time to position themselves. The Japanese had every reason to expect heavy ships inside the strait.

It would have been out of character for Admiral Nishimura to cancel the mission, and he did not. That choice was the correct one, for his unit had already been committed and would not have gotten away without substantial losses. But he also did not speed up his advance, which would have been his best chance at getting into the strait before Kinkaid's fleet had completed preparations. You can call this foolish or purposeful. The latter supports the notion that Admiral Nishimura had determined to sail to his doom. He did so in the expectation that his sacrifice would open a way to overall victory.

The Nishimura unit continued plowing ahead—the battleships, accompanied by destroyer *Shigure*, at a stately pace; cruiser *Mogami* with the scout force, at speed. At 9:45 p.m., Kurita sent a message reporting his fleet on track to pass through San Bernardino Strait after midnight and to be in a position on the Pacific side by 6:00 a.m. It was too far away to cooperate with Nishimura, who expected to fight two hours earlier, and even though Nishimura might now have *slowed* his advance to compensate for Kurita's delay, all continued as before.

PT boats, radio call sign "Martini," were grouped in three-boat sections to defend the approaches. The sections were given specific waters to patrol. As the Japanese neared, PT leader Commander Robert A. Leeson concentrated them. The biggest grouping—five sections with nearly half of Leeson's boats—idled along the shore just where one entered the Surigao Strait. PT tactics were to keep the boats throttled down to minimize noise, ships darkened to minimize their visibility, and keep a sharp watch until they detected the enemy. Then the PTs would head for attack position, going to battle speed only for the final torpedo run. Each boat carried four torpedoes. Japanese sailors dreaded the PTs and called them "devil boats." And as Lieutenant Commander Tanaka Tomo of the *Michishio* told interrogators later, the PT boats had been like mosquitoes.

First up would be PT Section 1, off the end of Bohol Island just before eleven o'clock. A lookout aboard destroyer *Shigure* reported torpedo boats to starboard. Ensign Peter R. Gadd in *PT-131* actually picked up the Japanese flotilla on radar and began stalking them together with *PT-130* and *PT-152*. They were still several miles away when *Shigure* and Rear Admiral Shinoda's *Yamashiro* fired star shells to illuminate the PTs. The latter battleship then followed with real ammunition. Shinoda's first salvo straddled the fragile, wooden-hulled PTs. Gadd's devil boats went to twenty-four knots and bored in. Admiral Nishimura ordered a turn to comb the tracks of any torpedoes in the water. The *PT-152* would be badly damaged, while Nishimura emerged unscathed. At 11:30 p.m., Nishimura reported to Kurita and Combined Fleet that he had engaged torpedo boats but continued his advance.

PT-130 lost her radio to a shell that passed through the boat without exploding. She made her best speed to another PT section, where *PT-127* copied her report and passed it up the line. Oldendorf got the message at 12:26 a.m. It was his first definite news the Japanese were coming.

Mogami and the scout destroyers saw the pyrotechnics of Nishimura's fight with the Martinis, and they soon became involved. The ships passed through squalls, then encountered Lieutenant (Junior Grade) Dwight H. Owen's Section 3. In *PT-151*, Owen identified Captain Toma's cruiser and several destroyers and thought he saw a battleship. He got off one torpedo before *151*, caught in searchlight beams, had to retreat under a smoke screen. *PT-146* also managed to launch a torpedo. Both *PT-190* and the *146* boat thought they had scored many 40mm gun hits on the Japanese. On the other hand, due to Japanese radio jamming and bad atmospheric conditions, it would be several hours until Ensign Edward S. Haugen of *PT-190* could get off his report on the enemy. And by that time, the battle had intensified.

The two Japanese units joined up, with *Mogami* coming into line behind the battleships and the three destroyers taking station ahead. This was not accomplished easily. The ships had just been assigned to the Nishimura unit and had never worked together. Toma on the cruiser kept furnishing imprecise position data, leaving his recognition lights dark, while the Imperial Navy's radars were too primitive to eliminate the ambiguities. Thinking the *Mogami* an enemy, *Fuso* opened fire and hit the cruiser with a 6-inch shell. Fortunately it did not detonate.

A trio of American PTs guarded the western side of the strait's entrance. This was Commander Leeson's section. The PT boats had been filling the airwaves as sections reported the approach, then passage, of Nishimura's fleet. Leeson's unit, Section 6, had not gotten any action until now. Suddenly he had radar targets and crept up on what he thought were two battleships with several destroyers. In *PT-134*, Commander Leeson reached a distance of about 3,000 yards when enemy searchlight shutters opened up and his boat came under fire. The *134* replied with what she had—just light cannon of 20mm, 37mm, and 40mm calibers, which was not much against a major warship. Leeson launched three torpedoes and thought he obtained hits, but the Japanese steamed on unconcerned.

Commander Leeson's Martinis engaged after Captain Toma had reunited his scout force with Nishimura's battlewagons. In a confusing melee in the dark, further muddled by gunsmoke, shell flashes, squalls, and smoke screens, Leeson's PTs launched most of their torpedoes but were unable to see any results. About an hour later, when the Japanese 2nd Diversion Attack Force sped up in Nishimura's wake, *PT-134* had no torpedoes left. The Japanese passed sections of torpedo boats and managed to avoid any damage. It was impressive that Nishimura managed to transit the narrow waters at the entrance to the Surigao at all in the face of the devil boats. The PTs fought determinedly and ten of them were hit, but just one (*PT-490*) was damaged seriously enough that she had to be beached and abandoned.

Next up to fight were the Allied destroyers. Jesse Oldendorf had essentially lined the strait on both sides with squadrons of tin cans ready to pounce. The moon set just after midnight. The sea remained calm, the sky partly cloudy, and a light breeze blew from the northeast. Visibility was at two miles, though that mattered less to the Allies with their radars.

In addition to his own vessels, Oldendorf had the benefit of the ships of Destroyer Squadron 54, which had been on ASW duty and had asked to participate. Captain Jesse B. Coward divided his squadron by divisions and put some ships on each side.

Destroyer *McGowan* made first contact on her SG radar at 2:38 a.m. The enemy were 39,700 yards away and almost due south. Commander W. R. Cox got on the TBS to radio the news. The contact faded but returned. More ships picked up the Japanese, tracking them, filling the ether with notices. Captain Coward recorded firing his eastern group's torpedoes at exactly thirty seconds past 3:00 a.m. Ships in the western group put their torpedoes in the water ten minutes later. Nishimura's warships also detected the Americans and opened fire at 3:01, straddling Coward's destroyers, which began to retreat.

Commander Nishino in the *Shigure* remembers so many torpedoes churning the water, their phosphorescent wakes lit the strait like daylight. Despite the fact that the Allied warships appeared exactly like tin cans launching torpedoes, Nishimura took no countermeasures except to shoot at them. He increased speed to twenty knots, with no zigzagging. He did communicate with Vice Admiral Shima, whose Fifth Fleet, coming up fast, was now in TBS range, and who could see the flashes on the horizon as the battle intensified, and Nishimura told his own ships that they would be entering Leyte Gulf.

Suddenly a torpedo struck the *Fuso* amidships to starboard, extinguishing her searchlights. She fell out of formation. Rear Admiral Ban Masami and Captain Hirata Tsutomu, the executive officer, plunged into damage control. Boiler rooms flooded, and the ship listed.

At 3:20 a.m., Nishimura ordered a simultaneous turn to starboard. Ironically, analysts at the U.S. Naval War College, painstakingly reconstructing and charting all the torpedo tracks, concluded that if the *Yamashiro* had held to her eastern course, the battleship would have outrun the torpedoes aimed at her. *Yamashiro* received one hit, but her captain, Rear Admiral Shinoda, consulting executive officer Captain Ozaki Toshiharu, told Nishimura she'd not been affected. *Mogami* took station behind the flagship.

Admiral Nishimura ordered Captain Takahashi Kameshiro, leading his destroyer unit, to prepare for torpedo action. At that exact moment, two torpedoes blasted the destroyer *Yamagumo*, and she simply exploded. Captain Takahashi went down with his flagship. Then it became *Asagumo*'s turn. Commander Shibayama Kazuo, the destroyer's skipper, realized she had been hit in the port bow but found the ship could still manage ten to twelve knots. Shibayama began to make his way south, back down the strait. Commander Tanaka Tomo of the *Michishio* ran out of luck as well. The destroyer leader, struck amidships by at least one torpedo, quickly began settling. Tanaka would be rescued and taken prisoner. The torpedoes were from the U.S. destroyers *McDermott* and *Monssen*, making theirs one of the most successful single torpedo attacks of the war.

Nishimura sent a fresh dispatch at 3:30 recording destroyers and torpedo boats, the damage to *Yamashiro*, and the fact that a pair of his destroyers was hit and adrift.

But the damage had been worse than that. Of the Japanese escorts, only the *Shigure* still fought—and she lived up to her nickname, the "Miracle Destroyer." Commander Nishino watched from the bridge as three torpedo wakes closed in on his vessel and seemed to join on the starboard side, right below the bridge. But there was no hit, no explosion, nothing. Either the torpedoes had passed underneath the ship or they had failed to explode. This is a mystery of Surigao Strait. Captain Coward, the U.S. destroyer commander, had instructed his skippers to set their torpedo depth at six feet, which ought to have ensured damage to *Shigure*. If the torpedoes had been duds and bounced off, collision shocks should have occurred. Neither happened. Perhaps the *Shigure* had steamed through wakes of torpedoes that had already passed.

Then U.S. Destroyer Squadron 24 mounted yet another torpedo attack. Captain Kenmore M. McManes split his force of six tin cans into two attack groups that struck in sequence. Kinkaid's fleet missed no tricks this night. McManes's force included the Australian destroyer *Arunta*, whose skipper, Commander A. E. Buchanan, led the second group. Allied tin fish filled the water. One of McManes's torpedoes hit the *Yamashiro* amidships. She lost way and listed to port. Admiral Nishimura indicated the battleship was in danger when he ordered the rest of his unit to attack independently. How much power the Nishimura unit could muster by this point is uncertain. The destroyer *Asagumo*, her bow compromised, wasn't going to make any more attacks. Miracle destroyer *Shigure* headed south to check on the *Fuso*. Only cruiser *Mogami* remained in position and in fighting shape. Somehow, Captain Ozaki's damage-control teams made progress against *Yamashiro*'s wounds and she made way again. Soon the battleship reached eighteen knots speed. Nishimura headed into battle. The *Mogami* and *Shigure* came to her support. (While some accounts have the destroyer *Asagumo*, damaged as she was, coming up too, Commander Shibayama, her skipper, told Imperial Navy researcher Chihaya Masataka that after being torpedoed, the ship went south.)

Battleship *Fuso* limped along down the strait. She settled in the water with a magazine flooding. Sailors in the number one powder room suddenly realized the water dripping into their compartment was coming from above. The list inclined more sharply to starboard, and now the bow submerged. Admiral Ban Masami finally ordered "abandon ship." An ordeal began for the survivors. Seaman Kato Yasuo, perhaps the longest-serving crewman (he'd been on the *Fuso* since 1938), wept openly as he jumped into the water. His watch stopped at 3:25 a.m. The ship went down by the bow, with *Fuso*'s stern elevating as the nearly 700-foot-long battleship stood on her keel end. Kato could see the ship's rudder against the night sky. Once she had submerged,

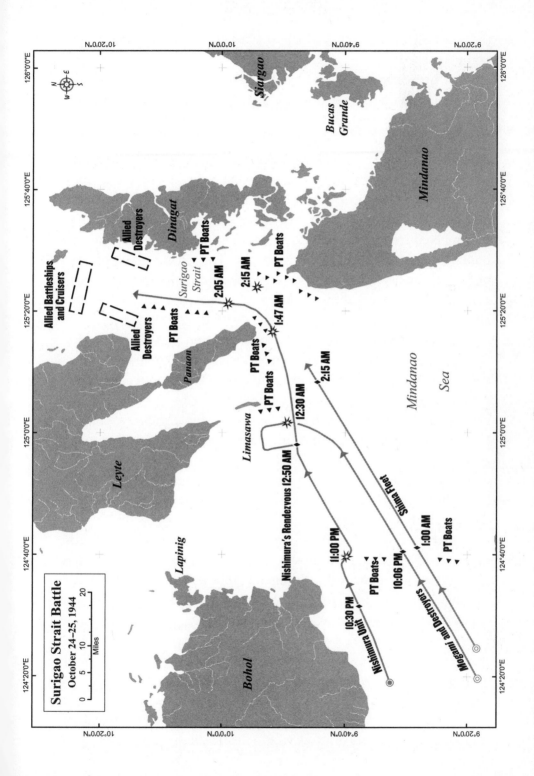

the vessel began leaking oil, which soon caught fire from conflagrations raging internally.

Destroyer Squadron 56 lined up for its shots next. Led by long-faced Captain Roland N. Smoot, who studied the charts and determined the exact place where each of his sections would make their attacks, the squadron sped to its positions. Commander Joshua Cooper's *Bennion* numbered among Smoot's ships. Her experience would be emblematic of this sea fight. The future head of the U.S. Navy, chief of naval operations James L. Holloway III, sailed in the *Bennion* as gunnery officer. He had joined the ship barely two weeks earlier at Manus. Holloway remembered streaming rain after dark. The weather was warm and humid, and the rain provided brief respite. The sea was glassy and the night obscure. Suddenly there were star shells and flashes on the horizon. Then there were ships, and Smoot's vessels maneuvered for position.

Cooper's destroyer had the second position in her section. He ordered Holloway into action. The young officer estimated flashes covered 20 percent of the horizon in his gun director optics. The magnification of a Mark-37 was by a factor of twelve to fourteen. "I could clearly see the bursting shells on the enemy ships," he recalled. The first destroyer in their column launched her torpedoes at 10,000 yards. *Bennion* loosed five fish at 5,600. By then, the *Yamashiro* filled the entire viewing lens. The destroyer turned away into a smoke screen, but behind her, the *Albert W. Grant* came under fire and suffered damage, including 39 dead and 119 wounded.

Just then, there came a ripple of fire from several thousand yards' distance. The CIC reported nothing on radar, but big American ships always fired simultaneously. Lieutenant Holloway instantly concluded the ship had to be Japanese and shifted target. Commander Cooper decided the enemy—she was heavy cruiser *Mogami*—offered a fine target for the *Bennion*'s five remaining tin fish. Two of them hit. Commander Cooper was awarded the Navy Cross and Lieutenant Holloway a Bronze Star.

In the face of such devastation, the attack no longer qualified as a naval maneuver. Nishimura's pell-mell advance more resembled closely a handful of teammates in a sack race to their deaths—because one damaged battleship, a battered heavy cruiser, and one Japanese destroyer were up against Jesse Oldendorf's main body of half a dozen battle-wagons and eight cruisers. The Allies' big guns were about to open fire.

It was at that moment that Admiral Nishimura learned that Shima Kiyohide's 2nd Diversion Attack Force had entered the Surigao Strait too. Shima was barely twenty miles away.

RETIRING TO PLAN SUBSEQUENT ACTION

The Shima fleet, from which so much was expected, though it possessed so little, anchored at Coron Bay in the evening on October 23. Vice Admiral Shima Kiyohide had barely recovered from his frustration at having his fleet tossed like a baseball thrown around the infield after a strikeout. So many dispatches had flown back and forth between Manila and Combined Fleet headquarters, and at one point the admiral had gotten so irritated he'd considered going to sea so he could profess to be out of communication. But the matter had finally been settled to his satisfaction. Better yet, C-in-C Toyoda had given Shima the opportunity to choose his own course of action.

Perhaps Combined Fleet took a chance giving Shima his head. Like so many others, the admiral thought of decisive battle as a fight against another fleet, not against transports. As he explained, the Japanese fleet should not "waste itself in piecemeal action against transports." And anyway, Shima thought, during the long approach of the main force from Lingga, the Allied transports would leave. Shima believed any competent commander would share his judgment.

Here again is evidence of the high command's failure to sell the Imperial Navy on its selection of invasion shipping rather than battle fleets as the targets of decisive battle. But just how "competent" was Shima Kiyohide? The Navy evidently thought he was competent enough. Though Shima had had only middling class rank at Etajima, he passed both levels of study at the Naval War College before reaching lieutenant commander, had served at the NGS (twice) and on Combined Fleet staff in addition to others, and had been aide-de-camp to an imperial prince. He began as a torpedo specialist but found his true calling in radio. Not only was Shima an expert, but he had instructed in the subject, and not just at the radio school but as adjunct at the torpedo and gunnery schools, with the JNAF, and back at the communications school as chief instructor. Indeed, the admiral's last post before taking up the reins at Fifth Fleet in February 1944 had been as its superintendent.

Admiral Shima's seagoing experience was another matter, quite the opposite of Nishimura's. He had seen no shipboard assignments for a decade after 1923, a period during which technological advances transformed the Imperial Navy. By then a captain, Shima commanded light cruiser *Oi*. A year there, more shoreside billets, and then he took charge of Minesweeper Division 19 as a rear admiral in November 1940. Shima's most noteworthy wartime experience had come during the Battle of the Coral Sea, when he had led the invasion force that occupied the Solomon island of Tulagi. A couple of months later came command of a cruiser division. The three years from 1940 to 1943 were his longest stint of sea service. This put the radio maven on the sea during the period of Japanese supremacy, at the moment of balance, and then into the beginning of the Navy's decline. At Leyte, Shima Kiyohide enjoyed a reputation as a relatively young admiral (at fifty-four) attuned to technological developments. When Admiral Shima told historian John Toland that his radars had been lousy, he knew what he was talking about.

Toyoda had left the admiral to decide his own role. Shima's radiomen overheard Combined Fleet concede Kurita's fuel problem and change X-Day to October 25. Toyoda's departure orders for the Ozawa decoy mission on October 20 also reached Fifth Fleet. At Mako, Shima realized it was not too late to join Ozawa, and he took advantage of being in port to ask Combined Fleet for a determination. Shima claims Hiyoshi never replied. Instead the Fifth Fleet commander got information copies of a message in which Mikawa's chief of staff recommended the Shima fleet be used in conjunction with either Kurita's or Ozawa's outfit.

For Shima, these were the most nervous hours of the entire operation. He recounts that a staff officer advised him to go with Kurita, and Shima sent a dispatch to that admiral with ideas for their cooperation. Again, no answer, until October 22, when the Second Fleet commander (Kurita) sent a laconic reply merely describing his intended schedule. Kurita did not discuss how they might cooperate. The force commander seemed to assume Shima would proceed independently. Consulting with chief of staff Rear Admiral Matsumoto Takeshi, and looking at the messages between Kurita and Nishimura, Shima discovered his Etajima classmate had sailed for the Surigao Strait with a weak attack unit. He knew his own destroyers would need to refuel before the penetration operation. Coron Bay offered the logical place for that. Admiral Shima decided he would take the southern route and reinforce Nishimura. From the X-Day traffic, he knew when to time his arrival at Leyte.

Commander Mori Kokichi, torpedo officer on Admiral Shima's staff, hoped to find a tanker awaiting them at Coron Bay. He was disappointed. The admiral had to refuel his destroyers from the cruisers before setting out again in the early hours of the new day, October 24. That put him in the Sulu Sea, headed south, just when the Nishimura unit was discovered and the Kurita fleet assailed in the Sibuyan Sea.

Rather than suffering attack itself, Admiral Shima's detached destroyer division fell victim to the American scout bombers. Originally, Shima had wanted to recall Destroyer Division 21 from its detached mission before it got sucked into repeat Tokyo Express runs. Trying to preserve radio silence, Admiral Shima elected to send the order to Captain Ishii Hisashi via floatplane to Manila, where it could be put on broadcast radio. Instead the plane overturned in the water when landing and the dispatch never reached Captain Ishii. As a result, Shima's destroyer division bypassed Coron, speeding southeastward off Panay Island, where it would be caught by the same Task Force 38 air search that discovered Nishimura. Ishii's command ship, the *Wakaba*, would be bombed and sunk. Ishii himself and the ship's skipper, Commander Ninotaka Kanefumi, were able to reach destroyer *Hatsuharu*. Ishii retired to Manila, but Admiral Shima never knew, and even upon entering battle, he continued hoping the destroyers might join him.

By midmorning, Admiral Shima's fleet had set a fast pace. He learned American long-range bombers were over Mindanao and headed his way. The grandly titled 2nd Diversion Attack Force kept awaiting discovery and attack. Shima adopted a ring formation with Captain Miura Hiyao's light cruiser *Abukuma* in the lead, the outer ring of four destroyers on the quarters, flagship *Nachi* in the center, and heavy cruiser *Ashigara* following. They never saw the planes.

Just before noon, with Shima off Panay, a U.S. B-24 saw and accurately reported his force. The fleet commander suffered no ill consequences from the sighting. Admiral Shima advanced his timetable and increased speed to twenty knots. At 5:45 p.m., he circulated his battle plan by flag signal: The fleet would penetrate Leyte Gulf at 3:00 a.m. on October 25, making twenty-eight knots. The force would increase speed and change formation at designated times on its approach. Commander Mori of the staff reported later that Shima had wanted to go even faster but fuel consumption had made that impossible.

Vice Admiral Shima worried about Allied submarines. He had warned his ships that morning and again as they entered the Mindanao Sea near sunset. He updated the fleet by blinker signal, supplementing the bare-bones battle plan with information on Allied forces they expected to encounter. The data was an underestimate. Commander Mori, standing on the bridge of the *Nachi*, would be startled at about 10:00 p.m. when lookouts began reporting PT boats shadowing them. It was not subs, but torpedo boats that were the real threat. Admiral Nishimura confirmed that directly a couple of hours later in the message where he reported PT boat attacks.

After more than 2,000 miles, many scares, and much to-ing and fro-ing about missions, now the "stepchild" Shima fleet pressed into narrowing waters only about an hour behind the Nishimura unit, which was fighting for its life not far ahead.

The 2nd Diversion Attack Force steamed at twenty-four knots. At 11:55 p.m. Vice Admiral Shima ordered the fleet to be ready to make twenty-eight knots immediately, and full battle speed on fifteen minutes' notice. After midnight, the vessels entered a hard rainsquall. Only about forty miles separated the two forces around 1:00 a.m. when Commander Mori and others began to see the horizon lit by gun flashes. Battle was near.

WHATEVER RELATIONSHIP EXISTED between the two Etajima classmates Shima and Nishimura, in the darkness of Surigao Strait that night, Shima Kiyohide had become Admiral Nishimura's lifeline.

But many of the Japanese sailors in Shima's fleet had real reason to fight—for friends right ahead of them in the strait to comrades fallen in the nobility of failure. Shima's screen commander, Rear Admiral Kimura Masatome, had skippered a heavy cruiser under Nishimura in the Solomons. The flag captain, Rear Admiral Kanoka Empei, was a classmate of Hirata Tsutomu, an executive officer on the *Fuso* right ahead of them. The *Nachi*'s skipper had the same relationship with Kuno Shuzo, chief of the T Air Attack Force, and Inoguchi Rikihei, the First Air Fleet staffer.

In addition, many of their mates were driving other ships in Sho right now, including battleships *Yamato* and *Nagato*, cruisers *Atago* and light cruiser *Yahagi*, and aircraft carrier *Zuiho*. Destroyer leader Kimura, renowned for his successful evacuation of the Japanese defenders of Kiska Island in the Aleutians, surely also wanted revenge for the spring 1943 Battle of the Bismarck Sea, in which the Allies had massacred the troop convoy he escorted to New Guinea. Many hopes and fears came together in the Surigao Strait that night.

By 2:45 a.m., the Shima fleet neared the entrance. The ships had been making twenty-two knots. Entering by dead reckoning, the heading changed to north-northeast at 3:11. They were early, actually, blinded by a rainsquall, and made the turn too soon. Destroyer *Ushio* nearly ran aground as a result. A few minutes earlier Admiral Shima had asked Nishimura by TBS for an update. His silence was ominous. Meanwhile Shima ordered a speed increase and a turn to starboard to make a proper entrance into Surigao.

The turn marked the beginning of the Fifth Fleet's nightmare. Commander Leeson's PT section guarded the waters at the strait's mouth. Two Martinis had used up their torpedoes by now. The other was Lieutenant (Junior Grade) Isadore M. "Mike" Kovar's *PT-137*. The *137* had been incapacitated by an auxiliary generator malfunction, which had disabled both her radio and her radar, so she almost missed the party. Kovar had used only one torpedo when Nishimura sped by, shooting uselessly from behind at destroyers that had already passed. Now, at about 3:24 a.m., he glimpsed what he thought was a destroyer coming back down the strait; it was probably *Asagumo*. Mike Kovar took his PT to 900 yards from the enemy and launched one torpedo. The Japanese saw *PT-137* too, illuminated her, and opened fire.

Kovar felt devastated when his tin fish sped underneath the vessel. But destroyer leader Kimura's flagship, the light cruiser *Abukuma*, had the third place in Shima's formation, and it was passing on the far side of Kovar's fight. Captain Hanaka Takuo, *Abukuma*'s skipper, suddenly spotted a torpedo wake to port just 500 yards away. Hanaka ordered an emergency turn, but it was already too late. The torpedo slammed into the ship under the bridge, killing thirty sailors and cutting speed to just ten knots. Unable to keep up, Captain Hanaka dropped out of Shima's formation and turned his cruiser to head for safety. A couple of Kimura's destroyers had to take evasive action to avoid collision with the wounded *Abukuma*. Both Hanaka's ship and the destroyer *Shiranuhi* saw *PT-137* and took Kovar's boat under fire.

Admiral Shima responded by increasing fleet speed to twenty-eight knots. His vessels really had bones in their teeth now. Once he cleared the entrance, Shima ordered his force into battle formation. Their course was directly into the strait, then northeast. The four destroyers took station behind Shima's heavy cruisers. Captain Inoue Yoshio of Destroyer Division 18 in the *Shiranuhi* assumed command of the screen in the absence of Rear Admiral Kimura, stuck on the *Abukuma*.

At 3:44 a.m., a Fifth Fleet staff officer got on the TBS to inform Nishimura that they were in the strait and that help was on the way. It is not clear if the battleship commander heard their news. By now, sailors on Shima's warships could see and hear gunfire and could see that vessels ahead of them were in flames. The voice radio crackled with the survivors' battle transmissions.

The gunfire Shima could see came from two sources. Nishimura's remnants were one, with *Yamashiro* opening up at 3:52, soon turning to port to open her broadside, and *Mogami* doing the same to starboard. But the answering fire, far more deadly, came from Kinkaid's battleships and cruisers. Against a dozen Japanese 14-inch and half that number of 8-inch guns, the Allies ranged sixty-four cannon of 16 and 14 inches, thirty-five 8-inch guns, and fifty-four 6-inch guns. Shock and awe would be a fair description of that cannonade.

Sailors on the Allied cruisers and battlewagons were increasingly anxious through the midwatch, as the battle seemed to unfold to the south without them taking part. Admiral Oldendorf led the fleet into battle formation at 1:52 a.m. So far there were Martini reports but nothing more substantial. Fifteen minutes later, the battleship *West Virginia* saw gun flashes. Oldendorf, in the heavy cruiser *Louisville*, did not yet see the fighting, but there would clearly be a battle. *West Virginia* went to general quarters at 2:32. Within minutes, most everyone could see gunfire, and destroyers reported their first surface contact at 2:41. The enemy were visible on radar at 3:04. Six minutes later the *West Virginia*'s gunnery radar had the target, which it never lost, and gunnery had the firing solution by 3:33—as Nishimura struggled desperately against the destroyers. Despite the confusion of many Allied destroyers and some Imperial Navy warships cutting through almost the same water, at least on the *West Virginia*, the Combat Information Center and gunnery control agreed the Allied ships were clear.

At 3:51 the Allied cruisers opened fire. Australian Navy Captain C. A. G. Nichols saw nothing of the fall of shot for the first salvos. But starting with the third, the bell that rang on the bridge of his heavy cruiser *Shropshire* at the moment when her shells should be impacting coincided with a flash on the radar screen. Australian *Shropshire* began straddling the target on that salvo. Overall, the heavy cruisers shot more than a thousand 8-inch shells. The light cruisers contributed their usual incredible volume of fire (*Columbia*, for example, pumped out 1,147 rounds within eighteen minutes, which works out to a twelve-gun 6-inch salvo every twelve seconds).

The battleships opened fire a minute later. Nishimura's ships must have endured a hurricane. On the battle communication phones of *West Virginia*, gunnery officer Commander C. M. Hardison could be heard chuckling. He reported a hit on the first salvo.

For all that American know-how, the *Pennsylvania* could not find a target and never used her main battery. The *Mississippi* was flagship for the battle line, led by Rear Admiral G. L. Weyler. It proved embarrassing that her Mark-3 fire control radar had trouble. Chief gunner Commander Richard Lane finally got a bead on the Japanese and the battleship fired a broadside, but at that moment Admiral Weyler ordered cease-fire. Battleship *Maryland* set her guns by observing the splashes of shells fired by the *West Virginia* and got off half a dozen salvos totaling forty-eight 16-inch shells. The *West Virginia*, *California*, and

Tennessee were all equipped with the late-model Mark-8 radars and had firing solutions long before Weyler gave them the okay. The range started at 22,800 yards. *California* and *Tennessee* got off sixty-three and sixty-nine rounds, respectively. The latter had orders to hold fire until the flagship, ahead of her, opened it; but when *West Virginia* commenced fire from just behind her, the *Tennessee* took that reference point instead and began shooting. *West Virginia* would be the champ, loosing ninety-three rounds. The Allies halted their fire when the *Yamashiro* was seen to capsize and sink, about 4:19 a.m.

On the Japanese side, the *Mogami* launched torpedoes at 4:01 a.m. Captains Toma and Hashimoto had both been killed. The cruiser's top gunner now commanded the ship and guns both. *Yamashiro* shot with all her turrets. Besides destroyer *Grant*, no Allied ship suffered any damage. Nishimura's flagship, on fire from stem to stern, turned to port at about 4:10 and headed south. Afire herself, the *Mogami* turned to starboard and started down the strait too.

Into this maelstrom steamed Admiral Shima. The visibility remained poor, with periodic squalls. Ahead he could see blue flares. He assumed they were American since Japanese star shells usually burst in yellow. Allied destroyers had laid a smoke screen. Their heavy ships and Nishimura's remnants were on the other side of it. A single battleship of the *Fuso* class lay there, illuminated by the flare. She was afire and there were explosions. To raise morale in the Nishimura unit, Shima took to the voice radio and announced his fleet had reached the battle zone. Again, no reply. He increased speed to twenty-eight knots, then to thirty—the maximum practical for a formation. About 4:00 a.m., the fleet passed what Shima took to be a pair of *Fuso*-type battleships. One had to be that vessel in her death throes, but the *Yamashiro*, now far ahead with *Mogami* nearby, was engaging the Allied forces. The other warship was a chimera or her identity was mistaken—the damaged *Asagumo* was somewhere around there.*

---

*U.S. official historian Samuel Eliot Morison writes the "two battleships" were the severed front and rear of the ship *Fuso*. Anthony Tully argues convincingly that this was not possible. Morison and Tully agree the ship was *Fuso*, which is significant because some recent accounts of Surigao Strait have reversed the identities of the two Japanese battleships.

The 2nd Diversion Attack Force came upon a destroyer, dead in the water. She blinkered, "I AM DESTROYER SHIGURE. RUDDER IS DAMAGED AND UNDER REPAIR."

Shima's radars showed the Allies ahead of them. Close in, to starboard, was another ship in flames, seemingly a hulk. Vice Admiral Shima ordered his fleet to attack, and he turned to starboard to bring his ship's torpedo tubes to bear. That was when someone noticed the "hulk" was actually under way—it was *Mogami*. Commander Mori, the torpedo staff officer, recalled that everyone on the bridge was too focused on their impending torpedo attack. Only after the tin fish were away did they realize *Mogami* had power. Captain Kanoka ordered the rudder hard over and the engines into reverse but far too late. *Nachi* sliced into *Mogami*, holing her starboard bow and flooding the anchor windlass compartment. The last-minute actions at least prevented the collision from being even worse. Shima's flagship headed south for some minutes to review the ship's condition, establishing that speed now had to be held to twenty knots, not so good in a battle.

Mori advised Shima that the Nishimura force had been almost totally destroyed. "Up ahead the enemy must be waiting for us with open arms," Mori argued. "It is obvious that the Second Striking Force will fall into a trap."

This marked the end of madness. The Japanese southern wing had been overwhelmed by superior force. Vice Admiral Shima recoiled down the strait and out to sea. Shima reported to Mikawa and for the information of others: "THIS FORCE HAS CONCLUDED ITS ATTACK AND IS RETIRING FROM THE BATTLE AREA TO PLAN SUBSEQUENT ACTION." That information from Admiral Shima was oddly misleading— "concluding" the attack under the Sho plan suggested a successful mission. The high command could have been left thinking Shima had actually mounted an attack inside Leyte Gulf. A communications specialist ought not to have sent such an ambiguous dispatch. A later message detailing the extent of the damage to himself and the Nishimura unit perhaps clarified his meaning.

Allied cruisers and destroyers pursued them down the strait. Destroyer *Asagumo* sank. On the way out, the Japanese had to run the gauntlet of the PT boats once more. Torpedo boats attacked the *Shigure* and the *Mogami*, and with dawn came the airplanes. They finished off *Mogami*, and, a day later, Army Air Force planes would sink the hapless *Abukuma*. Admiral Shima regrouped at Coron Bay. This time a tanker awaited him. Shima believed he had been saved by a trick. With planes of the Seventh Fleet's escort carriers in sight, a young communications lieutenant who had been born in Hawaii had gotten on a U.S. Navy air radio frequency and broadcast an emergency recall—supposedly JNAF carrier planes were assailing their base ships. Shima recalls watching the Grummans as they turned and flew away.

The death ride of the Nishimura unit ended with nearly total annihilation. When the news reached Hiyoshi, Combined Fleet staff chief thought of Nishimura, "It was just like him. Headstrong." But Nishimura's force had actually accomplished something instrumental to the Japanese mission. The Surigao Strait lay on the far side of Leyte Gulf from where Kurita would appear. Admiral Kinkaid's Seventh Fleet tarried long into the night to finish off Nishimura's ships. As dawn approached, the mighty fleet had just begun its return. But when the sun rose, the Kurita fleet struck.

CHAPTER 9

TALLYHO . . . CARRIERS!

Commander Thomas Hamilton had known Bull Halsey at Annapolis. At the time, Halsey had commanded the naval academy's station ship, *Reina Mercedes*, while working as boxing coach. Tom Hamilton had admired his aggressive style. He himself was an Annapolis football star who had kicked the Navy to an undefeated 1926 season and was immortalized as the model for a stained-glass window in the chapel. Presently, Hamilton served as executive officer aboard *Enterprise*. When that ship's prow turned north on the night of October 24, Commander Hamilton applauded because he knew that meant Halsey would hunt Japanese carriers.

Though Pete Mitscher resumed tactical command of Task Force 38, when the night search confirmed Ozawa's presence, Halsey ordered, "FORM LEO." That short message at 2:40 a.m. had a scripted meaning—the fleet would immediately pull together the warships constituting Task Force 34, Vice Admiral Willis A. Lee's battleship action group.

The Third Fleet leader intended Ching Lee's surface force as a foil against any enemy attempt to engage Halsey's fleet with surface ships. Its formation had been rehearsed only once. Now, carried out at night, in the midst of a major naval battle, this would not be a simple evolution. It required all the aircraft carriers and their remaining escorts to slow to ten knots while the fast battleships and their screen pulled away.

The whole story of the run north, the role of Task Force 34, and the destruction of the Ozawa fleet makes up one of the great what-ifs of the Leyte sea fight. And it's the last piece to the puzzle of how the Japanese got to do what they did.

THE OZAWA PLOY

Aboard *Enterprise*, the routine would be very much like that on the other carriers when Commander Hamilton crafted the ship's daily plan for October 25. His provided for crewmen to awaken at 3:30 a.m. Half the crew would breakfast ten minutes later and the rest at 4:15. The dawn general quarters—now standard in the U.S. Navy—would start at 5:29, an hour before expected sunrise. Early-morning searches would cover seven vectors out to 275 miles, each with a TBM Avenger as scout covered by a Hellcat for protection. Several night fighters would follow as radio relay planes. The search would launch shortly after six o'clock.

Once the scouts were airborne, Big E would begin clearing the deck, putting up a strike package to be able to respond to any sighting. The group, thirteen dive-bombers, seven torpedo bombers, and sixteen fighters, would orbit fifty miles to the north. "Dog" Smith led the package. The portents so thrilled Tom Hamilton that he scribbled a note on the typewritten master for the mimeographed order of the day: "Today may be the biggest in our Navy's history. *Enterprise* will set the pace."

Wind blew from the northeast with brisk (thirteen- to sixteen-knot) breezes. The weather would be generally clear with only a few clouds.

Jerry Bogan's other aircraft carriers had similar standing procedures. The *Franklin* put up its own strike package, the two light carriers lesser flights. Admiral Halsey was short one carrier group—Slew McCain's 38.1, which the Bull had sent to Ulithi for rest, then recalled—which meant the overall task force numbered five fleet carriers plus an equal number of light ones. At 4:30 a.m., Pete Mitscher ordered all the carriers to prepare deckload strikes and start arming them, as well as to be ready to launch both the strike packages and combat air patrols with dawn. Ted Sherman's 38.2 group put up packages totaling 101 airplanes with the redoubtable David McCampbell of *Essex* as attack coordinator.

Despite the Japanese gains in distance during the interval required to form up Task Force 34, Task Force 38's maneuvers in the night left the carrier fleet in an enviable situation at morning. Ozawa's fleet was headed north, barely 150 miles from Halsey's armada. Commander

McCampbell's ready-strike group, orbiting seventy miles from their own force, could virtually see the Japanese.

The first sighting came from an *Intrepid* plane at 7:10 a.m. Admiral Mitscher ordered immediate attack. They were after a pretty cool customer.

The island of Kyushu had long produced some of the finest Japanese naval officers, Ozawa Jisaburo among them. During the nineteenth century, the Satsuma clan had been powerful on Kyushu, and it joined with others to fight the power of the military dictators, or shoguns, who claimed to exercise authority in the name of the emperor. Among some of the Meiji Restoration reforms were the creation of both the Japanese Army and the Imperial Navy. Where other clans sought dominance in the Army, many Satsuma clansmen joined the Navy. By 1886, when Jisaburo was born in Miyazaki prefecture, the Meiji upheavals had ended, but the navalist tradition on Kyushu was stronger than ever. So going Navy and entering Etajima were natural choices for him.

Ozawa graduated with the class of 1909. His middle ranking (45 of 179) did not do justice to his analytical mind, his brightness, or his adaptability. Samuel Eliot Morison, the American naval historian, said of Ozawa that he would have done just fine in the U.S. Navy. Agawa Hiroyuki, biographer of the renowned Japanese commander in chief Yamamoto Isoroku, named Ozawa as one of only two officers qualified to replace Yamamoto—and the other man (Yamaguchi Tamon) had already perished. Denizens of the Zoo at JICPOA had this to say about Ozawa Jisaburo at the height of the Pacific war:

HE IS CONSIDERED AN IDEAL FLEET COMMANDER. . . . HE KEEPS FORGING AHEAD UNTIL HIS OBJECTIVE IS GAINED. A GOOD STRATEGIST, HE IS VERY PAINSTAKING AND THOROUGH. . . . A MOST SIGNIFICANT FACT ABOUT HIM IS THAT HE IS CONSIDERED A "WIN OR LOSE" TYPE, CAREFULLY CALCULATING WHEN MAKING HIS PLANS AND THEN WILLING TO RISK ALL ON THEM.

That is certainly what Vice Admiral Ozawa was up to in the Sho operation.

The graduation cruise Japanese officers take after leaving Etajima found Midshipman Ozawa aboard the training ship *Soya*, and that experience, in fact, became his first exposure to Yamamoto, who was a ship's officer at the time. Afterward, young Ozawa Jisaburo served aboard the Navy's flagship, battleship *Mikasa*.

But his real devotion was torpedoes. By the time Ozawa made lieutenant commander, in 1921, he had done the torpedo school's basic and advanced courses, led a torpedo boat division, and completed both levels of study at the Naval War College. Ozawa commanded more destroyers, was an instructor at the torpedo school, and served on a destroyer squadron staff and on the Navy General Staff—all before 1930. Then he took six months off for an extensive tour of Europe and the United States.

During that trip, Commander Ozawa made a special study of the Battle of Jutland, reading everything he could find on the subject, speaking to veterans in both Germany and England. Ozawa decided that the best histories are done by the defeated, because victors always want to keep secrets about their actions. Ozawa argued this was true for Japan's sea battles in the Russo-Japanese War as well as for the British in World War I. That aside, he discovered that an important aspect of the fighting at Jutland had been the concentrated torpedo attacks by destroyer units, of which the Germans had made great use. The Japanese suspected that the British were designing an oxygen-powered torpedo to overcome previous deficiencies. At the Kure Torpedo Institute, engineers solved the problems of oxygen power for torpedoes and the Imperial Navy produced a high-speed tin fish it called the "Long Lance" (Type 93). U.S. intelligence believed Ozawa made his reputation in Imperial Navy circles by advocating for this weapon.

Upon returning from his Jutland inquiry, Ozawa briefly served at the head of several destroyer units before returning to the Naval War College as an instructor. Now a captain, he next commanded the heavy cruiser *Maya*, and then the battleship *Haruna*. It would be after that assignment that Ozawa, newly minted rear admiral, went to Combined Fleet headquarters as chief of staff. He fought in the China Incident as leader of Cruiser Division 8 before his appointment as director of the

Yokosuka Torpedo School in 1938. There, he presided over the introduction of the Long Lance torpedo and its new doctrine manual.

Admiral Ozawa's other big contribution to Navy tactics came little more than a year later, when he led carriers for the first time. The Imperial Navy was rapidly increasing its stake in air forces, with new aircraft designs (the Zero was a brand-new airplane then) and big fleet carriers. Ozawa's Carrier Division 1 would be the first to achieve sinking scores against multiple battleships in fleet exercises. The idea of concentrating carrier divisions into a single striking force is one that Admiral Ozawa formally proposed. That the Navy thought highly of Ozawa can be seen in his promotion to vice admiral in November 1940 and his assignment to lead its most prestigious cruiser unit, and also in its selection of Vice Admiral Ozawa as director of the Naval War College in September 1941.

What happened next also demonstrates the importance of Admiral Ozawa. The Navy Ministry yanked him from the newly appointed position almost immediately. By then, Japan stood on the brink of war and its plans for offensives were far advanced. After barely a month at the head of the War College, the Navy tapped Ozawa to lead its Southern Expeditionary Fleet, the important covering force for all the Japanese offensives into Southeast Asia and the Philippines.

In this capacity, Ozawa would be in on the destruction of the British battleships *Prince of Wales* and *Repulse*; he would lead the Japanese invasions of Borneo, Java, Sumatra, and the Andaman Islands; and he would conduct raids into the Indian Ocean. After a break of just a few months in the summer and fall of 1942, the Navy brought Ozawa back to replace Nagumo Chuichi in command of the *kido butai*, the carrier force also known as the Third Fleet, which would be the aviation component of the Mobile Fleet that Ozawa also headed.

As he had done before, Vice Admiral Ozawa devised tactics and techniques suitable for Japan to fight. With the Mobile Fleet before the Philippine Sea, it was Ozawa who had advocated taking advantage of the longer range of JNAF carrier aircraft by attacking with them while Allied fleets were still too far away to use their own planes. It had not been the admiral's fault that the JNAF proved too weak to lay a glove on the Allied fleet.

Before Sho, Ozawa had intended to restore the carrier force, then sail to Lingga and reunite the Mobile Fleet, operating as it had at the Battle of the Philippine Sea. Preparations for that voyage were under way when the Allies moved against Taiwan and the Philippines. Ozawa had plumped for his role as a lure, a reduced mission to make the surface attack forces that much stronger. When Combined Fleet activated the air-only Sho for the Battle of Taiwan, Ozawa had prepared his air groups in a timely fashion while hating every bit of it.

ONE KEY MISTAKE took place even before the guns began shooting. Admiral Ozawa took his flagship, light cruiser *Oyodo*, to fuel at Tokuyama on October 15. He then brought the Mobile Fleet together at Yashima anchorage, where Ozawa moved his flag from *Oyodo* to the fleet aircraft carrier *Zuikaku*. The admiral probably did this to free up the light cruiser and strengthen his slim surface strength. But the *Oyodo* had been designed with service as a flagship in mind, and the cruiser had facilities for staff and extra communications gear for a fleet commander that *Zuikaku* did not have. And Ozawa did not realize, as he worked within cramped quarters on the carrier, that *Zuikaku* had something wrong with her radio transmitters. The carrier admiral reckoned—and later told his U.S. Navy interrogators—that Imperial Navy communications were bad *onshore*, due to poor technical ability, equipment, and other reasons.

When word came that the Americans had started landing at the mouth of Leyte Gulf, Ozawa sent senior staff officer Ohmae Toshikazu to Kure to confer once again with Combined Fleet higher-ups. The high command agreed the Mobile Fleet needed some sort of air arm to be credible, even as a decoy. As a result, Combined Fleet recalled the carrier air groups that had been flying under Admiral Fukudome's command, and the remaining planes came to Oita, where Ozawa had sent the vessels of his Carrier Division 3. In inclement weather, cranes loaded them aboard the ship, finishing the morning of October 20. There were no aircraft for the battleship-carriers *Ise* and *Hyuga*.

The fleet left base via the Bungo Strait late that afternoon, with the *Oyodo* now in the role of leading Rear Admiral Edo Heitaro's 31st

Escort Squadron. Admiral Ozawa set a five-minute interval between zigzags and, when day dawned, began to use floatplanes for antisub scouting, starting with those from *Oyodo*. There were submarine alerts every day. Somehow in waters saturated with U.S. submarines, it did not translate into what Ozawa wanted: sighting reports sent to Allied commanders.

On the morning of October 22, Rear Admiral Nomura Tomekichi's hybrid battleship *Hyuga* intercepted what he understood to be Task Force 38's voice radio. From Manila, Admiral Mikawa's radio operators got a bead on the same transmissions. Plotting the bearings gave Ozawa his first inkling of where Halsey might be. In preparation, Ozawa had his own ships refuel under way, and in keeping with the Japanese experience at this stage of the war, fuel proved a headache for the Ozawa fleet. All went without incident until about one in the afternoon, when Commander Kawabata Makoto's *Kiri*, a small destroyer of the latest type, refueled alongside *Oyodo*. A swell took Kawabata's ship at the beam and pushed her over, severing the fuel hose and the lines connecting the two ships.

Kiri got just twenty tons of precious oil. High seas also frustrated Captain Mudaguchi Kokuro of the *Oyodo* when he tried again later that day. The fleet received just a third of the oil it expected. Ozawa was operating with two replenishment units, each with a big tanker. He was forced to cancel the entire refueling effort when a submarine contact developed toward evening. *Zuikaku* and light cruiser *Tama* cast off and made emergency turns. A destroyer counterattacked. The next refueling now loomed even more important.

On his mission, Admiral Ozawa kept to character. Stubborn, silent, strong-willed, Ozawa paced the bridge of flagship *Zuikaku*. Hour upon hour, nothing happened. So he innovated. The radio deception plan would be especially elaborate. Several lengthy dispatches, from different radios, using different call signs, were involved. Ten or more signals typical of aircraft transmissions were to suggest carriers. Cruiser *Oyodo*, assigned to participate because Allied intelligence would know she had been the Combined Fleet's flagship, would send a series of messages to Admiral Matsuda's hybrid battleships. In the evening of October 22, Ozawa had another lengthy dispatch transmitted specifically so Allied intelligence might intercept it and establish his position. Breaking radio silence failed. The Allies' vaunted Ultra network completely missed the deception. The Zoo's Ultra summary for October 23 noted the Imperial Navy's carriers at sea, but hedged the judgment with qualifiers such as "apparently" and "unknown," which made clear its deduction had no basis in evidence. The first appearance in the Ultra of any element associated with the Ozawa fleet came on October 24, and at the time, it concerned only its refueling groups.

By then, it was the very day of battle. Commander Yamazaki Jintaro led destroyer *Akikaze*, fresh from refitting, to the replenishment group escort. He continued to steam south as submarine *Sterlet* (Commander Orme C. "Butch" Robbins) caught the oiler *Jinei Maru*. Some 69 sailors drowned. Ultra intercepted Yamazaki's dispatch reporting the rescue of *Jinei Maru*'s captain and 113 other crew. *Akikaze* and another escort took them to Oshima.

Admiral Ozawa put his worries about fuel on hold while feeling his way southward. A full set of searches went to a distance of 300 miles, ending with a 40-mile dogleg. The ships were alerted for battle from 6:18 a.m. onward, and antiaircraft positions were fully manned. The admiral, whose nickname in the fleet was "Gargoyle" for his stony countenance, showed no reaction when they received a sighting report of Task Force 38 carriers from the First Air Fleet in the Philippines, or when his own scouts confirmed the information with better location data. Then, and only when Ozawa had become confident his fleet had been spotted, did he send his own planes to add to the hell of the *Princeton*.

Here is a mystery of Leyte Gulf: Early this day Halsey had only suspicions about Ozawa's presence. Yet the Japanese admiral acted based upon a belief that his lure had worked—that a scout had spotted him. But no U.S. aircraft filed any sighting of Ozawa before late afternoon. *Oyodo* noticed that scout at 4:42 p.m. Captain Mudaguchi added that it was an SB-2C Helldiver that made a strafing run on his ship from thirty degrees to port, giving the report a concrete character. U.S. Navy interrogators pressed Ozawa about the morning sighting and the admiral insisted he had it right. Ozawa said he had seen the scout planes himself.

"I expected complete destruction of my fleet," Ozawa told U.S. interrogators, "but if Kurita's mission was carried out that was all I wished." He lacked confidence in the success of his decoy mission but knew it was the only thing they could do. That, too, was characteristic of Ozawa. His only sign of agitation was a slight shaking in his hands. The JNAF scout confirmed the Halsey fleet at 11:15 a.m. Half an hour later, Ozawa's carriers turned into the wind to launch. Shortly after noon, the cool Ozawa came around to a northwest course, but no Allied attack materialized.

Out of options, at 2:40 p.m., the main body commander pulled his own version of forming the battleship task force. Ozawa directed Rear Admiral Matsuda Chiaki to separate, take most of the destroyers, and operate as an advance force to make a night torpedo attack. Matsuda complied. In the dusk, lookouts saw flashes against the horizon. Staff thought it could be from the pyrotechnics of JNAF attacks on the Halsey fleet. Admiral Matsuda thought the sky looked more like an electrical storm and felt that even more strongly as darkness gathered. Matsuda also had radar indications of aircraft, however. The occasional flashes persisted until about nine o'clock. Deciding to observe strict radio silence, Matsuda made no report. But he shaped a course toward the lights. Around 10:30 p.m., as Matsuda expected to close with the phantom fleet, Admiral Ozawa recalled the vanguard, planning an early-morning rendezvous.

Meanwhile, the main body turned due west toward Cape Engaño. This marked a departure from standard carrier tactics, in which the force launching a strike against an adversary heads away from the enemy to put maximum distance between the sides. Instead, Ozawa maneuvered so as to maintain a constant distance from Task Force 38.

But that did not last. Suddenly the *Oyodo* reported an American scout plane and its strafing attack. Admiral Ozawa turned the fleet due north. Elated, he dashed off a dispatch to Combined Fleet, Kurita, Mikawa, and everyone else that the Americans had found him and were tumbling for the lure. That transmission failed to go through. The *Zuikaku*'s communication problems cost the Imperial Navy dearly.

The *Zuikaku* overheard the message where Admiral Kurita reported his decision to withdraw temporarily in the Sibuyan Sea. This must have tried Ozawa's stolidity when he learned of it at about eight o'clock. He had already sacrificed the carrier air groups, deliberately kept his fleet in harm's way, detached his biggest surface ships as bait, all to enable the Kurita fleet's penetration mission, and now they were turning away. Ozawa ordered a course change too, northeastward toward Empire waters.

With Admiral Matsuda's advance force dangling, the main-body commander altered course again around midnight, coming around to the south-southeast to rendezvous with the vanguard unit. Admiral Matsuda had not been able to find the Allies in the dark, so his attack mission turned into a bust—probably just as well since his warships were no match for the escort of even one of Halsey's task groups.

It was on Ozawa's 140-degree heading that the night scout from *Independence* found him after two o'clock. There is no indication the Japanese were aware of this sighting, since Ozawa coolly maintained his course. Once the Matsuda vanguard unit rejoined, at about dawn, the admiral began evasive maneuvers for the first time. The fleet turned through many points of the compass to head, first northeast, then to the northwest, and the *Zuikaku* crew went to battle stations at 5:30 a.m.

A couple of hours after dawn, all doubt evaporated. At 7:13, lookouts saw American air scouts. Ozawa knew Halsey's attack would begin shortly. The one bit of good news—a dispatch from Kurita showed he had gone through the San Bernardino after all and was engaging the Allies off Samar. At 7:45, Ozawa ordered his fleet to prepare for air attacks. The Gargoyle would need all his faculties.

THE SACRIFICE OF THE MOBILE FLEET

Airman John Yeager of the *Essex* would always remember October 25 as the day he and his comrades raised a lot of hell. That wouldn't be obvious at first—Mick Carney later admitted to Bill Halsey, "I chewed my fingernails down to my elbows," while awaiting news of the first wave. But the combat power of the Third Fleet had grown enormously, and after the happy hunting against Kurita the day before, the pilots were on a roll.

The lead attack that Dave McCampbell managed set the tone. The Japanese detected about eighty planes inbound at 8:17 a.m. Barely ten minutes later, the strike arrived overhead. Ozawa launched what fighters he had, but the powerful strike force simply brushed aside the dozen or more interceptors. Ozawa's only defenses would be maneuver and flak. He ordered fire opened at 8:23 a.m.

In contrast to the *Musashi* earlier, the Ozawa fleet had no compunction about using the dangerous *sanshikidan* shells from the 14-inch guns of *Ise* and *Hyuga*. Flak began assailing the strike aircraft as far as ten miles away. *Enterprise* fliers found the fire surprisingly accurate, and far enough downrange that the Japanese could take more than one shot. The powerful explosions were unnerving but not especially effective. The huge shells destroyed no planes, and the same went for the rockets the Imperial Navy had installed so assiduously on its big ships. Their firing angles and slant ranges were so restrictive that they served primarily to disrupt attackers' aim. The conventional medium and light flak was another matter. *Enterprise* crews observed intense fire and shell bursts in many colors. Avenger pilot Robert Barnes decided the flak was "the most intense I have ever seen." As he went in, "all ships were firing everything they had . . . every ship you flew by was shooting at you." TBM crewman John Underwood of the *Lexington* remembered the flak as "awesome." Given the fierce opposition, it is fortunate that only eleven American warplanes were lost—Halsey's assault had involved 527 sorties (cruiser *Oyodo* claimed twenty-seven planes were shot down).

Dave McCampbell would be only the first Task Force 38 strike manager. This offensive was different from the fight at Philippine Sea. Engaño was carried out at such short range that Admiral Mitscher could rotate coordinators and keep up a constant, well-directed assault. Here, McCampbell had the leisure to fly home to refuel and return to resume his coordination role. Commander Theodore H. Winters, the *Lexington*'s air group boss, estimates spending six to six and a half hours orbiting the Ozawa fleet that day. The Japanese were less than 100 miles away. Mitscher sent his planes at Ozawa in five waves starting with this early-morning attack. McCampbell's strike pitched the Ozawa fleet immediately into turmoil. First into Davy Jones's locker would be Commander Yogata Tomoe's destroyer *Akitsuki*. On that vessel Lieutenant Yamamoto Heiya was chief boilerman. He had a bad feeling about this sortie—third time, unlucky—as *Akitsuki* had survived a couple of tight scrapes already. In any case, there had been so many phony submarine and other alerts that he and the fifty-odd sailors in the boiler gang were exhausted. In addition, Ozawa had maneuvered so much throughout the day on the twenty-fourth that it had added to their burdens. Commander Yogata's vessel sailed with Matsuda's vanguard force. There had been no battle, but the chief engineer, maintaining eighteen knots, kept switching orders to prepare for twenty-four or not. The boilermen were constantly to-ing and fro-ing.

Suddenly Yamamoto heard the noise of flak, then sounds of battle. Moments later a bomb burst in the engine room. Before the battle, the boiler gang had neglected to close and seal the hatch between the compartments. More explosions followed; then steam and smoke poured in, causing real confusion. The space became unbearably hot, with fires *above* them too. When the fumes became noxious, Yamamoto and a few boilermen pushed their way up, despite how scalding the ladders were, and became the only survivors. The lieutenant reported to Commander Yogata, his ship otherwise undamaged, who wondered why *Akitsuki* had lost power. Yamamoto's burn injuries stunned the skipper. Suddenly the destroyer lurched and listed. At 8:57 a.m. the *Akitsuki* rolled over and sank.

From the *Oyodo* sailors saw the destroyer emit innocent-looking white smoke, but the color changed to oily and black after just six minutes. Observers on the cruiser thought the *Akitsuki* had simply blown up. The entire episode took less than ten minutes.

Similar scenes played out elsewhere. *Essex* torpedo bombers went after the battleship *Ise* and claimed three hits. The Japanese recorded nothing more than near misses on her. Torpedo bombers from Task Force 38 carriers *Belleau Wood* and *San Jacinto* rolled into attacks on the light cruiser *Tama*. Captain Yamamoto Iwata's (no relation to any of the others in our story) cruiser had been helping protect the Japanese light carrier *Chitose*. For her trouble she suffered a torpedo hit in a portside boiler room, which left the ship temporarily dead in the water.

Dive-bombers and torpedo planes from the *Essex* took on the

Chitose. Captain Kishi Yoshiyuki's carrier would be challenged by three events in quick succession. Sources differ on whether these were bomb hits, near misses, or torpedos, but Lieutenant John D. Bridger's Helldivers claimed a dozen hits and the Avengers of Torpedo 15 insisted two of their fish struck home.

The carrier's executive officer, Commander Yano Kanji, plunged into efforts to save the ship. He managed to right half of the steep thirty-degree list, but he could not restore power lost from two flooded boiler rooms. Then the rudder failed, and the vessel had to steer by engines. When an engine failed too, *Chitose*'s speed, which had already dropped to fourteen knots, fell off even more. Before Yano could accomplish anything else, the *Chitose*'s list increased more, and just an hour after her initial wounds, the ship sank. Captain Kishi and more than 900 crewmen went down with her. Captain Matsuda Gengo's *Isuzu* plus destroyer *Shimotsuki* teamed up to rescue another 600 sailors.

In the Japanese formation, Captain Sugiura Kuro's *Zuiho* steamed on the port quarter of Ozawa's flagship. Emmet Riera of the *Enterprise* led his Helldivers to bomb her. There were three misses off the stern and a 500-pound bomb hit aft, which jammed the rear elevator. The ship took a slight list, rudder control failed, and a fire started in the hangar deck. But Commander Eguchi Itozumi's repair teams were so effective that by 8:55 a.m.—within twenty minutes—the list had been righted, the fires stopped, and the steering restored.

Fleet carrier *Zuikaku*'s purgatory would be more intense as Rear Admiral Kaizuka Takeo maneuvered the ship. (Ozawa had no use for superseding his ship captain.) Kaizuka went twenty-four knots, turning violently. Lookouts counted forty bombers plus ten torpedo planes. Someone spotted a torpedo on the starboard beam. Barely five minutes later, another track appeared up the ship's throat—from port, astern. Just then one or several 500-pound bombs hit on the port side, amidships. Then a torpedo impacted amidships. Fires started on the hangar deck. The number four generator room flooded. That and consequent damage disabled the rudder, cut power to the helm, and shorted out the secondary switchboard controls. Soon one of the port engine rooms flooded and the ship acquired a marked list, her speed depending solely upon a single propeller.

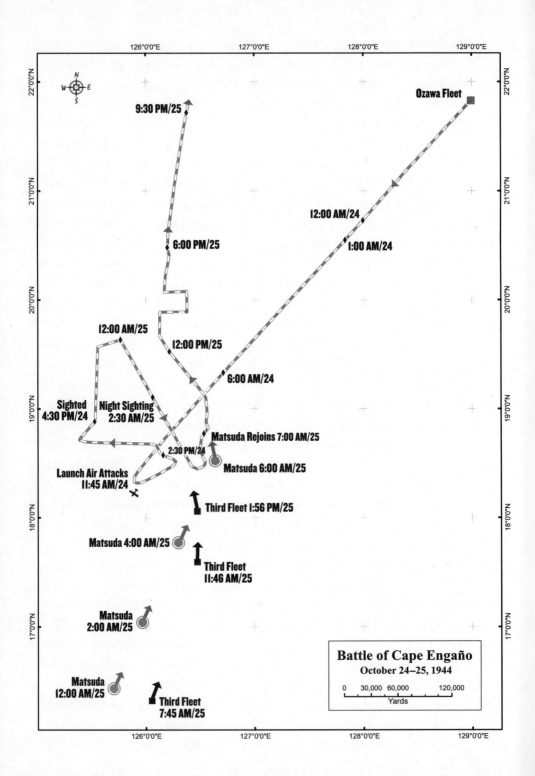

Battle of Cape Engaño
October 24–25, 1944

At first damage control worked effectively. By nine o'clock, when Admiral Kaizuka ordered a cease-fire, signaling the end of the air attack, helm control had been restored, the fires were out, counterflooding had corrected the port list from a dangerous twenty-nine and a half degrees to a mild six, and the vessel could make good speed again, albeit on only two shafts. On the other hand, the *Zuikaku*'s radio transmitters had ceased functioning altogether.

The latter seriously affected fleet commander Ozawa. Chief of staff Obayashi advised the admiral to transfer his flag. Ozawa refused. He expected the fleet to be destroyed, so he would go down with his flagship. Senior staff Ohmae appealed to his good sense, and Ozawa still resisted.

Seven *Lexington* torpedo planes had been too late for the first wave. Airman John Underwood was the belly gunner in one of those and had missed the launch because hangar crews had trouble slinging her torpedo properly. The planes finally got away, flying parallel to a small second wave from *Enterprise*. Big E Helldivers and *Lexington* Avengers went after Kaizuka's carrier, which had just finished moving ammunition from the water-threatened aft magazines to the starboard side. *Zuikaku* mustered all her speed, and gunners poured out fire. Crewmen saw two torpedos off the stern. The carrier emerged unscathed, but the TBMs believed they had hit with three fish. Underwood and his crewmates received the Distinguished Flying Cross.

Most of the second wave concentrated against light aircraft carrier *Chiyoda*. She was the vessel skippered by Captain Jyo Eichiro, one of the Navy's kamikaze advocates and formerly aide-de-camp to Emperor Hirohito. The Helldivers were from *Lexington* and *Franklin*. They bored in from 10:10 a.m., slapping Jyo's carrier with four bomb hits. Suddenly the *Chiyoda* lost power, like the others, but this time nothing that executive officer Kumon Shigenori tried seemed to work. The warship drifted. A few planes went after the *Zuiho*, and in one of the few instances where these proved effective for the Japanese, the carrier's antiaircraft rockets were instrumental in driving them off.

With Imperial Navy warships being destroyed, and *Zuikaku* without radios, Admiral Ozawa finally listened to Captain Ohmae's pleas. Thanks to swift repair work, Captain Yamamoto's cruiser *Tama* had gotten under way again just as the second attack rolled in. Light cruiser *Isuzu* sailed with her. Rear Admiral Matsuda was trying to organize a tow for the crippled *Chiyoda*. What to do? The fleet still needed Ozawa's leadership. When Captain Ohmae asked again if he would transfer—and said "Please!"—Gargoyle agreed. At 9:44 a.m. *Zuikaku* signaled *Oyodo* to come alongside, but they postponed the transfer minutes later as the gunners fired upon the new attack planes. Another transfer attempt failed at 10:14. A dozen minutes later, Captain Muda-guchi was actually able to stop and put a boat in the water. Admiral Ozawa and eleven staffers climbed down to the cutter, which also picked up a downed pilot. At 10:54, Ozawa raised his flag on board the cruiser *Oyodo*. He had come full circle.

The *Zuikaku* managed eighteen knots, but it was not enough for Rear Admiral Kaizuka to position his ship to recover CAP fighters. The nine remaining planes had to ditch. Ozawa instructed the *Tama* to head home independently and tried to regroup the remaining ships with him. A little after noon, the *Zuikaku* increased to twenty knots and an hour later to twenty-four. She seemed to be in good condition.

The *Zuiho* now held the port quarter position, with Rear Admiral Matsuda's *Ise* completing a triangle. Battleship *Hyuga* now lay thirty miles to the rear, trying to protect the *Chiyoda* while *Isuzu* towed her. When Admiral Ozawa discovered a third attack wave headed his way, he reluctantly recalled those ships and left the light carrier to her fate.

This third mission, coordinated by Commander Ted Winters, put more than 200 aircraft up against the Mobile Fleet. Ozawa's force, punier by the minute, was creamed. Winters set *Lexington*'s planes against the *Zuikaku*. Aircraft divided to hit from both sides at once. He thought the carrier smothered. Beginning at 1:15 p.m., pilots pressed home their attacks. Within the space of eight minutes, half a dozen torpedoes slammed into the hapless warship from both sides. The assault left the carrier powerless and settling in the sea. Rear Admiral Kaizuka ordered all hands on deck at 1:27, preparatory to abandoning ship. The captain addressed his crew, the Imperial Navy ensign was lowered, and a bugler played the "Kimigayo." Crewmen began leaving just before 4:00 p.m. About a quarter of an hour later the *Zuikaku* slowly rolled over to port and sank, stern first. Destroyer *Wakatsuki* and escort *Kuwa* rescued a bit more than half the carrier's crew. Some 842 sailors were lost, including Rear Admiral Kaizuka.

Zuiho's cruise also ended in a nightmare. Captain Sugiura could hardly maneuver. Strike coordinator Winters directed the attack planes from the *Enterprise, San Jacinto,* and *Franklin* at her. At 1:17 p.m., *Enterprise* planes hit the carrier with a torpedo right under the bridge. Sugiura would be wounded. A bomb struck the after elevator. A little more than ten minutes later, the really massive strike washed over Sugiura's weakened ship—a torpedo hit starboard, another bomb, and seven near misses, followed by dozens of claimed near misses from subsequent serials of aircraft. Lieutenant Wistar Janney of the *Franklin*'s VT-13 won the Navy Cross for putting the new torpedo into the *Zuiho.*

On the Japanese carrier, executive officer Eguchi Itozumi had little chance against the extensive damage. Speed dropped until the *Zuiho* drifted, only to be hit by Task Force 38's fourth strike, with yet more near misses. Already by 2:10, every available sailor had been summoned to the pumps. *Zuiho* sank about an hour later, though Sugiura had time to save the emperor's portrait and most of the crew—more than 750 men. It was Commander Eguchi, caught in the blasted bowels of *Zuiho*, who did not survive. He would be the seniormost of 215 men lost.

For Task Force 38's fifth-wave attack, Admiral Mitscher considered the Japanese defenses so beaten down that he ordered the fighters to fly in a strike role, armed with rockets or 1,000-pound bombs. That assault connected around 4:15 p.m., to be credited with two torpedo and six bomb hits on the battleships, plus sinking a destroyer. The claims seem to have been illusory.

What is interesting about the last three Task Force 38 strikes—the ones that finished off two of the four Japanese aircraft carriers—is that they were mounted by an incomplete and reduced U.S. striking force. Admiral William F. Halsey no longer sailed alongside. The Bull had left—taking Jerry Bogan's Task Group 38.2 and Ching Lee's Task Force 34 with him. Halsey's absence reflected the gravest emergency for the Allies at the Battle of Leyte Gulf.

BULL'S RUN

When Admiral Halsey decided on his run north he had some confidence the Japanese strength represented by the Kurita fleet had been countered. They had been seen to turn away. The dilemma lay in whether that much was enough. If Kurita continued to flee, unquestionably it was. If not, the situation could become dicey. Admiral Halsey held to his decision to head north with all three groups, including the vessels that would have formed Lee's fast battleship armada.

Admiral Halsey arranged his chase from midafternoon on October 24, with the Kurita fleet under fire. Halsey's misinformation regarding enemy losses, though not so immense as Japanese delusions in the Taiwan battle, were enough to hold a mistaken impression of Kurita's true strength. That led the Third Fleet commander into error. Halsey understood his aviators had sunk a *Yamato*-class battleship, three cruisers, and a destroyer, while damaging all the other battleships and reducing their fighting power. From this, he deduced that the Kurita fleet would be hampered if it turned east again.

In part, history has burdened William F. Halsey with an impossible mission. The three task groups of Third Fleet spent most of that day circling the waters where the *Princeton* fight took place. This put the fleet roughly 260 nautical miles from the San Bernardino Strait. If Halsey's message *had* been an action order, and Vice Admiral Lee had separated his task force in, say, two hours (very quick) and made the run to San Bernardino Strait at twenty-four knots—a fast fleet speed— Task Force 34 could have arrived off the San Bernardino at about 6:00 a.m. on October 25, five hours *after* the Kurita fleet passed that way.

At this moment the Kurita fleet had already attacked farther south. To block Kurita and force a battle, Ching Lee would have had to steam the whole way at a full battle speed of thirty-three knots. But four of the six battleships in Lee's force were not rated higher than twenty-eight knots. His choices would have been to go hell-for-leather, dropping ships along the way, and reaching the San Bernardino with just the *Iowa* and *New Jersey*, or to make a stern chase after Kurita had passed into the Pacific. There were questions either way.

Part of the lambasting Halsey has endured comes from his Seventh

Fleet counterparts who *assumed* the Third Fleet commander had issued an action order. They are not the only ones. Admiral Nimitz and General MacArthur thought the same. Some of Halsey's own officers, including operations chief Brigadier General William Riley and radio unit boss Commander Gilven Slonim, thought, at the evening operations conference, that Task Force 34 would be together before morning. They were right, but it was not for the purpose of going after Kurita.

The storm over "Bull's Run" comes to a point when we discover that Admiral Halsey *actually knew* that Kurita had turned around and was headed east once more. Most disturbing of all—and missing from standard accounts of Leyte Gulf—were a pair of Pearl Harbor dispatches marked "Ultra. From CINCPAC," and "This is Ultra from CINCPAC," which were sent during the night and recorded radio direction-finding fixes for the locations of Japanese naval radio transmissions inside or on the *Pacific* side of the San Bernardino. Nimitz sent both messages to Halsey for "action." They originated close to dawn.

Nimitz's use of the word "Ultra" in these messages was a grave breach of security. It can only be explained as an attempt to indicate the authoritative source of the information and simultaneously demand, without actually saying so, urgent action. That Nimitz would take the risk of compromising the Ultra source in an operational message is astonishing. It is also an index of how serious he deemed the situation to be.

None of those warnings, however, induced Admiral Halsey to change his mind. When he did form Lee's fast battleship force, it was for the same purpose Ozawa had used Rear Admiral Matsuda's hybrid vessels, as an advance guard. Soon news began to flow, interspersed with Third Fleet pilots' tallyhos! On sighting the vaunted Japanese carriers anew, Halsey was anxious to be at them.

Admirals Nimitz, Kinkaid, and everyone else ought to have been in no doubt regarding Halsey's intentions. Ten days before, at the height of the Taiwan battle sequence, the Third Fleet commander had briefly been distracted by the appearance of a Japanese force (Shima, misidentified as representing the forward echelon of the carriers) and had had to be prodded by Kinkaid and called back by Nimitz. On the twenty-first, Halsey had complained of his operations being restricted by the need to cover Leyte. He had wanted freedom for more offensive action.

CINCPAC had called him to task again. But Halsey had a basic order that allowed him to make a Japanese fleet his target, if one materialized—and his experience taught him that aircraft carriers were the heart of fleets. Now that he had carriers in front of him, there was nothing else he could arguably do but go after them.

The irony here is very sharp. At the Battle of Leyte Gulf *both sides* made a mistake. Moreover, both sides *made the same mistake.* And each made its mistake *for the same reason*! The Japanese let the desire to attack fleets get in the way of their asserted goal of destroying invasion forces, and they did it because tradition taught that fleets must be the primary target. Bill Halsey left the San Bernardino Strait unguarded because he wanted to keep his force together to attack the enemy carrier fleet he had learned was the main threat.

The Third Fleet commander, enjoying the chase, waited on news of his first strike wave when other reports began to flood in. At 6:48 a.m. on October 25—almost precisely the moment the Japanese began attacking off Samar—Halsey received word of Kinkaid's fight in the Surigao Strait. The Seventh Fleet chief added a question: "IS TF34 GUARDING SAN BERNARDINO STRAIT?" Halsey's reply that it was not stunned Kinkaid.

Then, at 8:22 a.m., Halsey got the delayed news of Japanese battleships and cruisers attacking jeep carrier units outside Leyte Gulf. That had been sent in real time, of course, at 7:07. Only eight minutes later came Kinkaid's appeal, "FAST BATTLESHIPS ARE URGENTLY NEEDED AT LEYTE GULF AT ONCE." Around nine o'clock, with the Seventh Fleet's jeep carriers almost on the ropes, Halsey learned Kinkaid's details of the Kurita fleet and its attack, with further messages asking for immediate strikes by carriers and the fast battleships.

Bill Halsey replied that he was engaging the Japanese carriers and that he had ordered Slew McCain to the aid of the Seventh Fleet. Halsey added his position, thus indicating the physical impossibility of fast battleships helping Kinkaid. The Third Fleet boss also wondered at another Kinkaid dispatch, one delayed in transit, revealing that Seventh Fleet had expended much ammunition at Surigao. Halsey describes this as "so astonishing I could hardly accept it," implying that had he known he would have acted differently.

Three things are worth comment. First, the earliest Kinkaid could have realized his ammunition situation would have been before dawn, say, about 4:15 a.m., following the Surigao cannonade—and probably a bit later due to the time required to take inventory. That coincided with the moment in the predawn hours that Vice Admiral Lee finished assembling Task Force 34, so Halsey could have sent them immediately, but the distance to San Bernardino from where Third Fleet happened to be, roughly the same as the previous afternoon, would have consumed about the same transit time. Within those parameters Admiral Lee might have been able to intervene by six in the afternoon—still too late to do any good. In his responses to Kinkaid's increasingly anxious appeals, Halsey was already making the "too late to do anything"–type argument. There is no reason to suppose that, resistant to sending Lee's battleships, the Third Fleet commander would have done so now. Halsey's account seems aimed at the reader.

Second, delays kept the message from Admiral Halsey for hours after the Surigao fight. The Third Fleet's admiral records getting this information at 9:22 a.m. Not only did this automatically hold up a Third Fleet response, but the delay was entirely avoidable. Because MacArthur's communications plan provided for messages between the fleets to go over SOWESPAC circuits, the Kinkaid dispatch went to a radio relay station at Manus, and there joined a queue to be re-sent in the order received. This delay cost vital time.

The other thing is that Admiral Kinkaid was being disingenuous too. His big ships had plenty more ammunition than he let on. Exhaustive postwar study by the Naval War College established that the Seventh Fleet battleships at Surigao expended a total of 282 14- and 16-inch shells in the battle. *After* the fight—and counting *only* armor-piercing shells—Kinkaid's ships still had about 300 16-inch and almost 1,100 14-inch rounds. He was certainly not out of ammunition. The best you can make of this from Kinkaid's point of view is to say he must not have known his ships' status right after the battle. But if not, *he had no business making that claim.* What *was* true—that the Seventh Fleet battleships in Surigao were at the opposite end of Leyte Gulf from the new threat, probably five hours away—was a point Kinkaid's messages *did not make.*

The tone in Seventh Fleet dispatches became increasingly desperate. At about 10:00 a.m., Kinkaid sent a message in the clear, not even bothering to encode it: "WHERE IS LEE. SEND LEE."

Then came the message that has reverberated down the years, sent by Admiral Chester Nimitz, not Kinkaid. "WHERE IS REPEAT WHERE IS TASK FORCE 34. THE WORLD WONDERS. TURKEY TROTS TO WATER."

Halsey could not believe that CINCPAC would send him such a message, and he was right. The confusion arose because anonymous communications officers, when preparing the signal, padded it with spurious text to confuse enemy code breakers. The "turkey trots" language had been obvious filler, but the "world wants to know" part was so close to the true events of the situation that radiomen on flagship *New Jersey*, worried it might be actual text, left it in. The filler contained an implied criticism. Commander Slonim pointed that out to Halsey.

Bill Halsey felt like Nimitz had hit him in the face. He turned red, threw his cap on the deck, and demanded to know how Nimitz dared. Admiral Carney ran up and grabbed Halsey's arm. He practically *did* slap the fleet commander in the face.

"Stop it!" the chief of staff exclaimed. "What the hell's the matter with you? Pull yourself together!"

Halsey stalked off to his cabin with Mick Carney right behind him.

THE THIRD FLEET commander might have been right, but the world did want to know about this battle, this key battle, upon which so much depended. Perhaps not the whole world, but at least Franklin Delano Roosevelt, which, from an American naval officer's point of view, amounted to the same thing.

FDR had a command center called the Map Room. A Navy captain, John L. McCrea, had set it up in early 1942, starting with just two file cabinets, situated on the ground floor of the White House, next to the Diplomatic Reception Room. President Roosevelt often stopped by in the morning or at night, or both.

Many, many messages, dispatches reflecting developments in every theater of the war, flowed through the president's Map Room. The duty officer made choices as to which ones to plot on maps, which to post on bulletin boards, and what simply went to file. FDR had been attentive to the Pacific action since the onset of the Taiwan air battle. Unlike Winston Churchill and his Soviet or German counterparts, Roosevelt almost never put his hand directly into naval or military affairs. In the Pacific war, he had not done so between a certain moment in the Guadalcanal campaign, late in 1942, and the recent conference President Roosevelt had held at Pearl Harbor. But seeing the traffic on the Taiwan battle, the president had sent a cable to Admiral Halsey congratulating the Third Fleet.

Map Room officers posted dispatches reporting the landings in Leyte Gulf, and they continued to follow the Japanese reaction. When the sub *Darter* saw the Kurita fleet and reported its movements, it would be posted in the Map Room. Copies of subsequent reports were circulated or posted too, including one of the Ozawa carrier force and another of the Nishimura unit. The president thus knew about all three major Japanese fleet units.

In the evening on October 24, the message containing the aerial sighting of the Japanese carriers would be not only posted, but forwarded to Mr. Roosevelt and to his naval aide, Admiral Wilson Brown. Kinkaid's brief notice that he was engaging Imperial Navy surface forces in the Surigao Strait would be hand-carried to the president. CINCPAC's Ultra messages giving positions on the Pacific side of the Philippines were stamped "SPECIAL DISTRIBUTION" at the Map Room. So, FDR knew about the security breach too. When the Japanese fell upon vulnerable jeep carriers, the Map Room exhibited great concern. A staffer annotated the initial message in that series with the location of the action and the local time in the Philippines.

Franklin Delano Roosevelt also wanted to know the answer to the question Chester Nimitz put to William F. Halsey. Later, he put Map Room analysts to work on a chronology explaining the precise sequence of events at Leyte Gulf. But the president said nothing in public.

IN FLAG PLOT on the *New Jersey* the mood darkened quickly with the parade of messages. Despite the excitement of the chase and the destruction of Ozawa, news of an emergency down south and Kinkaid's appeals for fast battleships caused concern. Faces paled at the idea that the emergency might have something to do with Third Fleet decisions. And now Nimitz's admonition made the situation clear. Mick Carney returned after nearly an hour with Halsey, bearing orders to turn the fast battleships around. Intelligence officer Carl Solberg recalled, "Halsey had no choice. . . . He had to comply." At 10:52 a.m., Vice Admiral Lee with Task Force 34 began turning south accompanied by Admiral Bogan's carriers.

The forces were on the new heading by 11:15 a.m. Bill Halsey's next message warned they could not arrive in the Leyte area before about eight the following morning. No exaggeration—at this point the Halsey force lay roughly 440 nautical miles from the San Bernardino Strait. Even at twenty-four knots that meant more than eighteen hours, which put arrival at 7:00 a.m., and Leyte lay even farther away. What actually happened was that Admiral Lee refueled destroyers and then divided his force, with fast battleships *Iowa* and *New Jersey* sent ahead at very high speed to sweep the approaches to the San Bernardino during the night, then proceed along the coast of Samar to Leyte. The main force took the direct route to Leyte.

The Third Fleet commander instructed Admiral Lee to detach four cruisers and ten destroyers to join Ted Sherman's Task Group 38.3. Admiral Sherman had felt little effect from the withdrawal of ships of his escort that had gone to Task Force 34. Sherman writes that he preferred to pose a surface threat to Ozawa, recommending to Pete Mitscher that this ad hoc surface action group be committed to the chase. E. B. Potter, biographer of Mitscher's staff chief Arleigh Burke, contends that Sherman's suggestion was not for a surface pursuit but for ships to take derelict carrier *Chiyoda* in tow, and that Mitscher's idea was to attack instead. Admiral Mitscher issued that order at 2:15 p.m.

Be that as it may, the last three strike waves of the Battle of Cape Engaño thus occurred in tandem with a surface pursuit. Under Rear Admiral Laurance T. DuBose, four cruisers and nine destroyers made speed toward the enemy. They came up on the *Chiyoda* just as the air coordinator, Ted Winters, was heading back to roost. Commander Winters supplied DuBose with the right bearing to reach the Japanese ship and stayed a bit longer to spot the fall of shot for the surface attackers. About 4:25 p.m., the U.S. warships began shooting. The *Chiyoda* went to her final resting place half an hour later. There were no known survivors.

DuBose resumed his pursuit. By now the Ozawa fleet, its vessels having sustained varying amounts of damage or mechanical malfunctions, were strung out over many miles. Admiral DuBose worried about a continuation of the pursuit. Ozawa had two battleships, after all, and his strongest vessel was a heavy cruiser. But Admiral Mitscher persisted. The cruiser-destroyer group steamed on into the gathering dusk. DuBose, helped by a couple of night fighters from the *Essex*, got a bead on several Japanese destroyers in the twilight. Led by the *Hatsuzuki*, the Japanese ships were picking up survivors from Ozawa's sunken carriers. The American cruisers commenced firing at 6:52 p.m. The *Hatsuzuki*, wearing the pennant of Captain Amano Shigetaka, who led a destroyer division, maneuvered as if she were launching torpedoes. Taking no chances, DuBose turned away to evade. Both sides repeated that maneuver, and the American admiral ordered his own destroyers to attack with torpedoes. The cruiser force resumed firing at 14,000 yards' range and steadily drove nearer. *Hatsuzuki* held on as Captain Amano played for time for the other escorts to escape. The cruisers stopped shooting and the Japanese destroyer sank at nearly nine o'clock.

Though the engagement with the U.S. cruisers marked the last contact with Third Fleet, it might not have been. From the *Oyodo*, lookouts could see the horizon lit by gun flashes to the south. At 7:52 p.m., Admiral Ozawa received Captain Amano's report of a surface engagement. Always one to support his men, Ozawa turned back to support the embattled *Hatsuzuki*. The cool Ozawa regrouped Matsuda's two battleships—just as the American DuBose had feared—with *Oyodo*, and the destroyer *Shimotsuki*, coming to a heading just west of south at about 9:30. Having just had his entire carrier force blown out from under him, Ozawa wanted to fight. On the way down, the *Wakatsuki*, one of Amano's survivors, joined up. They continued searching for DuBose until just before midnight, when Ozawa reluctantly retraced his steps and headed for safety.

Considering the actions of top Imperial Navy commanders, in the context of Ozawa's historical studies, he seems very much like a Japanese Franz von Hipper, the precise and careful leader of the German battle cruisers at the Jutland battle the young officer had studied so assiduously.

SUBMARINE ALARMS

Ozawa's defiant turnback marked the last act of the aero-naval battle between his main body and Halsey's Third Fleet. But it was not the end of the ordeal for this element of the Japanese force. Now came the submarine offensive.

The Allied submarine campaigns, incredibly damaging to Tokyo's hopes, had progressed to the point where commanders had sectioned off Pacific geography into broad areas in which not only individual subs but also so-called wolfpacks assumed patrol positions. Vice Admiral Charles A. Lockwood led the submarine fleet stationed at Pearl Harbor, and he had two wolfpacks totaling six boats to the east of the Philippines at the time of the Leyte battle. Both were headed for the region the Allies called "Convoy College," basically off the northern edge of the Philippines, in the Luzon Strait. The zone around Leyte and to the north had been ruled off-limits to subs because of the invasion.

But when Admiral Lockwood learned of the high probability that there would be a carrier battle off Cape Engaño, he asked CINCPAC for permission to send his wolfpacks into the proscribed waters. Chester Nimitz denied the request. The on-scene commander, Admiral Mitscher, however, was happy to get submarine cooperation. Subs had been major contributors to hurting the Japanese at the Philippine Sea battle, and as early as Midway, submarines had offered a helping hand in a carrier battle. Mitscher sent a message inviting help, which led Admiral Nimitz to relent. Unfortunately, all this happened too late for the subs to take full advantage, although they would still prove to be a thorn in the sides of their enemies.

Admiral Lockwood ordered the subs into a line to search out the

Japanese. Commander John P. "Beetle" Roach led three boats, *Haddock*, *Tuna*, and *Halibut*. It was Commander Ignatius J. ("Pete") Galantin's *Halibut* that made first contact. Galantin had had a ringside seat as warplanes assailed Ozawa's battleships and the cruiser *Oyodo*. At 5:42 p.m., the *Halibut* saw what it thought were the pagoda masts of a battleship coming his way and decided it was the *Ise*. Galantin maneuvered for an hour to set up a shot, and eventually emptied six torpedo tubes at the target, with the crew hearing five explosions. The *Ise* actually saw two torpedoes in the water at one point, and several more another time, but none hit her. Clay Blair, redoubtable chronicler of the U.S. submarine war, believes the victim was really destroyer *Akitsuki*, but, as related here, the *Akitsuki* had been sunk by aircraft much earlier in the day.

Before midnight (local time) at Pearl Harbor, Admiral Nimitz had received word, not only of the attack on the *Ise*, but of *Halibut* plus Roach's *Haddock* trailing Japanese battleships, and of a boat from the other wolfpack, *Jallao*, sinking a Japanese light cruiser. That would be the damaged *Tama*, struggling on her own to reach home. Lieutenant Commander Joseph Icenhower, on his very first patrol as a sub skipper, rode on the surface when his *Jallao* picked up the contact on radar. Captain Yamamoto Iwata's *Tama* struggled at reduced speed, but she was nearly fourteen miles away. Icenhower gave chase, as did Commander Bernard A. "Chick" Clarey in the *Pintado*. The *Jallao* got there first and loosed seven torpedoes, and the *Tama* disappeared beneath the waves. Clarey was close enough to confirm the cruiser had sunk. The news must have set Nimitz at ease about agreeing that subs could operate here.

There were another half dozen boats in the Luzon Strait, and a gauntlet of a dozen between the Ozawa fleet and home. A muddled contact report from the *Halibut* put the *Trigger* in a poor position to catch Admiral Matsuda's battleships the next morning. Commander Vernon L. "Rebel" Lowrance in the *Sea Dog* got another shot at Matsuda on October 28, after the Japanese battleships refueled from the *Takane Maru*, but the hermaphrodites providentially zagged away from the torpedoes in the water. They were steaming too fast for Rebel to chase. His report, picked up by Butch Robbins in *Sterlet*, led to one more attempt northeast of Okinawa, but it was again frustrated by Matsuda's speed. Remnants of the Ozawa fleet were near home now. They reached Empire waters safely. Matsuda entered Kure on October 29.

Finally the play came full circle to Ozawa's replenishment group. *Takane Maru* had boiler troubles, restricting her to a very low speed, so she was ordered to Kure for repairs. Code breakers at FRUPAC, benefiting from reading the Japanese transport ("*Maru*") code for so long, kept up a stream of updates on the oilers. They reported the demise of *Jinei Maru*, the boiler problems of her consort, movements of a couple of her escorts on October 26, and Combined Fleet orders to the oiler the next day. *Takane Maru*'s boiler problems cut her speed to well within the cruising capabilities of the U.S. submarines. Commander Frederick J. Harlfinger in the *Trigger* picked up *Takane Maru* and attacked her on October 30. The oiler saw one of *Trigger*'s torpedoes break the surface, so she turned away, whereupon escorts counterattacked and forced the *Trigger* to dive deep.

But Harlfinger's contact report enabled the *Salmon* to renew the attack. Two torpedoes struck the *Takane Maru*. Again, the escorts counterattacked, damaging Lieutenant Commander Harley K. Nauman's boat, forcing her to surface and fight with guns. At one point Nauman and a Japanese coast defense ship passed each other no more than fifty yards apart, firing everything down to machine guns. While all this distracted the escorts, Butch Robbins crept up again. At one in the morning, his *Sterlet* put four torpedoes into the hapless *Takane Maru* and sent her to Davy Jones.

THE IMPERIAL NAVY had its own submarines, and they too had their role to play in the Sho plan. The Japanese undersea service had been in flux for months, since its Sixth Fleet headquarters had been caught on Saipan, wiping out the sub fleet commander and his entire staff. Vice Admiral Miwa Shigeyoshi subsequently moved over from the bureau handling sub construction to reconstitute the fleet headquarters.

Miwa had been flotilla leader for some of the I-boats surrounding Pearl Harbor when the war began but had not had a billet at sea since he fell ill in 1942. A great deal had changed since then. At his ship-building post, Admiral Miwa had actually witnessed some of that, because virtual attrition had especially affected the Imperial Navy's submarine force. Allied dominance in the air and, increasingly, on the surface had forced the Sixth Fleet to repurpose submarines as undersea transports, not weapons. Miwa's shipbuilders actually converted some boats and designed a new class of subs without torpedo tubes so they could carry more supplies to bypassed island garrisons. In their desperate search for new weapons, the Japanese were also creating a manned torpedo they called the *kaiten*, and more subs were taken out of service to be prepared as mother ships for them.

There were service problems too. During the July 1944 command conference, Admiral Miwa found out that most of the boats (nine of fourteen) lost during the Marianas campaign had been pulled out of the Indian Ocean, where crews knew nothing of the latest American antisubmarine warfare tactics. Many of the others were crewed by sailors fresh from submarine school. The high loss rate sharpened the need for new crews, exacerbating the newbie problem. Admiral Miwa's fleet contained fifty-five submarines, but fifteen of them were engaged in training. That was virtual attrition too.

Basic directives for the Sixth Fleet for Sho had been issued on August 20, 1944. Combined Fleet Operations Order No. 87 set target priorities and designated half a dozen preplanned deployment zones, giving Admiral Miwa wide discretion to dictate final deployments. Increasing the confusion regarding Sho objectives, the submarine priorities were to sink aircraft carriers, battleships, and troop convoys—the opposite of other directives. However, Order No. 87 also emphasized flexibility and provided that the subs had to be ready to attack in strength in conjunction with penetration operations, and that Allied moves might require the submarine fleet to act in strength in unanticipated directions.

That very thing happened when Halsey's Third Fleet started the Taiwan air battle. Combined Fleet instructed Admiral Miwa to deploy off Taiwan immediately. Suddenly the effects of virtual attrition became very apparent. The strength of the Sixth Fleet did not even amount to the forty submarines on Miwa's active list. Seven boats were working up after construction or refits. Four subs were converting to *kaiten* carriers. An equal number were in the Indian Ocean. Another seven boats were in service as transports. Four submarines were overdue from their war patrols or transport missions. Commander Kudo Kaneo's *I-12* had been sent on a harassment mission to the waters between the U.S. West Coast and Hawaii. The Sixth Fleet's list of fifty-five submarines suddenly shrank to barely more than a dozen, fourteen to be exact. Of those, three boats, which had been operating off Morotai or Ulithi, were still on their way back and could be used only after upkeep in harbor.

Admiral Miwa organized his force into several groups. The *I-26* and *I-45* left on October 12, and the *I-54* and *I-56* on the fifteenth. They headed for Taiwanese waters, essentially the Luzon Strait. Miwa wanted them to deploy in a search line from east to west and work their way south along the Philippine littoral. Eight more submarines left port by October 21. By then, the Sho surface and air operations were in full swing. Lieutenant Masuzawa Seiji's *RO-109* sailed from Kure on October 23. Masuzawa had joined the ship just over a week earlier. That same day Lieutenant Uesugi Kazuo assumed command of the *RO-112*, which he took to sea on October 23. Thus, on top of their other disadvantages, the Japanese had some crews and captains who hardly knew each other.

In the *I-26*, Lieutenant Commander Nishiuchi Shoichi was an experienced skipper who had sailed the Indian Ocean, in addition to Australian and Solomons waters. Sixth Fleet ordered him to a position southeast of Leyte on October 20, later moving him to east of the gulf. Allied Ultra on October 24 reported positions of three Japanese submarines established by direction finding, including one east of Leyte. The next day, still east of Leyte, Nishiuchi reported seeing four U.S. carriers. These were the small escort carriers of Task Unit 77.4.1, familiarly called a "taffy." A sub, presumably *I-26*, made a torpedo attack against the escort carrier *Petrof Bay*. The jeep carrier evaded the torpedoes with luck—one passed along each side of her hull. One of Taffy 1's escorts destroyed the attacking submarine. The *I-26* was never heard from again.

The mystery of what happened to the *I-26* set the tone for the Japanese submarine experience at Leyte. Lieutenant Commander Nakayama Denshichi of the *I-54* disappeared after a message on October 23. On the twenty-eighth, actually, a Japanese submarine tried to get inside the screen of Task Group 38.4. She was discovered only 600 yards away by the destroyer *Helm*. That warship and the *Gridley* cooperated to destroy the sub, identified after the war as the *I-54*. Morinaga Masahiko, among the top sub aces in the Imperial Navy, skippered the *I-56* and became one of the only ones who succeeded in bringing his boat back. Commander Morinaga fired at an Allied convoy on October 24 and at the escort carrier *Santee* the next day. Destroyer counterattacks forced him into an extraordinarily deep dive, and when the sub surfaced again, an unexploded hedgehog depth charge was discovered caught on her deck.

Despite their misfortunes, Japanese submarines had a bit of an impact—but paid a considerable price for it. During the pursuit of the Ozawa fleet in the Luzon Strait, one of the American subs trailing the Japanese surface ships turned away and lost her position after sighting an enemy periscope. Off Samar Island, where the American jeep carriers would fight to the death with the Kurita fleet, sailors reported that a submarine appeared right inside their formation during the evening after the big battle. The destroyer escort *Eversole* fell victim to an I-boat, while the light cruiser *Reno* and an LST would be damaged.

Sixth Fleet had one more arrow in its quiver: a direct attack with the *kaiten* suicide torpedoes. The *kaiten* was a Long Lance torpedo modified to be driven by a human pilot—and indeed the early trainees were all student aircraft pilots who were unmarried and volunteered for the suicide torpedoes. A class of 200 pilots began training in August 1944. Admiral Miwa held a formal ceremony to honor the Kikusui unit, as the mission force was called, led by Sublieutenant Nishina Sekio, a coinventor of the suicide torpedo. Captain Ageta Kiyoi of Submarine Division 15 led the mission. The pilots were presented ceremonial swords, a dinner was given in their honor, and religious services were held for them on November 8. Admiral Toyoda attended the dinner and send-off. After that the mission began, with submarines *I-36* and *I-47* going to the U.S. anchorage at Ulithi, and the *I-37* to nearby Palau. Each boat carried four *kaiten*.

No attack took place at Kossol Roads (Palau). Allied code breakers identified the *I-37* and passed warnings down the chain of command, resulting in her destruction on November 19. The Ulithi attack took place the next morning. Commander Orita Zenji in the *I-47* launched four *kaiten*, which succeeded in entering the atoll. Captain Ageta had sailed in Lieutenant Commander Teramoto Iwao's *I-36*, and that boat had trouble with her *kaiten*. Two would not separate from the sub, while a third was found to have extensive leaks. A total of five human torpedoes made the actual attack. One, believed to have been piloted by Lieutenant Nishina, blew up the tanker *Mississinewa*. Allied cruisers and destroyers, with fire and depth charges and by ramming, seem to have destroyed all of the other *kaiten*.

Not by aircraft or by submarine did the Imperial Navy defeat MacArthur's return. Admiral Ozawa had done his part to pull Bill Halsey offsides, and the unfortunate admirals Nishimura and Shima had kept Bill Kinkaid busy until the crack of dawn. All that considerable sacrifice had had the purpose of setting up the power play, the attack of the Kurita fleet.

With the dawn, that Japanese armada sped down the east coast of Samar, shifting formation as it bore down to attack Leyte Gulf. All of the Sho operation had come down to one cosmic roll of the dice.

CHAPTER 10

"CLOSE AND ATTACK ENEMY CARRIERS!"

Kurita Takeo graduated from the naval academy one class behind Ozawa Jisaburo. Smart, Kurita ranked twenty-eighth in his class—though he did not place as well as Mikawa Gunichi, who was third. Nevertheless, Kurita got his wish; his first service training would be the basic course at the Yokosuka Torpedo School, and his early seagoing tours were with cruisers and big ships.

It was a long way for a boy from Mito. Born a little after the cherries blossomed in the spring of 1889, Takeo had been inculcated with a philosophy of *jen*, an amalgam of civility, charity, and kindness—a contrast with his name, which means "warrior." Kurita would be the kind warrior, though the lightning thrusts of his sword led enemies to think of him more like Hotspur.

Like Nishimura Shoji, Kurita spent most of his career at sea. His longest shoreside posts would be at the Torpedo School, where Takeo served as an instructor several times, including as chief instructor from 1935 to 1937. He also spent a few months doing the short course at the Naval War College. Marked for leadership, he was still a lowly lieutenant when he took command of destroyer *Shigure* in 1920. After that, Kurita never again served on a staff, in the Navy Ministry, or anywhere else except directing a ship or unit (and instructing in torpedoes, or helping design them). He first led a destroyer division in 1930, commanded the light cruiser *Abukuma* in 1935, and skippered battleship *Kongo* in 1937. Kurita achieved promotion to rear admiral in 1938. His destroyer flotillas fought in the China Incident and kept the seas clear during Japan's 1939 troubles with Russia.

His sailors loved Kurita. Approachable and considerate within a naval service known for hard discipline, Kurita always seemed distinctive.

Petty Officer Koitabashi Kosaku, an *Atago* survivor pressed into service as a lookout aboard the *Yamato*, recalled that "I never heard a negative word about Admiral Kurita . . . He was a great man." Destroyerman Commander Terauchi Masamichi, who skippered the *Ukikaze*, also thought Kurita a bit of a cosmopolitan. His wardroom served Western-style food at lunch, Japanese fare at dinnertime.

In the lead-up to Leyte Gulf, Kurita knew the flak defenses of his warships had been strengthened, and the vessels themselves had been well trained—by him. The admiral's remarks to his senior commanders at Brunei indicated a certain fatalism, but also a modicum of hope.

Hope? Why should a Japanese admiral expect a miracle this late in the war, with the Allied intelligence advantage, their technological prowess, and their great preponderance of power? It can only be that Kurita expected to make a miracle happen. Of course, the Combined Fleet would help him—the sacrifices of other fleet elements were all aimed at getting Kurita's gunnery ships into contact with the enemy—but ultimately everything stopped at the fleet commander's door. From this the most reasonable inference is that Kurita *had a plan* to get at the enemy. All of which takes us back to the Battle of the Sibuyan Sea. Chief of staff Koyanagi Tomiji pointed out that until Yamamoto at Pearl Harbor, a "gambling philosophy" had never before existed in the Imperial Navy. Gambling then had been justified in terms of disrupting long-established U.S. war plans. Now, three years later, gambling, for Kurita, had the purpose of Japan neutralizing Allied advantages by means of doing the unexpected. The bid to take losses became part of the gamble, one officially sanctioned by Combined Fleet. As for tactics, not only Ozawa Jisaburo studied the Germans at Jutland. Kurita had also been interested in the German use of battle turnaways at Jutland and had discussed the subject with his chief of staff.

That said, it had been a shock at the Sibuyan Sea to witness the destruction of the "unsinkable" battleship *Musashi*. The damage to heavy cruiser *Myoko*, also distressing, fit more within Kurita's expectations. By this stage the leader of the Kurita fleet can fairly be regarded as rattled if not gun-shy. The fleet had lost one of its five battleships and had damage to others, 40 percent of heavy cruisers were damaged or lost too, and almost 30 percent of Kurita's destroyers had had to be detached to cover crippled warships or carry survivors to safety. In particular the loss of flagship *Atago* hurt. Kurita and Koyanagi in postwar interrogations, and Shima in an interview, *all* drew attention to the fact that the Second Fleet lost roughly half its expert radiomen in the *Atago* sinking, while the physical fact that Admiral Kurita had to change ships, twice, to end up on the *Yamato* had to have had an effect. Plus, for all her splendid attributes, the *Yamato* had not been prepared as a fleet flagship and so lacked the necessary communications equipment.

Though the preliminaries had rattled Admiral Kurita, he nevertheless persevered in his determination to perform a miracle, even with the difficulties he was faced with. And the fleet commander sailed with a resentful subordinate in a flagship not fully suited to her sudden role. Plus, at the moment Kurita made his battle turnaway in the Sibuyan Sea, he had failed to inform Nishimura. That mistake could not be rectified. Kurita's general schedule message sent in the evening did not induce Nishimura to slow his own progress. This would afford Kinkaid additional time to respond. No one knew how this would play out.

Japan's entire battle hopes now lay on the shoulders of just one man. Beneath his stolid countenance, Kurita exhibited many qualities of the best leaders. His reputation in the Imperial Navy was for coolheadedness. But Vice Admiral Kurita offered more than that. Sharp, aggressive, and thoroughly professional, Kurita kept up with technical trends and calculated probabilities to a nicety. So his understanding of the possibilities was coupled with determination to carry out the mission. In command of the Second Fleet, Japan's most powerful force at this stage of the war, Vice Admiral Kurita had trained his crews to a fine edge, prepared his warships for battle, and studied the Sho plans long and hard. He had made some mistakes and the Allies had advantages, but if the mission could be carried out, Kurita Takeo was one of the best men to do it.

CLOSE ENCOUNTER

Admiral Kurita expected to have to fight his way through the San Bernardino Strait. That morning, even before the Sibuyan Sea battle,

Kurita had warned his fleet to have all its torpedo crews prepared for action in the evening. He sought to anticipate transiting the strait and ordered the fleet to abandon its ring formation before the waters narrowed. The current flowed at eight knots.

Shortly after 9:00 p.m., Kurita ordered vessels to be ready for twenty-eight knots immediately and full power within fifteen minutes. In the narrows, the warships should show recognition lights. Beginning around 9:30 Kurita's ships formed a single line ahead for passage. At 10:24, the admiral issued instructions for course and heading to be followed once debouching into the Pacific.

Accounts differ on the light situation. Despite Allied scouts' reports, some Japanese accounts insist the transit took place in darkness. But the action report of battleship *Yamato* records a bearing taken on the San Bernardino Island lighthouse. Kurita told interrogators there had been bright moonlight. In his diary, Ugaki Matome recorded dim moonlight through a cloudy sky. Contemporary sources note a quarter moon, setting during predawn hours, with overcast moving in, and a light wind from the northeast. The light lay just two miles from the *Yamato*.

Orders to prepare for sudden battle had been issued at 10:48. The fleet still felt jittery. At 11:40 Vice Admiral Ugaki suddenly ordered his battleship division to maneuver to evade torpedoes. At half past midnight the column emerged on the Pacific side of the Philippines.

This marked the moment that sailors either dream of or fear. An Allied fleet—say, Ching Lee's Task Force 34—could be there set to pounce, already in battle line, astride Kurita's course so that his T was crossed. Admirals Kinkaid, Nimitz, and quite a few others thought this precisely the situation. Had it been so, there would have been a sea fight to rival Jutland. Unlike the torpedoman Kurita, Vice Admiral Lee was a gunner. As the supervisor of the American fast battleships even when they were not gathered in Task Force 34, Lee had been a stickler for keeping the gun batteries aligned and calibrated, and all these U.S. ships had the latest, Mark-8 fire control radars. Commander Lloyd M. Mustin, Lee's staff gunnery officer, attests that on numerous practice shoots the fast battleships landed nine-gun salvos at 40,000 yards with the shells clustered within 300 yards of each other.

Lee led six battleships to Kurita's four. The *Yamato* had slightly greater range, more armor, and a heavier weight of shell. *Nagato* was also well armored but had fewer guns. Her 16-inch weapons were outperformed by the 16-inch armament of the U.S. fast battleships. The *Kongo* and *Haruna* possessed inferior 14-inch guns and less armor and were significantly older. All the American battleships had a speed advantage over the Japanese. In a night battle, radar represented a decisive advantage for Lee, who could have stood off and shelled Kurita until the Japanese were weakened and then finished off by lighter forces. After the war, however, Allied technical experts were astonished at the sophistication of the Imperial Navy's specially developed night optics. And, in this battle for the first time, the Japanese had radar, too—not so advanced as the U.S. Mark-8, but worth something. Plus, Kurita had been assiduously training his fleet in night surface tactics for months, whereas Lee's task force had been concerned primarily with protecting aircraft carriers.

Kurita was well supplied with fast, heavily armed cruisers, which, unlike the American ones, had torpedoes. Their Long Lance tin fish had the speed and explosive power to seriously impact Lee's battle line, while the Japanese heavy cruisers had the endurance, power, and armor to last long enough to put those torpedoes in the water. On the other hand, Admiral Lee's light cruisers could pump out such a volume of fire that the Japanese might be blinded by shell splashes if not actually blown to bits. In short, this would have been a battle royal, its outcome difficult to predict.

But the San Bernardino Strait would not be the place or the time. There were no defenders when the Japanese fleet spilled into the Pacific. Vice Admiral Hashimoto Shintaro led the formation with his Cruiser Division 5. The other heavy cruisers were next, with the battleships bringing up the rear. Flagship *Yamato* sailed in seventh position among ten heavy ships. A few minutes after midnight, Kurita received Mikawa's report on the latest conditions at Leyte Island. Upon exiting the strait, Admiral Kurita directed a change of course to the east. At 12:40 a.m., he ordered radar ranging. The *Nagato* soon reported a contact, but ten minutes later Rear Admiral Kobe Yuji, her skipper, sheepishly retracted—with news his radar had spotted an island.

After about an hour, Kurita altered two points to starboard to parallel the Samar coast. Less than a dozen miles from shore they passed in the darkness. At 1:55 a.m., the admiral had his fleet assume a surface search formation. By three o'clock the Kurita fleet, heading southeast, felt ready for anything.

A few minutes later Captain Shiraishi Nagayoshi's Division 2 destroyer *Akishimo* collided with another, the *Shimakaze*. Fortunately the warships merely bumped each other. *Akishimo* skipper Lieutenant Commander Nakao Kotarou reported her fighting ability unimpaired. The admiral paced the bridge of *Yamato*. Still suspicious that Ching Lee or another Allied officer lurked just beyond the horizon, Kurita permitted himself no rest. Half an hour before dawn, the Japanese were eighty miles from the lighthouse on Suluan Island, which was now almost directly south of them. Approaching daylight meant a renewed Allied aircraft threat. Kurita ordered his ships back to ring formation.

Then something happened. When the news reached Combined Fleet headquarters, Admiral Kusaka records that the staff were so overjoyed they "almost stood on [their] head[s]."

ADMIRAL KINKAID'S JEEP carriers had orders to conduct three air searches at dawn. One of them, he intended to overfly the San Bernardino Strait. Kinkaid had also instructed the leader of his escort carrier force, Rear Admiral Thomas L. Sprague, to have a strike force ready to fly out of the Surigao Strait in search of the ships fleeing Nishimura's debacle. Collectively, the eighteen jeep carriers in Admiral Kinkaid's Seventh Fleet were armed with 235 fighters and 143 torpedo bombers, about the strength of one of Halsey's carrier groups. Sprague's airmen began preparations at about 4:15 a.m.

The jeeps, or "escort" carriers, were arrayed in several elements. In the system the U.S. Navy had developed, each bunch of ships was called a "task unit," and an assortment of task units made up a "task group"— equivalent to the Third Fleet carrier groups. A collection of task groups made up a fleet. Kinkaid's fleet had task groups for his battleships and cruisers, the invasion forces, and the escort carriers. The Navy's abbreviation for an escort carrier was "CVE" for "Carrier (CV), Escort," which, old swabbies would explain, stood for "Combustible, Vulnerable, Expendable." Admiral Sprague's agglomeration of CVEs formed Task Group 77.4. He also led one of the CVE groups, Task Unit 77.4.1. It was nicknamed "Taffy 1."

Sprague's Taffies were located in a line off of Leyte Gulf, roughly southeast to northwest, each ten to twenty miles from its neighbor and all about the same distance from the Leyte land battle they supported. There were three Taffies, with Sprague's own being the southernmost. Taffy 2 under Rear Admiral Felix B. Stump steamed at the center. To the north lay Rear Admiral Clifton A. F. Sprague—amazingly, no relation to his commanding officer—with Taffy 3. The Taffies were generally aware of the Surigao battle, but they captured only snippets from the low-frequency radios of the TBS system. For example, just before 3:00 a.m. Taffy 2 overheard Admiral Oldendorf discuss engaging Nishimura. Destroyer escort *Roberts* of Taffy 3 overheard a report that the Japanese in Surigao Strait were retreating in disarray.

Flight operations began before dawn. The CVE *Gambier Bay*, of Taffy 3, started to launch fighters at 4:57 a.m. Scheduled missions began soon after. Taffy 3 had to maintain the combat air patrol over Leyte Gulf itself. The *St. Lo*, a Taffy 3 ship, put up the day's first antisubmarine patrol at 5:30. Taffy 1 sent out the strike mission against the Japanese remnants of the Surigao battle. Taffy 3 sent out a second patrol for subs plus a support group for all her flights, and a combat air patrol for her own safety. At 6:30, Rear Admiral Clifton "Ziggy" Sprague ordered Taffy 3 ships to secure from general quarters, beginning a routine day. He set a cruising disposition and sat back. At 6:37, the CVE *Fanshaw Bay* heard Japanese voices on the Taffy air defense net. Ziggy Sprague had no idea a Japanese fleet already had him almost on the ropes.

SUDDENLY, A LOT OF THINGS HAPPENED
NEARLY ALL AT ONCE

Kobe Yuji of the *Nagato* ordered his crew to prepare for daytime battle. Japanese practice was for ship captains to decide when to order action stations, and Kobe's battleship appears to have been the first to do so. That took place at 6:17 a.m.

Barely five minutes later—still before sunrise—*Yamato*'s radar detected American warplanes. While the Taffies were standing down from general quarters, the Japanese were clearing for battle. By 6:35, airplanes could be seen from the *Nagato*. After that, more and more ships chimed in—cruisers *Chokai* and *Noshiro* had planes on radar at 6:39, heavy cruiser *Haguro* at 6:40. One minute later, Captain Sugiura Kaju of the *Haguro* ordered flak action. On the *Yamato*, two TBM Avengers were visible. Light antiaircraft opened fire but quickly ceased.

That was the moment an enemy fleet appeared. The development was the most dramatic on the heavy cruiser *Kumano* of Cruiser Division 7. Commander Hirayama Shigeo, the gunnery officer, dozed at his post on the control tower. The days of frantic action, by this point, had taken their toll on the crews, all of whom had been at their posts longer than twenty-four hours. Hirayama, as it happened, felt chagrined because he had also been dozing at the moment Kurita's cruisers were slaughtered in the Palawan Passage. He'd been determined not to succumb again, but there it was, and here he was.

Commander Hirayama woke up with the dawn. Suddenly he saw movement and looked up—a carrier-based torpedo bomber, a Grumman, as the Japanese often called the sturdy Avengers, coming from the west. Hirayama wondered what the Grumman was doing there and ordered machine-gun crews to shoot. The plane lumbered away. A Japanese lookout watched it go, then, on that heading, suddenly saw a mast against the horizon. Hirayama also looked, with his much less powerful binoculars. He could see the mast too. Hirayama hastened to report to the skipper, Captain Hitomi Soichiro, and the commander of Cruiser Division 7, Vice Admiral Shiraishi Kazutaka, who wore his flag in the *Kumano*. At 6:52 a.m., the cruiser reported to Admiral Kurita, "ENEMY STRENGTH SEVEN SHIPS."

Though maneuvering to execute a change of formation, the Kurita fleet had yet to shift away from its arrangement in ship divisions across a line of bearing. The admiral ordered his ships to prepare for sixteen knots on twenty minutes' notice. Even as planes began popping out all over, Kurita held to his intention, changing course to nearly due south.

At that moment, chief of staff Koyanagi reckoned the fleet had reached a point only sixty miles from Suluan Light. The fleet commander ordered readiness for maximum speed.

The *Kumano*'s report actually came a bit late, among a flood of similar sightings. The reports almost make sport of who saw the Allies first, much like fighter pilots with their "Tallyhos." The *Yamato* carefully puts her first sighting at 6:44.5 a.m., with that being about the only time anything is logged at a half-minute interval. Perhaps that was because battleship *Kongo* puts her glimpse of masts at 6:45, and *Nagato* has this at 6:41, possibly making up for her mistaking an island on radar for the enemy fleet the night before. Battleship *Haruna* saw masts at 6:50, heavy cruiser *Haguro* at 6:44, *Tone* at 6:47, and light cruiser *Noshiro* at 6:49. Several of the ships reported multiple masts. Range estimates were more than sixteen miles.

The first sighting aboard *Yamato* came from a lookout high in the crow's nest. Fleet operations officer Otani Tonosuke climbed up there to see for himself. The staff gunnery officer went to gunnery control to check what the high-power optics might reveal. Admiral Kurita and other senior officers mulled over whether the masts might be the Nishimura or Shima fleets exiting Leyte Gulf for their anticipated rendezvous. But officers were doubtful—and presently Commander Otani reported flight decks. That could only mean aircraft carriers. Not only did the lookouts spot them; Otani saw two himself.

THOSE FIRST MINUTES on the bridge of the *Yamato* must have been amazing. With the war nearing the end of a third year, with every advantage of combat power, intelligence, resources, and military technology in Allied hands, Japan was nearly exhausted. Under these conditions the Japanese could hardly expect to compel battle much less obtain favorable conditions. Yet here, off Samar, by dint of incredible sacrifice and not a little sleight of hand, the Imperial Navy had overturned the strategic balance. Not only had the Japanese forced a surface engagement; they had contrived to have one in which they had the superiority, against the very kinds of vessels the Japanese had the greatest interest in eliminating.

News of warships galvanized Admiral Kurita. Chief of staff Koyanagi saw some officers literally crying with joy. Kurita's report notes, "It was definitely established that the masts belonged to ships of a gigantic enemy task force including six or seven carriers accompanied by many cruisers and destroyers." Imperial Navy practice, unlike the American, had been to mix admirals and staffs with ship commanders and their crewmen. Though large, the bridge on the ersatz Japanese flagship filled with bodies: the ship's skipper, Rear Admiral Morishita Nobuei, his helmsman, navigators, lookouts, and orderlies; Vice Admiral Ugaki and his staff; and Admiral Kurita and his. All their voices competed for attention. The Sho mission loomed before them. But now, here, an enemy surface fleet lay open to attack. Koyanagi immediately thought of Kurita's "miracle" speech, recording, "We moved to take advantage of this heaven-sent opportunity."

The admiral had to make a quick decision. Ugaki, standing right there, writes his diary stiffly in the third person. He supplies the snide remark "Actions of the fleet headquarters were also apt to lack promptness." The admiral writes this after noting the weather was poor, there had been no news of Allied forces—reports from JNAF floatplanes and from Mikawa at Manila had been held up by slow communications—and, of course, that the fleet had expected to break into Leyte. (Ugaki's notation that the JNAF scouting report was seriously delayed conflicts with Yamato's action report, which logs that message arriving before 5:00 a.m.)

But Admiral Kurita found himself faced with discrepant information. On the one hand, there were masts on the horizon. On the other, no reports suggested the presence of Allied warships there. Despite that, Koyanagi writes that Kurita's orders came "instantly." Actually thirteen minutes elapsed between the sighting and Kurita's order "CLOSE AND ATTACK ENEMY CARRIERS," and one minute later, the execute, "ATTACK!" It is a judgment call whether this is slow.

Ugaki's recollections continue in this vein—the fleet orders called for battleship and cruiser divisions to attack with destroyers to follow. Ugaki felt this conflicting, and Kurita's reasoning is unknown. In thirteen minutes the fleet commander can hardly be expected to write a detailed directive (orders to the destroyers were issued at the twenty-minute mark, still too little to expect extensive instructions).

About the only new information Kurita received, at 6:52 a.m., came from heavy cruiser *Tone*. Captain Mayuzumi Haruo reported the enemy attempting to retreat. Admiral Kurita could see that himself. He did not know the course of the American force, but that hardly mattered since they soon turned. Kurita believed it a starboard turn because when the aircraft carriers heeled, their flight decks became visible, full of planes. The wind blew from the northeast. Kurita set a fleet course of 110 degrees in order to come upwind of the Americans, reducing the range while keeping to their windward.

As for fleet deployment, the Second Fleet could have maneuvered into column with the battleships behind its starboard wing, the heavy cruisers of Cruiser Division 7; or to port behind the two ships of Cruiser Division 5. Either would have consumed time, and that would mean that the Americans could be expected to get farther away. Kurita was already at long range from his adversaries, but *any* line-ahead battle formation would sacrifice one of Japan's best advantages in this action—the speed of Kurita's cruisers. All of them except the *Haguro* were designed to sustain speeds of thirty-four or thirty-five knots (and the *Haguro*, thirty-three). In a stern chase, that speed would be an important consideration.

Conversely, to have maneuvered into fleet formation would have meant restricting the overall speed to that of the ships that were wounded in the Sibuyan Sea. *Yamato* had damage from three bombs, forward. Down at the bow, she could make only twenty-six knots. The *Nagato*'s damage knocked her down a knot from design speed, to twenty-four. The *Haruna*, too, had significant restrictions. Admiral Koyanagi refers to propeller-shaft damage from near misses at Midway that were never quite repaired. (But there are instances of near design speed recorded after the Midway battle.) Perhaps the violent evasive maneuvers in the Sibuyan Sea somehow jarred her repair loose, cutting thirty and a half knots to just twenty-five or twenty-six. Either way, this impediment explains why Vice Admiral Suzuki Yoshio, leader of Battleship Division 3, made no effort to keep the *Haruna* in formation, instead taking off in the *Kongo* on an easterly heading, seeking to fulfill Kurita's intention to stay upwind of the U.S. carriers.

The Kurita fleet had encountered a worthy opponent, they thought. Here, to make for Leyte without fighting would leave those carriers to fling endless bolts from the sky at Kurita's fleet. Having just endured what he had in the Sibuyan Sea, Kurita's desire to strike back dovetailed with his interest in preventing unfettered air attacks *and* his secret plan to engage task forces if at all possible. As Koyanagi put it, they could potentially put a net around four or five carriers, two fast battleships, and at least ten heavy cruisers. The admiral informed Combined Fleet and Southwest Area Fleet, "BY HEAVEN-SENT OPPORTUNITY WE ARE DASHING TO ATTACK THE ENEMY CARRIERS. OUR FIRST OBJECTIVE IS TO DESTROY THE FLIGHT DECKS, THEN THE TASK FORCE."

A crucial element in Kurita's calculation would be the identity of his adversary. His lookouts, Commander Otani, and Kurita himself had seen aircraft carriers. Kurita assumed these were *fleet* carriers with thirty-three knots speed, not the thin-skinned jeeps, which could not make more than twenty if you fueled them with nitroglycerin. From top admiral to ordinary seaman, no Japanese surface ship crew had ever fought a battle against a jeep carrier. The Imperial Navy's surface fleet had no notion of the habits of the CVEs, their vulnerabilities, or their tactics.

A criticism often leveled at Kurita is that he did not wait to form a battle line. But the gripe is appropriate only if the Japanese *knew* they faced jeep carriers. Here, if the Second Fleet commander stopped to maneuver into line ahead, and the enemy were fleet carriers capable of thirty-three knots, there would have been no battle. The initial sightings were already at maximum range. Kurita's big battlewagons could not match that speed, and a battle line would have held back his cruisers. The Americans would simply have disappeared over the horizon. Ko-yanagi again: "In a pursuit the only essential is to close the gap as rapidly as possible and concentrate fire upon the enemy." The one solution that worked no matter the identity of the adversary was a general chase in which Kurita's cruiser divisions could profit from their speed. General chase was no error.

Another criticism needs mention because of things that happened later. Referring to Kurita, Morison contends that "complete surprise seems to have deprived the Admiral of all power of decision, and the result was a helter-skelter battle." The discussion here demonstrates, in my view, that Admiral Kurita *did* consider his decision at the outset of combat. There would be many reasons why this action became helter-skelter, but an alleged refusal of Kurita to decide is not one of them. We will presently see two real errors the Japanese made—both attributable to Kurita Takeo's decisions, not the lack of them.

The last element that seems to have confused battleship leader Ugaki would be Kurita's instruction for destroyer formations to bring up the rear. The pair of flotillas accompanying the fleet amounted to more than a dozen ships. They, too, were much faster than the battleships. If the enemy amounted to nearly twenty vessels, evading wildly, and there were going to be another half dozen Japanese heavy cruisers obstructing the range between Kurita's battleships and the enemy, holding back the destroyer flotillas had merit in terms of preventing confusion among his gunners. Throwing another dozen warships into the battle zone would impede tracking the quarry. In addition, Koya-nagi notes, *maneuvers had shown* that fast battleships in a daytime action could easily escape torpedo attack because they would see the launch and then go to full speed to avoid it. The destroyers—and this illustrates how Imperial Navy leaders had begun thinking—would simply be burning that much more oil. Here again the misidentification of Taffy 3 as a fast-carrier unit exerted an influence on Japanese tactics.

Professionalism lies precisely in officers' sense for leaders, developed from service together, which permits abbreviated messages. Ugaki had just had two months of focused training under Kurita and had been under his command for half a year. Before that, he had watched Kuri-ta's performance from an exalted height at Combined Fleet. Ugaki ought to have had a feeling for Kurita's instincts. He did not. This lack of perspective, plus Ugaki's carping about the Sho mission of destroy-ing transports (where the subordinate writes as if Kurita rejected his views when the latter completely agreed), and his claiming not to under-stand a fine point of destroyer tactics the fleet had apparently learned from maneuvers, all indicate that Ugaki indulged his resentment, let resentment blind him to his superior's moods, and failed to apply his professional judgment.

In any case, this Japanese officer had quite limited exposure to the front lines of this fierce war. Ugaki had led Battleship Division 1 for just eight months. It was his only wartime command. He had participated in just one battle—two if you count the hapless attempt to express reinforcements into Biak on the eve of the Philippine Sea battle—and his leadership had not been especially stellar. Most of the admiral's time had been spent as an instructor, as a naval attaché, or on staffs.

Admiral Ugaki told his diary that he protested to chief of staff Koyanagi because "I feared the spirit of all-out attack at short range was lacking." But, in fact, there could be no all-out attack at short range *except* if Kurita ordered a general chase. Ugaki's diary here smacks of cynical rationalization, compiled to lambast his commanding officer. But because his is an authentic voice, many historians have simply repeated Ugaki's take on these matters.

At 6:58 a.m., four minutes after the *Nagato* broke out her battle flag, the *Yamato* opened fire. After ordering maximum battle speed, at 7:03 Kurita sent: "CRUISER DIVISIONS, ATTACK!"

ON THE ROPES

Ziggy Sprague paced the deck of his flagship, the *Fanshaw Bay*. He needed to submit an operations schedule that would inform the air support commander what missions, strikes, and patrols Taffy 3 would carry out. Rear Admiral Sprague had come to flag plot early that day to work on the schedule. The aircraft commander, Captain Richard Whitehead on Kinkaid's flagship, *Wasatch*, monitored all of Task Group 77.4, which was under Rear Admiral Thomas L. Sprague, whom Ziggy knew as a stickler for detail. The two Spragues had known each other since they were midshipmen at Annapolis, from which Tom graduated in the top tenth of the class of 1918, with Ziggy just behind at the quarter mark. The Taffy 3 leader knew the operations schedule would be more than humans could accomplish, with sailors pushing into the night, so getting the priorities right seemed important. Ziggy was also new at this. Until the Great Marianas Turkey Shoot, he had skippered the fleet carrier *Wasp*. Sprague's first op with the little CVEs had been the Morotai landings, where he had figured in the loss of destroyer escort *Shelton* and submarine *Seawolf*. That rankled.

Suddenly a message tore Cliff Sprague away from his preparations. One of the Avengers on antisub patrol described an enemy fleet, the Kurita fleet. The plane was one of the radar-equipped Avengers used for night missions. From the *Kadashan Bay* of Taffy 2, Ensign Hans L. Jensen had been startled when his radarman told him of a big mass of blips to the north, and he went to investigate, even though the location lay outside their patrol zone. He sent his report to *Natoma Bay*, the flagship of Rear Admiral Stump's Taffy 2. Then Ensign William C. Brooks of the jeep carrier *St. Lo* saw the enemy too. Jensen's initial report had been garbled in transmission; Brooks supplied full details.

Ziggy thought the pilot had screwed up and was reporting units of Halsey's fast battleship force. Admiral Sprague quotes himself, talking into the squawk box, "Air Plot, tell him to check his identification."

"Identification of enemy force confirmed," Brooks replied. "Ships have pagoda masts."

Confirmations piled up rapidly. Japanese voice transmissions were heard on the radio net; sailors reported seeing bursts of exploding antiaircraft shells against the horizon. At 6:45 a.m. radar on Rear Admiral Sprague's flagship registered the same targets. Shortly thereafter, lookouts reported seeing pagoda masts too.

Ziggy Sprague had been in tight places before. At Pearl Harbor, he had had to thread his way through the wreckage of the Japanese attack to get his oiler, the *Tangier*, out of the base. Target ship *Utah*, moored right next to *Tangier*, would be blasted by the attackers. Right after, the *Tangier* spent harrowing weeks accompanying clumsy U.S. attempts to succor Wake Island, when it very much seemed like the relief efforts would lead to the first-ever clash at sea between aircraft carriers. Sprague had then taken the *Tangier* to the South Pacific, where she served as mother ship for PBY Catalina patrol planes right through the Coral Sea action, which *was* the very first aero-naval battle. But those episodes paled next to Ziggy's predicament off Samar.

Admiral Sprague details the thoughts rushing through his head: The Japanese would continue to parallel the Samar coast down to Leyte Gulf and send some cruisers to finish off Taffy 3. He didn't think his thin-skinned CVEs could last more than fifteen minutes against this heavily armed and armored enemy. But if Taffy 3 could get the Japanese to home on it, Sprague reasoned, their arrival at Leyte might be delayed long enough for help to arrive.

As had Kurita, Sprague made crucial decisions in the very first moments. At 6:50 a.m., he ordered a turn from a northerly course to one directly east, toward rainsqualls in the distance. He increased speed to sixteen knots, then to the maximum eighteen. Minutes later he ordered all carriers to launch available planes against the Japanese. Ziggy also asked for planes that had gone off on missions to be returned so they could join in. Worried ship identifications might be mistaken— probably a result of the Morotai tragedy—Admiral Sprague cautioned his crews to verify targets before dropping weapons. At 6:57, hoping to confuse enemy gunners, he ordered CVEs to make smoke. Moments later Admiral Sprague extended that order to all vessels. The first warships reached the shelter of the rain just about twenty minutes after spotting the Japanese.

All were within the squall by 7:15 a.m. At that point the Taffy 3 commander ordered his escorts to attack. He also altered course to the southeast. Ziggy wanted to draw Kurita farther away from the San Bernardino Strait, the presumed Japanese escape hatch.

The other Taffies of Tom Sprague's task group acted to support the embattled force. Felix Stump's Taffy 2 launched its own air strikes. The night before, in the expectation of mounting air attacks to finish off the Nishimura unit and Shima fleet, Admiral Kinkaid had instructed Task Group 77.4 to load the Grummans with torpedoes rather than bombs. Tom Sprague's Taffy 1 had already sent a strike group after those remnants, but Stump had not, and now his planes could quickly be rearmed. The action this fateful morning was all catch-as-catch-can, planes taking off in ones, twos, or more, whenever they could, and returning to rearm and go out again.

Desperation focused the crews. One officer aboard the jeep *White Plains* had gone to the ship's store the previous day and bought a whole case of gum, intending to share it with his friends and the sailors of his division. With the battle he began to chew gum furiously, one stick after another. By nightfall he had gone through the entire case—and he'd not shared any of it.

William Kunstler (no relation to the famed lawyer) was a machinist's mate with the torpedo squadron aboard the *Kitkun Bay*. He awoke that morning to misty storm and overcast gray sky. He'd just been relieved and was headed for breakfast when his CVE called "battle stations." The mate reached his post, where flashes could be seen on the horizon. At the next set of gun flashes he asked a friend who had a watch to give him a mark and he started counting. Kunstler got to seven and had just decided the shot had to be over (beyond the CVE) when there was a huge explosion right next to the ship. Geysers from exploding shells were everywhere. They had colors, too. A seaman on the *White Plains* cried out, "They're shooting at us in Technicolor!"

GENERAL CHASE ORDERS put much of the onus on the Japanese cruiser commanders. The most important unit here was Vice Admiral Shiraishi Kazutaka's Cruiser Division 7. His ships took off pell-mell after Taffy 3, dashing to match Sprague's turn to the east. In thirty minutes they would cut the range by half. Shiraishi was determined to succeed. He knew that Koyanagi Tomiji, an Etajima classmate, watched closely from Kurita's nearby flagship.

Admiral Shiraishi obtained his initial sighting data from Mayuzumi's *Tone* at 6:47 a.m., followed almost immediately by news that the Americans were changing course. Shiraishi clearly anticipated the decision Kurita would make. His actions did not at all conform to Ugaki Matome's complaint that units were slow to act due to uncertainty about what the command would order. Shiraishi did not stand around complaining that the orders were obscure, unexplained, or slow. Rather, at 6:52, *before* Kurita's decision (when *Tone* reported the enemy moving to escape), the admiral ordered a course of due south and an increase to number four battle speed (thirty-one knots). A minute later Shiraishi instructed his cruisers to prepare for gun action to port. At 6:57, he ordered full speed. Two minutes later he changed that to maximum battle speed (thirty-five knots). It was then that Kurita came on line with formal attack orders.

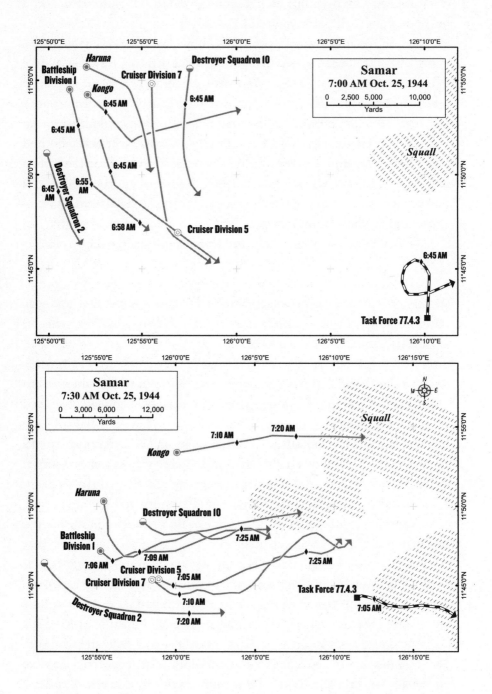

Shiraishi Kazutaka had a lot to do with Cruiser Division 7's fighting spirit. He had held the command for nearly half a year, so the Lingga training with Kurita was his time to become familiar with the men and the ships. The fifty-two-year-old admiral had trained as a torpedoman, but Shiraishi had spent most of the decade before Pearl Harbor in staff jobs—in China, with the NGS, at Combined Fleet. Only for one year did he command a cruiser. When war came, Shiraishi had been chief of staff to Vice Admiral Kondo Nobutake, who then held Kurita's job as leader of the Second Fleet. Shiraishi had been at several naval actions, most notably at Midway, during the Guadalcanal campaign, and in Japan's invasion of Indonesia. But he had never held a position of command during those campaigns.

He was desperate to get into the action, but duty had called Shiraishi away. In 1943, the Navy had used his staff experience, making Shiraishi the chief of research at the War College. Finally, he had obtained a seagoing command, Cruiser Division 7. The responsibility weighed heavily, and he felt lucky to be backed by fine warships and good sailors.

The fight began well. This cruiser force entered the lists with determination. Shiraishi's heavy cruisers were formidable warships, every one of them capable of slaughtering a CVE. *Suzuya* opened fire first, at destroyers, at 7:00 a.m. Five minutes later Shiraishi's flagship *Kumano* signaled the rest of the division that they were closing the distance to the enemy. The admiral radioed, "INTEND ENGAGE TO STARBOARD." Five minutes later he ordered his cruisers to open fire. Captain Mayuzumi first used *Tone*'s main battery to starboard at 7:13.

Almost simultaneously American planes appeared and fought using whatever they had. Avengers of Taffy 3 were armed with either bombs (if they had been intending to head for air support over Leyte) or depth charges (if on antisub flights). Only Admiral Stump's Taffy 2, at first, seemed able to get many torpedo-armed planes up. Fighters strafed with their machine guns. Those armed with light bombs and rockets for ground support expended them against warships instead. Unlike Halsey's big carriers, the CVEs were equipped largely with older-model Wildcats, but they did their best. Like gnats or mosquitoes, the planes became a constant distraction for Japanese in the chase, at first by one plane or two, later by fours, and, as the morning wore on, in real attack groups of twenty, thirty, or more warplanes.

The experience of Lieutenant (Junior Grade) L. E. Waldrop of the *St. Lo* illustrates how distracting the planes could be. Waldrop had launched for a ground-support mission with eight 100-pound bombs and two rockets on his Wildcat. He made for the scene of the action and, with Taffy 3 hidden inside the squall, went for a group of four Japanese heavy cruisers, the Shiraishi unit. Waldrop's bombs were not big—at that weight they would barely scratch a cruiser—so he was very careful with them. On two attack runs, the pilot released no munitions at all. Then he dropped half his bombs on each run, then combined rockets and machine guns in his passes, and finally made a pair of strafing runs. When Waldrop landed he found a three-foot gash carved out of his wing. Squadron mate Lieutenant (Junior Grade) Fields dropped depth charges ahead of a heavy cruiser and watched her run over them, but the ship showed no sign of damage. Lieutenant (Junior Grade) J. H. Gore, also of the *St. Lo*, dropped his little bombs over a heavy cruiser too. He thought five of them made a pattern along her deck. Then the ship sped past him.

Admiral Shiraishi led the cruiser column in the *Kumano*. Second ship was Captain Teraoka Masao's *Suzuya*. Teraoka made an odd fit. A submariner until that summer, he had joined the ship only at the beginning of September. Teraoka had to depend on the expertise of his chief gunner, Commander Tachikawa Hideo. A smoke screen grew around Taffy 3. At about 7:10 a.m., a U.S. destroyer charged out of it. Tachikawa fired *Suzuya*'s 8-inch guns when the range dropped below 11,000 yards. *Suzuya* was looking for her first hit when the destroyer shot back.

Neither Teraoka nor Tachikawa knew it, but they were facing a three-quarter Cherokee/Creek Indian. Commander Ernest Evans, skipper of the destroyer *Johnston*, had been born in Muskegee, Oklahoma. His mom still lived in Tulsa. Evans believed the purpose of escorts—to interpose themselves between their charges and the enemy—justified the torpedo attack he intended. That initiative reflected well on Commander Evans, who had fought every step of the way to get where he was. Enlisting in the National Guard right out of high school, he joined the Navy from there, applying to Annapolis as an enlisted sailor. In the stiff and quietly prejudiced U.S. Navy of the late twenties and thirties, Evans's open ambition and clear determination earned him a nickname, "the Chief." That did not prevent the Navy from relegating the Cherokee to a post at the helm of a tugboat, but in 1941, he'd been sent to the China Station just ahead of the coming war, and the Chief ended up as the executive officer of the USS *Alden*, the Asiatic Fleet veteran of the Battle of the Java Sea. Succeeding to command of that ship, Ernest Evans had achieved his métier, and he took the *Alden* to the Gulf of Mexico, where he met Ziggy Sprague, then staff chief of the naval district. Now Commander Evans had a new *Fletcher*-class destroyer, and with his *Johnston*, he was determined to defend Sprague's jeeps. Junior officers viewed Evans as a bull-voiced firebrand who spouted orders, his mastery and skill sparking the crew to fight like demons. Once the destroyer got within a distance of 9,000 or 10,000 yards, Commander Evans launched torpedoes, anxious to get them off before the Japanese crippled him. The ten fish were set for maximum range and a slow speed with a narrow spread.

Commander Hirayama Shigeo, chief gunner on Shiraishi's flagship, the *Kumano*, had been dozing again when the action began. As he went to his battle station, in the main gun director high in the conning tower, Hirayama could see carrier-based torpedo planes. He wondered where they had come from. He remembered the weather as clear, with few clouds and little wind. Once he could use his gun director, he could actually see the planes taking off from the Taffy 3 jeeps. Captain Hitomi Soichiro had ordered Hirayama to shoot at the CVEs. His flak guns barked at the planes. They could see destroyers, but no one paid them any mind. But in fact the *Johnston* was launching her torpedoes.

Japanese gunners shot at the jeep carriers. The flagship designated the target at 7:10 a.m. Fire commenced right away. By 7:16 a.m., lookouts were reporting one of the jeeps on fire. A couple of minutes later Shiraishi ordered fire shifted to a different CVE.

Kumano may have ignored the destroyers, but other ships did not. Light cruiser *Noshiro*, leading Destroyer Flotilla 2 to take station behind the Japanese battleships, opened fire at an enemy "cruiser" at 7:14 a.m. Moments later, she estimated the range at 20,500 yards.

Battleship *Nagato* contributed a 16-inch salvo. The *Johnston* suffered several 14-inch hits around this time, which must have come from battleship *Kongo* since the *Haruna* checked fire at 7:13. Captain Sugiura Kaju's heavy cruiser *Haguro* saw a destroyer begin shooting at that instant. Sugiura thought she was aiming at him. (On the *Johnston*, Commander Evans had told his gunners to focus on the lead Japanese cruiser, the *Kumano*.) So *Haguro* rigged for starboard gun action and loosed a broadside at 7:15. The *Yamato* would not be heard from until 7:21, and then only with her 6-inch secondary armament.

Commander Evans's warship would be among the first that morning to benefit from the weaknesses in Japanese gunnery. One shortcoming is directly attributable to mistaken identification of Taffy 3 as fleet carriers, battleships, and cruisers—the Japanese used armorpiercing shells. These were optimal against battleships, but very wrong to use against small destroyers and even smaller destroyer-escorts. Compiling lessons learned in the battle, Tom Sprague noted that he could not find a single record of the detonation of a Japanese armorpiercing shell. The 14-inch shells that fell on the *Johnston* thus caused minimal damage. Compounding that error would be the extremely tight pattern of shell fall. Americans made estimates of 200 to 300 yards, even down to 50 yards, for salvo dispersion. This made it harder to aim. A wider dispersion pattern meant greater chances to straddle, hence quicker zeroing in.

Despite the hurricane of enemy shells, the *Johnston* stayed afloat. Lieutenant Robert C. Hagen, her gunnery officer, estimated they made as many as forty 5-inch shell hits on the *Kumano*. The shells were too small to inflict critical damage, but they killed Japanese sailors caught in the open and interfered with Commander Hirayama's own gunfire. *Johnston*'s torpedoes accounted for the crippling damage. About 7:24 a.m., *Kumano* lookouts spotted several torpedo wakes to starboard. One tin fish hit Hitomi's cruiser and blew off her bow forward of frame 10. At first, the crew thought they had been struck by planes; then they realized the Cherokee destroyer had gotten them. Hirayama decided those American destroyers were very daring.

Johnston's torpedo put Vice Admiral Shiraishi out of business. Captain Hitomi needed to assess the wounds. Executive officer Sanada Yuji led counterflooding to stabilize the ship. The chief engineer, Commander Moriyama Sakae, decided the cruiser would still be able to make twelve knots. That relieved Captain Hitomi, but Admiral Shiraishi needed a vessel able to race after Taffy 3. He called for a cutter to transfer his flag and for the *Suzuya* to come alongside and take aboard himself and half his staff. Shiraishi designated his flagship at 7:41 a.m. But nearly a dozen Grummans peppered *Suzuya* with bombs. A near miss to port aft and she lost a propeller. Teraoka's cruiser suddenly found her maximum speed cut to twenty-three knots. Still the ship stopped smartly. Captain Teraoka might have been a submariner, but he was a good ship driver. Shiraishi had only just completed his transfer at about 8:00 a.m. and already he was trapped again.

Admiral Shiraishi's energetic pursuit degenerated. First, he ordered the *Kumano* to follow the column; then his new flagship was crippled too. In a bid to minimize damage, Captain Teraoka cut *Suzuya*'s speed more, to fourteen knots. Cruiser Division 5 still chased the Americans with two ships. Shiraishi could have attached *Tone* and *Chikuma*, his last two cruisers, to Division 5, but he did not. Instead, at 7:32, Shiraishi ordered Captain Norimitsu Saiji of the *Chikuma* to assume command and continue the chase. The *Tone* wore out four 8-inch gun sleeves, expending 419 rounds. *Kumano* now received orders to retire from the battle zone.

Much later the anxious vice admiral would succeed in moving his flag again, to heavy cruiser *Tone*. That was just as well, because Norimitsu's *Chikuma* never came back. Planes from Admiral McCain's Task Group 38.1, finally appearing in the Samar battle, caught her. As it turned out, Captain Mayuzumi's *Tone* would be the *only* one of Shiraishi's heavy ships to return. The *Suzuya* would be finished off by Taffy planes. Captain Hitomi's *Kumano* moved off toward safety, recrossing the Sibuyan Sea to Coron Bay, and would endure a lengthy ordeal. Halsey's warplanes would hit her, leaving the cruiser badly damaged. She made temporary repairs at Manila. The *Kumano* survived *three* sub attacks on her withdrawal to Taiwan but succumbed to a fourth, new damage, and had to be towed back to a bay on Luzon's west coast. Planes from the Halsey fleet sank her there on November 25.

The Leyte experience seared the proud Shiraishi Kazutaka. His powerful cruiser division was blasted to practically nothing; thousands of sailors perished in his first wartime command. The *Tone* would not survive the rest of the war either. Nor would Shiraishi's hometown—he was a native of Nagasaki.

After Leyte, the Imperial Navy put Shiraishi in charge of the care and feeding of merchant marine sailors, an ignominious end to a fighting sailor's career. Small wonder that Allied intelligence interrogators found Shiraishi "a broken and sad old man" who "continually gazed into space and seemed unable to concentrate."

WHILE THE THREAT from Japanese cruisers might be diminishing, that could not be apparent to Ziggy Sprague. The admiral swore expletives at Bull Halsey, who had failed to block the San Bernardino. But Sprague quickly appreciated his situation, had sound judgment, and took practical measures.

Coming out of the squall, he saw the Japanese had followed outside him on the arc of a circle rather than just punching forward to cut him off. But since they were so much faster, their warships were closing the range anyway—with "depressing rapidity," to 25,000, then 20,000, then 15,000 yards. The volume and accuracy of the Kurita fleet's fire sharpened until Sprague again thought his jeeps could not endure another five minutes.

Rear Admiral Sprague had already mobilized his airplanes for ad hoc air attacks. The smoke screen had been an inspired idea, and the CVEs had benefited from the cover, combined with the squall. Now Sprague warned his plucky little CVEs—each of them had a single pip-squeak 5-inch gun—to prepare for surface engagement. He took the example of Cherokee Evans and ordered his destroyers to hit the Japanese with torpedoes. Evans had initiated, and now Sprague directed— it was a veritable "Charge of the Light Brigade."

By 7:30 a.m. the Taffy 3 jeeps had launched ninety-five fresh planes. Some left with no bombs at all, intent on buzzing the enemy for effect.

ABOARD SEVENTH FLEET flagship *Wasatch*, Admiral Kinkaid read a detective novel and awaited reports he anticipated from Task Group

77.4 and a cruiser-destroyer force he'd sent to mop up Nishimura's and Shima's cripples. The news of the new fight raced up Kinkaid's chain of command. The morning of joyously following the demise of Surigao's remnants went forgotten amid the emergency of the battle against Kurita.

Kinkaid discovered that the big Japanese fleet—Americans had been calling it the "Center Force"—was back, and it was a bigger surface unit than anything Allied sailors had ever encountered. The initial airplane sighting made that quite clear. By 7:07 a.m., Admiral Kinkaid was so alarmed he sent Halsey another dispatch, not even encoded: "ENEMY [BATTLESHIPS] AND CRUISER REPORTED FIRING ON TU 77.4.3 FROM 15 MILES ASTERN." The Seventh Fleet commander needed to get Halsey's attention. Unbeknownst to Kinkaid, it was now, at this moment of disaster for Taffy 3, that Halsey received Seventh Fleet's triumphant report of engaging the Japanese at Surigao Strait. At the moment Kinkaid's message went out, Halsey understood him to be happy, not desperate.

Rear Admiral Sprague also sent a message in plaintext—not encoded. The White House Map Room noted the transmission's garbled radio call sign. But two features indicate it came from Ziggy Sprague: a notation that the Japanese warships had divided into two formations, generally accurate but visible only to someone on the scene, and the identification of Japanese strength as four battleships and eight cruisers. The latter figure corresponded to Kurita's six heavy plus two light cruisers and differed slightly from what pilots Jensen and Brooks had reported. That, too, was visible only to someone on the scene. Despite the garbled call sign, FDR's Map Room correctly attributed the message to Taffy 3.

This period featured heroics from Ziggy Sprague's warships, desperation aboard Kinkaid's flagship, and nonchalance on board Halsey's. At 7:25 a.m., Admiral Kinkaid put Sprague's position into another message, repeating his appeal, "REQUEST IMMEDIATE AIR STRIKE. ALSO REQUEST SUPPORT BY HEAVY SHIPS." In this message Kinkaid inaccurately "revealed" for the first time that his heavy ships were low on ammo. Just two minutes later, Kinkaid put Sprague's latest information into yet another dispatch to Halsey, repeating his appeal for air strikes and heavy ships.

In this ten-minute period, the Seventh Fleet commander bid for help he had to know could not be forthcoming. The situation would be rendered far worse by U.S. communications foul-ups—news of the ammunition "crisis" on Kinkaid's battleships did not reach Halsey until 9:22, and that regarding Kurita's attack strength came only a little sooner, at 9:03. But Kinkaid certainly got Chester Nimitz's attention, if not Halsey's. The CINCPAC sent out the famous message that led Bull Halsey to stomp on his hat (and send the battleships). Equally significant, Nimitz sent a message to U.S. Navy commander Admiral Ernest J. King reporting that radio intercepts indicated a surface naval battle in progress at Taffy 3's position and with the Japanese in Kurita's strength.

Fortunately for all the Allies, by that time, the real situation would have morphed once more.

COMMANDER WILLIAM D. THOMAS, leader of the screen, sailed on the *Hoel*. Her skipper, Commander Leon Kintberger, at first focused on laying smoke. Sailors groused it made them a target, but the enemy seemed more intent on the carriers. They could see gun flashes from the big Japanese ships and hear the shells pass overhead, sounding like boxcars, on their trajectory toward the jeeps.

Then Commander Thomas received the order for a torpedo attack. Commander Amos T. Hathaway needed to take his *Heermann* across the Taffy formation to reach attack position. In the rain and smoke, *Heermann* nearly collided with destroyer-escort *Samuel B. Roberts*. The destroyers turned toward Kurita's fleet and began their runs.

On the TBS, Thomas passed the attack order to the four destroyer-escorts, which made up the rest of his screen. He called them "little fellows." Lieutenant Commander Robert W. Copeland of the *Roberts* was not sure if the term referred to all of the ships or whether they should be attacking separately or in tandem. Commander Thomas told him the "big fellows" would go first, then the destroyer-escorts. The *Roberts* followed *Heermann* anyway.

Hoel led the *Heermann* on another audacious attack. The *Johnston*, hit three more times by 6-inch shells (variously attributed to *Kongo*,

Yamato, or a light cruiser), had been gravely damaged but left untouched long enough that Commander Evans could jury-rig means to steer the ship, power for seventeen knots, and maintain gunnery control for three of her five guns. Evans operated in support of Commander Thomas's other vessels.

The *Hoel* went after the nearest enemy battleship, *Kongo,* and launched on her at about 7:27 a.m. Rear Admiral Shimazaki Toshio, *Kongo*'s captain, had been preoccupied with marauding aircraft. Moments before, they had disabled the ship's main range finder. The battleship went into the squall and ceased fire just before *Hoel*'s torpedo launch. Shimazaki had skippered his battlewagon for more than a year, including the Philippine Sea slugfest, and though he'd spent half the war as a naval district staff chief, he had also led destroyer units and commanded cruisers. He knew how to steer a ship. When crewmen saw torpedoes in the water a little after 7:30, Shimazaki evaded immediately to the southeast.

The *Hoel* became the bull's-eye for a host of Japanese forces, causing her to soon after lose guns, fire control director, and the port engine, and get her rudder jammed in a hard starboard turn. Before long, the number of heavy-caliber hits on this tin can approached a staggering two dozen. But, like Shimazaki's *Kongo,* she soon returned to the fray. Commander Kintberger powered his ship up again and went after heavy cruiser *Haguro,* against which she launched her last five torpedoes at about 7:53 a.m. *Hoel* had been shot up so badly that torpedomen had to aim manually, with no bridge communications. Also, contributing three deadly torpedoes were destroyer-escorts *Raymond* and *Dennis.*

Meanwhile, the *Heermann* moved up for her own torpedo strike—and had to put her engines into emergency back full speed to avoid a collision with the *Hoel.* Just a few minutes before observing *Hoel*'s torpedo launch, *Heermann* commenced her own. On her bridge, Amos Hathaway turned to *Heermann*'s officer of the deck, Lieutenant Robert F. "Buck" Newsome, and said, "Buck, what we need is a bugler to sound the charge!"

Commander Hathaway also targeted the *Haguro.* Captain Sugiura Kaju's cruiser had been firing at escort carriers, the *Johnston,* and the *Hoel,* and she picked out the oncoming destroyer plus the small boys now beginning to appear too. The skipper's sangfroid had become legendary—perhaps a Japanese Cherokee Evans. Sugiura had been one of the "miracle captains" running Tokyo Express missions out of Rabaul, with destroyers shot out from under him, but who came back for more. He stood with the Navy's premier torpedomen.

Instantly aware of three torpedo tracks when they appeared to starboard, Sugiura evaded them handily. That was a boon for Vice Admiral Hashimoto Shintaro, who had the flag of his Cruiser Division 5 in *Haguro*, and who thus avoided the need to find a new flagship, which had bedeviled his comrade Shiraishi as well as fleet commander Kurita. He was about to face that threat again.

TORPEDOES IN THE WATER

The incessant hovering of the airplanes and the escorts accounted for much of the disorganization of the Japanese pursuit—more so than any decisions made by Kurita Takeo. Admiral Shiraishi's story shows that nicely.

But there is always an exception. Seeking the full cooperation of battleship commander Ugaki Matome, and from abundant goodwill, Admiral Kurita permitted Vice Admiral Ugaki extraordinary liberties. In the Japanese fleet, unit commanders often supplanted ship captains on their own vessels, making the skipper a sort of supernumerary, while the senior officer issued direct orders. Admiral Kurita not only led the Second Fleet; he had also directly commanded a cruiser division (wiped out en route to Leyte by the Allied sub attacks) and therefore had been in charge of the helm of his then flagship *Atago*. Now he was entitled to lead the *Yamato*, which in practice meant giving free rein to chief of staff Koyanagi.

Submarine ambush had put Kurita on the bridge of the *Yamato*, Vice Admiral Ugaki's flagship of Battleship Division 1. Ugaki could supplant the behemoth's skipper, Rear Admiral Morishita Nobuei. But Kurita's appearance on the scene trumped that. Suddenly it was Ugaki who was the supernumerary. That did not sit well with the battleship driver, a dour sort of fellow. Lookout Koitabashi Kosaku said of Ugaki,

"Men loved him or hated him. He was seen as arrogant." Sometimes arrogance is just smarts. Here it's hard to decide which.

After just a salvo or two from *Yamato*, Admiral Ugaki complained. The fleet chief of staff, he asserted, knew little about gunnery. Ugaki had taught that subject in service schools and demanded he be given back the tactical command of his two ships. Like others of Ugaki's claims, this one amounts to less than advertised. Yes, Ugaki was a gunner and Koyanagi a torpedoman, but the comparison ended right there. In truth, Koyanagi had far more practical experience both in battle and at sea. Ugaki Matome had not commanded a warship since 1938—and even then, it had only been the vintage battleship *Hyuga*. At that time, Koyanagi skippered an old ship too, the cruiser *Iwate*, but he had gone on to lead a destroyer division and captained the heavy cruiser *Atago*, the battleship *Kongo*, and two different destroyer flotillas. At the helm of the *Kongo* off Guadalcanal—with Kurita in charge—Koyanagi had conducted the single most devastating Japanese battleship bombardment of the war. He had also participated in the Japanese evacuation of Guadalcanal. To say Koyanagi was not familiar with gunnery was absurd. In addition, Kurita Takeo had been with Koyanagi off Guadalcanal. Indeed, Koyanagi had been his flag captain, and the two had sunk the *Hornet* together. They were intimately familiar. Koyanagi had been Kurita's chief of staff for more than a year.

Conversely, here was Ugaki, the man who scribbled in his diary that deployment of the destroyer flotillas forward—which would have confused the gun layers—would have been a proper combat tactic. No expert gunner would have agreed. For weeks at Lingga, Ugaki had been an irritant. Tellingly, Kurita had seen fit to employ someone else—the *Musashi*'s Captain Inoguchi—as his special adviser on gunnery. Now Ugaki's complaint made it Kurita's call. Should he vest command in Koyanagi or Ugaki?

Admiral Kurita was tired, beyond exhaustion. He had supervised the fleet personally, on the bridge continuously since he'd come aboard the *Yamato*. Before that, while flagship *Atago* still floated, Kurita had begun his bridge vigil when the fleet entered dangerous waters. By now he had been on duty more than seventy-two hours. Kurita had to know of Ugaki's restiveness. The battleship admiral made no secret of his concerns—about the Sho goals, Kurita's idea of making *Yamato* the fleet flagship, the war games, the Combined Fleet's attempt to reassign the *Nagato*. It was unthinkable that Koyanagi, so close to his fleet commander, would not have kept Kurita apprised of Ugaki's thinking. In most of these cases, Kurita had taken Ugaki's point and played the issues as the battleship admiral wanted. Now that they were in combat, Ugaki wanted control. By all rights and prerogatives of the Imperial Navy, the fleet commander should have charge. And Kurita knew Koyanagi well, trusting his judgment. Acceding to Ugaki meant overruling his own chief of staff. Yet Kurita wanted earnestly to keep the peace. He made another of those quick judgments that Ugaki accused the fleet commander of being incapable of.

Out of exhaustion multiplied by urgency, Admiral Kurita let Ugaki take command.

Here came a true error. For Japanese prospects at Leyte, Kurita's error would have horrific consequences within the hour, and the outcome of this sea fight lay balanced on the edge of a knife.

THE TORPEDOES THE *Haguro* avoided spelled the beginning of disaster for Kurita Takeo's whole enterprise. They were early arrivals in a succession of American torpedo attacks. And because he had vested tactical command in Vice Admiral Ugaki, those torpedoes were going to afflict Admiral Kurita.

Chronometers were approaching eight o'clock when a "cruiser" burst from the smoke screen. Admiral Ugaki ordered the *Yamato*'s gunnery officer, Captain Kuroda Yoshio, to fight enemy ships ahead and to starboard. *Yamato*'s main armament and her 6-inch secondary guns took an array of enemy ships under fire. A target identified as a "destroyer," likely the destroyer-escort *Raymond*, appeared, following the *Heermann* and *Hoel* out of the mist and smoke. Before long, Kuroda had instructed the 5-inch heavy flak guns to join. The enemy loosed their torpedoes at battleship *Haruna*, but once she evaded, those deadly tin fish were suddenly headed right for *Yamato* and, behind her, the *Nagato*.

What happened next is a key error of the Leyte battle. Ugaki

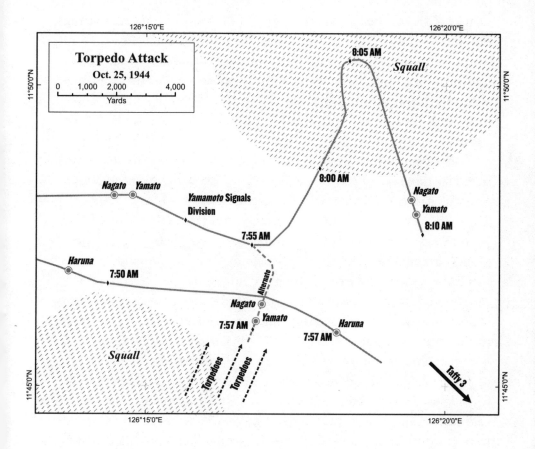

Matome, of course, predictably attributes it to Admiral Kurita. Turning to "fan the torpedoes" had long been a staple of evasive tactics. The helmsman could turn a ship toward torpedoes or away from them. The idea was to minimize the vulnerability of a ship by reducing the size of its target profile relative to the course of the torpedo. Which way to turn always depended on the situation. Here a starboard turn meant turning *into* the torpedoes that were running them down. That turn kept the ship headed toward Taffy 3. The port turn meant putting the ship on the same trajectory as the fish, but ultimately away from her prey. The battleship could not outrun the torpedoes, so she had to wait them out, until they either got ahead of her or expended their fuel and sank. A port turn also exposed the battleships' rudders and screws— their motive power—to potential damage in the middle of a high-speed chase.

Lookouts saw the oncoming wakes of torpedoes off the starboard side. The *Yamato* and *Nagato* turned to port, to almost due north, *away from* the American carriers that Kurita wanted so badly to bag. Ugaki's diary claims his fleet commander ordered that turn. Then, other torpedo tracks appeared to port, and torpedoes paralleled the Japanese battleships on *both* sides for nearly ten minutes. *Yamato* and her consort did not dare veer from a straight course.

We are left to deduce who made the decision, since there is no explicit record. Historian Robert Lundgren argues the turn to port was the only option because otherwise the battleships would have collided with the *Haruna*, which had been arcing to the south of them.*

Other depictions differ. While the ships were close just before the torpedo wakes appeared, the *Haruna* had already begun turning southeast as a result of a Kurita order at 7:46 a.m. A starboard turn would have put the *Yamato* and *Nagato* ships behind her, not on a collision

---

* Lundgren plots *Haruna* headed almost directly east, with the Ugaki unit converging on a southeast heading. He also locates the *Hoel* ahead and to the east of both Japanese units, and moving to the southwest. This chart differs from long-standing accounts of these events, including those of Samuel Eliot Morison and James A. Field, who chart these events in the fashion described here. Lundgren uses his analysis to defuse Ugaki's implicit anger at Kurita. But I believe Ugaki's anger had the purpose of hiding his own responsibility.

course. By 8:00 a.m. *Haruna* lay four nautical miles from *Yamato* steering a still-divergent course.

Historian Ito Masanori attributes the choice to Rear Admiral Morishita Nobuei. The logic here is simply that Morishita was captain of the *Yamato*. This is unlikely for several reasons. First, because of the practice of marginalizing ship commanders, Morishita likely did not have the helm. Second, as Kurita explained right after the war, ship drivers usually made their own choices in evading attack—but the *Nagato* maneuvered in a fashion identical to *Yamato*. That suggests a unit order. Morishita had no authority to make a decision that would affect another vessel. And last, Morishita Nobuei had a reputation as a crack ship handler, held in very high esteem, and this is a mistake he would not have made.

As a matter of fact there *is* a signal—the *Nagato* records it at 7:53 a.m.—where the *Yamato* orders the other vessel of Battleship Division 1 to evade torpedoes. That would be Ugaki, the division commander, not Morishita. Equally to the point, Kurita Takeo, who would have been intent on staying on top of those U.S. carriers, would have realized that turning to port meant extending the torpedoes' threat-time envelope, with Taffy 3 gaining sea room every minute. Called upon to evade torpedoes in this same battle, both the *Kongo*'s Shimazaki Toshio and the *Haguro*'s Sugiura Kaju chose the turn to starboard, not port.

The person on *Yamato*'s bridge who most lacked experience as a ship driver was Ugaki Matome—the very fellow who had staged a scene to wrest tactical command from Kurita. It is not likely that Ugaki, having gained control, would relinquish it for this decision. It is also true that the battleship boss, in the San Bernardino Strait the night before, had ordered a similar maneuver to counter an imagined torpedo threat. And there is the 7:53 a.m. order to the *Nagato*. The notion that Ugaki ordered the turn is a deduction, but a reasonable one.

As for Ugaki's blaming Kurita, the problem there is the fact of his open animosity toward the fleet commander. Ugaki's diary is studded with "recollections" aimed at Kurita, a number of them disingenuous or else based on superficial analysis, and this alone makes it difficult to agree with the accusation. In this case, there *was* a signal to the *Kongo* to evade torpedoes at 8:00 a.m., and that must have come from

Kurita. But it seems to be a warning. By that time, the ships Admiral Ugaki controlled had been settled onto their contrarian course for five minutes.

The Japanese behemoths were safe, but suddenly they were *seven miles* out of position. Kurita could no longer see what was happening, and Ziggy Sprague obtained a considerable advantage as a result. Kurita's concern is evident in the fact that now, in a sky dominated by desperate, marauding U.S. aircraft, he had *Yamato*'s aviation officer launch a floatplane at 8:12 a.m. Commander Ito Atsuo, the air officer, must have warned against putting up a plane in this hostile environment, but Kurita suddenly had no options.

NOW THE PROBLEM became one of making up for lost time. At 8:03 a.m., Rear Admiral Kobe Yuji of the *Nagato* had both his main and secondary batteries shoot at a "cruiser." The 6-inch secondaries loosed the first of five salvos a minute later. Within a couple of minutes, gunnery officer Commander Inouye Takeo noticed the cruiser on fire and listing.

Suddenly, the American planes took center stage. Not until 8:22 did the *Yamato* speak up again. Then her 18.1-inch guns engaged an American "battleship." She saw a carrier on fire at 8:23, and her secondaries engaged a "cruiser" at 8:34. Sure enough, contact with the *Yamato* floatplane would be lost at about 8:30.

The outside rim position on the turning Japanese wheel continued to be held by the *Kongo*. Rear Admiral Shimazaki believed he had already sunk an "*Enterprise*-class" aircraft carrier—Japanese ship identification remained terrible throughout. The problem would not be confined merely to the airmen who had fought the Battle of Taiwan.

In any case, the *Kongo* had suffered damage to her ten-meter range finder already. Commander Noguchi Yutaka, gunnery officer, either effected a repair or crafted a jury-rigged version, because shortly after 8:00 a.m. both primary and secondary batteries were in action. Noguchi thought *Kongo* had neutralized another U.S. carrier at about 8:10, leaving her listing and afire. Suddenly, in the far distance (24,700 yards) the ship spotted vessels of Taffy 2. She resumed shooting at Ziggy

Sprague's escorts. Noguchi's gunners used up 211 of her 14-inch armor-piercing shells plus 48 of the special 14-inch flak rounds and 272 rounds for the secondary armament.

Commander Gondarira Masao sailed as gunnery officer in battleship *Haruna*. Although the ship had a speed impediment, Rear Admiral Shigenaga Kazutake contrived to gain by cutting inside other Japanese pursuers. *Haruna* would end up the farthest advanced of Kurita's battleships. Gondarira had his primary and secondary guns all firing at a cruiser shortly after 8:00 a.m., though controllers soon pronounced their target a carrier, not a "cruiser." At 8:09, the gunner recorded hits on his first 14-inch salvo and a straddle on the third salvo of the vessel's 6-inch battery. Shortly thereafter Shigenaga, too, sighted Stump's Taffy 2 in the distance. Commander Gondarira reset his turrets for gun action to port. At 8:13, *Haruna* opened fire at eighteen nautical miles range. Over the next hour, Gondarira fired on several different targets, alternating between Taffy 2 and Taffy 3. His gunners expended 95 armor-piercing rounds plus 72 of the special flak shells and 353 munitions for the secondary armament.

Kurita's behemoths might be out of position—and he himself struggling to regain a grasp of the battle—but with radar control, his battleships could get in some licks, even at long range. And some targets were still nearby, such as the "cruiser" the 6-inch battery engaged shortly after half past eight. At 8:40 a.m., Commander Kuroda recorded the "cruiser" sinking. Five minutes later the *Yamato* regained sight of three U.S. carriers. By 8:54, one, most likely the *Gambier Bay*, seemed to be on fire. At 9:05, the superbattleship would steam through waters where the carrier had sunk. Wreckage, rafts, life preservers, and many survivors marked the area. The *Nagato* recorded this as a U.S. light carrier of the *Independence* class. The *Yamato* expended 100 of her 18.1-inch armor-piercing shells (plus 24 of the antiaircraft versions) and 127 rounds of 6-inch ordnance. *Nagato*'s consumption amounted to 45 armor-piercing and 52 high-explosive 16-inch shells, 84 of the antiaircraft type, and 133 shells from secondary.

Despite the imperfections of Japanese gunnery and their use of the wrong ammunition, the cannonade took its toll. Admiral Kinkaid resorted to another plaintext appeal at 8:29 a.m.: "MY SITUATION IS

CRITICAL FAST BATTLESHIPS AND SUPPORT BY AIR STRIKE MAY BE
ABLE PREVENT ENEMY FROM DESTROYING CVES AND ENTERING
LEYTE." Delays continued to prevent these messages from reaching
Halsey in a timely manner, but the Third Fleet commander had seen
enough by 8:48 a.m. that he ordered Slew McCain into action.

Taffy 3 now played with another squall, on a west-southwest course.
Admiral Sprague's escorts were arrayed in a rough arc in between his
escort carriers and the Japanese. Wounded ships were beginning to fall
out of formation. The Kurita fleet held positions analogous to the
outside lines of a right triangle. Across the baseline were the destroyer
flotillas and—bringing up the rear—the *Yamato* and *Nagato*. Arrayed
down the sideline were the four remaining heavy cruisers and the two
ships of Battleship Division 3.

Tone led the cruiser column. Captain Mayuzumi's ship immediately
attracted the attention of American planes, leading to repeated attacks.
A strafing fighter plane skewered the bridge, inflicting many casualties,
including Mayuzumi himself, hit in the right thigh by a machine-gun
bullet. A surgeon attended to the captain right on the bridge, for Mayuzumi refused to leave his post. The other major damage, inflicted by
splinters from a shell that fell in the sea nearby, took place right after
the captain had ordered torpedoes launched. A shell splinter ignited
oxygen flasks on two torpedoes in the number three mount, setting a
fire. Only the immediate launching of the torpedoes prevented detonation and much greater damage. This was part of an exchange with a
"light cruiser," believed to be *Heermann*. Mayuzumi recorded a
destroyer exploding at 8:45 a.m. In fact, Amos Hathaway's tin can,
though grievously damaged, never sank. The *Hoel* did, at 8:55, as did
the *Johnston* (but not until 10:10) and the destroyer-escort *Roberts* (at
about that same time).

Third in column had been Captain Sugiura in the *Haguro*. Shortly
after 8:00 a.m. a concentrated assault by ten planes blasted her. *Haguro*
sustained slight damage from a hit aft, but the more dangerous was a
direct hit on the number two turret. Thirty sailors expired around the
8-inch guns or within the protected area of the barbette. Commander
Ono Itaru saved the ship by instantly flooding the magazine serving

that turret, closing antiflash doors to prevent any spreading ignition of explosives. Flash detonations like that had destroyed British battle cruisers at Jutland and were probably responsible for the 1943 loss of the Imperial Navy battleship *Mutsu*. Executive officer Ono earned his pay that day.

Sugiura continued pursuing the jeeps, making twenty-eight knots and drawing closer every minute. *Haguro* had one CVE under fire, observing her listing sharply to starboard and sinking. By 8:52 a.m., there were several more in view, laying smoke and trying to flee. Sugiura took them under fire too, as well as a destroyer that tried to close. On the sixteenth salvo (78 rounds) against the new targets, gunnery officer Sato Hiroshi saw hits on the bow, amidships, and on the after section. Already on fire, the jeep blew up. Sato thought *Haguro* had badly crippled another CVE too, but her effectiveness against a third remained unknown. The cruiser also launched eight torpedoes. She consumed 582 armor-piercing and 211 high-explosive rounds for her 8-inch guns.

Around ten minutes before nine, a coordinated air attack played havoc with the Japanese warships. The *Tone* and the *Haguro* managed to outwit the attack planes. Mayuzumi Haruo wanted to make a torpedo attack and the two cruisers set up, but Rear Admiral Hashimoto Shintaro of Cruiser Division 5, in the *Haguro*, did not fancy wasting Long Lance fish against the little carriers. Hashimoto had *Haguro* stand down. *Tone* followed suit.

Captain Tanaka Jyo's *Chokai* took a bomb in the forward engine room. She dropped out of the chase, and twenty minutes later, Tanaka informed Kurita she also had a damaged floatplane. Just after nine o'clock, simultaneous attacks from Grummans off both sides made a torpedo hit unavoidable. At least one torpedo hit *Chikuma*'s stern, with a burst of flame and a waterspout as tall as the cruiser was long. Sailors aboard *Tone* could see light 23mm flak guns blown into the air by the force of the blast. At 9:07 a.m., Captain Norimitsu Saiji reported to Admiral Kurita that his cruiser had become unnavigable. Strenuous efforts were made to control the damage. Speed fell to eighteen knots, then to nine. She would be attacked again later in the morning, and planes would finish her off that afternoon.

SALVATION

The plucky, resilient men who crewed Rear Admiral Clifton Sprague's ships were brave, resourceful, and inspired. The Japanese made no end of mistakes, from ship identification to ammunition. They made use of radar-ranged gunfire for the first time, and that helped diminish accuracy too. Plus the weather remained a good friend to Ziggy Sprague, repeatedly enabling his hard-pressed ships to shelter from Kurita's guns.

For all of that, though, time had started to run out. Almost his last gambit was to order destroyer-escorts *John C. Butler* and *Dennis* to abandon their guard posts on the starboard side of the formation and join the other escorts trying to stave off the Japanese.

At first, some thought their ships could be inundated just from the waterspouts kicked up by all that action. The CVE *White Plains* became an early victim. One salvo's near misses created enough concussion to toss airplanes together. Two Wildcats just taking off were blown together like pieces of paper and ended up as junk on the flight deck. The rainsqualls were a blessing. Kurita's fleet concentrated its fire on the destroyers, visible because they were laying a smoke screen, and later because of their torpedo attacks.

Historian James D. Hornfischer has written movingly of the last stand of the tin can sailors, and their courage, skill, and determination are magnificent. But their luck is equally impressive. The *Heermann*, for example, having nearly collided once (with the *Roberts*), and then a second time (with *Hoel*), continued her violent maneuvers and almost crashed into the escort carrier *Fanshaw Bay* and then the *Johnston*. All the while, she remained the target of many enemy ships. Yet she survived.

The Japanese flotillas were in action by now, with light cruiser *Yahagi* and Destroyer Flotilla 10 ships engaging "destroyers" from 8:35, just the moment of *Heermann*'s near collision with CVE *Fanshaw Bay*. Commander Terauchi Masamichi, on the *Yukikaze*, felt the fleet had done nothing except allow itself to be attacked. He was happy for action.

The jeep carriers were careening around too, thus *Fanshaw Bay*'s near mishap. Carrier *St. Lo*, just renamed to honor Americans fighting in Normandy, endured several near misses early in the fight. Captain T. B. Williamson's *Kalinin Bay* suffered her first damage from near misses too, but the Japanese hit her with an 8-inch shell that swam through the sea to hole her below the waterline. Flooding almost incapacitated the forward engine room but did not. *Kalinin Bay* would be hit fourteen times. Thanks to the Japanese belief that they needed armor-piercing shells, the CVE still floated.

Worst off would be Captain Walter V. R. Vieweg and his CVE *Gambier Bay*. Japanese cruisers first targeted her right when she emerged from the early squall. Vieweg tried to steer the ship for the place the last enemy salvo had hit, chasing the shell splashes for a good half hour. But his luck ran out at about 8:10 a.m., when an 8-inch shell struck the flight deck just behind the after elevator. By then, the first outliers of Rear Admiral Stump's Taffy 2 were visible on the horizon to the southeast. The Japanese hardly let up. Another hit came near the bow.

But the critical damage followed a 14- or 16-inch shell that impacted in the water, just feet away from the ship, and then detonated below the surface. The shock ruptured the hull and let water into the forward engine room. In the time required for the black gang—the engineers— to secure those boilers, the flood had already reached their waists. It increased quickly. The *Gambier Bay* lost speed, with the Imperial Navy closing in even faster. After 8:45, when more hits compromised the aft engine room and the ship went dead in the water, the Japanese were down their throats. One of the Japanese cruisers, probably *Tone*, brazenly closed to within 3,000 yards of the stricken CVE. Captain Vieweg gave orders to abandon ship at 8:50. Only five minutes later, somewhat to the north, the blasted carcass of the *Hoel* rolled over and sank.

Survivors watched as Japanese warships continued pounding the wreck. Suddenly looming over them was the bulk of the superbattleship *Yamato* herself, followed by *Nagato*. The *Gambier Bay* actually sank at 9:07 a.m. Ships of Destroyer Flotilla 10 made their own torpedo attack at 9:05 but from extremely long range. There would be no hits.

Meanwhile Kurita's crews closed on the other CVEs. Ziggy Sprague's sailors held to their tasks in a most amazing way, their fighting spirit undiminished. The classic bit of bravado comes from Chief Gunner Jenkins, a flak battery officer aboard the *White Plains*. "Hold on a little longer, boys," he shouted. "We're sucking them in to 40mm range!"

The Kurita fleet did not feel that brave. They were confronted by a renewed air threat, a strike including sixteen Avengers that Taffy 2 had launched a quarter of an hour earlier. This attack would be the one to inflict important injuries on the *Chikuma* and *Chokai*. Captain Sugiura or Mayuzumi, of the *Haguro* or *Tone*, could have told Admiral Kurita the Americans were in extremis, but apparently they assumed the C-in-C knew everything. Kurita did not. Poor observation and scouting by the Japanese cruisers left Kurita in the dark.

At 9:11 a.m. the admiral ordered his fleet to regroup with him, setting a course near to due north. As soon as the message went out, the *Yamato* put her helm over to assume the new course.

"I HAD EXPECTED to be swimming," recalled Admiral Clifton Sprague. He heard a lookout shout that the Japanese were getting away. If anything, Ziggy Sprague thought the Japanese would be barreling down upon him. Sprague saw it with his own eyes but still could not believe it. "It took a whole series of reports from circling planes to convince me. And still I could not get the fact to soak into my battle-numbed brain."

Many American sailors reacted the same way. Possessing every advantage, the Kurita fleet turned around and sailed the other way. It proved more complicated than that, of course, but the turnaway off Samar on the morning of October 25 became a key event in the Leyte Gulf battle. It needs to be looked at from several perspectives.

The mind of Kurita Takeo needs a better probe than to assert he had no powers of decision this day, or that he panicked, or whatnot. The admiral had reason to think himself out of touch at 9:11 a.m. By dint of their unfortunate counter to the torpedoes, *Yamato* and *Nagato* were so disadvantaged that only radar-directed gunfire remained possible. Floatplane scouts had been sent out but disappeared. Data from subordinate commanders was sparse. Direct observations—such as speeding past the sinking *Gambier Bay*—disclosed only bits of information. Rear Admiral Koyanagi's postwar interrogation would be the first time he learned that Japanese cruisers had been less than 10,000 yards from the U.S. carriers when *Yamato* recalled them. Similarly, Koyanagi told his interrogators that the Kurita fleet had not been able to close the range against fast carriers, only to be stunned to discover they were CVEs. Kurita seconded that view in his own interrogation. This underlined the importance of Japanese misidentification of the Taffy 3 ships. Much later Koyanagi wrote, "If we had known the types and number of enemy ships and their speed, Admiral Kurita would never have suspended the pursuit."

What Kurita *did* know was fuel. He told the interrogators that he had enough fuel and ammunition to get into Leyte Gulf—that "there was no consideration for how to get home." But the high-speed chase was emptying his ships' tanks, especially those of the destroyers. The fleet could not sustain battle speed for very long. If they were to turn away, fuel became an issue immediately. And there was the hurt to the fleet itself. Four of the six heavy cruisers with which Kurita had burst through the San Bernardino just hours earlier were now at assorted stages of sinking. An equal number of tin cans—effectively a third of his destroyer strength— were standing by the damaged ships. The Allied air attacks, from the beginning a nuisance, were getting stronger by the minute.

New losses piled atop those already suffered. That amounted to a strong consideration but not the central one. Operations staff officer Otani had expected the fleet would be met by Allied forces—read Kinkaid's battleships—as it passed the bottom of Samar toward Leyte. While the fleet proceeded south, lookouts did, in fact, report sighting a *Pennsylvania*-class battleship with escorting destroyers, but the Japanese gave it a wide berth. Commander Otani believed the entire fleet would perish. Admiral Kurita's remarks at Brunei before sailing can be viewed the same way. If losses had been the central factor, Kurita would not have reacted the way he did when he obtained radio intelligence.

Both the Owada Group and Combined Fleet headquarters supplied intercepts that informed Kurita of some of the pleas sent out by Tom Kinkaid and Ziggy Sprague, which reported texts appealing desperately for battleship intervention and carrier air strikes. Matching reports came from the radio intercept station at Takao. These supplemented

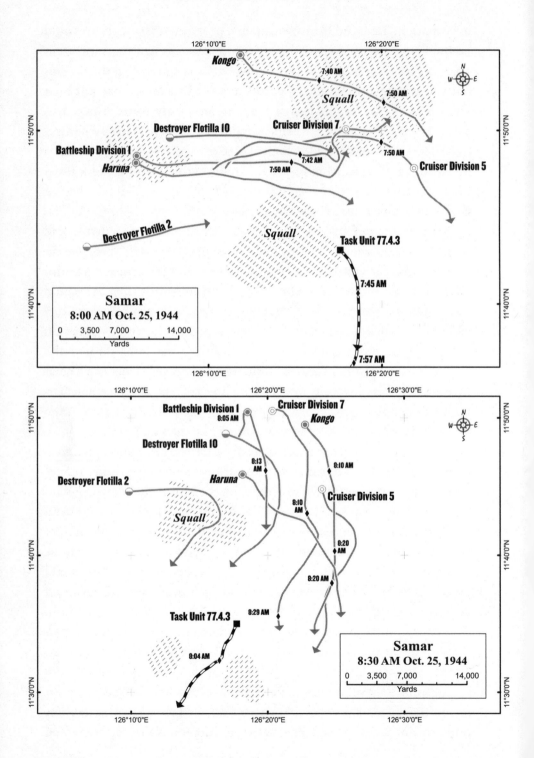

Samar
8:00 AM Oct. 25, 1944

0   3,500   7,000   14,000
Yards

Kongo
7:40 AM
7:50 AM
Squall
Destroyer Flotilla 10
Cruiser Division 7
7:50 AM
Battleship Division 1
Haruna
7:42 AM
7:50 AM
Cruiser Division 5
Destroyer Flotilla 2
Squall
Task Unit 77.4.3
7:45 AM
7:57 AM

Samar
8:30 AM Oct. 25, 1944

0   3,500   7,000   14,000
Yards

Battleship Division 1
8:05 AM
Cruiser Division 7
Kongo
Destroyer Flotilla 10
8:13 AM
8:10 AM
Destroyer Flotilla 2
Haruna
8:10 AM
Cruiser Division 5
Squall
8:20 AM
8:20 AM
8:29 AM
Task Unit 77.4.3
8:04 AM

an intercept the Kurita fleet itself had obtained at 9:00 a.m. that adverted the Taffies still under attack. Immediately upon receipt of the Owada Group intercept, at 11:20 a.m. Admiral Kurita ordered his fleet around to the southwest to proceed to Leyte Gulf. Shortly after the hour he notified Combined Fleet, "WE ARE DETERMINED TO EXECUTE THE PLANNED PENETRATION OF LEYTE GULF DESPITE ANY ENEMY AIR ATTACKS WHICH MAY BE ENCOUNTERED."

While this was happening, the JNAF struck back with the first really effective kamikaze mission, aimed at the very same Taffy 3. During the hour before Kurita made his second run on Leyte Gulf, the special attack unit led by Lieutenant Seki Yukio struck hard, sinking the jeep carrier *St. Lo*, 800 of whose crew were rescued, and damaging the *Kitkun Bay*, *Kalinin Bay*, and *White Plains*. This single attack signaled the onset of a new way of warfare in the Pacific. Late that afternoon Mikawa sent a dispatch in which the Southwest Area Fleet discussed these attacks. He reported one carrier—a "regular carrier"—damaged but otherwise results unclear.

The next stage of the disintegration of the Sho plan came with news of another carrier task group sighting, one to the east of the San Bernardino. At 12:36 p.m., Kurita ordered his fleet around to the north to chase this new enemy. The admiral discussed the option with his staff, including Koyanagi and Otani, and determined on that course of action. He reported to the high command that once he had engaged the new carrier fleet he would withdraw through the San Bernardino Strait.

Meanwhile, the alleged carrier force was actually a phantom, as probably was the sighting of a Kinkaid fleet *Pennsylvania*-class battleship. Ugaki suggested the report, from a masthead lookout, might be Nishimura, successfully exiting Leyte. Koyanagi disagreed. Kurita sent a floatplane to investigate, but it got shot down. As in the Taiwan air battle, the atrophy of Japanese skills at warship identification helped create an unmitigated disaster. Word soon came on the radio of the destruction of the Nishimura unit and the failure of the Shima fleet.

AT HIYOSHI THE succession of reports fueled a roller-coaster ride. The previous day Admiral Toyoda had managed not to show concern when the Kurita fleet had turned back, though he had agreed to the "divine guidance" dispatch. Chief of staff Kusaka, one of those few officers who believed in transports as targets, had been dissatisfied but not angry. Headquarters knew it could not direct the fleet from Hiyoshi and realized Kurita must have had reasons for his action. Senior officers expressed more concern with Nishimura and Shima—the former for not coordinating more closely with Kurita, the latter for not ordering Nishimura to wait for him so they could make a combined sally. News of the losses deepened their gloom.

Then, early that morning, Combined Fleet staff had nearly stood on its head, electrified at news the Kurita fleet had encountered an enemy carrier fleet. Officers were overjoyed. No one had thought an enemy carrier fleet would appear within visual range—and as Kusaka observes, the Samar battle actually represented the first time in the Pacific war that a large enemy fleet was encountered within eyeshot. Captain Fuchida claims he himself felt disgust and believed the quarry were merely the small jeep carriers, taken all out of context by his colleagues. "This cannot be happening," he recalls thinking.

Fuchida uses a hunting-dog analogy: Trained his whole life to hunt, the dog rushes after a hare. Following similar instincts, naval officers unthinkingly attacked at the first sight of the enemy fleet. Fuchida notes that the operating forces and Combined Fleet headquarters were both full of officers trained to hunt. Admiral Toyoda was all smiles. Admiral Kusaka thought it a golden opportunity. Radio intercepts showed the enemy begging for help. No one at Hiyoshi was about to chastise Kurita and remind him of his mission to actually penetrate Leyte Gulf.

When news came of Kurita regrouping—then heading north—fleet headquarters was at a complete loss.

Admiral Toyoda, thousands of miles away, did not feel right giving orders in a tactical situation that changed from minute to minute. The "divine guidance" message had been more of a strategic directive, applying to all Japanese forces, not only Kurita. After the war Toyoda refused to criticize Kurita for the withdrawal.

At 5:15 p.m., NGS chief Admiral Oikawa radioed: "REPORT MADE TO THRONE CONCERNING TODAY'S BATTLE DEVELOPMENTS IN PHIL-IPPINE AREA. HIS MAJESTY EXPRESSED DEEP SATISFACTION WITH

THE VIGOROUS ACTION OF THE FIRST STRIKING FORCE IN DEALING THE ENEMY A CRIPPLING BLOW."

Only in the evening, at 7:25 p.m., did Toyoda send a directive message:

IF THERE IS AN OPPORTUNITY TO DO SO, THE FIRST DIVER-SION ATTACK FORCE WILL CONTACT AND DESTROY WHAT IS LEFT OF THE ENEMY TONIGHT. THE OTHER FORCES WILL COORDINATE THEIR ACTION WITH THE ABOVE. 2. IF THERE IS NO CHANCE OF ENGAGING THE ENEMY IN A NIGHT ENGAGE-MENT TONIGHT, THE MAIN BODY OF THE MOBILE FORCE AND THE FIRST DIVERSION ATTACK FORCE WILL PROCEED TO THEIR REFUELING POINTS.

By then the Kurita fleet had already passed through the San Bernardino on its way home. Allied forces bearing down on them included Vice Admiral John S. McCain's Task Group 38.1 speeding from the east—and within strike range by late afternoon. Halsey, with Bogan's Task Group 38.2, Lee's Task Force 34, and the splinter unit Task Group 34.5, were all speeding down from the north.

The pursuit had begun.

CHAPTER 11

SEA FIGHTS AND SHIPWRECKS

The disappointment of the ultimate surface battle surged with the pain of the relentless Allied pursuit as the fleet retreated. Leyte Gulf had been a sea fight without precedent in the Pacific war, indeed, in all of World War II. Much more had been on the line for the Japanese, who were hoping their actions would stall the Allied offensive in the Pacific, at least long enough for Japan to achieve a new synthesis of tactics and combat power. Instead the battle led to the shipwreck of Japanese naval strategy. And that disaster culminated with the Allied mop-up operations following the battle.

Crewmen of the *Tone* saw the heavy cruiser *Chokai* stopped in the water as they complied with Admiral Kurita's order to regroup. Commander Matsuzaki Tatsuji's destroyer *Fujinami* had been detailed to escort the big ship. Instead, Matsuzaki stood by as *Chokai*'s troubles multiplied. Eventually *Fujinami* evacuated the crew from the crippled cruiser. Matsuzaki torpedoed the *Chokai* to end her ordeal.

The *Chikuma* staggered away from the battle area and was hit again by another wave of Grummans from escort carrier *Kitkun Bay*. New damage from two torpedoes brought her to a halt. Destroyer *Nowaki*, assigned to recover survivors, stayed late into the day at her side. Commander Moriya Setsuji then set off for Coron Bay. Like the promised land, Coron Bay represented salvation for Imperial Navy sailors terrified of the Allied juggernaut. But there would be no salvation for Moriya's destroyer. A night scout plane from the carrier *Independence* saw *Nowaki* at 10:40 p.m. Bull Halsey reacted by detaching several of his fastest ships, cruisers *Biloxi*, *Miami*, and *Vincennes* and destroyer *Miller*, and they caught the Japanese destroyer before she could enter the San Bernardino Strait. The Americans opened fire at 12:54 a.m.

and quickly dispatched Moriya, his destroyer, and the *Chikuma* survivors.

Captain Teraoka Masao's *Suzuya* never escaped the battle scene. As she made her way back home, a strong formation of warplanes assailed *Suzuya* in the forenoon, and a near miss to starboard ignited torpedoes, which led to secondary explosions and spread to ammunition lockers. At 11:30 a.m. Vice Admiral Shiraishi transferred his flag to cruiser *Tone*, and Teraoka reluctantly ordered "abandon ship" just before noon. The destroyer *Okinami* stood by to rescue survivors, including the captain and more than 400 crew, but more than 650 sailors went missing or were dead. At 1:22 p.m., the cruiser turned on her starboard side and sank.

Less than ten minutes later a new wave of American aircraft arrived to persecute the *Okinami*, now laden with helpless survivors. Commander Okino Tan, the destroyer's skipper, suspended rescue efforts while the planes attacked. There were several near misses. Okino withdrew but returned afterward to pick up more men. A huge formation of nearly 100 airplanes appeared, but they ignored the *Okinami* and kept their distance. Around five o'clock Okino received orders to rejoin the Kurita fleet. A small flight of planes harassed him again. With dark coming and no information on the enemy, Commander Okino decided to leave.

Okinami passed through the San Bernardino alone, stopping briefly to recover thirteen seamen in a lifeboat from the cruiser *Tone*. Next morning the destroyer would be hit by airplanes in the Sibuyan Sea. Nearly thirty sailors and *Suzuya* survivors were killed in the attack, and the ship sustained damage around the stern, taking on 150 tons of water. After 11:00 a.m., Commander Okino ran into the damaged destroyer *Hayashimo*, which had stopped and had just five tons of fuel left. *Okinami* herself had barely ninety tons, but Commander Okino gave some of it to the other ship. *Okinami* continued to Coron Bay, was attacked again along the way, and later escorted the crippled *Kumano* to Manila.

Kurita Takeo led his battered fleet west, through the San Bernardino, also headed for Coron Bay and oil. Early morning found them off Panay. The weather was fair and the sky clear. Carrier aircraft made contact first, following the oil trails of wounded ships with leaking bunker tanks. A hundred planes came in waves before 9:00 a.m. With thirteen killed and forty wounded, the *Yamato* suffered more casualties on October 26 than in the Battle of Samar. A bomb casing splinter wounded chief of staff Koyanagi in the right leg. *Yamato* used up fourteen more of those *sanshikidan* special flak shells. She sustained a couple more bomb hits and *Haruna* some near misses, but the main victim would be Captain Kajiwara Sueyoshi's light cruiser *Noshiro*. A torpedo hit caused the ship to halt and list dangerously. Attempting to correct the tilt by counterflooding, Captain Kajiwara ordered the forward magazines to be flooded. After 10:00 a.m., another wave hit the already damaged *Noshiro*. She settled by the bow. Kajiwara and several hundred sailors were rescued by destroyers *Hamanami* and *Akishimo*.

Another heavy cruiser headed to Coron was Captain Hitomi Soichiro's *Kumano*, which had limped away from battle, at times doing no better than two knots. Some of the planes aiming for Kurita that morning peeled off to blast the *Kumano* instead. With her damaged bow, the ship could hardly maneuver, and *Kumano* suffered hits and a near miss that left her without steam pressure, with most of her boilers off, and with a turbine damaged. Damage repair restored some of the power, and that afternoon, remnants of the Shima fleet joined *Kumano* for the last leg into Coron. Hitomi stayed there just long enough to refuel and then left for Manila.

As Admiral Kurita maneuvered under these new air attacks, he gave up the idea of making for Coron Bay. Heavy cruiser *Myoko*, damaged on the way to Leyte Gulf, was already there. She was meant to leave for Brunei in the afternoon. Early on the twenty-sixth, Captain Ishihara Itsu of the *Myoko* received fresh orders: Await the arrival of the Kurita fleet. Shortly before 11:00 a.m., the instructions morphed again. Kurita now ordered Ishihara to depart for Brunei immediately. Escorted by destroyers *Naganami* and *Kiyoshimo*, the *Myoko* left.

The final victims of the Allies mopping up after Leyte were ships from the Shima fleet and Cruiser Division 16. Heavy cruiser *Mogami*, barely afloat after the Surigao Strait fight, lost its way and then was jumped by planes of Taffy 1. The light cruiser *Kinu* was smashed as she tried to get a Tokyo Express into Leyte Island.

Meanwhile, the grounded *Hayashimo* turned into a Japanese nightmare. She had been damaged by air attack during the afternoon of the Samar battle, losing fuel, radio, compass, and more. The next morning came an attack by Grummans. Skipper Lieutenant Commander Hirayama Toshio suffered wounds. Captain Shiraishi Nagayoshi, commanding Destroyer Division 2, took direct command. At one point, Hirayama and Shiraishi thought they could steam the damaged destroyer, stern-first, all the way to Coron, but instead she was grounded to wait for fuel. Destroyer *Fujinami* would be sent back to succor the vessel, with *Shiranuhi* as a rescue ship on October 27, and both of them were sunk by American aircraft. *Fujinami*'s loss was especially tragic since she carried survivors from cruiser *Chokai*. The partially sunk hulk of the *Hayashimo* lay perched on that reef through the end of the war.

Combined Fleet headquarters took a hand, finally, at 11:34 a.m. on the twenty-sixth. Admiral Toyoda ordered heavily damaged ships to return to the Inland Sea, ones able to be repaired at Singapore to head there, and vessels requiring emergency repairs to obtain them at Hong Kong or Keelung, on Taiwan. The former had two dry docks suitable for vessels up to 10,000 tons, and Keelung had another.

The *Nachi* followed Combined Fleet's prescription but obtained her emergency repairs at Manila, instead. That turned out to be a fatal mistake. Allied subs sat around Manila to trap the unwary, while carrier planes picked over the environs even as they avoided the city. The *Nachi* lay in Manila Bay on November 5 when *Essex* planes sent her to the bottom of the sea.

Kumano followed the prescription too, but also stopped at Manila. The planes and subs hunted *Kumano* like a burglar in the night. Eventually they caught her.

AS HAD HAPPENED with the Taiwan air battle, the Japanese put an unreal face on the Leyte action. Broadcast on October 26, Radio Tokyo's commentary asserted that "Japanese forces now have complete air and sea superiority on and around Leyte."

The details are of some interest: "The Imperial fleet, which patiently held back its desire to engage in battle in order to pile training upon training, has finally been given the chance to manifest its power. The

Imperial fleet saw an opportune moment to deal a death blow upon the enemy fleet, and boldly and fearlessly sailed out to challenge a battle with the main strength of the enemy fleet."

The newspaper *Asahi Shimbun* also said this on October 26: "The fact that the United States Navy has suffered two successive defeats of the greatest magnitude in less than two weeks in the Pacific theater of war indicate either a complete lack of ability and recklessness of the enemy High Command, or some factor other than strategic is dictating the conduct of the enemy's recent operations."

Navy minister Yonai would be more candid about the reality of the situation. "When you took the Philippines," he told interrogators in November 1945, "that was the end of our resources."

Americans learned of these momentous events in a series of official communiqués from the U.S. Navy, CINCPAC, and General MacArthur's Southwest Pacific theater command. General MacArthur proved quick to release news of the Allied landing in the Philippines, and Admiral Nimitz at Pearl Harbor put out a communiqué the same day announcing the Japanese advance to battle through the Sulu and Sibuyan seas. This series of CINCPAC press releases (nos. 163 to 166) gave a running account of events, which, despite the fact that these reports are often distorted, provided a surprising level of detail on the Japanese side.

Kurita's turnaway in the Sibuyan Sea received mention. Lavish detail would be devoted to the attack on the Ozawa fleet. Nothing whatsoever was said about the Battle of Samar. The first mention, only a vague intimation, appeared on October 27 (October 28 in the Philippines) in a Navy Department release:

1. According to latest information received, the following U.S. Naval vessels, in addition to the USS *Princeton* (light carrier) have been sunk during the recent operations in the Philippines:
   2 escort carriers
   2 destroyers
   1 destroyer escort
2. No details have been received.
3. Next of kin of casualties aboard the above vessels will be notified as soon as possible.

That constituted the entire release.

Finally, on October 29, Admiral Nimitz released CINCPAC Communiqué No. 168, which contained the first explicit declaration that a battle had taken place. More than that, CINCPAC declared that "although still subject to revision as more information is received, [reports] indicate an overwhelming victory for the Third and Seventh United States Fleets. The Japanese fleet has been decisively defeated and routed. The second battle of the Philippine Sea* ranks as one of the major sea battles of World War II."

IN TOKYO, AT the Diet, the foreign minister's private secretary, Kase Toshikazu, happened to be meeting with senior politicians when the Leyte landings began. Kase announced the invasion to the assembled group. Consternation followed—along with intense anxiety about the role of the Imperial Navy. That was cleared up a few days later. Admiral Toyoda put out an order of the day for public consumption. But the Navy could not admit the truth without revealing the falsity of the spin it had put on the battle, starting with the Taiwan action. So it continued to claim a fictional victory. The real story it kept within a very tight circle. The Japanese government persisted in acting as if the armed forces were succeeding.

The Leyte battle had effectively ended the first round of Tokyo's search for a diplomatic solution to the war. Prime Minister Koiso had pursued opening up dialogue through the Soviet Union, with which Japan had a nonaggression pact. Koiso had not been very serious, and he achieved nothing before Leyte. The battle results were evident to others, even if they were kept from the Japanese people. On November 7, Joseph Stalin took the occasion of the anniversary of the Russian Revolution to denounce Japan as an aggressor. The road through Moscow, at least for the moment, had been blocked.

---

*Only later did Americans begin calling this huge action the Battle of Leyte Gulf. In October 1944, alluding to the Great Marianas Turkey Shoot—aka the Battle of the Philippine Sea—the "second battle" nomenclature prevailed. Japanese commentators persisted much longer in using the Philippine Sea tag.

The following day Koiso declared that the Battle of Leyte would decide the outcome of the war and that Japan had determined to hold the island. Resorting to hyperbolic rhetoric, Koiso invoked the classic Japanese hero Hideyoshi and the decisive battle that had led to the Tokugawa era to dramatize Leyte. Military leaders who doubted their ability to win this fight were not pleased.

Private secretary Kase meanwhile consulted with *jushin* figures in his effort to bring realistic information to Foreign Minister Shigemitsu. Kase met with Admiral Okada Keisuke. The admiral replied quite frankly: The fleet would be entirely at the mercy of the Allies. Japan could not replace its losses in pilots and planes. Even if aircraft carriers could be built—and Kase appears to have been unaware of Japan's alarming steel shortage—the trained pilots were missing, stockpiles were largely exhausted, and essential war matériel was running out. Kase notes, "It was clearly no longer possible to continue the struggle, let alone mount another offensive on the high seas."

WAS LEYTE GULF a "decisive battle"? Official historian Samuel Eliot Morison punts on that question, arguing that "decisive" is a relative term, concluding that Midway had been more decisive. But he also argues that Leyte "did decide" the fact that the Allies would rule the Pacific through the end of the war. Admiral Chester Nimitz, on the other hand, had no doubts, even just a few days after the battle.

There are at least two ways in which conditions that existed prior to this battle were transformed. First, before Leyte the Imperial Navy had been a potent weapon waiting to be used. Every Allied commander in every theater of war had to consider the possibility that weapon could be aimed at him. After Leyte the Japanese fleet was expended, a collection of units to be repaired, retrained, and reconstituted, and which would return at a lesser level of power. It would be a weapon suited to a different kind of war. That change was decisive.

Second, the ultimate failure of the Imperial Navy to exact a price from its adversary using conventional methods brought to a head the tactical/technological/strategic dispute that had been building on the Japanese side. This was the effort to find a way around the virtual attrition that increasingly hampered Tokyo's war effort. The need to find ways to make inferior weapons count, against a technologically advanced enemy, received a great impetus from the fleet's failure at Leyte. Failure enshrined the "special attack," the kamikaze. Paradoxically, the huge victory at Leyte put a new kind of enemy in the face of Allied forces, making for one of the great challenges of the war. That too was a decisive development.

A collateral point is that the Imperial Navy had explicitly aimed for a decisive battle through its Sho plan. In important ways the battle disarmed the Japanese fleet. That result displayed the bankruptcy of the long-standing Japanese doctrine. Even those officers inclined to resist the special attack methods had to be chastened by the failure of their forces in a conventional role. That, too, softened the way for kamikaze tactics.

There were a number of ways, some major, some not, in which Leyte had effects that nevertheless fell short of being decisive. The most obvious is the huge loss of Japanese combat ships. For a military balance in which the Allies had already attained significant superiority, and were adding to their forces at a faster rate, for the Japanese to incur an instantaneous loss of more than 300,000 tons of warships in exchange for barely 40,000 tons of Allied ones meant an acceleration of Allied superiority. Along with that huge loss went shrinkage in the pool of experienced sailors on whom the Japanese depended. The Imperial Navy suffered more than 118,000 dead in 1944, the largest number of them at Leyte Gulf, followed by the Marianas battle. That represents more than 43 percent of all Japanese Navy battle deaths for the war. Put another way, Navy casualties in 1944 equate to roughly two and a half times Japanese naval casualties for the entire period since Pearl Harbor, including very costly campaigns in the South Pacific.

No service could sustain such losses without deterioration of skills and capabilities. One can debate how decisive this impact was, but clearly it needs to be seen as major.

THE LEYTE INVASION crystallized the strategic dilemma President Roosevelt had mulled over at Pearl Harbor. The question had been how to isolate Japan, and the choices the Philippines versus Taiwan. Now there would be a campaign for Leyte, then landings on other Philippine islands, principally Luzon, but Leyte meant commitment. The Allies would still be fighting, on Luzon if not Leyte, when the war ended. The strategic aim decided at Pearl Harbor had been to blockade Japan by cutting its overseas supply routes. The Philippine campaign accomplished that, but merely in a haphazard fashion.

Douglas MacArthur's pitch had been misleading. Overselling the Philippines as the base for a blockade came easily to MacArthur—as easy as pretending to be interested in FDR's stamp collection. What MacArthur had really been after were his political preferences. That was something Franklin Roosevelt understood—and accepted. But what is so tragic is that one person's preferences had global consequences. The Japanese did not fall like a house of cards. In spite of the friendship the Filipinos had for Americans, an awful lot of hard fighting still remained. Every new target (or rather, island) would have to be invaded, adding up to multiple amphibious assaults. As a single contiguous landmass, Taiwan would have required only one invasion, reducing the complexity of the overall mission.

MacArthur had been deceptive on another level too: The Philippines were *not* the superior position from which to complete the blockade and encirclement of Japan. As Admiral Ernest J. King had argued, Taiwan would have been better for that purpose. Standard planning templates the Joint Chiefs of Staff employed show that control of Taiwan would have positively corked the bottle of the supply routes to Japan, whereas against a blockade applied from the Philippines a resourceful adversary could contrive an infiltration route—which is eventually what happened when imperial commanders began developing a seaborne infiltration route. In January 1945, Admiral Halsey would take his Third Fleet on a raid into the South China Sea precisely to interdict that coastal traffic. His mission demonstrated, among other things, that the blockade from the Philippines had to be *enforced*. A blockade from Taiwan simply could have existed. Standard search-and-strike tactics would have sufficed to choke off the Japanese supplies, with no special fleet action required to choke off Tokyo's supplies. While it is true that Japanese figures also understood the fall of the

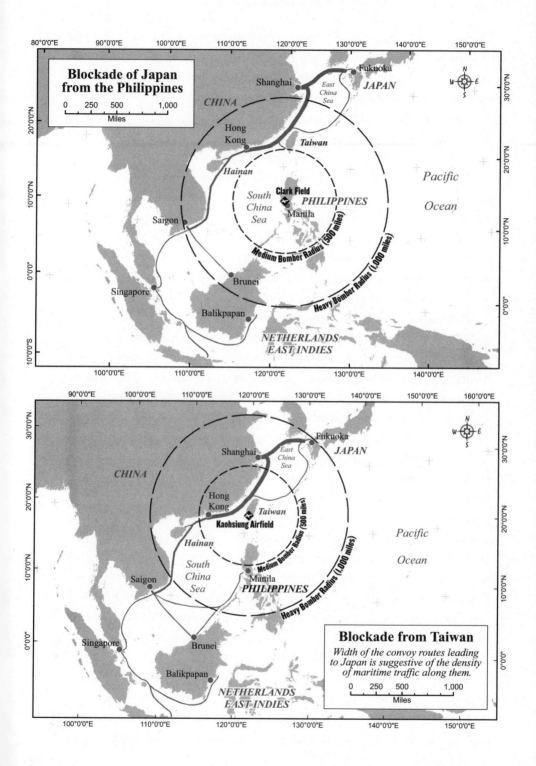

Blockade of Japan from the Philippines

0   250   500   1,000
Miles

CHINA

Shanghai

East China Sea

Fukuoka

JAPAN

Hong Kong

Taiwan

Pacific Ocean

Hainan

South China Sea

Clark Field

PHILIPPINES

Manila

Saigon

Medium Bomber Radius (500 miles)

Heavy Bomber Radius (1,000 miles)

Brunei

Singapore

Balikpapan

NETHERLANDS EAST INDIES

Blockade from Taiwan

Width of the convoy routes leading to Japan is suggestive of the density of maritime traffic along them.

0   250   500   1,000
Miles

CHINA

Shanghai

East China Sea

Fukuoka

JAPAN

Hong Kong

Taiwan

Kaohsiung Airfield

Pacific Ocean

Hainan

South China Sea

Manila

PHILIPPINES

Saigon

Medium Bomber Radius (500 miles)

Heavy Bomber Radius (1,000 miles)

Singapore

Brunei

Balikpapan

NETHERLANDS EAST INDIES

Philippines as cutting the Empire off from the south, it is also the case that imperial commanders actually began developing the seaborne infiltration route as time stretched from weeks into months. Hence the Halsey carrier raid.

The imperfect blockade had a marked impact. War termination in the Pacific could have resulted *if* a successful blockade had made it plain to Japanese leaders and commanders that further military operations were simply not possible. Instead Tokyo received the impression that it could continue a broken-backed war. This point should not be taken too far, since even with the imperfect blockade, at a certain point Japanese resources were going to give out. However, Washington did not have time for that. War-weariness on the *Allied* side, the end of the war in Europe, and the impatience of leaders led to demands for near-term results, and thus pressures for action.

Writing of the Pearl Harbor conference, Joint Chiefs of Staff chairman Admiral William D. Leahy said that the strategic decisions made were aimed primarily at avoiding an unnecessary invasion of Japan. By overselling the Philippines as an objective, however, Douglas MacArthur actually pushed American leaders in the exact opposite direction. Japan would have to be invaded if it could not be subdued.

Douglas MacArthur's preferred strategic option led ultimately to a Hobson's choice among horrific pathways. The general seems to have been discomfited by the consequences of his actions, at least to judge from how he falsified his letter to FDR. The burdens of the Hobson's choice *were* awful. The Philippine strategy led to the need for direct action, and the options included a strategic bombing campaign against Japan for massive death and destruction, invading the Home Islands, or employing the atomic bomb against the Japanese. Predictably this caused a lot of existential dread—invasion versus the A-bomb? A million casualties versus introducing a horrific, unthinkable weapon and actually using it against innocents? A course that led to the horns of that dilemma has to be ranked a decisive choice.

IN ADDITION, THERE are a number of questions, remarkable insights, gaps in vision, mistakes, and miscalculations that affected the actual fighting at Leyte Gulf that demand comment. The bottom-line question is this: Could the outcome at Leyte have been anything other than it was?

Imperial Navy planners have to be given credit for remarkable insight. That is, the NGS and Combined Fleet realized that a properly conducted operation could potentially reverse the numerous Allied advantages in terms of raw strength, technological superiority, intelligence, and command function. The Japanese understood the keys to attaining that position were an asymmetrical approach, compelling the Allies to pay attention to multiple threats simultaneously; accepting the high potential for losses; and mounting decoy missions. Naval leaders believed this a onetime opportunity and the high command attached it to a suitably important objective, the Philippines. In some sense a victory lay in the very fact that with the dawn of October 25, there would be an Allied carrier force under the guns of an Imperial Navy surface fleet. Every measure of the existing war situation thus turned inside out. That the Kurita fleet did not fully profit from that circumstance does not detract from its achievement.

Having said that, it is also necessary to observe that Imperial Navy commanders failed critically in setting goals for the Sho plan—or more accurately, they failed to mount an active effort to build a consensus among officers on their recast of naval targets. The NGS and Combined Fleet were within their prerogative to enshrine different objectives, but having done so, it became incumbent upon them to push officers to accept the new objectives. "Admiral Kurita's mission was complete destruction of the transports in Leyte Bay," Combined Fleet C-in-C Toyoda told interrogators. "In the orders there was no restriction as to the damage he might take." To leave the old understanding and new objectives on the table simultaneously inserted a source of uncertainty, which meant officers needed to be unflinchingly dedicated to the goal. Toyoda's trip to the Philippines in early October marked an effort to deal with that problem, but it ended up as a disaster that trapped the C-in-C away from headquarters at *the* critical moment.

Perhaps the uncertainty of the Sho objectives can be taken as evidence of the continued dysfunction of the Japanese high command. There were Army officers who firmly believed in the enemy fleet was the target, though invasion flotillas posed the greatest threat to Army troops. On the Navy side, there were officers who believed the opposite—that flotillas were the threat, not the fleets. But cooperation fell short of the unity of effort the top commanders promised Emperor Hirohito when he approved the execution of Sho. The Army's sudden switch of strategy to make the peripheral island (Leyte) rather than the prepared bastion (Luzon) the central front automatically created a Tokyo Express–type demand that was sure to increase its losses. In addition, the Army's procrastination in providing troops to reinforce Leyte, and its sudden aversion to a naval battle, call into question its entire purpose in the enterprise.

The Navy leaders made great progress in preparing their forces for Sho. They understood clearly that they lacked a unitary force, instead possessing the distinct, limited weapons of an air attack force, a submarine force, and a surface unit. But it was a major mistake, starting with Admiral Kusaka, to activate Sho only for the airplanes. The only way to obtain synergistic effects from the disparate arrows in the Japanese quiver was to employ the separate forces in a related space and together in time. An arrangement like that might have spared Kurita Takeo and other commanders some of their losses on their way to Leyte Gulf. The day of October 25, when the Allied escort carriers perished to surface gunfire and an air attack, and had another jeep narrowly evade a submarine torpedo attack, hints at the potential here.

Navy leaders were also responsible for the general weakness of antisubmarine warfare (ASW) tactics and forces in the fleet. The Japanese reluctance to devote serious forces and technological effort to ASW afforded Allied subs much greater freedom of action than they would otherwise have had. One of the impacts of this would be the loss of tankers, which essentially crippled all Japanese operations. Another was virtual attrition—the diversion of Japanese destroyers, submarines, and even big ships to transport duties rather than combat patrols. Allied submarines began specifically targeting Japanese destroyers, magnifying virtual with real attrition. That not only cut back ASW forces; it reduced the offensive torpedo capability of the destroyer flotillas at Leyte.

The diminished availability of destroyers to escort surface forces had some real consequences for the naval forces at Leyte. Kurita's fleet, for example, had less protection in the Palawan Passage, and similarly, the same proved true for Ozawa's fleet as it tried to escape from battle.

In addition, Japanese admirals underemployed what escorts they did have. From what we know of the Kurita fleet's training at Lingga, there were three or four, or more, gunnery exercises for every one that focused on ASW. Most likely this represents a general phenomenon. When the fleets sortied, the number of false submarine detections was considerable, and a good deal of them were attributable to lack of practice. During the battle, Allied submarines alone accounted for three Japanese cruisers sunk and two damaged, all of which were critical losses to the Kurita fleet, among them the admiral's very flagship, a singular event to which some attach very great importance.

Intelligence helped both sides at Leyte Gulf. Though the Allies never achieved the surprise they had often enjoyed, Japanese operations, and even their intentions, were almost an open book to Allied commanders. The intelligence units at Pearl Harbor, in Washington, and with MacArthur did an excellent job of keeping commanders apprised of Japanese moves. Their information ranged from whether or not it could be expected that the Imperial Navy would sortie if the Allies invaded the Philippines to observations of Japanese tanker traffic and what it indicated about naval operations. Even something as specific as warning of the activation of Sho had been seen, too, and taken into account. Intelligence difficulties have also been noted, as in the debate that raged over the true inventory of Japanese combat aircraft, or the number of training aircraft that should be regarded as suitable for combat. For all that, the spooks were no longer so important as they had been in the South Pacific or at Midway.

At the very height of the Leyte battle, Admiral Nimitz took a chance, possibly exposing Ultra in order to warn the fleets that Kurita had come through the San Bernardino Strait. That kind of move had been unheard-of in the European war. It can be read either as an index of the emergency Nimitz believed existed or as a measure of the diminished importance of intelligence in a world of Allied military might.

William F. Halsey did not respond to the intelligence because he fixated on destroying the Japanese carrier fleet. That basic structure ensured that the Japanese decoy plan would work. There will be more to say about this in a little while, but here the interesting point to reiterate is that both sides made a mistake at Leyte Gulf. Not only that, but both sides made the identical mistake, and for the same reason. The Japanese belief in decisive battle meant a focus on combat forces. Before the war they would have emphasized battleships, but they had come to rank aircraft carriers as the main combatants. Bull Halsey believed the same thing. He was bound to go after Ozawa just as Kurita had to fight Ziggy Sprague.

With all of this in mind, was another outcome possible? No. That's the short answer. There could have been a more diminished outcome—in the sense that it might not have been as great a slaughter of the Imperial Navy. Or it could have differed in that more damage might have been accrued by the Allies. The optimal case required an enormous number of things to go exactly right.

For the sake of discussion, let's assume that Combined Fleet held its hand during the Taiwan air attacks, began to gather the tankers to fuel the fleet very early on, and avoided tipping off Allied intelligence by keeping the Shima fleet in port. In this vision, Toyoda and Kusaka would throw everything at MacArthur when he began moving into Leyte Gulf, opening with a fierce hurling of air strikes between the Halsey fleet and the Taffies, on one side, and the JNAF air fleets, on the other. This new focus on the air forces and carrier fleets would most likely prevent much of an attack against the approaching Japanese surface fleet. Like before, Halsey would then discover Ozawa and take off after him, with the Third Fleet. Shima and Nishimura would arrive in Surigao Strait, mostly undamaged, and Kurita would happen upon Taffy 3. Let's also suppose that Kurita holds on, keeps up the pursuit, and arrives in Leyte Gulf.

We can speculate that the preliminary air battle, because the Japanese this time are concentrated and the Allied carriers are tied to the Leyte invasion, inflicts damage on some fleet carriers, some CVEs, and the *Princeton*. That's no detriment to Halsey destroying Ozawa's aviation ships, so that would happen, as before. In Surigao Strait, Shima and Nishimura would be destroyed again too. Admiral Kurita would catch the Taffies and engage them. They'd shake him up with the desperate air strikes, and the tin cans would make their brave stand. But Kurita, having sustained less damage on the way, is stronger by a battleship (*Musashi*), a cruiser, and at least one escort. Not a lot, but sufficient for him to feel more comfortable, and enough to keep up the pressure on Ziggy Sprague. Taffy 3 and perhaps Taffy 2 would suffer more losses.

Thus, the key question in this scenario becomes, does Kurita Takeo turn around?

THE BIGGEST CONTROVERSIES surrounding Leyte Gulf concern Admiral Kurita's turnaway and Admiral Halsey's pursuit of the Japanese carriers.

Because the question of why Kurita turned away is central to the what-if scenario being explored, from earlier, we will turn to that first. Top brass at Combined Fleet, admirals like Toyoda and Kusaka, refrained from criticizing Kurita Takeo, but they were among the few to do so. Vice Admiral Kurita himself certainly felt mortified. He had not long left to fly his flag. A little more than a month after the battle Kurita would be kicked upstairs, promoted to superintendent of the naval academy at Etajima. On January 10, 1945, Emperor Hirohito received Kurita in audience, thanking him for his service.

The issues surrounding Kurita's decisions were noted in Chapter 10. Kurita told interrogators later that he made up his mind based upon what good he could do inside the gulf, not the technical issues or inability to effectively communicate with the remaining ships of his fleet. The most recent floatplane report mentioned about thirty cargomen inside Leyte. That number is consistent with what we know of the logistics planning and practices of MacArthur's supply officers. The destruction of thirty transports and cargo ships, even with a pile of landing craft thrown in, was not going to make any difference in the tempo of Allied invasions. Leyte had been mounted by hundreds of transports, not thirty. To trade the flower of the Imperial Navy for that—because without fail Kinkaid's battleship fleet would have arrived right in the middle of Kurita's hypothetical rampage inside Leyte Gulf—just seemed wrong. He agreed with a question that postulated that one factor in his choice could have been the thousands of sailors who were spared because he chose against that battle.

But the story does not end there. On the bridge of *Yamato*, Admiral Kurita was beyond tired. In fact, he told Captain Hara Tameichi, "I made that blunder out of sheer physical exhaustion." Historian Ito Masanori concludes that Kurita held a general view that "death should not be invited unnecessarily" and held human life in great respect. Kurita reflected that his decision had seemed right at the time, but that in retrospect, he ought to have carried out his orders. With Ito, the admiral returned to the issue of exhaustion. The idea of striking another Allied task force was a mistake, Kurita declared—his own mistake, he said, since he held no staff meeting to consider the matter. "The destruction of enemy aircraft carriers was a kind of obsession with me, and I fell victim to it," Kurita told Ito. "I was, so to speak, the pitcher of the losing team."

One of the key elements in Kurita's decision to break contact with the Taffies had been a sighting report of a U.S. carrier group farther to the north. Kurita had taken off in search of it, realized the futility of it, and then finally simply canceled the operation. Former admiral Shima Kiyohide, who also survived the war, reports a very interesting exchange: Ito Masanori, *after* publication of his own book on the Japanese Navy, invited Kurita, Shima, and Ozawa Jisaburo to his home, where all four debated the events of Leyte. Shima recounts that he also received the sighting report, which establishes that this was not an invention of Kurita's, that there must have been a real message. As a communications specialist, Admiral Shima looked into this transmission after the battle, but he could not find any Japanese command that admitted to sending it. Shima decided this was a "ghost message" and attributed it to Kinkaid's Seventh Fleet. If so, the ghost message would rank as one of the most successful (and crucial) radio deceptions of the war. Also, one of the most secret, since no one has ever stepped forward to claim credit (which is a reason to doubt this ploy). In the absence of more concrete evidence, the more reasonable conjecture is that some naval unit sent a report discovered to be false and, in view of the enormity of the consequences, denied ever sending it.

Shima's overall analysis is worth noting. In his view, the first and foremost reason for the defeat at Leyte had been the squandering of airpower over Taiwan. Next to that he ranks the Japanese communications problem. Ozawa's decoy mission, though successful in its own terms, also depended upon Kurita knowing about it—and the surface admiral never learned anything directly from the decoy commander. Radio silence only complicated matters. Had Kurita known of Ozawa's achievements in a timely fashion, he would have had reason to doubt the ghost message and would have had better background information as he approached Leyte Gulf. As it was, his information came late and secondhand, via Mikawa in Manila. By the time Kurita knew of Ozawa's success, he had started for home. Shima Kiyohide, incidently, completely agreed with Kurita's decision to turn around.

In later days, Kurita clammed up, no longer speaking of his experiences, to the point that people began to call him the "Silent Admiral." Twice a year he visited the Yasukuni Shrine to honor the sailors who had died under his command. When John Toland came to Japan to research his opus on the Pacific war, *The Rising Sun*, Kurita Takeo refused to talk with him, instead asking Koyanagi Tomiji to speak in his place.

Not long afterward, toward the end of 1967, Kurita moved in with his son and began meeting periodically with a circle of men who had been with the seventy-eighth class at Etajima—midshipmen of the class Kurita supervised in 1945. It was among this group the admiral opened up. Kurita so cottoned to one of them, Oka Jiro, that he starting talking about a biography. Oka enlisted his comrades in the project. To this group, Kurita dismissed his previous explanation that the abandonment of the Samar action had been an error brought on by exhaustion. Instead, he reported thinking that he had come very far to achieve victory, and if he could catch a carrier group, it would go a long way. Both the decision to regroup and that to head north had been his alone. Kurita believed the ghost message came from Mikawa Gunichi. He dismissed the exhaustion argument as unworthy. No senior naval commander had a right to exhaustion. Be that as it may, Kurita had used that explanation not only with historian Ito and Imperial Navy officer Hara Tameichi, but also with Allied intelligence interrogators.

It's difficult to decide what to make of all this. I draw the following conclusions: Admiral Kurita did indeed make the decisions by himself. Sensitive to the sailors under his command, he carried the burden of the Leyte losses for the rest of his life, and it is probable that the growing death toll played at least some part in Kurita's decision to regroup— if not the one to withdraw. The latter choice, apart from the issue of the ghost message, can be attributed to Kurita's inability to revise his concept of naval war and decisive battle being about destroying warships. He had that in common with most of his fellow naval officers. Some bit of responsibility remains with the admiral, but the greater amount lies with higher commanders who sought to transform long-held tenets of Imperial Navy doctrine but did little to sell the program.

On the Allied side, William F. Halsey attracts similar levels of criticism. The notion that the San Bernardino Strait could have been shut tight and that the Kurita fleet could have been prevented from ever transiting it has so much allure. The controversy over "Bull's Run" also has some of the same features as that surrounding Kurita's withdrawal. Rather than the ghost message, we have the dispatches Admiral Halsey sent that discussed formation of the fast-battleship unit, Task Force 34. Americans dispute whether or not Halsey's colleagues were right to assume, on the basis of the warning message, that the fast-battleship unit had actually been constituted.

After the war, Admiral Halsey defended himself in interviews, articles, and his own memoir. It was a robust defense and the admiral never publicly admitted to be at fault. There are rumors he softened before his death in 1959, though there's no evidence to prove it. But the criticisms have been persistent and seem to revive with each new generation of scholarship on the war.

Halsey biographer Elmer B. Potter asks why anyone should think the Bull would do any differently—and he is right. The standing directives on the American side were very much like the Japanese doctrine for decisive battle. The enemy fleet was the target. Aircraft carriers, over the course of World War II, had been established as the most dangerous element of enemy fleets, and consequently, the enemy fleet should be the target. Chester Nimitz issued a basic order for Third Fleet's support to the Philippine invasion, which provided that Halsey should engage the Japanese fleet if it emerged to do battle. Halsey put that language into his instruction for his own sailors. He added only slight elaboration. Halsey's directive circulated back to Admiral Nimitz, to General MacArthur, and to Admiral Kinkaid. No one objected then.

Not only did no one object, but Admiral Halsey's method of operation was also on display for them for weeks before Leyte Gulf. His technique was to push every advantage. When air strikes in the southern Philippines went well, Halsey added the Manila area to his target list. When that had been saturated, he went for Coron Bay. Along the way he recommended advancing the timetable for the Philippine invasion and aiming at Leyte. No one objected there either. Then he went off to strike the Ryukyu Islands and Taiwan. He added days of battle against the Japanese on Taiwan and more strikes on the Japanese in the Philippines. Halsey was *rewarded* for that aggressiveness. Barely a week before the Leyte battle began, he received a commendation from President Roosevelt, an early version of what is known today as the "Presidential Unit Citation." Thus, it's hard to believe that when a Japanese fleet actually materialized, no one expected Halsey to go after it.

Part of Halsey's aggression was linked to his ideas about fighting the Japanese. Evan Thomas pictures Halsey as a product or tool of cultural hysteria: He bought the stereotypes about the Japanese and felt as infuriated as anyone after Pearl Harbor. But a bigger element was sheer professional competency and his development of a smoothly functioning military machine combined with a formula that taught that dynamic operations produced results.

Another level of this analysis concerns a different element of naval doctrine. One cardinal rule for U.S. officers concerned concentration of force. Such forces as existed were to be used together. Concentrated force achieved goals. American officers frequently criticized Japanese methods of creating many naval formations for an operation, thus dissipating their available force. Halsey had absorbed that doctrine too. The Big Blue Fleet evolved a very conscious technique of spreading heavy gunnery ships through the carrier units as core antiaircraft protection. Detaching the fast battleships meant diluting the force. Halsey was not about to do that without a damned good reason.

The situation during the afternoon of October 24 was that the Kurita fleet had turned away in the Sibuyan Sea in the face of Halsey's fierce air armada. The Japanese were badly damaged, having lost super-battleship *Musashi*. Meanwhile, scouts had seen the enemy Halsey had *really* wanted, the Japanese carriers. And they were pretty close. By Third Fleet reckoning, Kurita was not coming back, and if he was, he would be reduced by enough that Kinkaid's forces would be able to cope with him. Preliminary estimates were lurid: fifty-five bomber attacks on *Yamato*-class battleships for thirty-one hits. A half dozen other hits on battleships. Torpedo hits at 40 to 46 percent on battle-ships, 51 percent on cruisers. Even with air intelligence officers shaving away at the damage estimates, these were pretty high claims, and Halsey had some reason to feel confident.

Finally, there is Halsey's analysis of the position and navigation data once Kurita was through and fighting with the Taffies, who were beg-ging for help. Even the fast battleships, he argued, could not arrive in time to do any good. Reexamining positions and plotting courses and headway, as was done here, confirms the admiral's original argument. The run of the fast battleships had no military point, except to keep the ships out of battle altogether. The only value of Task Force 34, in the end, would be a psychological one, furnishing some aid and comfort to Seventh Fleet.

MANY OTHER ASPECTS of these events invite comment. The most important is that Leyte Gulf became a further demonstration of the transformation of warfare through technological dominance that be-came prominent in World War II.

The intelligence reporting, briefly referred to already, owed a very great deal to technological means, including both aerial photography and code breaking. (In the Pacific, unlike Enigma in Europe, Ultra de-pended much more on card-sorting devices—simpler machinery but just as technological.) The intelligence brought combat the closest it would come to dispelling the fog of war prior to the advent of the reconnaissance satellite.

Then came the acquisition of targets by electronic means. Radar furnished both Allies and Japanese their first sightings of the most important enemy forces throughout the battle. Technological devices—radar again—won the Battle of Surigao Strait for the Allies by means of controlling the aiming of guns. The Japanese themselves made their first use of (a less sophisticated form of) this technique at Leyte Gulf. Meanwhile another electronic entity, the radio, permitted a measure of close coordination among disparate forces that were widely separated in time and space. The combination of radar and radio for fleet air defense attained new heights of effectiveness in these battles, starting with the Great Marianas Turkey Shoot. In short, technological means endowed military forces with even greater powers.

That being said, technology did not eliminate the human factor. At least three major traumas of Leyte Gulf took place *because* of radio. The Combined Fleet command would be thrown into complete disarray because, in the case of Kurita's turnaway in the Sibuyan Sea, a field commander sought to inform headquarters of his actions without being able to provide sufficient context. Less than twenty-four hours later the same field commander, faced with a ghost message, made a decision that let his enemy off the ropes. Meanwhile, to reprise Halsey, the sequence of messages surrounding his decisions made about fast battleships had everything to do with the electronic medium but resulted in these vital weapons making very little contribution to monumental events taking place all around them.

While we are on this subject, a word is in order about Thomas C. Kinkaid. Beginning days before Leyte Gulf—indeed, while the Third Fleet still fought off Taiwan—Admiral Kinkaid showed a predilection for prejudgment and some prevarication. At a certain point, Halsey thought the Japanese fleet was reacting to the Taiwan battle and expressed an intention to fight it. Kinkaid immediately resorted to higher authority to force Halsey to abandon that idea. The Seventh Fleet commander did that again when he decided Halsey was not sufficiently dedicated to preinvasion attacks. That was before the Leyte battle had even started.

Kinkaid would be extremely methodical in the way he prepared and conducted the Surigao Strait battle. But when Kurita appeared opposite the Taffies, the radio stream resumed. The sequence of Kinkaid's messages reported an emergency to be sure, but they did so in a way that ignored the boundaries of what practical help Halsey could give him, again invoked higher authorities, brought aid and comfort to the enemy, misled colleagues regarding the ammunition status of his own battleships, and continued to sound the alarm after Kurita had left the scene. Messages sent in the clear not only indicated a state of emergency, but also aimed to mobilize higher commanders (Nimitz, MacArthur) to intervene. At the same time, those dispatches revealed Kinkaid's anxiety to the Japanese. They also suggested Kurita was still attacking after he had sailed away, demanding urgency from Halsey when the need for action was gone and the Third Fleet could do nothing more than it already was. All this can be interpreted as Kinkaid panicking, but that is not a very likely scenario. The sequence of Kinkaid's messages can also be seen as methodical, as were his actions at Surigao Strait, but the object was to use technology to shape the actions of another commander.

Dissonance among colleagues can be damaging, but it was much more tolerable on the Allied side, which enjoyed a marked superiority of force. But problems that had the effect of reducing the capability of an already inferior force are especially crippling. The obvious case on the Japanese side is the question of cooperation between Admirals Nishimura and Shima. The former's death in the battle eliminates any possibility of a definitive analysis of their differences. On the other hand, the small combat value of both the Nishimura and Shima forces raises the issue of whether Japanese possibilities would have been any greater with the fleets united. In view of the onrush of the Kurita fleet from the other end of Leyte Gulf, the much greater value of the one-two surge of the Japanese in Surigao Strait lay in their requiring Vice Admiral Kinkaid to delay before he could begin moving his battleships to confront a potential Kurita break-in from the north. The value of that delay cancels the impact of any dissonance that may have existed between the two admirals.

The dissonance that *was* damaging affected the Kurita fleet. The evidence here is quite asymmetrical. Kurita Takeo survived the war but left no record. Ugaki Matome made a record but did not survive the war. Given Vice Admiral Kurita's general attitudes toward subordinates and sailors, it is doubtful that he held any kind of antipathy for Ugaki. The battleship commander, on the other hand, puts so many backhand criticisms, snide remarks, and even omissions about Admiral Kurita in his diary that it is difficult to suppose that Ugaki had anything other than opprobrium for his commander.

The most important post in the Imperial Navy on the morning of the climax at Leyte Gulf was on the bridge of the *Yamato* when both Ugaki and Kurita were there, and the fact that the Japanese lost combat capability was because of Ugaki's resentment for his boss. Whether or not the inference deduced here (that Ugaki actually ordered *Yamato*'s disastrous torpedo evasion) is correct, Ugaki's demand of his superior to be accorded control of gunnery represented an explicit statement alluding to his resentment. That expression of simmering anger can only have upset Kurita, adding to his anxieties at the very moment the Second Fleet commander needed all his wits about him. A tense atmosphere on *Yamato*'s bridge added up to a diminution of Japanese battle ability in that moment. If it *is* true that Ugaki ordered the portside turn, then he directly holds an even larger share of the blame for Japanese failure at Leyte. Either way, some of the burden is his.

However, Admiral Ugaki might have felt more comfort and less resentful had he had not suffered losses of his own, specifically superbattleship *Musashi*. Ugaki had lived in that ship for more than a year while it housed Combined Fleet headquarters and recorded that he felt its loss as if losing a part of himself. The principal culprit for this is Ugaki's successor as Combined Fleet chief of staff, Kusaka Ryunosuke. Imperial Navy planning for Sho had specifically recognized JNAF weakness and provided for husbanding strength until the key moment. The Japanese had even war-gamed the specific scenario of an attack on Taiwan, concluding that withholding the air units was the proper strategy. Kusaka's haste to commit the air forces to an air-only Sho blunted the very instrument Kurita and Ugaki counted on to get themselves across the dangerous waters they needed to traverse. On the other hand, Admiral Kusaka gains some merit for his suggestion to send a secondary decoy force along the Surigao Strait route, which substantially complicated timing factors in the Allied defense of Leyte.

Presiding over it all had been Toyoda Soemu, the commander in chief. There is a question of whether Toyoda had been too passive—certainly his absence on Taiwan is what opened the door to Kusaka's throwing away the air arm in the precursor battle. Toyoda's reluctance to micromanage subordinates had often served him well and freed him to focus on the overall aspects of strategy, but one of the Imperial Navy's greatest mistakes was to change the nature of the decisive battle doctrine without selling the new objective to the officer corps. That task had been Toyoda's.

Despite all the mistakes, all the responsibility, all the squandering of forces, the Imperial Navy succeeded in reversing the basic strategic balance. For a moment on the morning of October 25, 1944, the unthinkable happened. In the face of every Allied advantage in intelligence, air and naval forces, technology, and raw combat power, a Japanese surface fleet of great intrinsic strength put American aircraft carriers under its guns. The development was so alarming that Admiral Chester Nimitz risked the Ultra secret to warn his frontline commanders of the enemy's feat. Courageous sailors in a handful of destroyers, escorts, and expendable aircraft carriers were the ones who turned back the Japanese armada. That was huge. The biggest naval battle in history came down to a few storm-beaten ships on whom the sun never set. Their story will be told forever.

ABBREVIATIONS

AIB	Allied Intelligence Bureau (SOWESPAC intelligence agency)
ASW	Antisubmarine warfare
ATIS	Allied Translator and Interpreter Section
CAP	Combat air patrol
CIC	Combat Information Center
C-in-C	Commander in chief (Japanese)
CINCPAC	Commander in chief, Pacific Ocean areas
CNO	Chief of naval operations
COMINCH	Commander in chief, U.S. fleet
CVE	Escort aircraft carrier
F-22	Combat Intelligence Division (COMINCH)
F-6F	Plane-type identifier for Hellcat fighter
FECB	Far East Combined Bureau (British intelligence agency)
FRUMEL	Fleet Radio Unit Melbourne (SOWESPAC communications intelligence)
FRUPAC	Fleet Radio Unit Pacific (Pearl Harbor communications intelligence)
IGHQ	Imperial General Headquarters (Japanese high command)
JAAF	Japanese Army Air Force
JCS	Joint Chiefs of Staff
JICPOA	Joint Intelligence Center, Pacific Ocean Area
JNAF	Japanese Naval Air Force
NGS	Navy General Staff (Japanese Navy command)
ONI	Office of Naval Intelligence
OP-16	Naval Intelligence Division (ONI), Navy Department

OP-20-G	Communications Intelligence, Navy Department, Washington, DC
PT	Patrol torpedo boat
SB-2C	Plane-type identification for Helldiver dive-bomber
SEFIC	Seventh Fleet Intelligence Center
SOWESPAC	Southwest Pacific Area (and command—MacArthur's theater)
TBM	Plane-type identification for the Grumman Avenger torpedo bomber
TBS	Talk between ships (short-range voice radio)
Ultra	Code name for Allied communications intelligence

ENDNOTES

PROLOGUE

8 "POSSIBLE ENEMY TASK FORCE": U.S. Navy, Hawaiian Sea Frontier, broadcast dispatch 21133, July 1944. Franklin D. Roosevelt Library (hereafter cited as FDRL): Roosevelt Papers: Map Room Files series, box 95. Vice Admiral Robert L. Ghormley, of Solomons fame (see *Islands of Destiny*), now led the Sea Frontier.

13 "A political picture-taking junket": D. Clayton James, *The Years of MacArthur*, vol. 2, *1941–1945*. Boston: Houghton Mifflin, 1975, p. 527.

16 "The blockade that I will put": Geoffrey Perrett, *Old Soldiers Never Die: The Life of Douglas MacArthur*. New York: Random House, 1996, quoted p. 405.

16 "In all my life, nobody": Mark Perry, *The Most Dangerous Man in America: The Making of Douglas MacArthur*. New York: Basic Books, 2014, quoted p. 271.

17 "It was both pleasant and very informative": William D. Leahy, *I Was There: The Personal Story of the Chief of Staff to Presidents Roosevelt and Truman Based on His Notes and Diaries Made at the Time*. New York: McGraw-Hill, 1950, p. 250.

17 "It was highly pleasing and unusual": Ibid., p. 251.

17 "He was entirely neutral": Douglas A. MacArthur, *Reminiscences*. Greenwich, CT: Fawcett Crest, 1964, p. 214.

18–19 "In preventing an unnecessary invasion of Japan" and "MacArthur and Nimitz were now in agreement": Leahy, *I Was There*, p. 251.

20 "As soon as I get back": Thomas J. Cutler, *The Battle of Leyte Gulf, 23–26 October 1944*. New York: Pocket Books, 1996, quoted p. 38.

CHAPTER 1. ALL IN

30 "He thought it advisable": Kase Toshikazu, *Journey to the Missouri*. New Haven, CT: Yale University Press, 1950, p. 74.

34 "I must remain on the mainland": Kido Koichi, *The Diary of Marquis Kido, 1931–1945: Selected Translations into English*. Frederick, MD: University Press of America, 1984, p. 398.

34 "While it would not be accurate to say": Toyoda Soemu Interrogation, in United States Strategic Bombing Survey (Pacific), Naval Analysis Division, *Interrogations of Japanese Officials* (hereafter cited as USSBS, *Interrogations of Japanese Officials*). Washington, DC: Government Printing Office, 1946, vol. 2, p. 317.

36 "Attacking and destroying the enemy fleet": IGHQ Directive No. 431, July 21, 1944. Imperial General Headquarters Navy Directives, vol. 2, pp. 67–68. U.S. Navy microfilm J-27.

36 **"Raiding operations"** et seq.: IGHQ Navy Directive No. 435, July 26, 1944. Imperial General Headquarters Navy Directives, vol. 2, pp. 71–84. U.S. Navy microfilm J-27.

37 **"To intercept and destroy the invading enemy"**: Combined Fleet, Top Secret Operations Order No. 83, August 1, 1944. Supreme Commander Allied Forces (SCAP), *Reports of General MacArthur: Japanese Operations in the Southwest Pacific*, vol. 2, pt. 1. Washington, DC: Government Printing Office, 1966, p. 329.

37–38 **"I agreed to the showdown battle"** and Bix opinion: Herbert B. Bix, *Hirohito and the Making of Modern Japan*. New York: HarperCollins, 2000, p. 481.

40 **"Unprofessional vindictive satisfaction"**: Wilfred J. Holmes, *Double-Edged Secrets: U.S. Naval Intelligence Operations in the Pacific in World War II*. Annapolis, MD: Naval Institute Press, 1979, p. 180.

43 **"Under present conditions"**: U.S. Navy, JICPOA, Letter, W. Holmes to W. Sebald, July 24, 1944. National Archives and Records Administration: Records Group 457 (hereafter cited as NARA: RG-457): Records of the National Security Agency: SRMN 009, "JICPOA-F-22 Administrative Correspondence, January 1942–September 1945," p. 193.

CHAPTER 2. THE LOWDOWN

44 **"KING HAS CONFERRED WITH NIMITZ"**: Ugaki Matome Diary, July 25, 1944, dispatch quoted in *Fading Victory: The Diary of Admiral Matome Ugaki, 1941–1945* (hereafter cited as Ugaki Diary), ed. Donald M. Goldstein and Katherine V. Dillon; trans. Chihaya Masataka. Annapolis, MD: Naval Institute Press, 2008, p. 436.

50 **"I placed my greatest reliance"**: Fukudome Shigeru, "The Air Battle off Taiwan," in *The Japanese Navy in World War II: In the Words of Former Japanese Naval Officers*, ed. David C. Evans. Annapolis, MD: Naval Institute Press, 1986, p. 341.

55 **"acute"**: Commander Terai Yoshimori interview. Naval Historical Center (hereafter cited as NHC): Records of the Japanese Navy and Related Documents, box 73, folder: "Interrogation no. 602."

55 **"If we are to win"**: Hasegawa Kaoru, *My Personal History: Two Lives*. Japan: Rengo Company Ltd., n.d. [1999], p. 16.

59 **"Had the U.S. Navy been dependent"**: Holmes, *Double-Edged Secrets*, p. 119.

65 **"Outline of operations"** et seq.: Combined Fleet Top Secret Operations Order No. 85, August 4, 1944. Supreme Commander Allied Forces (SCAP), *Reports of General MacArthur: Japanese Operations in the Southwest Pacific*, vol. 2, pt. 1, Washington, DC: Government Printing Office, 1966, p. 330.

67 **"I will recommend the idea"**: Nakata Seiichi, ed., *For That One Day: The Memoirs of Mitsuo Fuchida, Commander of the Attack on Pearl Harbor*. Kamuela, HI: eXperience inc., 2011, quoted p. 161.

69 **"Make the demons weep"**: Yonai Mitsumasa speech, September 9, 1944. Foreign Affairs Association of Japan, *Contemporary Japan*, vol. 13, nos. 7–9, September 1944, p. 851.

69 **"Japan's Fleet in Being Strategy"** et seq.: Ito Masanori, "Japan's Fleet in Being Strategy," *Contemporary Japan*, vol. 13, nos. 7–9, September 1944, pp. 638–44.

CHAPTER 3. BREAKTHROUGH AND EXPLOITATION

79 **"A dream come true"**: Harold L. Buell, *Dauntless Helldivers: A Dive-Bomber Pilot's Epic Story of the Carrier Battles*. New York: Dell Books, 1991, p. 331.

79 **"It was obvious":** Okumiya Masatake and Horikoshi Jiro with Martin Caidin, *Zero! The Story of Japan's Air War in the Pacific: 1941–1945*. New York: Ballantine Books, 1957, p. 243.

83 **"My decision to poke a strike":** William F. Halsey and J. D. Bryan III, *Admiral Halsey's Story*. New York: McGraw-Hill Book Company, 1947, quoted p. 199.

83 **"BECAUSE OF THE BRILLIANT PERFORMANCE":** Quoted ibid.

83 **"The South Pacific campaign had impressed us all":** Ibid.

86 **"The hell you do":** E. B. Potter, *Admiral Arleigh Burke: A Biography*. New York: Random House, 1990, quoted p. 187.

87 **"Those are Japanese installations"** et seq.: Ibid., quoted p. 202.

91 **"We have never made a dishonest estimate":** U.S. Navy, JICPOA, Letter, W. J. Holmes to W. J. Sebald, May 15, 1944. NARA: RG-457, SRMD-009, "JICPOA-F-22 Administrative Correspondance," January 1942–September 1945.

CHAPTER 4. BEST-LAID PLANS

95 **"Perhaps the most important single document":** Stanley L. Falk and Warren M. Tsuneishi, eds., *MIS in the War Against Japan: Personal Experiences Related at the 1993 MIS Capital Reunion, "The Nisei Veteran: An American Patriot."* Privately printed, Japanese American Veterans of Washington, DC, 1995, p. 29.

102 **"To depend entirely":** Ugaki Diary, August 9, 1944, p. 439.

103 **"Now we have something to study":** Ugaki Diary, August 17, 1944, p. 442.

104 **"The war is in its last stages":** Yoshimura Akira, *Build the Musashi: The Birth and Death of the World's Greatest Battleship* (trans. Vincent Murphy). Tokyo: Kodansha, 1991, quoted p. 153.

106 **"How is it that the headquarters, attack force":** Ugaki Diary, September 18, 1944, p. 458.

107 **"Our one big goal":** Koyanagi Tomiji, "The Battle of Leyte Gulf," in Evans, ed., *The Japanese Navy in World War II*, p. 360.

112 **"All-out decisive battle"** et seq.: JICPOA, "Estimate of Enemy Distribution and Intentions," September 4, 1944. NARA: RG-457, SRMD-010, pt. 2.

114 **"Across this wide Pacific"** et seq.: U.S. Navy, JICPOA, Letter, W. J. Holmes to C. G. Moore, September 22, 1944. NARA: RG-457, SRMD-009, "JICPOA-F-22 Administrative Correspondance," January 1942–September 1945.

115 **"It was not believed that the major elements of the Japanese Fleet":** Royal Navy: Tactical and Staff Duties Division, Historical Staff, Battle Summary no. 40: Battle for Leyte Gulf, 23rd–26th October 1944. B.R. 1736 (41). Admiralty, May 1947, p. 18, fn. 4.

117 **"The overall tanker movement picture":** JICPOA, "Estimate of Enemy Distribution and Intentions," September 18, 1944. NARA: RG-457, SRMD-010, pt. 2.

117 **"This is the first indication":** U.S. Navy, Commander in Chief, Summary of Radio Intelligence, October 17, 1944. NARA: RG-457, SRNS-0918, "Japanese Radio Intelligence Summaries 1944."

CHAPTER 5. DESTROY THE INVADING ENEMY

127 **"I was hardly in a position":** Toyoda Soemu, *The End of the Imperial Navy*. Tokyo: 1950, pp. 149–53 (U.S. Navy translation). NHC: IJN Records, Leyte Series, box 30, folder: "Senior Officer Comments," quoted from p. 1 of the source document.

136 **"Our fighters were nothing but so many eggs" et seq.**: Fukudome Shigeru, "The Air Battle off Taiwan," in Evans, ed., *The Japanese Navy in World War II*, p. 347.

137 **"If we had stayed in the administration office"**: Quoted ibid., p. 350.

139 **"Right he was!"**: Handwritten marginal note on JICPOA, "Summary of ULTRA Traffic 0000/12–2400/12 October," NARA: RG-457, SRMD-007, Summary, September 11–December 31, 1944, pt. 1, p. 94.

140 **"I am sorry to say"**: Admiral Teraoka Kimpei, Translated Extracts from the Diary of Teraoka Kimpei, October 10–20, 1944. NHC: IJN Records, Leyte Series, box 30, folder: "Senior Officer Comments."

140 **"These planes failed to find our fleet"**: ONI, OP-20-G Radio Summary, October 14, 1944. NARA: RG-457, SRMD-007, p. 100.

142 **"We were squarely in the dragon's jaws"**: Halsey and Bryan, *Admiral Halsey's Story*, p. 205.

144 **"A graveyard"**: Admiral Obayashi Sueo, interview with John Toland, December 23, 1966. Notes, Toland Papers, FDRL.

145 **"REMAINING ENEMY STRENGTH IS COMPARATIVELY LARGE"**: Colonel Hattori Takushiro, *History of the Greater East Asia War*, vol. 3. Tokyo: Masu Shobo, 1953 quoted p. 367.

148 **"Circling around at an altitude of two thousand meters"**: Denis Warner and Peggy Warner, with Seno Sadao, *The Sacred Warriors: Japan's Suicide Legions*. New York: Avon Books, 1982, quoted p. 81.

149 **"THE THIRD FLEET'S SUNKEN AND DAMAGED SHIPS"**: Halsey and Bryan, *Admiral Halsey's Story*, quoted pp. 207–8.

149 **"A campaign of mendacity unprecedented" et seq., including Japanese newspaper headline quotes**: Office of Naval Intelligence, *The O.N.I. Weekly*, vol. 3, no. 44, November 1, 1944. NARA: U.S. Navy Records, Microfilm Publication M1652, Roll 66, pp. 3523–28.

150 **"In order to understand the state of mind"**: C. Vann Woodward, *The Battle for Leyte Gulf: The Incredible Story of World War II's Largest Naval Battle* (reprint edition). New York: Skyhorse Publishing, 2007, p. 16.

150 **"It is erroneous to think"**: Federal Communications Commission, Foreign Broadcast Intelligence Service, "The 'Annihilation' of Task Force 38," Special Report no. 132, quoted p. 5. FDRL: Roosevelt Papers, Map Room Files, box 89, folder: "MR-300, Sec. 2: Warfare (Japan) January–December 1944."

CHAPTER 6. MacARTHUR RETURNS, SHO UNLEASHED

152 **"CENTRAL PHILIPPINES ATTACK FORCE"**: COM7THFLT-COM3RDFLT, 150542, October 1944. From U.S. Navy, Commander in Chief Pacific Command Summary (i.e., war diary, hereafter cited as CINCPAC Graybook), pt. 2, p. 2240.

156 **"Since this is the important battle"**: Stanley A. Falk, *Decision at Leyte*. New York: W. W. Norton, 1966, quoted p. 85.

156 **"A sortie from Singapore"**: ONI, OP-20-G Radio Summary, October 18, 1944. NARA: RG-457, SRNS-0919, p. 1952.

156 **"*Based on an analysis of U.S. communications*"**: ONI, OP-20-G Radio Summary, October 19, 1944. NARA: RG-457, SRNS-0920, p. 1.

163 **"I have returned!" et seq.**: MacArthur, *Reminiscences*, quoted pp. 252–54. With Philippine independence already scheduled for a moment in the near future, little

would be gained by advancing that event. On the other hand, giving this bit of patently political advice served to suggest to FDR that General MacArthur really had the president's interests at heart.

164–65 **MacArthur memoir versus his letter to FDR:** Letter, Douglas MacArthur to Franklin D. Roosevelt, October 20, 1944. Reprinted in MacArthur, *Reminiscences*, pp. 253–54. MacArthur's actual letter is in the Roosevelt Papers (FDRL: FDR Papers, Map Room Files, box 104, folder: "President's Secretary's File: War Department— General Douglas MacArthur, 1944–1945").

170 "WILL ADVANCE THROUGH SAN BERNARDINO STRAIT" et seq.: Combined Fleet Top Secret Dispatch 181110, October 1944 (from 1st Diversion Attack Force detailed action report [WDC 161641]). NHC: IJN Records, Leyte Series, box 30, folder: "G4: Miscellaneous Orders."

173 **Kurita "was vaguely aware":** Anthony P. Tully, *Battle of Surigao Strait*. Bloomington: Indiana University Press, 2009, p. 23. Historian Tully has made many contributions to the study of the Japanese Navy in World War II. A number of his contributions relate to the modern history of the Surigao Strait battle, including clarifying the identities of the Japanese battleships *Fuso* and *Yamashiro*, the positions of which are reversed in a number of histories. I agree with Tully on many points, including, as is related in Chapter 8, that Japanese cruiser *Nachi* collided with the *Mogami*, and not the other way around, another point of confusion in the histories. Here, however, and on a few other items our views differ. Nevertheless I want to acknowledge the work he has done here, on the Midway battle (in *Shattered Sword*), and on the Nihon Kaigun Web site, all of which mark him as one of the foremost historians of the Pacific war.

174–75 **"If the fleet does not take the offensive now"** et seq.: Ohmae Toshikazu, "Research Report on Questions Related to SHO Operations," n.d. (received in Washington, DC, on April 13, 1953), quoted p. 5. (Ohmae relied on records provided by Hattori Takushiro.) NHC: Japanese Navy and Related Records, box 30, folder: "Senior Officer Comments."

176–78 **"The war situation"** et seq.: Ito Masanori with Roger Pineau, *The End of the Imperial Japanese Navy* (trans. Andrew Y. Kuroda and Roger Pineau). New York: McFadden-Bartell Books, 1965, quoted pp. 100–1.

CHAPTER 7. "WITH CONFIDENCE IN HEAVENLY GUIDANCE, THE ENTIRE FORCE WILL ATTACK!"

182 **"It just operated all day long":** Naval Security Group, Albert M. Fishburn Oral History, September 22, 1983, p. 24.

182 **"Good indications" and "poor":** Joint Intelligence Center Pacific Ocean Area, "Summary of Ultra Traffic, 0000/20—2400/20 Oct 1944," in JICPOA, "Summary of Ultra Traffic, 11 September–31 December, 1944." NARA: RG-457, SRMD-007, pt. 1, p. 120.

185 **"She was a mass of billowing black smoke":** *Darter* Logbook 0533/23, October 1944, reprinted in Theodore S. Roscoe, *Pigboats: The True Story of the Fighting Submariners of World War II*. New York: Bantam Books, 1958, p. 339.

191 **"As you know, the war situation is grave"** et seq.: Inoguchi Rikihei and Nakajima Tadashi with Roger Pineau, *The Divine Wind: Japan's Kamikaze Force in World War II*. New York: Bantam Books, 2013, quoted pp. 6–9.

197 "TALLY HO": Paul Drury, "A Naval Aviator at Leyte Gulf: October 24, 1944, The Longest Day of My Life," paper presented at the conference World War II in the Pacific, Arlington, VA, August 11, 1994. Author's notes.

201–2 "ENEMY ATTACKERS ARE APPROACHING": Yoshimura, *Build the Musashi*, quoted p. 159.

208 "WE ARE BEING SUBJECTED": Battle Summary of 1st Diversion Attack Force in Operation SHO, in U.S. Strategic Bombing Survey (Pacific): Naval Analysis Division, *Campaigns of the Pacific War* (hereafter cited as *Campaigns of the Pacific War*), reprinted Appendix 89, p. 300.

208 "We had expected air attacks": Koyanagi, "The Battle of Leyte Gulf," p. 364.

208 "Like losing part of myself": Ugaki Diary, October 24, 1944, translations from *Sensoroku*, NHC: Records of the Japanese Navy and Related Translations: Leyte Series, box 34, folder: "Diary, VAdm M. Ugaki," p. 26. The published version of the Ugaki Diary (Goldstein and Dillon, eds., *Fading Victory*, p. 491) refers to this passage but does not reproduce it.

211 "gun-shy": John Prados, *Combined Fleet Decoded: The Secret History of American Intelligence and the Japanese Navy in World War II*. New York: Random House, 1995, p. 666.

211 "Zelig of sea battle": Evan Thomas, *Sea of Thunder: Four Great Naval Commanders and the Last Great Naval Campaign, 1944–1945*. New York: Simon & Schuster, 2006, p. 78.

212 "an exceedingly intrepid sailor": Kusaka Ryunosuke, translated extracts from *Combined Fleet* (Tokyo: Mainichi Shimbun Sha, 1952, pp. 225–46), p. 9. NHC: Records of the Japanese Navy, Leyte Series, box 30, folder: "Senior Officer Comments."

214 "OUR DAMAGES ARE NOT LIGHT": Ito and Pineau, *The End of the Imperial Japanese Navy*, quoted p. 108.

214 "UNDER THESE CIRCUMSTANCES": Koyanagi, "The Battle of Leyte Gulf," quoted p. 365.

214 "THEREFORE, HAVE DECIDED": Ito and Pineau, *The End of the Imperial Japanese Navy*, quoted p. 108.

215 "WITH CONFIDENCE IN HEAVENLY GUIDANCE": Battle Summary of 1st Diversion Attack Force in Operation SHO, *Campaigns of the Pacific War*, quoted p. 301.

215 "The meaning of that order was": Toyoda Soemu Interrogation. USSBS, *Interrogations of Japanese Officials*, vol. 2, p. 317.

CHAPTER 8. THE FIRST TEAM VERSUS THE RISING SUN

219–20 "In case opportunity . . . is offered or can be created": Samuel Eliot Morison, *History of United States Naval Operations in World War II*, vol. 12, *Leyte, June 1944–January 1945*. Boston: Little, Brown, 1958, quoted p. 58.

222 "It preserved my fleet's integrity": Halsey and Bryan, *Admiral Halsey's Story*, p. 217.

222 "We had long since decided": Special Notes by William F. Halsey, Note (a), p. 175, to "1944: The SHO Plan—The Battle for Leyte Gulf," Hanson Baldwin, *Sea Fights and Ship Wrecks: True Tales of the Seven Seas*. Garden City, NY: Hanover House, 1955.

222 "Here's where we're going": Halsey and Bryan, quoted ibid.

222 "They're coming through, I know": Carl Solberg, *Decision and Dissent: With Halsey at Leyte Gulf*. Annapolis, MD: Naval Institute Press, 1995, quoted p. 125.

223 "CENTRAL FORCE HEAVILY DAMAGED": Halsey and Bryan, quoted p. 217.

224 "I think you're right": E. B. Potter, *Admiral Arleigh Burke: A Biography*. New York: Random House, 1990, quoted p. 206.

225 "TONIGHT EVERY EFFORT WILL BE MADE": Southwest Area Fleet Dispatch 250008, October 1944 (Mikawa to Toyoda). NHC: Records of the Japanese Navy, Leyte Series, box 30, folder: "1st Striking Force (2)."

226 "Stepchild fleet": Ito and Pineau, *The End of the Imperial Japanese Navy*, pp. 116–17.

228 Tully dismisses argument on Nishimura versus Shima: Tully, *Battle of Surigao Strait*, pp. 54–55.

229 "Something dignified and inaccessible": Ibid., pp. 32–33.

231 "Something you dream about": Barrett Tillman, *Enterprise: America's Fightingest Ship and the Men Who Helped Win World War II*. New York: Simon & Schuster, 2012, quoted p. 211.

231 "Far more than credited": Tully, *Battle of Surigao Strait*, pp. 73–74.

233 "PROBABLE ENEMY LANDING FORCE IN CONVOY": Message, Kinkaid to Halsey, 240443, October 1944. FDRL: FDRP: Map Room Files, box 123, folder: "MR 450 (Section 7): Enemy and Foreign Ship Locations, Jan–Oct 1944."

242 "I could clearly see the bursting shells": James L. Holloway III presentation, "The Battle of Surigao Strait," author's notes; James L. Holloway III, interview with the author, August 11, 1994.

243 "Waste itself in piecemeal action": Admiral Shima Kiyohide, interview with John Toland, October 18, 1966. Notes, Toland Papers, FDRL.

251 "I AM DESTROYER SHIGURE": Thomas J. Cutler, *The Battle of Leyte Gulf: The Greatest Naval Battle in History: The Dramatic Full Story, 23–26 October 1944*. New York: Pocket Books, 1994, quoted p. 227.

251 "Up ahead the enemy must be waiting for us": John Toland, *The Rising Sun: The Decline and Fall of the Japanese Empire*. New York: Bantam, 1971, quoted p. 637.

251 "THIS FORCE HAS CONCLUDED ITS ATTACK": Morison, *Leyte*, quoted p. 233.

252 "It was just like him": Kusaka Ryunosuke, interview with John Toland, November 18, 1966. Toland Papers, FDRL.

CHAPTER 9. TALLYHO . . . CARRIERS!

253 "FORM LEO": Solberg, *Decision and Dissent*, quoted p. 149.

254 "Today may be the biggest in our Navy's history": Edward P. Stafford, *The Big E: The Story of the USS Enterprise*. New York: Dell Books, 1964, quoted p. 433.

255 "He is considered an ideal fleet commander": Joint Intelligence Center Pacific Ocean Area, Estimate Section Appreciation, May 29, 1945.

261 "I expected complete destruction": Ozawa Jisaburo Interrogation. USSBS, *Interrogations of Japanese Officials*, vol. 1, p. 220.

262 "I chewed my fingernails down to my elbows": Halsey and Bryan, *Admiral Halsey's Story*, quoted p. 218.

263 "All ships were firing everything they had" et seq.: Tillman, *Enterprise*, quoted p. 217.

263 "Awesome": Marcia Lane, "Gunner in Torpedo Bomber Recalls Battle of Leyte Gulf," *St. Augustine Record*, December 25, 2006.

271 "Ultra. From CINCPAC," and "This is Ultra from CINCPAC": Messages, Nimitz to Halsey, 241937 and 242005, October 1944. FDRL: Map Room Files, box 123, folder: "MR 450 (1) Sec. 7, Foreign and Enemy Ship Locations, Jan–Oct 1944."

272 "IS TF34 GUARDING": Message, Kinkaid to Halsey, 241914, October 1944. CINCPAC Graybook, p. 2246.

272 "FAST BATTLESHIPS ARE URGENTLY NEEDED": Message, Kinkaid to Halsey, 242239, October 1944. CINCPAC Graybook, ibid.

272 "So astonishing I could hardly accept it": Halsey and Bryan, *Admiral Halsey's Story*, quoted p. 220.

274 "WHERE IS LEE": Ibid.

274 "WHERE IS REPEAT WHERE IS": Solberg, *Decision and Dissent*, quoted p. 153. I have replaced the separators (aka "nulls") in the message with periods. The other piece of padding in this message, "TURKEY TROTS TO WATER," was so clearly not part of the actual text that it was deleted in the radio room.

274 "Stop it!": Halsey and Bryan, *Admiral Halsey's Story*, quoted p. 220.

276 "Halsey had no choice": Solberg, *Decision and Dissent*, pp. 154–55.

CHAPTER 10. "CLOSE AND ATTACK ENEMY CARRIERS!"

286 "I never heard a negative word": Thomas, *Sea of Thunder*, quoted p.175.

286 "Gambling philosophy": Koyanagi Tomiji, interview with John Toland, December 29, 1966. Toland Papers, FDRL.

290 "Almost stood on [their] head[s]": Kusaka Ryunosuke, Translated Extracts from *Combined Fleet* (Tokyo: Mainichi Shimbun Sha, 1952, pp. 225–46), p. 9. NHC: Records of the Japanese Navy, Leyte Series, box 30, folder: "Senior Officer Comments."

291 "Combustible, Vulnerable, Expendable": William T. Y'Blood, *The Little Giants: U.S. Escort Carriers Against Japan*. Annapolis, MD: Naval Institute Press, 1987, p. vii.

292 "ENEMY STRENGTH SEVEN SHIPS": Cruiser Division 7 Detailed Action Report: Leyte (WDC 161005). NHC: Records of the Japanese Navy, box 31, folder: "CruDiv 7."

294 "It was definitely established": Battle Summary of 1st Diversion Attack Force, *Campaigns of the Pacific War*, p. 302.

294 "We moved to take advantage": Koyanagi, "The Battle of Leyte Gulf," p. 367.

294 "Actions of the fleet headquarters": Ugaki Diary, October 25, 1944, p. 492.

294 "Instantly": Koyanagi, "The Battle of Leyte Gulf," p. 367.

294 "CLOSE AND ATTACK ENEMY CARRIERS" and "ATTACK": *Haguro* Detailed Action Report no. 5: October 23–26, 1944 (WDC 161747). NHC: Records of the Japanese Navy, Leyte Series, box 32, folder: "Cruiser Division 5."

296 "BY HEAVEN-SENT OPPORTUNITY": Message, 1st Diversion Attack Force to Combined Fleet, 250700, October 1944. Ito and Pineau, *The End of the Imperial Japanese Navy*, quoted, p. 128. The time of this message is recorded in the Detailed Action Report of battleship *Kongo*.

296 "In a pursuit the only essential": Koyanagi, "The Battle of Leyte Gulf," p. 367.

296–97 "Complete surprise seems to have deprived the Admiral": Morison, *Leyte*, p. 250.

298 "CRUISER DIVISIONS, ATTACK!": Cruiser Division 7 Detailed Action Report.

299 "Air Plot, tell him to check" et seq.: Clifton A. F. Sprague, "They Had Us on the Ropes," *The American*, April 1945, pp. 40–41.

301 "They're shooting at us in Technicolor": William T. Y'Blood, *The Little Giants*, quoted p. 160.

303 "INTEND ENGAGE TO STARBOARD": Cruiser Division 7 Detailed Action Report.

308 "A broken and sad old man" et seq.: USSBS, *Interrogations of Japanese Officials*, vol. 2, p. 569.

308 "Depressing rapidity": Sprague, "They Had Us on the Ropes."

309 "ENEMY [BATTLESHIPS] AND CRUISER": Kinkaid 7:07 a.m. Halsey and Bryan, *Admiral Halsey's Story*, quoted p. 219.

311 **"Buck, what we need is a bugler"**: Walter Karig et al., *Battle Report: The End of an Empire*. New York: Rinehart and Company, 1948, quoted p. 389.

313 **"Men loved him or hated him"**: Thomas, *Sea of Thunder,* quoted p. 175.

319–20 **"MY SITUATION IS CRITICAL"**: Kenneth I. Friedman, *Afternoon of the Rising Sun: The Battle of Leyte Gulf*. Novato, CA: Presidio Press, 2001, quoted p. 301.

324 **"Hold on a little longer, boys"**: Morison, *Leyte*, quoted pp. 284–85.

324 **"I had expected to be swimming" et seq.**: Sprague, "They Had Us on the Ropes," p. 116.

325 **"If we had known the types and number"**: Koyanagi, "The Battle of Leyte Gulf," p. 368.

325 **"There was no consideration for how to get home"**: Kurita Takeo Interrogation. USSBS, *Interrogations of Japanese Officials,* vol. 1, p. 45.

327 "WE ARE DETERMINED TO EXECUTE THE PLANNED PENETRATION": Message, 1st Diversion Attack Force to Combined Fleet, 251205, October 1944: Ito and Pineau, *The End of the Imperial Japanese Navy*, quoted p. 131.

328 **"This cannot be happening"**: Nakata, *For That One Day*, quoted p. 172.

328 **"REPORT MADE TO THRONE CONCERNING TODAY'S BATTLE:** Navy General Staff, NGS Chief Broadcast Dispatch, 251715, October 1944. Battle Summary of 1st Diversion Attack Force (WDC 161641), p. 33. NHC: Records of the Japanese Navy, Leyte Series, box 30, folder: "1st Striking Force (1)."

329 "IF THERE IS AN OPPORTUNITY TO DO SO": Message, Combined Fleet Dispatch Order No. 374, 251925, October 1944. From excerpts of the same summary battle report as reprinted in *Campaigns of the Pacific War*, Appendix 89, p. 306.

CHAPTER 11. SEA FIGHTS AND SHIPWRECKS

333–34 "Japanese forces now have" and "The fact that the United States Navy has suffered": *Contemporary Japan*, October–December 1944, vol. 13, nos. 10–12.

334 **"When you took the Philippines"**: Yonai Mitsumasa Interrogation. USSBS, *Interrogations of Japanese Officials,* vol. 2, p. 330.

334 **"According to latest information"**: Navy Department Communiqué No. 551, October 27, 1944, p. 255. U.S. Navy: Office of Public Information, *Navy Department Communiqués 301 to 600, and Pacific Fleet Communiqués, March 6, 1943–May 24, 1945*. Washington, DC: Government Printing Office, 1945.

335 **"Although still subject to revision"**: CINCPAC Communiqué No. 168, October 29, 1944, ibid., pp. 255–57.

336 **"It was clearly no longer possible"**: Kase, *Journey to the Missouri*, p. 95.

336 **"Decisive" and "did decide"**: Morison, *Leyte*, p. 337.

341 **"Admiral Kurita's mission"**: Toyoda Soemu Interrogation. USSBS, *Interrogations of Japanese Officials*, p. 317.

346 **"I made that blunder out of sheer physical exhaustion"**: Hara Tameichi, with Fred Saito and Roger Pineau, *Japanese Destroyer Captain*. New York: Ballantine Books, 1961, quoted p. 270.

346 **"Death should not be invited unnecessarily" et seq.**: Ito and Pineau, *The End of the Imperial Japanese Navy,* pp. 140–43, quoted at 141, 142.

BIBLIOGRAPHY

OFFICIAL SOURCES

AUSTRALIA

G. Herman Gill, *Australia in the War of 1939–1945: Royal Australian Navy, 1942–1945*. Canberra: Australian War Memorial, 1968.

JOINT CHIEFS OF STAFF

Grace Peterson Hayes, *The History of the Joint Chiefs of Staff in World War II: The War Against Japan*. Annapolis, MD: Naval Institute, 1982.

NATIONAL SECURITY AGENCY

Sharon A. Maneki, *The Quiet Heroes of the Southwest Pacific Theater: An Oral History of the Women of CBB and FRUMEL*. United States Cryptologic History, Series IV, World War II, volume 7, CCH-S54-96-01. NSA, 1996.

Ronald H. Spector, ed., *Listening to the Enemy: Key Documents on the Role of Communications Intelligence in the War with Japan*. Wilmington, DE: Scholarly Resources Inc., 1988.

UNITED KINGDOM

The Japanese Air Forces in World War II: The Organization of the Japanese Army and Naval Air Forces, 1945. Crown copyright 1979. (Published New York: Hippocrene Books, n.d. [1979]).

U.S. AIR FORCE

Haywood S. Hansell Jr., *Strategic Air War Against Japan*. Washington, DC: Government Printing Office, 1980.

Daniel L. Haulman, *Hitting Home: The Air Offensive Against Japan*. Washington, DC: Air Force History and Museums Division, 1999.

John F. Kreis, ed. *Piercing the Fog: Intelligence and Army Air Forces Operations in World War II*. Washington, DC: Air Force History and Museums Program, 1996.

Maurer Maurer, ed., *Combat Squadrons of the Air Force, World War II*. Department of the Air Force, 1969.

U.S. ARMY

All volumes: Washington, DC: Office of the Chief of Military History, dates specified Army in World War II Series: The War in the Pacific.

Philip A. Crowl, *Campaign in the Marianas* (1960).

M. Hamlin Cannon, *Leyte: The Return to the Philippines* (1953).

Roy E. Appleman, et al., *Okinawa: The Last Battle* (1948).

Army in World War II Series: The Technical Services

Karl C. Dod, *The Corps of Engineers: The War Against Japan*. Center of Military History, 1987.

Supreme Commander Allied Powers, *Reports of General MacArthur*, 2 vols., vol. II-2 in two parts. Washington, DC: Government Printing Office for Department of the Army, 1966.

Thomas M. Huber, *Japan's Battle of Okinawa*. Leavenworth Papers no. 18. Fort Leavenworth: Command and General Staff College, n.d. [1990].

U.S. NAVY

Communiqués, 1–300. Office of Public Information, United States Navy, 1945.

Communiqués, 301–600. Office of Public Information, United States Navy, 1945.

Navy Records

Richard W. Bates et al., *The Battle for Leyte Gulf, October 1944: Strategic and Tactical Analysis for the Naval War College*. Volumes 1, 2, 3, 5, and diagram book. Washington, DC: Bureau of Naval Personnel, 1957.

Robert L. Buckley Jr., *At Close Quarters: PT Boats in the United States Navy*. Washington, DC: Naval History Division, 1962.

Office of Naval Intelligence, *Index to All Japanese Naval Vessels* (ONI 41-42 I). December 1944 (U.S. Naval Institute Press reprint, 1987).

John C. Reilly, *Operational Experience of Fast Battleships; World War II, Korea, Vietnam*. Department of the Navy: Naval Historical Center, 1989.

Gerald E. Wheeler, *Kincaid of the Seventh Fleet: A Biography of Admiral Thomas C. Kincaid, U.S. Navy*. Washington, DC: Naval Historical Center, 1995.

United States Naval Operations in World War II (All volumes are by Samuel Eliot Morison and were published by Little, Brown on the dates indicated.)

Vol. 8: *New Guinea and the Marianas, March 1944–August 1944* (1953).

Vol. 12: *Leyte, June 1944–January 1945* (1958).

Vol. 13: *The Liberation of the Philippines, 1944–1945* (1959).

Vol. 14: *Victory in the Pacific, 1945* (1990).

U.S. STRATEGIC BOMBING SURVEY

Campaigns of the Pacific War
Interrogations of Japanese Officials

OTHER SOURCES

John A. Adams, *If Mahan Ran the Great Pacific War: An Analysis of World War II Naval Strategy*. Bloomington: Indiana University Press, 2008.

Agawa Hiroyuki, *The Reluctant Admiral: Yamamoto and the Imperial Navy* (trans. John Bester). Tokyo: Kodansha, 1982.

Thomas B. Allen and Norman Polmar, *Codename Downfall: The Secret Plan to Invade Japan*. Chatham, UK: Headline Books, 1995.

Christopher J. Argyle, *Japan at War, 1937–1945*. London: Weidenfeld Publishers, 1976.

Henry H. "Hap" Arnold, *Global Mission*. New York: Harper & Row, 1949.

Gerald Astor, *Operation Iceberg: The Invasion and Conquest of Okinawa in World War II—An Oral History*. New York: Donald I. Fine, 1995.

Albert Axell and Kase Hideaki, *Kamikaze: Japan's Suicide Gods*. London: Pearson, 2002.

Geoffrey Ballard, *On ULTRA Active Service: The Story of Australia's Signals Intelligence Operations During World War II*. Richmond, Victoria, Australia: Spectrum, 1991.

Daniel E. Barbey, *Battle Stations! Your Navy in Action*. New York: William H. Wise & Co., 1946.

———, *MacArthur's Amphibious Navy: Seventh Fleet Amphibious Force Operations, 1943–1945*. Annapolis, MD: Naval Institute, 1969.

James H. Belote and William M. Belote, *Titans of the Seas: The Development and Operations of Japanese and American Carrier Task Forces During World War II*. New York: Harper & Row, 1975.

———, *Typhoon of Steel: The Battle for Okinawa*. New York: Harper & Row, 1970.

David Bergamini, *Japan's Imperial Conspiracy*. New York: Pocket Books, 1972.

Herbert P. Bix, *Hirohito and the Making of Modern Japan*. New York: HarperCollins, 2000.

Robert W. Black, *Rangers in World War II*. New York: Ballantine Books, 1992.

Clay Blair Jr., *Silent Victory: The U.S. Submarine War Against Japan*. New York: Lippincott, 1975.

Carl Boyd and Yoshida Akihiko, *The Japanese Submarine Force and World War II*. Annapolis, MD: Naval Institute, 1995.

William Breuer, *Devil Boats: The PT War Against Japan*. New York: Jove, 1988.

———, *MacArthur's Undercover War: Spies, Saboteurs, Guerrillas, and Secret Missions*. New York: John Wiley & Sons, 1995.

Courtney Browne, *Tojo: The Last Banzai*. New York: Holt, Rinehart & Winston, 1967.

Harold L. Buell, *Dauntless Helldivers: A Dive-Bomber Pilot's Epic Story of the Carrier Battles*. New York: Dell, 1991.

Martin Caiden, *A Torch to the Enemy: The Fire Raid on Tokyo*. New York: Ballantine, 1960.

C. Raymond Calhoun, *Tin Can Sailor: Life Aboard the USS Sterett, 1939–1945*. Annapolis, MD: Naval Institute, 2000.

Gilbert Cant, "Bull's Run: Was Halsey Right at Leyte Gulf?" *Life*, November 24, 1947, pp. 73–86, 99.

Dorr Carpenter and Norman Polmar, *Submarines of the Imperial Japanese Navy*. Annapolis, MD: Naval Institute Press, 1986.

Worrall R. Carter, *Bullets, Beans and Black Oil: The Story of Fleet Logistics Afloat in the Pacific During World War II*. Washington, DC: Government Printing Office, 1953.

J. J. "Jocko" Clark, with Clark G. Reynolds, *Carrier Admiral*. New York: David McKay, 1967.

Basil Collier, *The War in the Far East, 1941–1945: A Military History*. New York: William Morrow, 1969.

Don Congdon, ed. *Combat: Pacific Theater: World War II*. New York: Dell, 1958.

Alvin Coox, *Japan: The Final Agony*. New York: Ballantine Books, 1970.

Alexander D. Corbin, *The History of Camp Tracy: Japanese WWII POWs and the Future of Strategic Interrogation*. Fort Belvoir, VA: Ziedon Press, 2009.

Robert J. Cox, *My Online Book: The Battle off Samar, Taffy III at Leyte Gulf*. www.bosamar.com, 2012.

Thomas J. Cutler, *The Battle of Leyte Gulf: The Greatest Naval Battle in History, The Dramatic Full History, October 23–26, 1944*. New York: Pocket Books, 1996.

Andrieu D'Albas, *Death of a Navy: Japanese Naval Action in World War II*. New York: Devin Adair, 1957.

Burke Davis, *Get Yamamoto!* New York: Random House, 1969.

———, *Marine! The Life of Chesty Puller*. New York: Bantam, 1964.

D. Colt Denfeld, *Hold the Marianas: The Japanese Defense of the Islands*. Shippensberg, PA: White Mane Publisher, 1997.

Roger Dingman, *Deciphering the Rising Sun: Navy and Marine Corps Codebreakers, Translators, and Interpreters in the Pacific War*. Annapolis, MD: Naval Institute Press, 2009.

Edward L. Drea, *In the Service of the Emperor: Essays on the Imperial Japanese Army*. Lincoln: University of Nebraska Press, 1998.

———, *MacArthur's ULTRA: Codebreaking and the War Against Japan, 1942–1945*. Lawrence: University Press of Kansas, 1992.

Bob Drury and Tom Clavin, *Halsey's Typhoon: The True Story of a Fighting Admiral, an Epic Storm, and an Untold Rescue*. New York: Atlantic Monthly Press, 2007.

Peter J. Edwards, *The Rise and Fall of the Japanese Imperial Naval Air Service*. Barnsley, UK: Pen & Sword, 2010.

Robert L. Eichelberger with Milton Mackaye, *Our Jungle Road to Tokyo*. New York: Viking Press, 1950.

Joseph F. Enright with James W. Ryan, *Shinano! The Sinking of Japan's Supership*. New York: St. Martin's Press, 1987.

David C. Evans, ed., *The Japanese Navy in World War II: In the Words of Former Japanese Naval Officers* (2nd ed.). Annapolis, MD: Naval Institute, 1986.

David C. Evans and Mark R. Peattie, *Kaigun: Strategy, Tactics and Technology in the Imperial Japanese Navy, 1887–1941*. Annapolis, MD: Naval Institute, 1997.

James J. Fahey, *Pacific War Diary, 1942–1945*. New York: Avon, 1963.

Stanley L. Falk, *Decision at Leyte*. New York: W. W. Norton, 1966.

Edward I. Farley, *PT Patrol: Wartime Adventures in the Pacific and the Story of PTs in World War II*. New York: Popular Library, 1962.

George Feifer, *Tennozan: The Battle of Okinawa and the Atomic Bomb*. New York: Tichnor & Fields, 1992.

James E. Field Jr., *The Japanese at Leyte Gulf: The SHO Operation*. Princeton, NJ: Princeton University Press, 1947.

Gregory G. Fletcher, *Intrepid Aviators: The True Story of USS Intrepid's Torpedo Squadron 18 and Its Epic Clash with the Superbattleship Musashi*. New York: NAL/Caliber, 2012.

Douglas Ford, *The Elusive Enemy: U.S. Naval Intelligence and the Imperial Japanese Fleet*. Annapolis, MD: Naval Institute Press, 2011.

Simon Foster, *Okinawa, 1945: Final Assault on the Empire*. London: Arms & Armour Press, 1996.

René J. Francillon, *Japanese Aircraft of the Pacific War*. New York: Funk & Wagnalls, 1974.

———, *Japanese Carrier Air Groups, 1941–45*. London: Osprey, 1979.

Benis M. Frank, *Okinawa: Touchstone to Victory*. New York: Ballantine Books, 1970.

Richard P. Frank, *Downfall: The End of the Imperial Japanese Empire*. New York: Random House, 1999.

Kenneth I. Friedman, *Afternoon of the Rising Sun: The Battle of Leyte Gulf*. Novato, CA: Presidio Press, 2001.

Richard Fuller, *Shōkan: Hirohito's Samurai: Leaders of the Japanese Armed Forces,*
1926–1945. London: Arms & Armour Press, 1992.

Ignatius J. Galantin, *Take Her Deep: A Submarine Against Japan in World War II.*
Chapel Hill, NC: Algonquin Books, 1987.

D. M. Giangreco, *Hell to Pay: Operation DOWNFALL and the Invasion of Japan,*
1945–1947. Annapolis, MD: Naval Institute Press, 2009.

Alton K. Gilbert, *A Leader Born: The Life of Admiral John Sidney McCain, Pacific*
Carrier Commander. Philadelphia: Casemate Books, 2006.

Donald M. Goldstein and Katharine V. Dillon, eds., *Fading Victory: The Diary of*
Admiral Matome Ugaki, 1941–1945 (trans. Chihaya Masatake). Annapolis, MD:
Naval Institute, 2008.

Ian Gow with H. P. Willmott, *Okinawa 1945: Gateway to Japan.* Garden City: Doubleday, 1985.

Edwin Gray, *Operation Pacific: The Royal Navy's War Against Japan, 1941–1945.*
Annapolis, MD: Naval Institute Press, n.d. [1990].

Thomas E. Griffith Jr., *MacArthur's Airman: General George C. Kenney and the War*
in the Southwest Pacific. Lawrence: University Press of Kansas, 1998.

William F. Halsey with J. D. Bryan III, *Admiral Halsey's Story.* New York: McGraw-
Hill, 1947.

Joseph T. Hamrick, *Technical Air Intelligence in the Pacific in World War II.* Cassville,
MO: Litho Printer, 2007.

Hara Tameichi with Fred Saito and Roger Pineau, *Japanese Destroyer Captain.* New
York: Ballantine, 1961.

Hasegawa Tsuyoshi, *Racing the Enemy: Stalin, Truman, and the Surrender of Japan.*
Cambridge, MA: Harvard University Press, 2005.

Hata Ikuhiko, Izawa Yasuho, and Christopher Shores, *Japanese Army Fighter Aces,*
1931–1945. Mechanicsburg, PA: Stackpole Books, 2012.

Hata Ikuhito and Izawa Yasuho, *Japanese Naval Aces and Fighter Units of World War*
II. Annapolis, MD: Naval Institute, 1989.

Hattori Takushiro, *The Complete History of the Greater East Asia War* (U.S. Army
translation), published in Japan by Hara Shobo, 1966.

Hayashi Saburo with Alvin D. Coox, *Kogun: The Japanese Army in the Pacific War.*
Quantico, VA: Marine Corps Association, 1959.

William N. Hess, *Pacific Sweep.* New York: Zebra, 1978.

F. H. Hinsley and Alan Stripp, *Codebreakers: The Inside Story of Bletchley Park.* New
York: Oxford University Press, 1994.

A. Hoehling, *The Franklin Comes Home.* New York: Manor Books, 1974.

W. J. Holmes, *Double-Edged Secrets: U.S. Naval Intelligence Operations in the Pacific*
During World War II. Annapolis, MD: Naval Institute, 1979.

———, *Underseas Victory, II, 1943–1945: The Tide Turns.* New York: Zebra Books,
1979.

Kevin C. Holzimmer, *General Walter Krueger: Unsung Hero of the Pacific War.* Lawrence: University Press of Kansas, 2007.

Horikoshi Jiro, *Eagles of Mitsubishi: The Story of the Zero Fighter* (trans. Shindo
Shojiro and Harold N. Wantiez). Seattle: University of Washington Press, 1992.

Edwin P. Hoyt, *The Battle of Leyte Gulf: The Death Knell of the Japanese Fleet.* New
York: Weybright & Tally, 1972.

———, *The Carrier War.* New York: Avon Books, 1972.

———, *Fighters of the Pacific War.* New York: Avon Books, 1984.

————, *Japan's War: The Great Pacific Conflict, 1853–1952*. New York: McGraw-Hill, 1986.

————, *The Last Kamikaze: The Story of Admiral Matome Ugaki*. Westport, CT: Praeger, 1993.

————, *Leyte Gulf: The Death of the Princeton*. New York: Avon Books, 1972.

————, *MacArthur's Navy: The Seventh Fleet and the Battle for the Philippines*. New York: Jove Books, 1991.

————, *McCampbell's Heroes: The Story of the U.S. Navy's Celebrated Carrier*. New York: Avon, 1984.

————, *The Men of the Gambier Bay*. Middlebury, VT: Paul S. Eriksson Publisher, 1979.

————, *Submarines at War: The History of the American Silent Service*. New York: Stein & Day, 1984.

————, *To the Marianas: War in the Central Pacific, 1944*. New York: Avon, 1983.

————, *Yamamoto: The Man Who Planned Pearl Harbor*. New York: Warner, 1990.

Frazier Hunt, *The Untold Story of Douglas MacArthur*. New York: Signet, 1964.

Ray C. Hunt and Bernard Nolting, *Behind Japanese Lines: An American Guerrilla in the Philippines*. New York: Pocket Books, 1988.

Allison Ind, *Allied Intelligence Bureau: Our Secret Weapon in the War Against Japan*. New York: Modern Literary Editions, 1958.

Inoguchi Rikihei and Nakajima Tadashi with Roger Pineau, *The Divine Wind: Japan's Kamikaze Force in World War II*. New York: Bantam, 1978.

Ito Masanori with Roger Pineau, *The End of the Imperial Japanese Navy* (trans. Andrew Y. Kuroda and Roger Pineau). New York: Jove, 1984.

D. Clayton James, *The Japanese Navy in World War II*. Annapolis, MD: Naval Institute, 1969.

————, *The Years of MacArthur: II: 1941–1945*. Boston: Houghton Mifflin, 1975.

Hansgeorg Jentschura, Dieter Jung, and Peter Mickel, *Warships of the Imperial Japanese Navy, 1869–1945* (trans. Anthony Preston and J. D. Brown). Annapolis, MD: Naval Institute Press, 1978.

Kumiko Kakehashi, *So Sad to Fall in Battle: An Account of War Based on General Tadamichi Kuribayashi's Letters from Iwo Jima*. New York: Ballantine Books, 2007.

Walter Karig et al., *Battle Report: IV: The End of an Empire*. New York: Rinehart & Company, 1948.

Kase Toshikazu, *Journey to the Missouri*. New Haven, CT: Yale University Press, 1950.

Kato Masuo, *The Lost War*. New York: Knopf, 1946.

Kawahara Toshiaki, *Hirohito and His Times: A Japanese Perspective*. New York: Kodansha International,

John Keats, *They Fought Alone*. Philadelphia: Lippincott, 1963.

Maxwell Taylor Kennedy, *Dangerous Hours: The Story of the USS Bunker Hill and the Kamikaze Pilot Who Crippled Her*. New York: Simon & Schuster, 2009.

George C. Kenney, *General Kenney Reports: A Personal History of the Pacific War*. New York: Duell, Sloan and Pearce, 1949.

E. Bartlett Kerr, *The Diary of Marquis Kido, 1931–1945: Selected Translations into English*. Frederick, MD: University Press of America, 1984.

————, *Flames over Tokyo: The U.S. Army Air Force's Incendiary Campaign Against Japan, 1944–1945*. New York: Donald I. Fine, 1991.

Dan King, *The Last Zero Fighter: Firsthand Accounts from WWII Japanese Naval Pilots*. Irvine, CA: Pacific Press, 2012.

Ken Kotani, *Japanese Intelligence in World War II* (tns. Kotani Chiharu). Botley, UK: Osprey, 2009.

Paul H. Kratoska, *The Japanese Occupation of Malaya, 1941–1945*. Honolulu, Universitu of Hawaii Press, 1997.

Kuwahara Yasuo and Gordon T. Allred. *Kamikaze*. New York: Ballantine Books, 1957.

Eric Lacroix and Linton Wells II, *Japanese Cruisers of the Pacific War*. Annapolis, MD: Naval Institute, 1997.

Raymond Lamont-Brown, *Kamikaze: Japan's Suicide Samurai*. London: Cassell, 1999.

Edwin T. Layton with Roger Pineau and John Costello, *"And I Was There": Pearl Harbor and Midway—Breaking the Secrets*. New York: Morrow, 1985.

William D. Leahy, *I Was There: The Personal Story of the Chief of Staff to Presidents Roosevelt and Truman Based on His Notes and Diaries Made at the Time*. New York: McGraw-Hill, 1950.

Robert Leckie, *Okinawa: The Last Battle of World War II*. New York: Viking Books, 1995.

———, *Strong Men Armed: The United States Marines Against Japan*. New York: Bantam, 1963.

Charles A. Lockwood, *Hellcats of the Sea*. New York: Bantam, 1988.

——— *Sink 'Em All: Submarine Warfare in the Pacific*. New York: Bantam, 1984.

Charles A. Lockwood and Hans C. Adamson, *Battles of the Philippine Sea*. New York: Thomas Crowell, 1968.

Robert Lundgren, *The World Wonder'd: What Really Happened off Samar*. Ann Arbor, MI: Nimble Books, 2014.

Douglas A. MacArthur, *Reminiscences*. Greenwich, CT: Fawcett, 1964.

Donald Macintyre, *Leyte Gulf: Armada in the Pacific*. New York: Ballantine Books, 1969.

Paul Manning, *Hirohito: The War Years*. New York: Bantam, 1989.

M. Ernest Marshall, *That Night at Surigao: Life on a Battleship at War*. Mechanicsburg, PA: Sunbury Press, 2013.

John T. Mason Jr., *The Pacific War Remembered: An Oral History Collection*. Annapolis, MD: Naval Institute Press, 1986.

James C. McNaughton, *Nisei Linguists: Japanese Americans in the Military Intelligence Service During World War II*. Washington, DC: Department of the Army, 2007.

Robert C. Mikesh and Tagaya Osamu, *Moonlight Interceptor: Japan's "Irving" Night Fighter*. Washington, DC: Smithsonian Institution Press, 1985.

John Monsarrat, *Angel on the Yardarm: The Beginnings of Fleet Radar Defense and the Kamikaze Threat*. Newport, RI: Naval War College Press, 1985.

Samuel Eliot Morison, *The Two-Ocean War: A Short History of the United States Navy in World War II*. New York: Ballantine, 1972.

Ivan Morris, *The Nobility of Failure: Tragic Heroes in the History of Japan*. New York: Farrar, Straus & Giroux, 1988.

Wilbur H. Morrison, *Above and Beyond, 1941–1945*. New York: Bantam Books, 1986.

———, *Point of No Return*. New York: Playboy Paperbacks, 1980.

Malcolm Muir, *The Iowa Class Battleships: Iowa, New Jersey, Missouri & Wisconsin*. Poole, UK: Blandford Press, 1987.

Kenneth Munson, *Aircraft of World War II*. New York: Doubleday, 1968.

Ivan Musicant, *Battleship at War: The Epic Story of the USS Washington*. New York: Harcourt Brace Jovanovich, 1986.

Naito Hatsuho, *Thunder Gods: The Kamikaze Pilots Tell Their Story* (trans. Ichikawa Mayumi). New York: Dell Books, 1990.

Nakata Seiichi, ed., *For That One Day: The Memoirs of Mitsuo Fuchida, Commander of the Attack on Pearl Harbor* (trans. Douglas T. Shinsato and Urabe Tadanori). Kamuela, HI: eXperience inc., 2011.

Nihon Kaigun Web site.

Oba Sadao, *The "Japanese" War: London University's WWII Secret Teaching Programme and the Experts Sent to Beat Japan* (trans. Anne Kaneko). Folkestone, UK: Japan Library, 1988.

Oka Shohei, *Fires in the Plain* (trans. Ivan Morris). North Clarendon, VT: Tuttle Publishing, 2001.

Okumiya Masatake and Horikoshi Jiro with Martin Caidin, *Zero: The Story of Japan's Air War in the Pacific, 1941–45*. New York: Ballantine, 1957.

Michael K. Olson, *Tales from a Tin Can: The USS Dale from Pearl Harbor to Tokyo Bay*. Minneapolis, MN: Zenith, 2010.

Orita Zenji with Joseph D. Harrington, *I-Boat Captain*. Canoga Park, CA: Major, 1976.

Pacific War Research Society, *Japan's Longest Day*. New York: Ballantine Books, 1972.

Albert Palazzo, *The Australian Army: A History of Its Organization, 1901–2001*. Melbourne: Oxford University Press, 2001.

Mark P. Parillo, *The Japanese Merchant Marine in World War II*. Annapolis, MD: Naval Institute Press, 1993.

Lawrence Paterson, *Hitler's Grey Wolves: U-Boats in the Indian Ocean*. London: Greenhill Books, 2004.

Michael Patterson, *The Secret War: The Inside Story of Code Makers and Code Breakers in World War II*. Cincinnati, OH: David & Charles, 2007.

Jack Pearl, *Admiral "Bull" Halsey*. Derby, CT: Monarch, 1962.

Mark R. Peattie, *Sunburst: The Rise of Japanese Naval Air Power, 1909–1941*. Annapolis, MD: Naval Institute, 2001.

Geoffrey Perrett, *Old Soldiers Never Die: The Life of Douglas MacArthur*. New York: Random House, 1996.

Mark Perry, *The Most Dangerous Man in America: The Making of Douglas MacArthur*. New York: Basic Books, 2014.

E. B. Potter, *Admiral Arleigh Burke: A Biography*. New York: Random House, 1990.

———, *Bull Halsey*. Annapolis, MD: Naval Institute, 1985.

———, *Nimitz*. Annapolis, MD: Naval Institute, 1976.

John Prados, *Combined Fleet Decoded: The Secret History of American Intelligence and the Japanese Navy in World War II*. New York: Random House, 1995.

———, *Islands of Destiny: The Solomons Campaign and the Eclipse of the Rising Sun*. New York: NAL Caliber, 2012.

Gordon Prange with Donald M. Goldstein and Katherine V. Dillon, *God's Samurai: Lead Pilot at Pearl Harbor*. Washington, DC: Brassey's (US), 1990.

Clark G. Reynolds, *The Fast Carriers: The Forging of an Air Navy*. Huntington, NY: Robert E. Krieger Publishing, 1978.

Matthew K. Rodman, *A War of Their Own: Bombers over the Southwest Pacific*. Maxwell Air Force Base, AL: Air University Press, 2005.

Theodore Roscoe, *Pigboats: The True Story of the Fighting Submariners of World War II*. New York: Bantam Books, 1958.

———, *Tincans: The True Story of the Fighting Destroyers of World War II*. New York: Bantam Books, 1960.

———, *United States Destroyer Operations in World War II*. Annapolis, MD: Naval Institute, 1953.

Sakai Saburo with Martin Caidin and Fred Saito, *Samurai!* New York: Bantam, 1978.

Henry Sakaida, *Aces of the Rising Sun, 1937–1945.* Botley, UK: Osprey, 2002.

———, *Japanese Army Air Force Aces, 1937–1945.* London: Osprey, 1997.

Hentry Sakaida and Takaki Koji, *Genda's Blade: Japan's Squadron of Aces, 343 Kokutai.* Hersham, UK: Ian Allen Books, 2003.

Richard Sakakida, as told to Wayne S. Kiyosaki, *A Spy in Their Midst: The World War II Struggle of a Japanese-American Hero.* Lanham, MD: Madison Books, 1995.

Howard Sauer, *The Last Big-Gun Naval Battle: The Battle of Surigao Strait.* Palo Alto, CA: Glencannon Press, 1999.

David Sears, *At War with the Wind: The Epic Struggle with Japan's World War II Suicide Bombers.* New York: Kensington Publishing, 2008.

M. G. Sheftall, *Blossoms in the Wind: Human Legacies of the Kamikaze.* New York: NAL Caliber, 2005.

Frederick C. Sherman, *Combat Command: American Aircraft Carriers in the Pacific War.* New York: Bantam, 1982.

Robert H. Sherrod, *History of Marine Corps Aviation in World War II.* Washington, DC: Association of the United States Army, 1952.

Shigemitsu Mamoru, *Japan and Her Destiny: My Struggle for Peace* (trans. Oswald White). London: Hutchinson, 1958.

John F. Shortal, *Forged by Fire: Robert L. Eichelberger and the Pacific War.* Columbia: University of South Carolina Press, 1987.

Leon V. Sigel, *Fighting to a Finish: The Politics of War Termination in the United States and Japan, 1945.* Ithaca, NY: Cornell University Press, 1988.

Paul H. Silverstone, *U.S. Warships of World War II.* New York: Doubleday, 1968.

John R. Skates, *The Invasion of Japan: Alternative to the Bomb.* Columbia: University of South Carolina Press, 1994.

Michael Smith, *The Emperor's Codes: Breaking Japan's Secret Ciphers.* New York: Arcade, 2000.

Peter C. Smith, *Fist from the Sky: Japan's Dive-Bomber Ace of WWII.* Mechanicsburg, PA: Stackpole, 2005.

Stan Smith, *The Battle of Leyte Gulf.* New York: Belmont Books, 1961.

———, *The Destroyermen.* New York: Belmont Books, 1966.

Carl Solberg, *Decision and Dissent: With Halsey at Leyte Gulf.* Annapolis, MD: Naval Institute, 1995.

Ronald H. Spector, *The Eagle Against the Sun: The American War with Japan.* New York: Vintage, 1985.

———, ed., *Listening to the Enemy: Key Documents on the Role of Communications Intelligence in the War with Japan.* Wilmington, DE: Scholarly Resources, 1988.

Russell Spurr, *A Glorious Way to Die: The Kamikaze Mission of the Battleship Yamato.* New York: Bantam Books, 1983.

Edward P. Stafford, *The Big "E": The Story of the USS Enterprise.* New York: Ballantine, 1974.

———, *Little Ship, Big War: The Saga of DE-343.* New York: Jove Books, 1985.

Adrian Stewart, *The Battle of Leyte Gulf.* New York: Charles Scribner's Sons, 1979.

Alan Stripp, *Codebreaker in the Far East.* London: Frank Cass, 1989.

Tagaya Osamu, *Aichi 99 Kanbaku "Val" Units, 1937–1942.* Botley, UK: Osprey, 2011.

———, *Imperial Japanese Naval Aviator, 1937–1945.* Botley, UK: Osprey, 2003.

———, *Mitsubishi Type 1 Rikko "Betty" Units of World War II.* Botley, UK: Osprey, 2001.

Evan Thomas, *Sea of Thunder: Four Commanders and the Last Great Naval Campaign,*
      1941–1945. New York: Simon & Schuster, 2006.

Barrett Tillman, *Enterprise: America's Fightingest Ship and the Men Who Helped Win*
      World War II. New York: Simon & Schuster, 2012.

————, *Whirlwind: The Air War Against Japan, 1942–1945.* New York: Simon &
      Schuster, 2011.

John Toland, *The Rising Sun: The Decline and Fall of the Japanese Empire.* New York:
      Bantam, 1971.

Toyoda Soemu, *Sekai No Nippon Sha (The End of the Imperial Navy;* excerpts translated
      by the U.S. Navy). Tokyo: 1950.

Anthony P. Tully, *Battle of Surigao Strait.* Bloomington: Indiana University Press, 2009.

Edward VanDerRhoer, *Deadly Magic: A Personal Account of Communications Intel-*
      ligence in World War II in the Pacific. New York: McGraw-Hill, 1978.

Milan Vego, *The Battle for Leyte, 1944: Allied and Japanese Plans, Preparations, and*
      Execution. Annapolis, MD: Naval Institute Press, 2006.

Denis Warner and Peggy Warner, *The Sacred Warriors: Japan's Suicide Legions.* New
      York: Avon Books, 1984.

A. J. Watts, *Japanese Warships of World War II.* Garden City, NY: Doubleday, 1967.

A. J. Watts and B. G. Gordon, *The Imperial Japanese Navy.* Garden City, NY: Doubleday,
      1971.

Ron Werneth, *Beyond Pearl Harbor: The Untold Stories of Japan's Naval Airmen.*
      Altglen, PA: Schiffer Publishing, 2008.

Arch Whitehouse, *Squadrons of the Sea.* New York: Modern Library Editions, 1962.

Ken Wiley, *D-Days in the Pacific: With the U.S. Coast Guard in World War II: The*
      Story of Lucky 13. Philadelphia: Casemate Books, 2010.

H. P. Willmott, *The Battle of Leyte Gulf: The Last Fleet Action.* Bloomington: Indiana
      University Press, 2005.

Charles A. Willoughby, *MacArthur, 1941–1951.* New York: McGraw-Hill, 1954.

John Winton, *The Forgotten Fleet: The British Navy in the Pacific, 1944–1945.* New
      York: Coward McCann, 1970.

————, *Sink the Haguro! The Last Destroyer Action of World War II.* London: Seeley,
      Service & Coy, 1979.

————, *ULTRA in the Pacific: How Breaking Japanese Codes and Cyphers Affected*
      Naval Operations Against Japan, 1941–45. Annapolis, MD: Naval Institute, 1993.

C. Vann Woodward, *The Battle for Leyte Gulf.* New York: Macmillan Company, 1947.

John F. Wukovits, *Devotion to Duty: A Biography of Admiral Clifton A. F. Sprague.*
      Annapolis, MD: Naval Institute Press, 1995.

Yahara Hiromichi, *The Battle for Okinawa* (trans. Roger Pineau and Uehara Masatoshi).
      New York: John Wiley & Sons, 1995.

William T. Y'Blood, *The Little Giants: U.S. Escort Carriers Against Japan.* Annapolis,
      MD: Naval Institute Press, 1987.

————. *Red Sun Setting: The Battle of the Philippine Sea.* Annapolis, MD: Naval Insti-
      tute Press, 1981.

Yoshimura Akira, *Build the Musashi: The Birth and Death of the World's Greatest*
      Battleship. Tokyo: Kodansha International, 1991.

————, *Zero Fighter* (trans. Kaiho Retso and Michael Gregson). Westport, CT: Praeger
      Publishers, 1996.

Lance Q. Zedric, *Silent Warriors: The Alamo Scouts Behind Japanese Lines.* Ventura,
      CA: Pathfinder Publishers, 1995.

INDEX